BOSS

CERMAK

OF CHICAGO

• •
•

A Study of Political Leadership

BOSS
CERMAK
OF
CHICAGO

A Study of Political Leadership

BY ALEX GOTTFRIED

UNIVERSITY OF WASHINGTON PRESS

Seattle · 1962

•

*This book is published
with the assistance
of a grant
by the Ford Foundation.*

•

•

*Designed by
Dianne Weiss*

. . .

To the Three Women in My Life

MY MOTHER, CHARLOTTE BRAUN GOTTFRIED

MY WIFE, SUE DAVIDSON

MY DAUGHTER, ERIKA

Biographers are fixated on their heroes in a very peculiar manner. They frequently select the hero as the object of study because, for personal reasons of their own emotional life, they had a special affection for him from the very outset. They then devote themselves to a work of idealization, which strives to enroll the great man among their infantile models....For the sake of this wish they wipe out the individual features of his physiognomy, they rub out the traces of his life's struggle with inner and outer resistances, and do not tolerate in him anything savoring of human weakness or imperfection; they give us a cold, strange ideal form instead of a man to whom we could feel distantly related. It is to be regretted that they do this, for they hereby sacrifice the truth to an illusion.

SIGMUND FREUD,
*Leonardo Da Vinci:
A Study in Psychosexuality*

The starting point of our present undertaking is neither to praise nor dispraise of the way power and personality interact upon each other. We began by observing Caesar; later we may bury him.

HAROLD P. LASSWELL,
Power and Personality

PREFACE

On march 10, 1933, in biting, near-zero temperature, the most spectacular funeral demonstration in the history of Chicago took place. The line of march was thronged by 500,000 spectators; 30,000 participated in the funeral procession proper; 23,000 attended ceremonies at the Chicago Stadium; another gigantic 50,000 witnessed the interment at Chicago's Bohemian National Cemetery.

The man so honored was Chicago's first and only foreign-born mayor, and the greatest boss that city has produced, Anton J. Cermak. He had not in his lifetime aroused a response so warm and devoted from the general public; and no doubt the dramatic circumstances of his death, together with the needs for mob emotional release created by the Depression, played some part in the great demonstration attending the departure of the "martyr mayor." But the enthusiasm did not survive overlong. Few public monuments to Cermak's name can be found today. The public was neither fully aware of nor much concerned with the monument Cermak himself created: the first cohesive city and state-wide Democratic machine in the history of Chicago politics.

Although some permanent tributes to Cermak's memory do

exist, they have in few cases been erected by the local and state governments in which he played so powerful a role, for so many years. It is his own ethnic group, the Czechs, who have insisted upon perpetuating his name. The city of his birth, Kladno, Czechoslovakia, placed a plaque on his first home; after its theft by the Nazis, the plaque was replaced with great ceremony. In World War II his countrymen, in memory of his services to the Allied cause in the first World War, succeeded in having a war craft named in his honor. Czechs also built the memorial at Bay-front Park, in Miami, where Cermak died after having been wounded by the assassin's bullet intended for President Roosevelt; here an annual memorial service is held. In Chicago there was a Cermak Post of the American Legion; and numerous other Czech societies bear Cermak's name.

Nothing could be more indicative of the peculiar ingredients of this politician's rise to power than his lasting prestige among his people. For Cermak "made" Chicago Czechs; and Chicago Czechs "made" Cermak. To a people hungry for a role in the political process, he gave the forceful leadership without which their dreams could never have been realized. From them he received the shrewd, disciplined, loyal support which carried him from his first obscure ward activities to the highest elective office the municipality could bestow.

In a work of this kind the author becomes indebted to many people. It would be impractical to list each of the dozens of persons who shared their knowledge of Cermak with me, in hundreds of interviews. I wish to thank all of these patient and generous people. Special thanks are due to those who made themselves available for extended interviews. They include the late Mayor Edward J. Kelly, Mayor Carter H. Harrison, Mr. John A. Cervenka, Mr. James C. Denvir, Mr. John Dienhart, Mr. H. C. Brodman, and several members of the Cermak family, including A. J. Cermak's daughter, Mrs. Frank Jirka.

Thanks are due to Professor Avery Leiserson for his great care in reading an early version of the manuscript, and for his incisive criticism.

I am indebted to the trustees of the Walgreen and Ford Foundations, without whose financial aid it would have been impossible to devote to the work the years it required. My debt is also grate-fully acknowledged to the University of Washington for grants from the Agnes H. Anderson Research Fund Committee and the Research Committee of the Graduate School.

Finally, I wish to express my gratitude to my wife for the editing of the final manuscript, and for many helpful suggestions in its revision; but above all, for her interest and encouragement over the years during which the book came into being.

As is customary, I assume sole responsibility for all statements of fact or value.

ALEX GOTTFRIED

Seattle, Washington
December, 1961

CONTENTS

xi

ILLUSTRATIONS

BOSS

CERMAK

OF CHICAGO

• •
•

A Study of Political Leadership

· 1 ·

FROM

KLADNO

TO

CHICAGO

In 1874, during the third great wave of Bohemian emigration, Anton and Catherine Cermak sailed to America. With them was their first-born, year-old son, Anton Joseph. Anton was twenty-five, his wife, twenty-six. They were physically vigorous, and already inured to hard work. Catherine was one of those quiet little women whose faces and personalities are recalled with difficulty. For all that, she had a kindly nature which was to serve her well in raising a family of six, under conditions of economic adversity. Her husband Anton was more striking, a man of medium height, with enormously powerful back and shoulders, bull neck, a thick, chunky trunk. His eldest son A.J. would one day bear a marked resemblance to him.

Bohemians had emigrated to this country in large numbers in the revolutionary period of 1848 and again in 1867, at the close of the Austro-Prussian War. Frustration of a desire for political independence; a strong movement against corruption in the clergy; the rebirth of national self-consciousness, in part a response to the conditions of the revolutionary European period and to the subsequent renaissance of the traditional language— all these were factors in Czech immigration. Many also came, in all periods, for economic reasons. It is to this class that Anton Cermak must certainly have belonged.

Anton Cermak was a coal miner, as his father had been before him. His lot was unenviable, as is the lot of coal miners the world over. Although the simple three-room home where A.J. was born was decent and substantial enough, employment in the Kladno mines was at times sporadic; and the situation following unsuccessful strikes was very conducive to movement to the United States.

Anton Cermak wished to escape the economic insecurity of the old country, but beyond this, he was not driven by the ambitiousness which was to drive his eldest son. Although he was never lazy, shiftless, or unwilling to provide for his family, he exhibited no outstanding desire to rise, materially or socially. When he and Catherine first arrived in America, they settled for a time in Chicago's then-major Bohemian center, known as Pilsen. Anton, although he was not a highly skilled worker, knew something of carpentry and masonry, and he was for a time able to find employment in the building of a Bohemian community center. But job opportunities for a greenhorn miner did not abound in the Chicago of 1874. Very shortly, the Cermaks put together their few possessions and moved again, this time the comparatively short distance of sixty-five miles southwest of the city, to Braidwood, Illinois.

The selection of this particular town was almost inevitable. Not only was it one of the most important coal-mining towns in the district, but one whole section of it—Lower Braidwood—was almost entirely inhabited by Bohemians. New to the country, unable to speak the vernacular, unfamiliar with laws and customs, the young couple automatically sought out their compatriots in Lower Braidwood. Upper Braidwood, or "The Grove," was populated largely by Irish and was considered by local Bohemians to be merely an adjunct. Lower Braidwood itself, however, was not 100 per cent Bohemian. There were other Slavs, Negroes, Germans, and several other groups, of which the Irish and the Italians were numerically most important after the Bohemians.

The town where A.J. was to spend the greatest part of his childhood and early youth had, at the time of his parents' arrival there in 1885, a population of 15,000, making it one of the largest and most important towns in Will County. It was larger and more influential, perhaps, than Joliet; and as a rule, when the county slates were drawn, Braidwood was considered. The local candidate was most often Irish. By 1890, however, the decline had begun, for coal operations had become less profitable and Braidwood was a one-industry town. Many of the neighboring towns were largely built up from Braidwood people and their Braidwood houses, the primitive foundations of which made possible their removal on rollers.

The town was set on flat, marshy prairie land, just off the main arterial highway to Chicago. It was dark and dirty, gray and drab. Houses were almost all small, frame, spindly, and unpainted, with sagging front porches and decrepit steps. There were no sidewalks. In the rain, streets and paths were like swamps, similar in their effect to the dank and slimy pits from which the men emerged.

Little wealth was in evidence, for the owners were largely absentee. The most imposing home belonged to the superintendent of the Chicago and Wilmington Coal Company, the corporation which largely owned Braidwood. The middle class was virtually nonexistent, consisting solely of small shop and saloon owners whose standard of living was not appreciably above the level of the miners. The broad base of the class pyramid was supplied by the pit employees.

Apart from whatever other consequences it may have had for young A.J., this simple class structure spared him at least one possible source of distress and misgiving—a continual comparison between himself and members of a numerous and prosperous middle class. In his work, in his recreation, at his school, A.J.'s associates were of the same economic and social background as he.

During the first dozen years of A.J.'s life, the family made several attempts to relocate in Chicago. These moves occurred when work was slow at the mines and green fields of seemingly better opportunity beckoned from the city. But each attempt failed; and the return to Braidwood at the time A.J. was twelve years old was the last such move until he himself left in 1889, never to return as a resident.

The house the Cermak family owned and lived in while A.J.

was at the Braidwood school was a frame, two-story building, no more nor less attractive than its neighbors. It had no parlor as such, for the (by then) large family required the use of every room but the kitchen for sleeping. The large kitchen, serving also as dining room and parlor, was the center of the household. Whatever heat was available came from its coal stove. There were no rugs; the furniture was sparse, plain, and inexpensive. Oilcloth covered the kitchen table; light, of course, came from kerosene lamps.

Like most of their Bohemian neighbors, the Cermaks had their little plot of land adjoining the house, about half an acre, used for modest farming. They also owned a cow, a pig, and some poultry. As the eldest son, A.J. had certain agricultural responsibilities; but he often neglected them to sneak off with the local boys for fishing on the banks of the neighborhood river.

About a city block from the Cermak house was the local Whiskey Row. At this time Braidwood had about ninety-nine saloons. Between thirty and thirty-six were located at this neighboring point. Almost certainly A.J., very early in life, came to know and accept such places as normal and desirable. For the transplanted Central European peasant and manual laborer, the saloon was not only natural, desirable, and free of moral stigma, but a virtually indispensable institution. It was the miner's social club, political forum, meetingplace, and theater all in one. It offered him his only escape from the physically exhausting and depressing as well as dangerous labor in the mines and from his otherwise bleak and impoverished existence. Here he might feel more a man among men than a human mole; here he might achieve social status among his peers by virtue of his capacity, strength, or wit.

The work of the coal miner has been, historically, among the most underpaid, physically destructive, and spiritually shattering of all occupations. Irving Stone, in *Lust for Life,* has described with great pathos the lives of Belgian miners not too far removed in time from Cermak's experience as a member of a mining community. Mining disasters, even today, with more efficient safety devices, stricter safety laws, inspection, and new technological devices, are by no means rare and are as fully horrifying in their consequences. This was the sort of work Cermak was to engage in as a young man, along with his father and brothers.

Meanwhile, he attended school—sporadically. Some accounts have credited Cermak with six years of elementary schooling; but the records in his Braidwood school do not bear this out. The first date of enrollment is January, 1883, when Cermak was nine years old. It is likely that prior to this date he attended a private Bohemian school. He was last dropped from the Braidwood public school rolls on May 1, 1885, one week before his twelfth birthday. Even over the period of enrollment, his attendance was irregular and infrequent. Thus, his formal English-language education in Braidwood consisted of less than two incomplete and intermittent academic years; probably his attendance at Chicago schools, if he attended at all, was as irregular.

Cermak's elementary-school career, although it is atypical of the men who become successful urban politicians, was not an unusual one for the Braidwood boys of his time.[1] By law and by the expressed command of most of their parents, the central activity of the boys was expected to be their schooling, but this was true only in an ideal sense. The boys knew that school was a very temporary stage in their lives, in spite of the verbal emphasis of their parents, and that in only a few years, when they were twelve or thirteen, their paths would lead out of the school and down into the mine shafts. In most cases, they looked forward to his prospect eagerly, not only because it signified at least quasi-adulthood, but also because it meant for the first time in their lives the personal possession of money.

Beyond this, school was not a very pleasant or stimulating place. The physical plant was adequate, as coal towns go—a white frame structure only nine or ten years old when A. J. matriculated. The teachers, however, were untrained and in most cases not particularly distinguished by sympathy or patience. Some had little to recommend them beyond the fact that they were literate and had become incapacitated in the mines.[2] Only the three R's were taught, and not in an inspiring manner. Traditionally, unorthodox behavior or unacceptable recitation were considered justifiable cause for application of the willow switches so sadly abundant in that vicinity. A.J. apparently did not think highly of his school as

[7]

a boy: at an early age, he announced to his mother his intention of quitting, on the grounds that he "knew more than the teacher." But this was his impression alone; there is no evidence that he was an exceptionally apt student, although he never fell behind the level of his age group in spite of his irregular attendance.

Most of the boys were expected to do certain chores when they were not in school. Parental discipline was strict, and the omission of these duties was punishable with a beating. Play was of the outdoor sort—games, gang warfare, fishing, hunting. The boys did not visit one another's homes; parents did not welcome young male guests. Children in general spent little time in the company of adults, and never on an even remotely equal footing. On these rare occasions when they accompanied their parents on a visit to someone's home, they were expected to be inconspicuous. They were not encouraged to take part in the general conversation; they sat silently or were dispatched outside to play.

We know that A.J.'s family was in typical Bohemian fashion a closely knit unit. Throughout his life Cermak continued to be in close contact with its various members and to be intimately bound up with their fortunes. His parents lived under his roof, even after marriage, until he was more than forty years of age. Although his mother was not an aggressive woman, it is certain that she had at least the influence springing from filial affection; during Cermak's career, when she is known to have interceded with him in behalf of friends, he usually granted her requests.

It was a home in which Bohemian culture predominated over the newer culture. Bohemian was the language of the home— indeed, to their last days, Anton and Catherine spoke very little English. The only books in the home were in Bohemian; in the evenings Anton instructed his eldest son in the Bohemian language. As an adult, Cermak showed a good deal of pride in his ethnic origin, a pride highly characteristic of Czechs and one undoubtedly handed on to him by his parents. Beyond this legacy, and that of his inherited physical endurance, A.J.'s parents had not too much to contribute to his future career. Although both parents were literate, they were not educated people, and their interests were limited. The father was not active in any political organizations in either Braidwood or Chicago. Nor did he take part in any union affairs, although Czechs generally in this country, and in Braidwood itself, have been ready joiners and organizers of trade unions. Both Anton and Catherine, in short, seem to have been simple people, resigned to spending the greatest part of their lives in the struggle for minimum existence.

As with the parents, so with the children—with the notable exception of A.J. None of A.J.'s five siblings—three boys and two girls—showed an active desire to distinguish himself in any way, although they were without exception willing workers if the occasion offered. In all probability, the lives of the brothers would have borne more resemblance to that of their father had it not been for A.J.'s influence. As it was, they made their way into the wood business A.J. founded in Chicago as a young man, and later into minor appointive political jobs. Although they were young men at the time Cermak began to gain political power, none of the brothers attempted to use this factor to any end beyond the retention of the above-mentioned positions. The two sisters married and bore children. Both were married to men of their own ethnic group and of their own general economic and social level.

But while Emilie, Joseph, Frank, Antoinette, and James were developing along the lines of the average run of men and women, their brother was forming the basis of the personality which would one day lead men and women. On the surface, his environment did not appear to offer him many opportunities toward this end. Yet it was not entirely without its advantages.

There is a saying among the people of Braidwood that their town is the only spot in the world where "Irishmen can speak Bohemian." Accurate or not, the remark provides an index to the ethnic composition of the town where A.J. spent his childhood and youth. In his political career, A.J.'s skill in dealing with different ethnic groups was to be one of the cornerstones of his success. His childhood and adolescent experiences in Braidwood were well suited to the birth of that skill.

The Irish were the older settlers in Braidwood. When the Bohemians first arrived, Braidwood had been almost exclusively Irish. In those days, clashes between the two groups were common, and "Bohemians dassn't put their heads out after dark."

By the time Cermak was of school age, although the enmity

persisted, the situation had in some other respects changed. The Bohemians had grown numerically strong enough to have formed their own community in Lower Braidwood. They constituted a larger ethnic entity there than the Irish, and there was no third or fourth group in sufficient numbers to challenge their supremacy. This situation was of considerable importance in Cermak's orientation. Instead of growing up as a member of one of many foreign groups living in a culture dominated by assimilated groups, as he would have in the city, Cermak grew up in an environment where his own culture was the dominant one. It was not merely in his own home, his neighborhood, or a number of scattered neighborhoods that the acceptable mores and customs were Bohemian, but in virtually an entire town. It may therefore be conjectured that he was to an important degree left free of that sense of cultural inferiority which so often affects members of the less assimilated groups of a large city. The feeling of adequacy was no doubt qualified by many factors, one of them the presence of the neighboring Irish, as representatives of a more generally dominant group. But this factor was in turn qualified by the circumstance that the Irish, as miners, were on the same social and economic level as the Bohemians.

The rivalry or enmity between the two groups was, as might be imagined, more active in the case of the gang-age boys. Ethnic gang warfare was more or less continual; the boys, with willow switches as weapons, frequently carried it to the very gates of the school.

But A.J. (or "Lossi," as he was nicknamed at the time) succeeded in breaking through the hostility. He managed to make friends with his estranged Irish neighbors. Among his closest boyhood chums he counted two MacElroys, a Sullivan, two Cunninghams, a Creighton, and a Muldowney. It is doubtful that he was personally motivated by the psychology of "If you can't lick 'em, join 'em." By all accounts he was more than able to take care of himself physically—a capacity that may account for his original acceptance among these youths.

From individual friendships he progressed to becoming the ringleader of the Irish boys. Whatever pugnacious qualities were responsible for his ascendancy are rejected by the surviving members of the boyhood gang in favor of such remarks as "He was full of life, highspirited"; "He was full of mischief"; "One kid who had more life than all the rest, and therefore was frequently blamed for things he didn't do." His intimate association with Irish cohorts continued unbroken until he left Braidwood for the last time.

When A.J. was twelve years old, the family made another of its hegiras to Chicago. Here, A.J. went to work in a sash-and-door mill, while his father worked in a lumber yard. The family lived in a swampy, unhealthy settlement known as Village of Kolaur, or "Goosetown," a Bohemian settlement. The environment was not much different from Braidwood, except that it was perhaps even more squalid. Goosetown too had its youthful gang; and A.J. once again became a leader. He is credited with having been very fertile in devising projects of the kind that most interested the gang—activities of the vandal or hooligan type. "He could always use his noodle."

This stay in Chicago lasted approximately one and a half years. At the end of that time, the family again returned to Braidwood; and A.J.'s childhood, with the beginning of his work in the mines, more or less came to an end.

Exactly how Cermak's entire development was affected by the marginal nature of these first thirteen years can only be surmised; but it is likely that some degree of insecurity was engendered by the conditions of extreme and chronic poverty and by the frequent moves between one town and the other, each move involving a different house or flat.

When the family was settled once more in Braidwood, A.J. entered the mines in the employ of the Chicago and Wilmington Coal Company. His first job was to open and close the trap doors at the pits. For this he was paid eighty-five to ninety cents a day. For a much longer period he worked at the job with which his obituaries and the old Braidwoodites most frequently connect him—that of a mule driver in the pits. One writer puts his wages on this job at $1.10 per day.[3] Old Braidwood miners say that mule drivers earned from $1.25 to $1.75. In any event, it was not a handsome salary, but it compared favorably with the earnings of the actual diggers, for whom $1.50 was a good average day's earning.

These mines were in the northern bituminous fields of Illinois, which had very thin veins as compared to those in southern Illinois. The market competition of the southern fields frequently caused the Braidwood mines to close, and also caused wages there to be much lower than those in the other fields. It was because of these factors that the percentage of Bohemian population was so high, for the Bohemian miners were willing to work where wages were lower and conditions more hazardous than were the miners from Anglo-Saxon or Western European countries.[4] During A.J.'s time, the mines either were closed all summer or else had so little work that only heads of families could get as much as one-half day a week of employment.

Rarely did the miners see daylight during the periods when they worked, except on Sunday. They left home before the sun rose, descended the 100- to 110-foot shafts, and worked nearly to the point of exhaustion. Usually three men worked in a room, often in slime up to their waists. At about six, one man would quit, go get dinner pails for his partners, and the men would eat in the mine. The work then continued until three or four in the morning; and after a few hours of rest, the cycle began all over again. A.J. from time to time mined instead of driving mules, for if one could get a good room it was sometimes possible to earn more at this job; and there was, besides, the comfortable sensation of being one's own boss.

There was little protection in this dangerous work from accident or death. Safety devices were primitive, and adequate insurance was too expensive. Each employee paid twenty-five cents a month into an accident fund from which compensation was granted in case of disability or death. If a man was crippled, he was eligible to receive five dollars a week; in case of death, the family received one hundred dollars.

Virtually no union for miners existed at this time, although the Knights of Labor had attempted to organize them. Strikes, however, usually only for better wages, were frequent and violent. More than once the militia was brought in. At one time violence reached such a pitch in the mines where A.J. was employed that coal cars were hurled into the shafts by the angry miners. Not much is known about A.J.'s participation in the major strikes, but it is known that he was the leader of one small, localized strike.

It was not until the late 1890's that the United Mine Workers effectively organized Braidwood.[5] Cermak's employment in the mines had ended by then, but his union-mindedness in this period is not doubted by acquaintances of those days.

The character of A.J.'s social life in this period was essentially unchanged from that of the prior period, except that with the graduation to manhood conferred by working in the mines, it took on some new forms. In the free hours of the daytime he was likely to be fishing in the Kankakee River or hunting in the surrounding prairies with his companions. Nighttime activities now, however, centered largely about the taverns, with an occasional nod being made in the direction of Saturday night dances. Attendance at the taverns was not confined to Saturday nights. Though minors were presumably not allowed, A.J. was "always in saloons when he was a kid." This was by no means unique in Braidwood. Nearly all the miners drank, some say to their last dime. Often Cermak and his cohorts did not have enough money to sit at the bar. On these occasions a giant can of beer would be bought and passed from lip to lip behind the saloon building. This was known as "shooting the can."

Although drinking was common enough, the alcohol did not affect everyone the same way. It affected A.J.'s conduct beyond doubt, but the effects produced by his conduct vary. Those who were attracted to him saw him as popular, spirited, and affable. He had "lots to say . . . he was a great lad for joking . . . he was well-liked." Others saw a different kind of person. This fellow could be described as a mean, rough customer. Even his admirers admit that he spent more than one night in jail. One such event occurred when he "sassed" the local constable, who asked him to leave a saloon, presumably because of drunkenness. On another occasion, he was incarcerated with several others because they disturbed the peace by running broomsticks up the sides of shingled houses. Liquor appears to have brought out all his latent brashness and aggressiveness. "When he had a little beer, he couldn't be handled by God, by the boss, by anybody." But the appearance of these characteristics did not depend altogether upon alcohol. He frequently engaged in brawls.

He didn't get along with people. He was always getting into fights. He thought he was a tough guy and could fight. He couldn't leave people alone, and most were afraid of him. Girls were very scared. He would always ask to take them home from dances, and they were afraid because he was mean and drunk. He would then "lay" for the girl and the boy who was walking her home, beat him up, and land in jail. The cop told me he never had to go into a tavern to haul him out. All he had to do was wait by the door, and soon he would be thrown out because he was making trouble.[6]

It is safe to say that the Cermak of this period was a lusty, brawling, drinking, pugnacious, undisciplined youth with a deserved reputation as a "tough fellow." He was not much hampered by consideration or sensitivity toward others. One day while he was a mule driver, a circus arrived in town. A.J. and another driver wanted to go to the circus but were hauling coal for a crew of Negro miners in Shaft "N." By some maneuver, A.J. managed to have the miners fired. Then he and his partner, having no coal to haul, were free to attend the circus.

It must be remembered, of course, that all of these incidents took place before A.J. was seventeen years old. Nevertheless, the incident mentioned above reveals capacities not so far removed from the sort which, employed toward the achievement of slightly more sophisticated ends, were to serve him often in his political career.

However, his audacity and aggressiveness were not always engaged in rowdyism, bullying, or buffoonery. In 1889, there was unrest among the mule skinners in his shaft, and at length a group of them decided to ask for a raise in wages, on threat of striking. None of them, however, wanted the unenviable role of negotiator, and it was Cermak who offered to take the responsibility of acting as their leader.

As a labor negotiator, the sixteen-year-old Cermak was not spectacularly successful. "So you want a raise, do you?" his foreman asked. "O.K., I'll give you a raise—right up the shaft."

He was fired on the spot. He immediately got another job on the surface of the same mine; but when his boss learned that he was harboring a "labor agitator," his new job ended the same day.

Shortly after this experience, Cermak boarded the boxcar which took him to Chicago, determined to make a new career.

ON

THE

MAKE,

1889-1902

UPON HIS arrival in Chicago in 1889, sixteen-year-old Cermak settled in Pilsen, the predominately Czech neighborhood where his parents had stayed temporarily upon their arrival from Bohemia. Taking up residence with an aunt, A.J. quickly found employment as a brakeman on the Elgin, Joliet, and Eastern Railroad. Next he became an employee of the street railway company, where his job consisted of riding an aged horse that helped pull the horsecars up a sharp incline on Blue Island Avenue.

During this period Cermak became a member of a gang of young men, almost exclusively Czech, who were known as "tough babies." His association with them was to continue for several years, well past the time of his marriage, and to contribute its bit toward the development of his political career.

Gangs of this type were common in Pilsen, and his membership in one was in conformity with the expected behavior for one of his age, economic group, and cultural-ethnic milieu. These gangs were saloon-centered rather than corner-centered, each gang having its favorite saloon and using it as a headquarters and base of operations. For Cermak, this was a continuation of the social orientation begun in Braidwood.

The activities of the gang bore other resemblances to the Braid-wood pattern. The high point of the week was attendance at Saturday night dances, a great many of which were held in the saloons and in the clubrooms of Czech social or benevolent societies. The purpose of attending dances was not terpsichorean, but rather the search for the excitement of physical combat. Gangs invaded dances in the territories of neighboring gangs, and the expected outcome was a massed fight. Although the gang members were violent, they confined themselves to fisticuffs: no guns, knives, or weapons such as chairs or tables were put into use.

Early in his stay in Pilsen, Cermak became the leader of his saloon gang, for reasons which are at least partially apparent. He excelled in the gang's two chief interests, fighting and drinking. Physically, he was extremely well adapted for gang brawls, being thick-bodied, broad-shouldered and heavily muscled. He delighted in combat. He had a great capacity for alcohol and could hold his liquor. This talent was to be an asset later in his career, when he was able to drink with any group and still exhibit perfect self-possession, thus appearing at one and the same time "one of the boys" and a steady and responsible public servant.

A.J.'s hold on the loyalty of his gang was to some degree responsible for his initial recognition by the party organization and for his first petty job with it. The fact that he controlled a small body of possible party workers and future, if not present, voters was persuasive reason for giving him this job, favors customarily going to individuals who have some sphere of influence, however limited. At the same time, his early membership in the formal political party structure served to reinforce and legitimatize his dominance in his gang. The very fact that he was "in politics" made him better known to persons outside his circle, thus increasing his prestige with his own followers, as did his connection with known power holders. As a man in regular contact with power holders, moreover, he was presumably in a position to bring benefit to his whole gang.

It thus became necessary for A.J. to perform in a dual representative capacity. In the eyes of his own followers, he was expected to represent their interests in dealing not only with the party but also with other groups contacted through the party;

while from the point of view of the party's functionaries, he was expected to represent the party in his dealings with all groups and especially to mobilize his own men in any situation exclusively for the party's benefit. From his own point of view, successful performance in this dual capacity built up his reputation with persons outside both groups and strengthened his position within them.

Although the saloon gangs included married as well as single men, Cermak ceased to participate in their public free-for-alls shortly after he married. By that time his relationship with the gang had assumed a different form. Gang life in the pattern just described, however, continued for at least three years, until 1892.

At that time the young man made an important decision. He quit his towing job, purchased the horse he had been using, and started his own business. In the Chicago where the self-made men of the nineties were preparing the Columbian Exposition to demonstrate to the world the virility of their laissez-faire culture, it was not strange that a young Czech-American should follow in the pattern. For it was evident that one path to power lay in the accumulation of wealth through private business. A wagon was also obtained, and at nineteen Cermak was in the hauling and wood business. The enterprise prospered from the beginning. Although he did not peddle with a pushcart, as some have thought, he did sell kindling wood, and to good advantage.

The wood was sold either by the carload or by the tub. This kind of business demanded rather close contact with customers. Everyone in the neighborhood needed wood, and many became acquainted with the wood distributors during the course of their frequent calls. The sales sometimes included a degree of personal service, such as lighting fires for the Jewish customers on their Sabbath.

With the push of two very advantageous contracts for waste wood, the business began to expand quickly. Eulogies have credited young A.J. with forty teams and forty men in two years' time, but this is an obvious device to create a myth. Nevertheless, within two years he became prosperous enough to marry; within four years he was able to build a home the equal of any in the area; and by 1902, when he entered the state legislature, he was considered a man of considerable means by his neighbors. Even then he had only five or six wagons and employed no more than twelve to fifteen teamsters.

A.J.'s marriage took place in 1894, when he was twenty-one years old. He married Mary Horejs, the eighteen-year-old daughter of Czech neighbors. Despite journalists' romantic accounts, the young couple did not meet in a restaurant, nor was Miss Horejs a waitress. By 1894 the Cermaks had lived across the street from the Horejses at Twenty-Fifth Street and Washtenaw Avenue, in Lawndale, for two years.

The young Mrs. Cermak had also been born in Bohemia and throughout her life was more at home speaking Bohemian than English. Prior to her marriage she was a seamstress in a tailor shop; and she had little formal education, less than A.J. Like A.J.'s mother, she was a plain, quiet woman, a homebody of a maternal nature. Czech associates say of her that she "gave herself no society airs" as A.J.'s fortunes rose. She never betrayed any wish to share the spotlight with her husband. On the contrary, she is recalled as having been acutely self-conscious and self-effacing, fearful of embarrassing her husband by her appearance, "always at the edge of a group," but watching A.J. with apparent pride.

For the first two years of their marriage the couple lived with the bride's parents. Their first home was built a block away from the homes of both their families. This was in 1896. At that time the business was transferred to the backyard of the new home. The Cermaks lived there through A.J.'s entire service in the state legislature, until his election as alderman in 1909. In this plain brick structure, Cermak had not only his business office for many years but his personal political headquarters.

Moving to Lawndale had not meant that A.J. dropped his friendship with his saloon companions of Pilsen. Even though he no longer joined them in their Saturday night escapades, he continued to see them. They frequently visited his new home in Lawndale. Cermak's home, even while he lived with his in-laws, was something of a male social center. It was not unusual for twenty or thirty men to congregate around the Horejs' barn of an evening to chat, swap stories, and drink beer from cans. These

Alderman Cermak,
secretary of the United Societies, 1913.

A. J. Cermak,
a few months before his death

sessions continued until his mother-in-law lost patience and dispersed the visitors with a tongue-lashing.

Mrs. Horejs was not prudish or overly sensitive. These gatherings were often noisy and boisterous. As more beer was consumed the jokes and the curses became louder; it was not unusual for physical violence—often not in anger—to result. Cermak was never effete. He joined willingly and even enthusiastically in the horseplay. One Saturday night, for example, dressed in a new suit, he greeted a friend who was bringing in his wagon. Some banter that was exchanged turned into a playful scuffle. This soon became quasi-earnest, and the outcome was a lusty struggle which included rolling through the dust and mud of the alley in locked combat from Washtenaw Avenue to Marshall Boulevard, a distance of about two hundred yards.

Such centers of male fellowship for Cermak were not limited to his barn. As in Pilsen, as in his official political work, saloons were important in his social life. When he was quite new in the neighborhood he made it his business to have an old resident squire him around to all the neighborhood places so that he might be introduced to people. Some of these taverns were in the remoter parts of the ward. In addition, he was anxious to meet members of the various local social and fraternal clubs. During this early period he joined at least four such organizations: Knights of Pythias, Foresters, Masons, and Zoldaks. The last was a social club of Czech businessmen of the sort who prided themselves on being the "better element."

Mention has been made of Cermak's earliest contacts with the Democratic party while he was a saloon gang leader in Pilsen. During that period his position in the political circle was manifestly lowly. He was still several years under voting age. Nevertheless, his value as a "ward heeler" had been sufficient to procure him the sporadic job of tacking up tax notices at the rate of five dollars a day.

Immediately upon moving to Lawndale, his new neighborhood, Cermak turned his attention, his business notwithstanding, to assessing the new situation in terms of relating himself to the existing party structure. Although he maintained his Pilsen gang connections and although this neighborhood was under the control of Adolph J. Sabath, a Czech Jew of considerable political power with whom he had had previous contacts, this was another ward, and his personal acquaintance was at first limited. He began consciously and assiduously to remedy this situation in the ways described above. Another early move in this direction was the attempt to create a grass-roots organization.

Lawndale was a new section, raw and undeveloped. Sidewalks, sewers, and pavements were lacking. Cermak wrote:

> I circulated around and got in touch with various people and we organized a little improvement association to fight for these improvements. I was made secretary and was thrown for the first time [sic] into a work of a semi-political nature. I noticed that my activities put my name more prominently before my neighbors and brought me a few customers who had not patronized me before.[1]

He soon made still other contacts. "During all this time . . . [he was] building himself a following among his people."[2] By 1894 he had become a driver, errand boy, and general factotum to an important local Democratic functionary named Cerveny.

"Fatty" Cerveny, a 450-pound wheel horse, was official West Town collector, an agent for Monarch Beer, and organizationally connected with the Carter Harrison faction[3] through his superiors, Sabath and Loeffler. It should be noted that this humble position was accepted by Cermak in 1894, by which time his business was fairly well established.

He continued as Cerveny's aide for six years, simultaneously operating his teamster business. Doubtless, in making the rounds with Cerveny, "rassling" books for Cerveny's clerks, A.J. received valuable political tutelage. He must also have enjoyed the sensation of meeting great numbers of party leaders and the attendant feeling of being "on the inside." There would seem to be scarcely any other explanation for his spending so much of his time in this work rather than in his growing business. It is improbable that he profited from his party status beyond the extent of the hire of one of his wagons by a ward yard.

His political activities were not, however, confined to assisting Cerveny. He also served directly on the party firing line. It could hardly have been otherwise in Chicago politics—then or since. One can say with assurance that any person holding a position such as Cermak had with Cerveny must be an energetic worker ın his home precinct. That Cermak was such a worker is shown by his successive precinct jobs—precinct election official, assistant precinct captain, and finally, getting his "own precinct" as captain. He was an outstanding success as precinct captain, for by 1902 he had received two more promotions in the ward organization. By this date he had served both as secretary and as chairman of the ward Democratic organization. Such promotions went only to those who were among the best and most loyal workers.

His successful party work was further rewarded in 1899 in more concrete political currency. He was appointed bailiff in a westside justice-of-the-peace court. This job he owed to the Harrison faction.

To have some idea of what was entailed in becoming an "outstanding success" on this important first step of the party ladder, a few aspects of Cermak's job as precinct captain should be detailed. The precinct captain is the basic unit of the urban political machine and the worker having the most direct and frequent face-to-face relationship with the citizen. His duties are divided, roughly, between those related to the election campaign and those which might be described as continuing activities. The first type of duty has been summarized as follows:

> To [precinct captains] are entrusted the execution of the extensive requirements of election routine, and the detailed supervision of the interests of the party in the localities. They are in charge of the naturalization, if need be, of the circulation of petitions, of the registration of voters, of the party canvass, of the distribution of party literature, of the whipping up of attendance at party rallies, of the task of bringing out the vote, of supervising the count.[4]

The canvass is one of their chief campaign duties, required in both primary and general elections. This is mostly patient and arduous leg work and doorbell ringing—it was especially so in the days before the ubiquity of the telephone. This tactic is indispensable to the success of the captain; he relies on this for getting to the voters his personal impression of the candidate.

Culminating the year-round, continuing responsibilities of the precinct captain are the various and exacting duties of election day. To this day all the energies and anxieties of the precinct captain are pointed. He feels that he must win at any cost, for defeat may result in loss of his job, sources of income and privilege, respect and prestige in the organization. Even if he prefers to win honestly (relying upon his canvass and his services to the voters), he often resorts to illegal methods if only because he has reasonable ground for fearing that the opposition may do so. Precinct election officials are appointed on a party basis, each party naming one half of the total number in the city. In odd-numbered precincts the incumbent party names two of the officials and the contending party chooses three, in even-numbered precincts the ratio is reversed. In addition to requiring party tests for precinct election officers, the statute prescribes that they must be residents of the precinct. These arrangements are often held responsible for the fact that from time to time criminals (from pickpockets to those convicted of election fraud) become precinct captains, and it is not surprising that recourse is made to the entire catalogue of illegal election practices.

The cataclysm of the election, however, occurs only periodically. To be properly prepared for a good showing the precinct captain must keep at his job all the year round. In many precincts the captain is a powerful person performing services and granting favors with a judicious eye toward votes. He tries to get jobs for individuals; he receives complaints about streets, alleys, and other governmental services. In a broader sense he acts as an intermediary between the citizen and the government, not only intervening with the law but often interpreting and representing the state to the individual. For many persons he is the only figure of authority ever seen in the flesh, except for the policeman.

He also acts as a personalized social service agency. This was much more important in Cermak's day, prior to the start of broad federal programs in this realm; but a Chicago study made in the 1930's showed that large numbers of precinct captains were still involved in distribution of coal, food, clothing, and rent money to needy clients.[5]

For all his energy, the tenure of the precinct captain is likely to be "short, nasty and brutish"—except when he belongs to a party or faction which has been securely entrenched for a long time. His career may be terminated after every election, for he serves at the pleasure of his immediate superior, the ward committeeman. There is sharp rivalry for the favorable notice of the ward leader.

Each of them hopes to control the ward some day. Each tries to spread out from his own precinct and pick up a personal following in the other precincts of the ward. . . . In due course some one of these precinct leaders wins his way to recognition as the right-hand man of the ward boss, while another, taking umbrage at this, begins to feel himself strong enough to "buck the machine." . . . The old machine usually wins, and the precinct leader who has matched strength with it goes into discard. Somebody else takes over the precinct in his place. . . . Most of the young hopefuls are eliminated in these ward insurrections. It is only the most capable who survive.[6]

This is the sort of endeavor in which Cermak emerged top man and a fledgling politician. A description of the type of man apt to succeed at this stage of the game is given by Gosnell, who says that

The ideal precinct captain is one who makes friends easily, who works hard and steadily, who gives absolute obedience, who is intelligent but satisfied with a subordinate role, who is not too demanding for himself and who does not ask too many questions.[7]

Apparently Cermak was able to convince his superiors that he approximated this ideal. But manifestly Gosnell's description scarcely fits a person of the leadership type—a type to which Cermak belonged, as his subsequent career demonstrates. Although he more than satisfied the needs of the organization with respect to his role as precinct captain, Cermak's inner disposition tallied in few respects with Gosnell's archetype.

This kind of political education was to be of great value in Cermak's future career. The years of countless face-to-face contacts with voters provided the basis from which he must have drawn a great deal of his "understanding" and "knowledge" of people—that is, the kind of understanding and the kind of knowledge which could be of political significance. Nor, in the future, could anyone ever accuse him of being an outsider, of lacking sympathy for the rank and file because he hadn't "learned the hard way."

His jobs as Cerveny's assistant and as bailiff were well suited to maintaining and strengthening his position in the local organization. On the one hand he was in a strategic position to perform favors for his constituents; on the other hand, continued success at the polls enhanced his standing in the organization. His promotions to secretary and later to chairman of the ward organization are clear indications of this.

In these subsequent quasi-administrative roles (although he continued to hold his base in his home precinct) his vista became wider and his responsibilities heavier. Although the frequent interaction with the voters in the precinct diminished, it was replaced by a much higher ratio of close contact with other precinct captains and the ward leader and his lieutenants. The ward club was the administrative hub of the ward machine. Here the ward leaders appeared *daily* and held court, listened to petitions, and dispensed favors. Cermak observed his chief closely. His principal task was an administrative one—to keep close check on the efficiency of the individual precinct captains and the health of the organization in general. The ward committeeman has other responsibilities. He has his own business office for nonparty affairs; he must constantly be in touch with city hall and maintain contacts with his peers and superiors. Therefore Cermak, the administrative assistant, was frequently in charge in the boss's absence.

An administrative assistant frequently replaces his chief in government and business. Cermak was in an enviable position to plan just such a succession. Not only was such a club a political headquarters, it was also a social center of considerable importance. Party workers and citizens of all descriptions lounged and spent time there. It was a place where one could come to know and be known by every working member of the machine and by large numbers of ordinary voters. In this situation Cermak was able to broaden his contacts, to improve and consolidate his position.

It appears that either objectively or instinctively A.J. evaluated the power potentialities of his total environment. In his social life, the sort of business in which he engaged, and his deliberate political work, he persistently moved in the direction of meeting and impressing an ever wider circle. By 1902 he was ready to reap his rewards in the form of nomination and election to his first elective office, that of state representative.

This event was of importance not only to A.J. but also to his Bohemian neighbors and followers, who played a large part in bringing it about. Before we follow his progress to the capitol, let us have a look at the people who came to regard A.J. as their leader and spokesman.

THE

CZECHS

OF

LAWNDALE

Cermak was a Czech not only by birth and parentage but by self-definition, by cultural, emotional, and political identification. The fact of Czechness assumes a central importance, first, because A.J.'s early claims to power and status occurred through his own group and were possible only in terms of his group; second, because the fact of Czechness and all that this implies may have had certain general influences on the kind of private and public personality Cermak became. An examination of these people and their institutions may also cast light upon the character, institutions, beliefs, and attitudes which are of importance in gaining group political power in the American urban environment.

A closer view of such an ethnic group as the Czechs seems particularly called for in view of the confusion concerning Slavic peoples which exists in the minds of most Americans. The totality of impressions held about the Czechs and other Slavic groups is often embodied, for the man on the street, in the value-loaded label "Bohunk," which carries with it a stereotype of a slow, plodding, dull-witted, broad-backed, unimaginative, insensitive, lowly paid work machine, a kind of subhuman species. With the informed American the case is not much better; for not only may this stereotype exist side by side with an awareness of the ethnic origins of Dvorak, Smetana, Chopin, Conrad, Turgenev, and Tolstoy, but also the fact that the term "Slav" refers to a number of differentiated groups is seldom recognized as a reality. Thus, although some may at one time have learned that the Slavs include Czechs, Russians, Ruthenians, Serbs, Croats, Slovaks, Slovenes, Bulgars, Poles, Montenegrins, Bosnians, and Dalmatians, but do not include Magyars (Hungarians); nevertheless, on the level of everyday experience the relevance of these distinctions tends to be disregarded or forgotten. It is very seldom taken into account that "there is no such person as a Slav, any more than there is such a person as a Teuton or a Celt . . . they are Russians, Poles, or what-not, as the Teuton is a German or a Swede or an Englishman."[1]

The Immigration Department at one time recognized eight Slavic groups, and this did not include all of them. Further, the differences between the various groups have certain consequences. One hears frequently expressions such as "the Slav vote in Chicago," which imply belief in one closely knit, homogeneous group, a group, moreover, which functions as a unit. That this is seldom the case is scarcely surprising.

The various Slavic nationalities are separated by distinctions of speech, historical experience, national self-consciousness, political aims, and often of religion. In American communities they have different churches, societies, newspapers, and a separate social life. Too often the lines of cleavage are marked by antipathies and old animosities . . . and a person who acts in ignorance of these facts, a missionary, for instance, or a political boss, or a trade-union organizer, may find himself in the position of a host who should innocently invite a Fenian from County Cork to hob-nob with an Ulster Orangeman, on the ground that both were Irish.[2]

Ask a New York Czech in what part of the city the Serbo-Croatians live. He does not know. Inquire of a Pole where the Czech quarter is located and the chances are he will have to ask a policeman. . . . In Chicago, Poles and Czechs professing the same faith bury their dead in a common cemetery . . . but the tie that binds in this case is not racial kinship, but religion.[3]

Some efforts toward Pan-Slavism have been made in Europe; but the enmities of the groups involved have not contributed to their success, any more than in the case of similar attempts at Slav unity in this country. The Slovaks and the Czechs, however, are very close not only geographically but linguistically. The Slovaks with the Czechs formed the reconstructed government in 1918, but prior to that time the Slovaks had no independent history.

By the fifth century Slavs occupied Bohemia; and by 870 they were organized into the powerful Moravian Empire. This was short-lived largely because of the Magyar invasions, which at last succeeded in completely subjugating the Slovaks. The Bohemians, however, kept their independence and formed a state. They retained independence until 1620. From early times Bohemia was the battleground between the Slav and the Teuton, since the Bohemians, westernmost Slavs, were surrounded by Germans on three sides. The Hussite wars of the fifteenth century were one great manifestation of this struggle. These wars stemmed in part from the preachings of Jan Hus, whose ideas anticipated the Reformation by fully a century but were also anti-German crusades.

Under the Hapsburgs and in the Counter-Reformation, Czech national life and language were almost eliminated. In the Germanization program everything Bohemian was rigidly suppressed, while bloody measures were taken to replace the dominant Protestantism with Catholicism. Bohemian political independence was extinguished for three hundred years. The fanning of revolutionary spirits throughout Europe in 1848 included a revolt in Prague. Although this was as unsuccessful as elsewhere in Europe, nationalism received a great impetus, and demands for recognition and autonomy or independence came to be made with increasing earnestness—always, however, in constitutional rather than in revolutionary forms. Complete independence was finally gained as a result of Woodrow Wilson's self-determination policy.

What kind of heritage did this sort of national experience leave? First, there is the fact of very mixed German-Czech culture. Not only have the two groups lived adjacent to one another for over a millenium, but they have intermarried, adopted one another's names and customs. So there have been Bohemian leaders with such German names as Reiger, Brauner, and Zeithammer; and men like Schmeykal, Taschek, and Chlumecky have led the German group in Bohemia. One writer is certain that propinquity resulted in acceptance of many German customs and culture characteristics, while at the same time the constant struggle against the Germans for national existence resulted in "a degree of aggressiveness . . . that is singularly lacking in the make-up of other Slavs."[4] Whether this is true or not, it is certain that this struggle is in part responsible for the Bohemian preoccupation with liberty, an interest covering both religious and political liberty, the two having been originally closely bound up together. These concepts are united in the symbolic figure of Hus, who is looked upon not merely as a religious leader but as a leader in the fight against political domination.

In the Hussite wars, the Bohemians faced most of the organized strength of Catholic Europe—that is, all of European Christendom. From that point on, opposition to orthodoxy has been "an important party of Bohemian life."[5] Freethinking is a philosophy, but it is also an indication of national character. There is among Bohemians at large a feeling of opposition to theocratic controls and a distrust of the clergy. Although the repressive policies of the Hapsburgs succeeded in turning nearly the entire country Catholic, once the people reached new shores they proved to be the least faithful to Rome of all immigrant groups. Estimates vary, but most observers judge that fully half of the Czechs in the United States in 1915 had given up Catholicism. A few found Protestant denominations, but the bulk of the dissenters became Freethinkers or agnostics.[6]

The political ideals of the Bohemians have been described as having for several centuries "approached nearer to those of England than any other of the greater European nations." They seemed early to have had considerable political capacities. They never recognized divine right; they elected their own kings who "were bound by what was practically equivalent to our modern constitutions."[7] Bohemians have been conscious of nationality for over five hundred years. This fact is central to an appreciation of the evolvement of much that is distinctive about them. Thus, their desire for political liberty came to be characterized more by the spirit of moderation and gradualism than by the revolutionary spirit of the early opposition to religious orthodoxy. During the incendiary nineteenth century, compromise rather than violent rebellion characterized their nationalistic strivings. This kind of spirit found its expression in the cool reception given the firebrands of other Slavic groups: Bakunin and effervescent Polish revolutionists were received in Prague with little enthusiasm.[8] The Bohemian weapons against the Austrian master were not those of the hero, but rather of the cautious, middle-class burgher. This attitude is best exemplified in the writings of their chief spokesman of the nineteenth century, Karel Havlicek, who believed that "a politician should act very much like a businessman."[9] This view, incidentally, is remarkably parallel to the views frequently expressed on the same subject by Cermak, as we shall see.

Bohemian civilization is older than that of the Germans or Austrians and is independent of it. Bohemian literature is one of the earliest in Europe; Bohemian elementary educational institutions antedate the establishment of such institutions in Germany and Austria; and the University of Prague was founded more than a half-century before any German or Austrian universities. A modern cultural revival began early in the last century, involving in the first instance the renaissance of the traditional language. One expert on the Czechs recognizes as the two national characteristics which distinguish them from all other Slavs their respect for religious freedom, symbolized by Hus, and their respect for education, symbolized by Comenius, another national hero, considered by some historians of education the true forerunner of modern philosophies of education. The school is said to be accorded a place of honor in Bohemian villages comparable to the place assigned to the prison or the church in some other Slavic villages. Some objective criteria of the regard for education exist in the literacy statistics for immigrants, which show the Bohemians to be among the most literate of all immigrant groups.[10]

Bohemians did not begin to come to the United States in any appreciable numbers until the revolutionary period of 1848. A large wave also occurred with the end of the Austro-Prussian War, in 1867, coinciding as it did with the end of the Civil War in the United States. The largest number of Bohemians arrived in the decade 1870-80, the period when Cermak's parents emigrated. The Czechs formed a significant immigrant group in this country by the turn of the last century when Cermak began his political career. Their greatest concentration at this time and since has been in Chicago and Cook County, and generally in urban areas. By 1920, the first and second generation Bohemians in Chicago had reached an estimated 200,000.

The Bohemians came as permanent settlers in family units. The families were and have continued to be relatively closely knit primary organizations in which group values and standards are to a high degree preserved. Although the father was nominally the head of the family, the position of the mother was not completely subservient, as in some ethnic groups. On the contrary, frequently the mother was the treasurer or guardian of the family exchequer and the disbursing officer. In other areas, such as churches and fraternal organizations, women were accorded if not equality, a high degree of participation.[11] Czech women, both married and unmarried, showed a greater tendency to be employed outside the home than women of other Slavic groups.

Both the women and the men showed qualities of immense physical endurance. Czech men did not often display their bodily power in their work, however: a disproportionate number of them, compared with other ethnic groups, had skilled occupations. To a high degree Bohemians in the United States have tended to concentrate in the relatively more individualized tasks—in offices, garment shops, their own crafts—rather than in great factories or other mass-production industries. (The miners, of course, are a notable exception.) Also, many were in the lower ranks of the business and professional groups, and the impulse to reach such burgher status was great. The most frequently found enterprises were grocery and similar provision stores, saloons, and banks— probably in this order of prestige.

Among the Czechs there was a very rapid rate and high percentage of naturalization. This can perhaps be partly accounted for by the heavy admixture of German and generally Western influences in the Czech culture. Czechs in this country have shown marked interest in trade unionism, not only readily joining existing unions but being instrumental in organizing some powerful locals, or even national unions.

Up to 1915 they were little interested in national politics and only in special cases in local politics. What interest and participation there was, was of the business sort, individuals sometimes becoming members of a local political machine or selling a vote. This being the case, in given localities it was not too difficult for the Czechs to be voted as a unit, the entire group feeling repaid when one of their members received recognition by nomination to a minor office. At the same time, Bohemians have been accused of being unusually harsh and critical of any of their group who attains a position of prominence or leadership. This attitude may be an expression of certain pessimistic resignation said to be caused by the centuries of national subjugation. The suspicion of current leaders undermined the ability of the Czechs to cooperate politically in their own country, where they were inclined to support with great devotion ideals and causes rather than persons. The inability to cooperate in the larger political arena is in striking contrast to the success of the Czechs at cooperative enterprises in the more communal areas of daily life. They are active, for example, in a great variety of cooperative economic organizations such as building-and-loan associations (with great assets) through the efforts of which Czechs have been enabled to own a much greater percentage of their homes than comparable ethnic units.

Prior to the Civil War, because of their fervent antislavery stand, they were heavily Republican. "Another reason for Republicanism has been the simple one that the Irish were Democrats."[12] However, in Chicago the Czechs have been Democrats in spite of the Irish. This has been explained on the grounds that inasmuch as the Republicans were the incumbents, the past experience of the Czechs required joining the opposition.

Czechs did not have representation in important political positions until Cermak's rise to power. Even compared with the Poles, who were a later group in Illinois, they fared poorly. As early as 1906, both parties in Illinois nominated Poles for state treasurer, while the sole claim of the Czechs was a congressman from Illinois. However, since the congressman, Adolph J. Sabath, was a Jew as well as a Czech, it is difficult to say to which group he was accredited.

Sociologists who have studied the American Czech community have made some comments about the Czech "national character" worth noting here, as follows: The Czech national character may be closely identified with the American national character. By

reason of their background and inclinations, the Czechs understand and accept the concepts of liberty, equality, democracy, and
justice; they readily subscribe to the business ideals of speed,
efficiency, and economy, showing "special aptitude" in what is
probably the central sphere of our culture, the practical aspects of
economic life.[13] "In another generation the Czechs will certainly
share as completely in our American life as the Irish, the Scandinavians and the Germans today."[14]

There is considerable controversy on the subject of Czech morals
and Czech attitude toward morals. The principal charges of
amorality seem to stem from misunderstandings of or objections
to the position of the Freethinkers. This is understandable, inasmuch as the position of atheists or agnostics in this country is never
an enviable one. (Some of the criticism of the Czech Freethinkers
comes, of course, from their own fellow countrymen.) This sect,
curiously enough, has many of the characteristics of an organized
religion—an ethical creed, a catechism, and its own "parochial
schools," teaching Czech language and history. Other charges of
amorality arise probably from confusion on the matter of Czech
drinking habits. Unquestionably, they may be said to drink a
great deal. However, this is a matter of cultural acceptance, not a
sign of the absence of morals. No social stigma is attached to
drinking among the Czechs, in contrast to more Puritanical
groups; if any objections are raised among their own members, it
is not from the standpoint of morals. Drinking is habitual, and
drunkards or alcoholics are rare. Violent brawls during the re-
current drinking bouts are not infrequent; but violence among
Czechs is otherwise rare.

Ordinarily Czechs are "conspicuously quiet, industrious, and
law-abiding," and are seldom guilty of homicide.[15] Crimes against
property are less rare. Czechs tend to be more aggressive than other
Slavs, but are also "mild, immovable, and stubborn."[16] They are
less litigious than other Slavs, but nevertheless extremely argu-
mentative. The indifference to danger of Czechs and other Slav
immigrants in United States' industries has been frequently noted.

Other features of Czech national character as it has been modified in the American environment can best be illustrated as we
examine the inhabitants of Lawndale, the Chicago Czech com-

munity where Cermak's career began and whence he received support to the end of his life. Lawndale had "developed as a distinctive unit in the pattern of Chicago, with a character of its own."[17] This was largely so because of a high degree of physical isolation from the rest of the city caused by large industrial plants, railroad yards, and similar barriers. On the north it is bounded by the elevated right of way of the Chicago, Burlington and Quincy Railroad. To the west it runs into the city limit, the giant Western Electric factories, the town of Cicero, and the right of way of the Belt Line Railway of Chicago. On the south it is hemmed in by industrial and public utility plants, and the Chicago Sanitary and Ship Canal. To the east it is shut off by the sprawling International Harvester Company and another belt railroad. "Lawndale is a residential island in a sea of industry."[18]

Despite this isolation, Lawndale was the heart of a fairly contiguous belt of Czechs reaching from the vicinity of the Loop southwest to the suburbs and beyond the boundaries of Cook County. In this wedge was located by far the largest Czech population of Chicago, Cook County, the State of Illinois, and the United States. In fact, it was the second Czech center of urban population in the world.

Lawndale was not a political or geographic subdivision, but rather a sociological category. However, contained squarely at the heart of it was the Twelfth Ward (now the Twenty-Second Ward). If Lawndale was the capital community of Chicago and Cook County Czechs, the Twelfth Ward was the nucleus of that capital. Cermak's power came to be firmly anchored upon this ward, although quite early in his career his influence began to spread over all of Lawndale and beyond. The distribution of Czechs in Lawndale and adjacent areas, in comparison to the Twelfth Ward, is shown in the accompanying table.

The section, sometimes called Ceske Kalifornie, is chronologically the fifth Czech settlement in Chicago. It was founded about 1880, just over a decade before Cermak settled there. By the 1920's it was one of the most densely populated areas in Chicago. Ever since its founding the Czechs were predominant. As late as 1930, 17.8 per cent of the population had been born in Bohemia; and of course the percentage is more than doubled when one includes the second and third generations. The Poles were the only other important national group, in 1930 representing 13.7 per cent of the population. No other group accounted for more than six tenths of one per cent of the total. "It is the Czechs who give the color and flavor to the community."[19]

DISTRIBUTION OF CZECHS IN CHICAGO IN 1914

Ward	Foreign-born	American-born	Total	Ward Population
10	10,332	11,611	21,943	61,446
11	3,954	4,604	8,558	67,900
12	13,447	16,983	30,430	66,082
20	1,284	1,046	2,330	61,459
29	4,740	5,002	9,742	83,691
34	9,247	9,846	19,093	70,630

Source: J. Horak, Assimilation of Czechs in Chicago, Ph.D. dissertation, University of Chicago, 1920, p. 19.

This being so, it is not surprising that one still sees evidence of Czechness on every hand. Czech names predominate on shop windows; Czech motion pictures are advertised on theater marquees; billboards and posters advise passers-by of a great variety of social and cultural events to be offered in Czech language or sponsored by Czech organizations. All these features still exist; one or two generations ago their influence was infinitely more pervasive. "If you ever walk on the street [Twenty-Sixth] between Kedzie and Crawford Avenues, nine out of ten you encounter will be of Czech stock," Cermak once commented.[20] Even today one hears English spoken with a distinctive lilt. Czech itself is heard frequently, and by no means always from septuagenarians; it is not unusual to hear it spoken on the street by parent and child.

The giant industries surrounding Lawndale gave employment to many of its people. The community also has its own Czech banks, breweries, and small factories. These are located largely on the main business streets, Twenty-Sixth and Twenty-Second (now named Cermak Road), and California, Kedzie, and Crawford avenues. On these same streets are located most of the Czech meetinghalls, Sokol gymnasiums, clubrooms, and reading rooms (there are several libraries in the community); the headquarters of

Freethinker societies and other local and national societies, and the offices of some of the Czech newspapers. Here, too, is the most important Czech meeting place, Pilsen Park, scene of festivals, bazaars, picnics, and political gatherings. This was the forum in which Cermak's voice was often heard. Here he appeared in each campaign; and here also occurred the free political picnics with which he frequently wooed his constituents.

The actual Main Street was the mile between Kedzie and Crawford avenues on Twenty-Sixth Street, in the geographic center of the area. In this mile Cermak had his real estate business. The bank and the building-and-loan association with which he was connected were also here. Later he was to have the county criminal court building and jail built on this street. This business area was only a community shopping center, rather than a regional one, largely because of physical barriers. However, for the same reason it was a "healthy, prosperous area." In 1935 it was twentieth among such districts in Chicago.[21] Because it was so difficult of access from other parts of the city, it contained no large motion picture theaters, department stores, or similar features. Also, its transportation facilities to other business areas and to the Loop were extremely poor. Therefore, it became relatively self-sufficient. Since many residents were, furthermore, employed in the community or at its edges, it was not uncommon to meet Lawndalites who hadn't been to the Loop in decades, or out of the community in years. Apart from this commercial area, there were only a few minor satellite business intersections.

Lawndale is definitely a low-rent, low-income area. Even in 1942, a relatively prosperous year, 50 per cent of the units rented for less than $25 per month; 85 per cent under $30 per month; and 96 per cent under $40 per month. At the same time, for the city as a whole, only 42 per cent of the rental units were rented for less than $30 per month. Despite the low-income, low-rental drabness, Lawndale is far from a slum. In 1942, by which time many of the dwellings were quite old, 97 per cent were either in good condition or needed only minor repairs. During Cermak's time, when most of the buildings were new, the situation was even more favorable.

Most of the single-family houses are one-story buildings in the

German Renaissance architectural style common to Central Europe. They occupy very narrow lots, usually not wider than twenty-five feet. The buildings are extremely close together, and there are narrow side yards and inconsequential front lawns. Often the small yards have been sacrificed in order to erect another building, or another wing. Sometimes one or more stories have been added. This has usually come about as a consequence of the drive to improve the economic lot. As soon as a family's dwelling was completed and paid for, these adjacent or overhead units were built as income-producing property. They were frequently let for stores, or flats, occasionally to roomers. For this end, the pleasure of a garden or yard was cheerfully relinquished, despite the fact that there were in Lawndale few parks and other outdoor recreation areas.

There were few conversions of residences for other purposes before 1920, and not nearly so many since then as in other parts of the city. The conversions that did occur were not of the kind which caused the introduction of business enterprises in residential areas. Nor have such conversions as have taken place caused the development of a large number of rooming houses and the concomitant transient population. This is unique for an immigrant area, and is in special contrast to the practices of other Slavic groups. In 1942, only 2.9 per cent of living units offered rooms for rent.

In this context, it should be noted that the above statistics are an index to the high degree of community stability, which finds further demonstration in the relatively long duration of dwelling occupancy. This applies both to renters and owners.

The 38.1 per cent of the dwelling units which are occupied by their owners have a median duration of occupancy of fifteen years and two months, while half of the tenant-occupied units were occupied more than three years and four months. . . . With long occupancy goes a local civic pride in one's house which is lacking in areas of transition.[22]

It is remarkable that in highly mobile Chicago, nine years after Cermak's death, nearly 40 per cent of home owners who occupied their residences in his territory had already been residents of Lawndale when he was at the peak of his power. This unusual neighborhood stability, it may be guessed, would simplify a leader's attempt to build a lasting political following, given the ability to represent community attitudes and desires.

HOME LIFE

Although the larger portion of the Lawndale Czechs lived in small, narrow, unattractive dwellings, the home, as is most often the case with Czechs, was an important part of life to every member of the family. A considerable portion of family income was spent upon it. If the interior of the home was fairly barren when first built, gradually cheap rugs came to cover scrubbed floors, and ugly plush upholstered chairs replaced utilitarian wooden ones. Often a piano, a violin, or other musical instrument was found in the parlor, while other items of dark-stained furniture, doilies, fancywork, and a great clutter of knickknacks completed the picture. Usually this portion of the house was reserved for guests, with the kitchen, as in Braidwood, serving the family as the *de facto* living room.

Family life and family ties in Lawndale, as elsewhere among Czechs, have always been strong. This was true despite the seemingly paradoxical penchant for joining societies and frequenting saloons. Family ties were more real than apparent, with a basic system of duties and loyalties which were seldom questioned, and yet did not require constant minor demonstrations. Thus, married children very often continued to live under the parental roof, or their parents lived with them. Cermak provides a case in point, having had his parents in his home until he was about forty years of age. Later in life he built summer homes for his married children, adjacent to the one he owned in Channel Lake, Illinois.

ECONOMIC ADJUSTMENT

"The economic adjustment of the Czech community is almost perfect."[23]

In their occupations the Lawndale Czechs reflected this adjustment. Since relatively few of them were peasant farmers upon their arrival, they largely became skilled artisans and shopkeepers. The second generation, in 1920, and an ever-increasing number since, in conformity with the general development of American culture, prefer white-collar jobs or professions. The Lawndalites ventured into almost every kind of business needed by the community and not pre-empted by large non-Czech chains. These businesses ran the gamut from banks, real estate, wholesale foods and retail stores, to light manufacture.

Conflicts in economic life were rare, although there was a definite antipathy for the Irish, which carried over into the economic realm, when the Irish were encountered in the process of earning a living. Jewish shopkeepers were few in Lawndale, in marked contrast to the Polish group, among whom Jewish shopkeepers predominated. Such Jewish shopkeepers as there were were nearly all Czech Jews, against whom there appeared to be a minimum of ill will.

The majority of Lawndale's intellectuals were foreign-born, while those in the arts were almost entirely so. The new culture did not appear to have encouraged the growth of such proclivities among second-generation Czechs.

SOCIAL ADJUSTMENT

Most groups, like most individuals, find it simpler to earn a living than to live the good life. For the Czech immigrant residents of Lawndale, the social readjustments which had to be made were relatively greater and more difficult than the economic ones.

Material well-being and progress still receive the greatest attention from the Czechs so that all other standards of conduct and social status and recognition are determined by the economic circumstances and the prosperity of a person. Czechs in Chicago are very practical and businesslike. They would not listen to any other than a strictly business proposition.[24]

Most of the Czechs arrived in Lawndale with economic resources comparable to Cermak's upon his arrival. The successful ones in business are truly self-made men, and as such are very proud of their achievements. They have a "great suspicion of everything that is intellectual or bears a mark of intellectuality."[25] Cermak shared fully in this attitude, although in him as in others there was also a certain ambivalence, for he keenly felt his own lack of formal education and constantly dwelt upon its great importance to the members of his family. On the other hand, Cermak early recognized the fact that, education or no, were he to become well-to-do he would be accepted at all levels of Lawndale society. And throughout his career, although his better-educated compatriots felt some aloofness and condescension toward this diamond-in-the-rough, there was no doubt about his welcome in almost all Czech homes.

So the eyes of the Lawndale businessmen were chiefly on economic advancement, on profits and interest and bank balances. They realized, however, that one good avenue to wealth and, hence, status was through gaining prestige among their own people. They realized that there was "much community spirit, patriotism, and solidarity among the people which [could be] to their advantage."²⁶ Cermak saw this very clearly. This was no doubt his meaning in his frequently repeated statement that "politics was good for my business." He knew that one path to prestige for himself—perhaps the only one—was through the political organization. That this prestige would be beneficial to his business interests and, in turn, that business success would cause additional status which could then be further used to consolidate and extend his political pretensions, seemed to be the round-robin calculation implied by his every move.

One element in the difficulty of social adjustment was the fear and suspicion of strangers. This is a phenomenon by no means restricted to Lawndale Czechs, but rather is unanimously observed by sociologists in the case of all groups seeking to adjust to an alien environment. In Lawndale, the hostility and anxiety was rarely manifested in overt conflict but rather showed itself in outward stolidity and aloofness in contacts with non-Czechs. Partially as an expression of this antagonism and fear, the group tended to be clannish. Given the physical make-up of Lawndale and the abilities of its people, it was not too difficult to be self-sufficient. However, there were some other ethnic groups in the midst of Lawndale, the Poles being notable from the point of view of numbers. With these fellow Slavs there was to be detected at the very least a showing of noninterest and neglect. This tended to disappear with the second generation, but considerable traces of this attitude remained.

The attitude of the Czechs toward Czech Jews has already been noted. Among their earliest political leaders we find William Loeffler and Adolph J. Sabath, both Czech Jews. Cermak's secretary for thirty years, later alderman and ward committeeman of the

Twenty-Second Ward, was Henry Sonnenschein, who remained a power in the same ward through the 1950's. Joseph Sabath, brother of the Congressman, was also a prominent Czech political leader. One of the earliest Czechs to gain prominence in Chicago politics—a staunch supporter of the elder Harrison—was another Czech Jew, Adolph Kraus. It should be stressed again, however, that it was in all probability their Czechness which made these men find acceptance, their Jewishness being overridden by that important factor. Each spoke Czech, and at least one made some effort to minimize awareness of his Jewishness.

Of other groups, oddly enough in the light of their historic enmity, the Lawndale Czechs seemed closest to the Germans. Undoubtedly, familiarity with the German language, literature, and customs was in part responsible for this. As we shall see, Cermak and his community became closely allied with the Germans in Chicago in their response to the liquor issue. This close working relationship was to continue for many years, though temporarily set back by differences flowing from divergent sympathies in World War I.

Whatever the role of historic propinquity in making for certain ties with the Germans, it did not operate to the same end in the case of the Hungarians. For the Magyars the Czechs maintained a cordial antipathy. Their attitude toward Italians in Chicago was marked by condescension or aloofness. It was for the Irish, however, a people with whom the residents of Lawndale had had little historical contact, that they reserved their bitterest contempt and hatred. In this observation there seems to be no minority view. The Irish were blamed for every misfortune and discomfort the Czechs found in Chicago. Indeed, to this day, "any American woman who incurs the dislike of a Czech is liable to be dubbed an 'Irishka.' "[27]

Given this kind of attitude toward non-Czechs, it follows that there was relatively little intermarriage, although again this was less true of the second and third generation. When intermarriage did occur, the non-Czech partner was most likely a German, or in some cases another Slav. Cermak, of course, married a Czech; both his sisters married Czechs; and although no definite information exists as to the ethnic origins of his sisters-in-law, the children of his brothers for the most part live now in areas of heavy Czech population. Of Cermak's three daughters only one, Lillian Cermak, originally married a Czech. Ella Cermak married a Canadian of Scottish origin; and Helen Cermak married an Irish-American—later, however, to divorce, and subsequently to remarry a Czech.

Although there was a great attachment among Lawndale Czechs to almost everything of a cultural nature that bore the stamp of Czechness, they made an exception of Czech literature. For a highly literate people, they showed little enthusiasm for books. One bookseller expressed it this way: "My best customers are clergymen and socialists. Old settlers seldom buy a book, their children, never."[28] This aversion, however, did not extend to periodical literature, which was avidly devoured.

The much-discussed alienation between generations existed in the community, but not to the same degree as in other immigrant communities. The American-born children to a considerable degree retained folk values and beliefs, one consequence of this appearing in the fact that there was much less delinquency among them than among such ethnic neighbors as the Poles,[29] the Russian Jews, the Lithuanians, the Slovaks, and the Irish.[30] These factors further accentuated the relative stability of the neighborhood.

Another major factor contributing to a nondynamic community was the prevalence, pervasiveness, and influence of the Czech press located in the neighborhood. From the very beginning of the community, the press and its editors were forces to be reckoned with. There were four main dailies in Czech. Nearly all Czech homes subscribed to one or more Czech dailies—in almost all cases, not because of any inability to read English.[31] Each of these four journals was spokesman for a well-defined political and social attitude, and represented a distinctive segment of political opinion. These divisions ran through all public questions, it being possible to find out "from a short conversation . . . to which one of the parties a certain person belongs."[32] There was one exception to these divergencies: on the matter of Czech-Slovak independence, there was complete unanimity, with press as with people.

The *Svornost* (*Concord*) was the journal of the Freethinkers. Founded in 1875, it accepted the capitalist society and opposed Socialism and organized religion—especially Catholic clericism.

The *Narod* (*Nation*) started in 1894 as the organ of the Catholics, was "very conservative politically and even reactionary."[33] It had a large circulation, well organized by the parishes. The Socialist paper, *Spravedlnost* (*Justice*) founded in 1900, had small circulation and traditional Socialist policies. The *Denni Hlastel* (*Daily Herald*), first published in 1891, was the paper of the businessman. It was conservative, "neutral," and indistinct. It allegedly attempted merely to "give the news." However, it at least equalled the *Svornost* in its enmity to Socialism and its bitternes toward organized labor. This analysis refers largely to stands taken on foreign rather than domestic or local issues. The interests in foreign affairs, especially Czechoslovak affairs, was notable even in the least educated. Conversely, little interest was manifested in domestic or local matters, at least as reflected in the contents of the dailies. This would seem to point to an indifference to local political matters, a view borne out by some observers.

> The masses seem to be excluded from all participation in political power and therefore they leave it to the businessmen and the ward politicians. This is especially true in city politics. . . . People feel that they are intentionally excluded from politics and consider it as something dishonest and dirty, full of fraud and favoritism, and they say that they would rather leave it to the lawyers and the Irish.[34]

There are, however, contrary views on this subject.[35] Actually, Czech participation in political life in Chicago goes back at least to 1883, when one of their numbers was nominated for alderman. He was nominated as a Democrat, and since before that time the Bohemians were closer to the Republicans, this marked the turning of the tide.

> The first political recognition given them was a stroke on the part of the Democratic wire-pullers to win the Bohemian vote. It "took" and the result was that today, of the 12,000 Bohemian votes cast, 8,000 are Democrat.[36]

By that time (1895) there were about 150 Czech political employees, by no means most of them from that new neighborhood, Ceske Kalifornie. Cermak was soon to join their numbers. We see that by the time he arrived in Lawndale, it was well ordained to which party he would give allegiance.

The Czech fondness for music, dancing, and beer found outlets in the Lawndale community as elsewhere. Often such activities were enjoyed as part of the program of one voluntary association or another. It has been remarked frequently, and with considerable justice, that these societies were most likely to have their headquarters over a saloon. However true this may have been, the Lawndale citizen, working hard all week toward his goal of rising on the economic ladder, had little patience with those who considered his Sunday behavior a desecration of the Sabbath and chose to be scandalized by it. In the periodic attempts to enforce the Illinois law forbidding the sale of alcohol on Sunday (the so-called Sunday-closing law), the Czechs of Lawndale had a powerful additional focus for unity. Cermak was not slow to see the political value of this attitude, and was to exploit it skillfully in the progress of his career.

Before leaving the area of social adjustment, a word must be said about one other tool of social stability: gossip. There was in Lawndale a great deal of attachment to the old ways; and as everyone knew everyone else and each person was interested in the affairs of every other person—what he was doing, how much money he had in the bank, whom he planned to marry—a high level of conformity to accepted mores was enforced by means of this verbal tool. "The standards and rules of conduct set by neighborhood organizations and the community of the foreign-born have to be carefully respected, if one wants to avoid severe criticism."[37] Cermak, in contrast to some Czech political pretenders, was very successful in avoiding this sort of political censure.

COMMUNITY INSTITUTIONS

The Czech proclivity for small and large social organizations has been remarked. This is not a purely Czech phenomenon; Italians, Germans, Poles, and others are noted for their many ethnic institutions. What distinguishes the Czech organizations is that they are primarily local, autonomous, and democratic, with membership in one of the many larger secondary federations being optional. On the other hand, the organizations of the Poles or the Italians, for example, are more frequently grouped into a few giant national orders, often under the auspices of the Catholic Church. In the Chicago area there were over 750 Czech lodges, societies, and clubs of every sort. The largest number of these were located in Lawndale.

In addition to the press, the chief types of Lawndale institutions were those that follow.

BENEFIT SOCIETIES

These were among the most important organizations. They were often made up of persons from the same Bohemian towns, and their chief purpose was to maintain a sense of group consciousness and well-being. In the twenties, all activities were conducted in the Czech language; more recently some English-speaking units were organized. In program the benefit societies were almost entirely social, although certain economic phases such as sickness and death benefits were common. These societies did, however, play their role as another face-to-face agency of social control, and "practically all have the desire to raise their status in the eyes of Americans and other races."[38] They also had an important function as discussion groups and as vehicles for the communication of ideas, attitudes, and stereotypes. In Cermak's time, of the more than three hundred groups, nearly one third were operated by Freethinkers. The units were nearly all very small; they had no permanent paid officers; and they used highly democratic procedures. Women enjoyed full equality of status. Cermak belonged to at least one, perhaps more, of such societies. He also founded "The Bohemian Charitable Organization," in 1910, and was its president for many years.

BUILDING-AND-LOAN ASSOCIATIONS

As imporatant as the benefit societies were the building-and loan-associations. The foundation of these groups was entirely economic. They were based upon an idea similar to that of the cooperative and were largely nonprofit-making. These organizations were also democratic in nature, with a high degree of membership participation in decision-making. Each had an elected board of directors, but usually there were no permanent offices or paid staff. Business was conducted at weekly meetings, when dues were paid. The usual payroll was from $1.50 to $25.00 per week. With this sort of overhead sizable dividends were possible.

Although, again, the Czechs had no monopoly on building-and-loan associations, their share of the total number in Chicago was remarkable. In 1912, there were 227 in Chicago with a capital of $19,327,848.47. Of these, 106 were Czech with a total capital of $10,106,132.18. By 1917 they had increased these figures to 125 units, and $15,000,000 capital. At this time there was an aggregate membership of 30,000. Cermak became president of one of these organizations in 1907.

FRATERNAL SOCIETIES

In 1922 there were about fifteen of these in Chicago, with many local lodges and most headquarters located in Lawndale. A few of these were Slovak. Of those that were Czech, only two were Catholic; the rest were controlled by Freethinkers. These organizations, like the benefit societies, were largely social in nature, although some had limited economic functions. They also sponsored considerable cultural activities. Many of them established schools, and almost all of them published periodicals. Cermak was an influential member of several of these societies.

THE SOKOL (FALCONS)

The Sokols were primarily physical culture associations, but were also deeply involved as transmitters of nationalistic and traditional values. They were rich and powerful, owning gymnasiums, libraries, halls, and publishing eight magazines in Chicago and its suburbs. Cermak was an avid and enthusiastic Sokolite. He was a member of the board of directors of Sokol Chicago, belonged to the American Sokol Gymnastic Union, and frequently and willingly offered his influence and services to the Sokols. He was outspoken in his praise of the "spirit of cooperation and the inculcation of ideals of discipline" which the Sokols were supposed to foster.[39]

RELIGIOUS INSTITUTIONS

The Lawndale Czechs were divided almost evenly between Catholics and Protestants or Freethinkers. Actually, the Protestants were very negligible in numbers and influence. Both Catholics and Freethinkers sponsored networks of organizations, newspapers, and other publications; both supported Bohemian-language schools.

However, whereas the Catholics were organized hierarchically, the Freethinkers' institutions were independent of one another. By 1895 the Catholics had eight schools and four newspapers; by 1922 they had nine schools and a junior college. By 1895 the Free-thinkers had four schools; in 1922 they had eighteen in Chicago and suburbs. Some of these offered only week-end or late afternoon sessions.

Of great significance was the relatively unimportant role played among Chicago Czechs by the clergy. Naturally, the half who were Freethinkers were totally unsubject to clerical influence; but the control of even the Catholic clergy was infinitely less than in other immigrant Catholic groups. Certainly Czech priests occupied nothing comparable to the positions of prestige and power pos-sessed in most other groups, nor did they appear to have attempted to exercise the intensity and scope of control which Polish, Italian, or Irish priests often did.

Cermak does not appear to have had any religious attitudes or loyalties. It is certain that he was not a Catholic; and although he has been variously described as a Presbyterian, Mason, and, most frequently, Freethinker, no one can point to any definite affilia-tion (even the evidence supplied by his family was inconclusive). It seems that for him religion as a concept and churchgoing as a spiritual expedient were both irrelevant. Yet his wife was a Cath-olic, as were his sisters and daughters. It is of some interest to note that upon the death of his wife (who predeceased him) there were first Catholic services at the home, then a Freethinker service in a hall. At the public funeral services held for Cermak himself in the Chicago Stadium, a rabbi, a priest, and a minister officiated. The case of the ascription of beliefs to a man, especially a public figure, after he is no longer able to speak for himself, by zealous friends and relatives and associates is so common, however, that one would scarcely think seriously of holding Cermak responsible for these churchly details.[40]

This was the community in which Cermak lived for more than forty years, from 1892 to 1933. Here was the tightly knit ethnic skein, where everyone knew everyone else, where the community was highly integrated by an involved honeycomb of institutions. Through countless face-to-face encounters, through multiple group membership, social, fraternal, athletic, and economic, Cermak moved among the people of the community, was conditioned by their beliefs, attitudes and preconceptions, and by their institutions. In turn, he came to speak for them, and they to identify with him as a symbol of group solidarity and group aspiration.

· 4 ·

STATE

REPRESENTATIVE,

1902-9

WHEN IN 1902 A.J. decided the time was propitious to seek his first elective office, it is noteworthy that he chose the avenue of representative for his district in the Illinois General Assembly rather than a municipal post.

It was a wise choice for several reasons. In the first place, since the office carried perhaps the least influence, there was likely to be much less competition for it than, for example, the much more desirable post of alderman. Second, there were four elective places from each district to the assembly, one senator and three representatives, as opposed to only two aldermen from each ward. Third, had he chosen to contest for the aldermanic post he would have had either to receive complete support from his ward organization—of which he was still a relatively junior member—or else to undertake to fight it. Since the senatorial districts are much larger, encompassing several wards, unless his organization intended to support another candidate there was little danger of challenging it. On the contrary, if his ward organization decided not to support him actively, there would be little reason for it to oppose him. Were he to be elected it would redound to the strength of the Twelfth Ward group. As a matter of fact, his ward organization did not usually have a candidate or make a full-fledged fight for this office. The district was so designed that control traditionally lay with the Irish groups in the northern part and Bohemians were rarely elected. Fourth, representatives were at that time still nominated by conventions rather than by primaries, and conventions are generally presumed to be easier, or at least less expensive, to manipulate. Fifth, his district traditionally elected two Democrats to the three seats to be filled. Finally, since the Bohemians were not in the habit of receiving representation in these offices, he could be fairly certain of getting the enthusiastic support of his compatriots.

Cermak gained this first important nomination with the help of the Zoldaks, a Czech social club of young, ambitious, ethnically conscious businessmen who, like Cermak himself, were "on the make." There was an important distinction, however, between Cermak and his fellow Zoldaks. Most of them were desirous of achieving status not only as businessmen of wealth, but also as decent citizens, pillars of the community. They were anxious on the one hand for the Bohemian community to be recognized by other ethnic groups and by "Americans"; but on the other hand, they were determined for the most part not to risk tarnishing their personal reputations by becoming soiled with the epithet of ward politician. When, therefore, they decided to seek a place for a Bohemian on the 1902 Democratic slate for representative from the Ninth District, none among them was so logical a choice as Tony Cermak, who already "knew his way around politics," and who was not at all shy about putting himself forward.

The Zoldaks made a deal with the incumbent state senator from the district, Edward J. Rainey (a good Irishman), offering to support his candidacy for re-election in their part of the district in exchange for Rainey's support in his part of the district. Cermak was one of the two candidates for representative nominated, and won by only one vote at a disorderly, brawling convention where he "got in with the strongest arm," according to a Czech associate. Cermak himself was under no illusion that his nomination was a reflection of a magnetic personality. Years later he said: "The real facts are that I won because we had organized the senatorial convention and got the nomination with one vote to spare."

The probability of election, once the nominations had been gained, was due to the curious system of cumulative voting used for election to the Illinois House of Representatives. In each district each voter had three votes for representative. He could present all three votes to one candidate or divide them among two or three. This system was useful for minority representation. If any group could gather one third of the votes in a given district (granted it had been able to have one of its members nominated in convention), it could be reasonably certain of electing one representative. To insure this, education of the minority-group voter was necessary, for each would have to cast all three votes for the favorite son.

Because of this system Cermak's election was almost assured by his nomination as a Democratic candidate. Chicago parties had long since accommodated themselves to this system of elections and traditionally worked out bipartisan arrangements wherein neither party nominated a full slate of three, but only the number reasonably certain of election. For the first time since the founding of Ceske Kalifornie, the Bohemians were to have a spokesman of their own in Springfield.

Despite the certainty of election, Cermak made a vigorous campaign. Never in his life did he neglect the opportunities for political prestige to be gained by campaigning. He won, one of two Democratic representatives elected in the district. Both ran well behind the single Republican. For his first success Cermak was indebted neither to the Sullivan nor the Harrison factions of his party.[1] He received support from his associates in the ward organization, in addition to assistance from the Zoldaks and other Czech groups.

Cermak was jubilant. Ten years of conscious and arduous party work had paid off. "When I was first elected to the legislature ... I walked down the street that morning with my head high in the air. I thought that every woman in the block was poking her head from the window to see me."[2]

But this was in familiar Lawndale and its adjacent territories, where he knew everyone and everyone knew him. When he reached Springfield, the bulky, untutored, twenty-nine-year-old ex-miner felt somewhat different. He was, he admitted, "quite

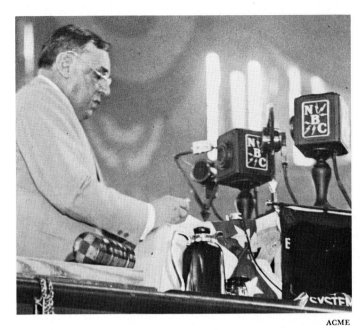

Mayor Cermak
welcoming Democratic delegates to Chicago
at the opening session of the Democratic Convention, 1932

On return from European tour, 1932.
Left to right: James A. Farley, Democratic National Chairman;
Vivian Graham, Cermak's granddaughter; Cermak;
Mrs. Frank Jirka, *Cermak's daughter; Frank Jirka*

*Selling the World's Fair
in a Limehouse saloon
on his trip to Europe in 1932.
Cermak is the center figure.*

*Miami Beach, Florida, 1932.
Seated left to right: Mayor Frank Katzentine of Miami Beach,
Mayor Cermak, Governor-elect Henry Horner of Illinois.
Standing, left to right: P. O. Wilson, Fred Snite,
William Tarradash, Fred Poor, and Fred Breit, all of Chicago.*

nervous when I got there." "When I took my seat in the House, on my right was a lawyer, and to my left a Harvard man and professor. I was scared to death." However, Cermak's usual self-confidence soon reasserted itself. "In a few days I became less impressed by the others," he told Judge Otto Kerner, a lifelong friend and political associate. "I believed I understood people better and had as much common sense."

Before Cermak ended his assembly service he was to emerge as one of the legislature's most influential members, as chairman of the Democratic steering committee and as floor leader. But during his first sessions he attracted little attention and had little influence or impact. He introduced only two bills, both inconsequential. Neither got past first reading. Owing to the Democratic minority in the assembly—the usual situation—and Cermak's own freshman status, his committee assignments in this first term were unimportant and not especially suited to his interests. He began his career slowly, cautiously. He was "amenable to party discipline, loyal to his chiefs, and adroit in carrying out orders." Lacking experience, he was at the start on the side of the Sullivan forces in the legislature, although he remained closer to the Harrison wing in local matters. His voting record reveals a high degree of party regularity.

Cermak was acutely conscious of his lack of education and social graces. Probably consciousness of his position as representative of Chicago Czechs made him tread warily at first. Besides, he had practically no forensic ability. This skill was never to be one of his major assets; even in later life he was often crude in expression and had difficulty with accents and pronunciation. But in 1902 the case was far worse; for until then he had spent his entire life among a bilingual, mostly foreign-language group. A proclivity for saying "hundert" instead of "hundred" was just one in a battery of linguistic errors.

Although A.J. voted generally with the Sullivan Democratic faction, his stand on a few measures should be noted. He was among those whose support and vote carried a resolution requiring the direct election of United States Senators, as well as bills calling for the use of voting machines and strengthening civil-service requirements. How is one to reconcile these stands with his later activity in behalf of free-flowing alcohol? These votes were cast during his first term and might have been the result of a naive support of good government. What seems more important, however, is that the Czechs at that time, although anxious as a group to gain power, held quite positive attitudes toward such early reforms. Much of this interest was later sublimated to the drive for prestige; but during this period the reforming Chicago Municipal Voters League believed that, regarding reform, "the races [*sic*] most responsive to its appeal are the Scandinavian, German, Irish and Bohemian." Perhaps A.J. merely bowed to the will of his constituency on these questions.

Cermak was re-elected in 1904. This was the year of the Theodore Roosevelt landslide, and the Republican majority in the assembly was greater than ever. A.J. was the only Democrat from his district to be elected this time. In a disastrous year for his party, he succeeded in an election which saw the defeat in his district of Hartnett, an Irish Democrat, and Marek, a nonorganization Slav. In many ways this was a great personal triumph for Cermak: he learned that he could defeat the Irish with unified Bohemian support. But Bohemian support was not enough, unless it was buttressed by a party organization.

In this assembly a noticeable improvement in committee assignments is seen. He was appointed to nine committees as against five in the previous assembly, several among the more influential ones. A few were of special interest to him because he was a member from Chicago and because of his private and political interests. Membership on the building-and-loan associations committee was important not only because of the high incidence of such organizations among his Czech constituents, but because—perhaps by reason of his committee experience—the very next year he was himself to found such an organization. His place on the Chicago charter committee was strategically useful since the perennial question of the relationship of Chicago to downstate was very live at the time. Cermak always had a deep concern in this matter, perhaps because of some belief in home rule but more concretely because of its intimate connection with possible control over the sale and consumption of liquor. During this session another proposal for a new Chicago charter was presented, and eventually passed both

Houses. Cermak, despite his belief in home rule, made yeoman efforts to defeat the proposal, because he was unable to have included in it a provision for free bar permits.

In this period he became involved in an operation—closely related to his stand on liquor—which was to be the foundation for his rise to power in the legislature. He took a leading position in an organization known as the United Societies for Local Self-Government, which had recently come into being.

At this time the adherents of liquor laissez faire were being attacked not only on their flanks by the new charter but frontally by main assult in Chicago. In 1906 Democratic Mayor Dunne, campaigning for re-election, was threatened with impeachment if he failed to enforce the state law that required the closing at one o'clock of all places where liquor was sold. In addition, he felt some fear from zealous and efficient newly elected Republican State's Attorney John J. Healy. At any rate, he enforced the law or attempted to do so. The reaction to this decision was typical of Chicago. There was great protest, much anguish expressed, and many angry threats, especially by the representatives of the foreign-born. The Germans took the lead; and the editor of the influential *Abendpost* quickly called a meeting of leaders of the aroused ethnic groups. These people were aggrieved not only because their numbers wanted saloons to remain open late and on Sundays but because the new curfew affected the large number of halls and clubrooms belonging to ethnic societies where liquor and beer were served.

A protest parade was arranged. It was a huge success. Many tens of thousands marched in it. The next time the city council met the order was amended—in effect, rescinded, inasmuch as late permits were henceforward to be issued.

Encouraged by their success, the German leaders called together a convention of representatives of ethnic groups. All of the major groups were represented in the persons of officers of individual societies. There were Germans, Bohemians, Italians, Poles, Belgians, French, and Hungarians. They agreed to organize permanently as the United Societies for Local Self-Government. An executive committee was elected, mostly German but with representation for Bohemians and others. A German was imported from New York to serve as secretary, but the presidency was given to an Irish lawyer. The German leadership felt it was impolitic to have as president an individual with a "foreign" name.

The executive committee and the officers were elected for one year. The next year, 1907, a good many politicians were delegates to the convention, because the United Societies had quickly shown its strength and had already started to indorse political candidates. When the new executive committee was elected, it developed that one faction among the Germans, who were in the majority, opposed the re-election of Zarner, the incumbent secretary. The leader of this faction approached a Czech member of the executive committee and offered, in exchange for support of the faction's candidate for president, to support a Czech for secretary. The deal was accepted; and Cermak—a delegate and member of the newly elected executive committee—was able to convince the Czech delegation that he was its logical candidate. Doubtless his strength in the ward organization, his membership in the legislature, and especially the membership on the Chicago Charter committee added weight to his argument. His active electioneering was successful.

Cermak and Zarner were both nominated. Cermak won by five votes. He was to hold this position until the advent of Prohibition and beyond. The secretary was the only permanent official and was in charge of the Societies' administration. From this point on, Cermak was recognized as the official spokesman of the Societies and, by inference, the most authoritative of the "dripping wets" in Chicago and Illinois.

Cermak's position in the legislature was now greatly enhanced. Henceforth, speaking for the United Societies, he was a power, not only while a member of the assembly but for the most of his career. At various times the Societies boasted a membership of several hundred societies and claimed to represent several hundred thousand individuals. When the Societies spoke, politicians and public officials listened. Not only did it claim votes, but it had money. The largest sums were supplied by brewers, some by distillers. The money was to be used to influence legislation and to elect favorable legislators, judges, and other officials. It was collected by Cermak, and presumably he distributed it to candidates who were acceptable. Few of the members of the Societies were aware of this arrangement; no one questioned Cermak about the distribution of the money, not even the brewers who were footing the bill.

Cermak was not slow to recognize the tremendous usefulness of this new office for his own political advancement. Nor did he show the slightest embarrassment at the fact that for a great many years he was simultaneously a public official and the recognized representative and lobbyist of a pressure group. At no time was he loath to raise the cry of personal liberty in the name of his organization. Though it increased his prestige in some quarters, this role did not endear him to certain other influential groups, who nevertheless recognized his power.

As leader of an organization which assumed the misleading name of *United Societies*, Cermak aroused and organized the underworld to enforce its demand for a wide open town. For a quarter of a century, any politician, whatever his party, who dared to support any measure that would curb the license of those antisocial hordes, was immediately confronted by Cermak, snarling and waving the club of the underworld vote.[3]

He was again re-elected in 1906. Although the House was Republican, 89 to 61, Cermak's committee assignments were, if anything, more favorable than in the previous terms. Of special importance, because of the very high degree of control over Chicago affairs exercised by the legislature, was his membership on the committees on elections, credentials, municipal corporations, and judicial apportionment. He found a place again on the committee on building-and-loan associations. At this time his interest in such institutions was transferred from the simple desire to protect his constituents' welfare to a more personal concern, for in 1907 he became president of the Lawndale Building and Loan Association. The same may be said for his membership on the committee on banks. It is certain that he had cordial relations with the bankers in his district from an earlier time; but in 1908, he himself became a director of the Lawndale National Bank. His relationship with the business community was further strengthened by his election as a director of the Twenty-Sixth Street Business Men's Association.

In this term the number of bills he introduced markedly increased. The thirteen bills he presented also had greater success than earlier attempts. One became a law; one was passed by both houses but later vetoed; two were passed by the House but not by the Senate. As for shepherding legislation through his chamber, his record was four out of thirteen, quite a respectable legislative batting average.

A.J.'s function as representative of the United Societies was best fulfilled not via the direct legislative line but rather through manipulating committees and individual legislators and attempting to influence political opinion.[4] He was omnipresent at committee hearings, where he was unabashedly the "Voice of Liquor." On the floor of the House his vote on any issue was recognized as indicating the Wet line.

In 1908 Cermak was elected for a fourth term. In this term he received the most favorable committee positions of his assembly career, including the highly significant chairmanship of the Democratic steering committee. His prestige, which prior to this time has shown persistent growth, now reached its highest point.

He spent much energy in 1908 working for the defeat of a new probation law, and was blamed by Municipal Judge McKenzie for being singlehandedly responsible for its ultimate defeat. The following year he was employed in fighting another version of a Chicago charter because of inadequate safeguards for "personal liberty." He had taken a similar position in 1904 before accession to his United Societies office, and in 1907 he and the Societies were largely responsible for defeating a charter referendum. In 1909 most of his opposition was centered upon hearings before the Chicago charter committee. We see here an illustration of the very strategic committee memberships he enjoyed.

In 1909 Cermak became one of the performers in the notorious Lorimer Affair. This involved the election by the general assembly of a United States Senator. Briefly, Albert J. Hopkins, the incumbent Republican "sun-burst Senator" from Aurora, had won the preferential primary. However, another Republican, William Lorimer, the notorious "blond boss" from Chicago's west side, desired the seat. The Democrats also had a candidate. The assembly remained deadlocked for five months but finally on the ninety-fifth ballot Lorimer was elected. He received 108 votes, 53 from Democrats.

The election caused tremendous repercussions. Talk of bribery was rife. There followed investigations by the general assembly and the Criminal Court of Cook County, and extended hearings in the United States Senate. On July 14, 1912, the Senate declared Lorimer's election invalid and he was ousted from that body.

Cermak had been one of the Democrats who voted for Lorimer. He appeared before the assembly investigating committee and was cleared. However, Republican Speaker Edward D. Shurtleff accused him of buying votes for Lorimer, and Representative Charles A. White accused him of accepting money in exchange for his vote.

Most of the Democrats who voted for Lorimer dropped out of politics subsequently, but Cermak was never proved guilty. Nevertheless, his hearing was believed by some to be a whitewash. Testimony had been given that the chief briber was Lee O'Neil Browne, a Democratic leader with whom Cermak was closely associated; and this, for some, was sufficient proof of his guilt. The testimony of several persons who were present during the notorious election provides a more complex view. Not only was Cermak an associate of Browne, but he also was a personal friend of Lorimer, as were most other representatives from Chicago's west side. Money was passed by Lorimer supporters and also by Hopkins' backers. Cermak's friendship with Lorimer, however, provides no positive proof of guilt.

An analysis of the politics of the election complicates the issue still further. Although Hopkins had received a majority of the votes in the advisory election, he did not win a majority of the senatorial districts. Besides, he was notoriously unpopular. As a result, there was much opposition to him, and many candidates were introduced with the object of stopping him. It was considered impossible to elect a Democrat, and a number of Republicans were put forward, including Speaker Shurtleff and Governor Deneen. When neither of these was any longer a possibility, sentiment focused upon Lorimer; and the five-month stalemate was broken.

The question, then, still remains unanswered: did Cermak receive money for his vote? Obviously it is possible; and the same can be said of buying votes for Lorimer. At the same time the political situation just described, as well as other purely personal and political factors, can also account for his vote. In due course we shall see that through his entire career Cermak was a skillful manipulator of bipartisan deals. His vote for Lorimer could be viewed in the light of the expectancy of patronage, added to the factor of their friendship. It is noteworthy, too, that he was only one of fifty-three Democrats who had voted for Lorimer; and one might add that elections of this kind were not unusual prior to the change in the method of electing senators. But whatever the truth of the matter, it is a fact that Cermak was plagued with accusations relating to Lorimer until the end of his life.

Despite these difficulties, Cermak emerged from the assembly a recognized party leader. Given the impression he made upon colleagues and observers in Springfield and the disadvantages under which he labored, how did he accomplish this feat? First, his colleagues must be noted. Although they included a few men of high caliber, the usual assemblymen then—and perhaps now—was indifferent, cautious, frightened, or venal. "A common attitude was to let George do it. If a man had guts and determination he was respected." Cermak, in addition to being reportedly "above average intelligence," was "not afraid of God, man and devil."

Many persons of integrity speak well of Cermak as a legislator. Judge John P. McGoorty, who had an adjoining seat in the House, assessed him this way: "Cermak was a good member. He had a good attendance record on the floor and in committee. He had judgment, common sense, and public spirit. Though he was close to the boodle-boys, he did not gang up with those who were working for their own interest. I never knew him to be associated with undesirable legislation."[5]

Although he did not speak often, and then had difficulty in expressing himself, his voice was "big, booming," and he entered debate explosively. "He had tremendous driving force." "He was like a powerful animal with other animals; and he just shook them off." Perhaps most important—"He had eyes only for his objective." Cermak's "objective," however, was highly complex and not compassed by the career in Springfield.

During these years his three children, all girls, were born. Since all his life he was known as not merely a devoted but a doting father, it is reasonable to suppose that he spent a good deal of time within the family circle. By this time his parents and siblings, too, had joined him in Lawndale.

For several years after his election he continued to hold his police-court job. He also held on to the chairmanship of his ward organization. Nor did he neglect his contacts with the ordinary voters. Therefore, he continued to visit, with frequency, the ward clubroom, the saloons and the ethnic halls.

Besides the business strides in banking and building and loan, he founded and became senior partner in the real estate firm of Cermak and Serhant in 1908. He continued to own the original wood and hauling business, though by this time it was operated by his brother. As if his life were not already amply filled, Cermak ran a successful race for the office of alderman of the Twelfth Ward in 1909. Since he was sitting in the legislature, this caused no little complication as will presently be seen.

In sum, the years from 1902 to 1910 were full in experience. From freshman member to Democratic leader in the House; from childlessness to a family of five; from kindling-wood business to a real-estate firm, presidency of a building-and-loan association, and directorship of a bank; from a private advocate of personal liberty to the authoritative, elective representative of the most potent Wet pressure group; and from the general assembly to the more strategic city council.

Not only were these years of experience but of ever-expanding responsibilities and the corresponding personal growth to meet them. In the party organization he had moved from the lowliest rung of the hierarchy to the leadership of the ward club, and finally to ward committeeman. As ward committeeman he was empowered to sit with the mighty of the local party and to share in decisions of the first importance.

As public official, he advanced from insignificant appointive offices to four successive terms in one elective office, and then demonstrated his growing power by a fifth election to a more important one. As assemblyman his representativeness for the first time went well beyond the boundaries of his neighborhood, ward, and own ethnic group. The senatorial district was much greater in area, and its population was much more heterogeneous. It included, in addition to the Czechs and Germans of the Twelfth Ward, Poles,

Irish, and others. Thus, the young politician had his first important experience in what Professor Merriam has aptly called "group diplomacy." This training was already illustrated in the mechanics of his first nomination. Further practice was gained during his rise to leadership in the Democratic caucus of the House. And probably the most rewarding training of all was the role as spokesman of the United Societies.

But his acknowledged leadership of the Wets pushed his representativeness even beyond the geographic confines of his district. As "Mr. Wet" his voice represented the claims of the organized liquor interests in Chicago, Cook County, and the State of Illinois. In this role, at least, he had skyrocketed from precinct to all-state significance.

Finally, A.J. had made giant strides as a public figure among the Czechs. At the start of the period he was only a young, ambitious compatriot in a not overly respectable business, with a few political connections. He was only one of several ambitious Bohemians striving for the position of authoritative representative of the solid Czech bloc of Lawndale, the large groups adjacent, and generally the entire Czech community in Cook County. Among these men Cerveny, Cervenka, Sabath, and Loeffler have been mentioned; at least one more, Edward Novak, should be added. Because of his consecutive elective successes, business growth, and United Societies position, well before the end of this eventful decade Cermak was to stand as equal with most of them and superior to some. Early in his legislative career "He was as important as Cerveny. During this time the people recognized that Tony was climbing, and they were proud. He was popular in the ward. The Bohemians would go to him."

In Cermak's rise one can identify a constant series of adaptations to the necessities of changing situations as he claimed power as Wet, Bohemian, and party functionary. Further, his continued choices of business tended to blend with the pattern of the urge for power. Real-estate man, banker, building-and-loan association official, each required a multitude of face-to-face contacts with persons in situations where very important decisions were at stake for them. Nor should it be overlooked that each of these enterprises was located prominently on Twenty-Sixth Street. Thus, in the very heart of Czechtown, the name and face of Cermak were difficult to avoid.

One must consider the rather prodigious tasks of coordination these many activities required. At first glance the difficulties of successfully handling so many jobs would appear insurmountable. Yet there is ample evidence that Cermak had not only a firm grasp of the broad outlines of each of his responsibilities but an extraordinary mastery of detail. This can be understood if we recognize that these enterprises for Cermak were in fact one. The whole complex was not a disjointed, unrelated welter of activities. On the contrary, it represented a highly integrated pattern of behavior consistently directed to one end: an ever broader sphere of influence and control. Each of the parts—Wet, Bohemian, party functionary, successful businessman—reinforced and made more secure the other roles. Each was a bastion in a well-constructed fortress, contributing its share to the power position of a potential center of influence in the Cook County Democratic political machine.

· 5 ·

BOSS

OF

LAWNDALE,

1909-12

WHILE still serving in the general assembly Cermak began to yearn to consolidate most of his manifold activities in Chicago. In order to do this he ultimately had to give up his seat in the legislature. Considering all his other activities, it does not seem that this should have been much of a sacrifice. But A.J. apparently found it intolerable to be without an elective office. Therefore, in 1909 he became candidate for alderman of the Twelfth Ward.

His desire for a seat in the city council in place of his by now influential position in the legislature was not caused entirely by a wish to cease commuting to the state capital and to ease his problems of coordinating his various responsibilities. Objectively, an aldermanic post was a greater prize than that of state representative. The local position at that time represented a higher salary and greater patronage. In those days the city budget was greater than that of the state, and more significantly, perhaps, the money expended was for services which were readily observable by the voters. Because the city council enjoys broad powers, "the aldermen are in a position to recommend certain appointments and to supervise the administration of city affairs within their respective wards."[1]

Cermak became alderman in April, 1909, filling a seat left vacant by a Republican. His growing power in his own ward was resoundingly demonstrated in a decisive victory for a normally Republican seat. He won by 2,000 votes; the former Republican incumbent had posted a 3,400 majority in the previous election. Cermak decided against resigning his legislative office and attempted holding both offices simultaneously. This aroused great controversy and much criticism from the press and from organized adherents of reform and good government. These skirmishes lasted more than a year. The repercussions were so serious that a movement arose in the United Societies to remove Cermak from office. This, however, did not succeed, never even coming to a vote.

Soon after his election, Cermak explained his position. Not only did he think his dual office-holding was not illegal or immoral, he believed it his *duty* not to resign from the legislature. He maintained that he had publicly announced during his campaign for the city council that he would resign from the legislature whenever it adjourned *sine die*. However, since this had as yet not occurred, there was no reason to resign, unless in the meantime he should be re-elected to the city council—the vacancy he had been elected to fill had only one year to run. If he were to resign he might be accused of receiving the full $2,000 salary without finishing the job for which he had been paid. (At no time during this controversy did it seem to occur to him that he might refund a portion of his salary.) He thought he would be derelict in duty were he to resign and leave his district underrepresented.[2] Finally, he did not see why membership in the city council would prevent him from fulfilling his responsibilities in Springfield. These arguments, if vulnerable to careful analysis, undoubtedly sounded convincing to many. Considering the fact that sessions of the legislature were brief, his last point was difficult to overturn.

Replying to his chief critic in this case, the powerful Municipal Voters' League, he went on to amplify his defense. The governor had just convened a special session of the legislature, and Cermak had tendered him his resignation. But the governor had pointed out that a special election to name Cermak's successor would cost about $5,000 or $6,000, and had advised him to retain his seat.

I now believe that owing to the fact that under the law as it now is, as I am receiving no compensation, and further I am chairman of the Democratic steering committee in the House of Representatives and being pledged to assist in the passage of a direct primary law that under the circumstances I am justified and, in fact, believe it my duty to complete the special session . . . although I have attended the special session of the legislature promptly and regularly, at an expense to myself, I did not during that time miss one meeting of the city council or of any committee of which I am a member, endeavoring at all times to do my duty in such manner as I believe to be for the best interest of the people of the 12th Ward and the city of Chicago.

I have given my entire time to the duties of alderman, and I have no other interest to serve.[3]

Despite attacks, A.J. was able to retain both positions. He finally resigned on April 5, 1910, following his re-election to a full term as alderman.

In 1909-10, then, in addition to the other positions he held, Cermak was an alderman. By 1908, he had also become ward committeeman, an office he was to keep for the remainder of his life, and one of major importance to his continuing political success.

WARD COMMITTEEMAN

To gain this office had required years of apprenticeship in party warfare. It is from the ranks of the most persistent and industrious of the precinct captains, after intensive struggle, that committeemen emerge. Once entrenched, a committeeman can rarely be dislodged. ". . . it is practically impossible to defeat a ward boss in a metropolitan community where the spoils tradition is deeply rooted. . . . Tidal waves of public opinion may sweep the city-wide leaders from their posts, but the ward leaders are safe in their little islands."[4] The long tenure of ward committeemen is the result of a number of factors, the most important being control of spoils and patronage, political experience, and prestige of the position, the inertia of the rank and file, plus a helpful long-standing confusion regarding the legal status of the committeeman.[5] Regardless of his legal status, in actual fact the committeeman is close to being the feudal lord of his local political domain.

Cermak greatly enlarged his clutch of power with the attainment of this new office, as a glance at some of the duties of the ward committeeman will show. To begin with, the committeeman is a member of the judicial circuit convention which nominates the slate of twenty circuit-court and twenty-eight superior-court judges. This comes to almost one per ward committeeman. He is also a member of the county central committee, which selects delegates to the state convention, where nominations for justices of the Illinois Supreme Court, trustees of the University of Illinois, and delegates-at-large to the national convention are made. He is a member of the congressional district committee in which his ward is located. These committees are empowered to fill vacancies for congressman if a nominee dies or is unable to run. Finally, he belongs to the city committee which has similar vacancy-filling powers.

In making the slates just mentioned, the committeeman participates as a matter of legal right. But—depending upon the strength of his ward—he is prominent in the construction of all local primary tickets. Despite primary laws, he has a major influence on nominations for nearly all local offices. This means in effect that most officeholders, not only judges, are under obligation to the ward committeeman. Any committeeman has what amounts to a veto over the nomination by his party of residents of his ward. To fight one's ward boss for nomination is to court almost certain defeat.

Another source of power for these officials is the control they hold over ward boundaries. Although by law redistributing by the city council is mandatory every ten years, such is the influence of the ward committeeman in the council that they have little to fear from this requirement. Traditionally, a number of committeemen are at the same time aldermen. Often, enough of them are in the city council to delay redistricting. Nor is it uncommon for one of their number to be chairman of the council committee charged with preparation of new wards. However, even if the committeeman and the alderman are not the same person, most aldermen are completely "owned" by their committeemen. From 1910 on, Cermak "owned" every alderman from his ward. Aldermen do not consider it wise to go against the committeeman's desires in matters of redistricting.

When redistricting is finally forced, extreme gerrymandering is practiced in order to protect the committeemen's vested interests. Rotten boroughs are not rare. Wards are also frequently skewed in order to divide ethnic groups. This device was important in the long control of Chicago politics by the Irish. Cermak was himself to use it in 1931.[6]

Usually the ward committeeman is the sole agent for distribution of patronage in his ward, and normally in this function he has a high degree of autonomy. Ward committeemen, by virtue of their connections "downtown," are in a position to grant many favors to individuals or to groups, much greater in value and scope than those at hand to precinct captains. The ward committeeman "is likely to be a center for the distribution of office, contracts, perquisites, tax-adjustments, favors, and sundry spoils."[7]

On the infrequent occasions when a ward boss is overthrown, it is often in connection with a change in the ethnic composition of the ward. The leaders of the new group, as it grows in numbers, with greater and greater urgency demand the position for one of their own until the existing power holder is swept from control. However, there is often a considerable time lag between the new ethnic composition of a ward and the deposition of the ward committeeman of "foreign" affiliation.

This was the situation in the Twelfth Ward at the start of Cermak's career. For many years the ward had been largely Irish and German, and control remained in the hands of these groups. Later, it was connected to the Harrison faction of the Democratic party through Loeffler and Sabath, both Czech Jews. It was, therefore, not unnatural that finally a non-Jewish Czech should capture the ward.

FACTIONAL AND PARTY ALIGNMENT

Hardly had Cermak become ward committeeman than his influence began to spread over areas adjacent to and farther removed from his own ward. Although A.J. roughly resembled the typical ward leader in some overt respects, he differed in his unique psychological drives and in the qualities he developed as a politician. Thus, while the others remained ward bosses, or failed even to maintain this power position, A.J. became the boss of Illinois.

How did A.J. use the added leverage of his ward boss-ship? What sides did he choose in the election battles of this period, and how successful was he? What additional weight did his United

Societies position give him? We should bear in mind Cermak's earlier bifactional allegiances with Sullivan-Brennan[8] in state matters and with Harrison in city matters. After 1910 he was less able to support the Sullivan group, for his influence in state matters was reduced after leaving the legislature. But Cermak knew that currently Sullivan controlled most of the Democratic ward committeemen. He was in a first-class dilemma, for the faction with which he was normally allied in city matters was growing weaker in the city. Further, a mistake in alignment at this time would be particularly crucial, since he wanted to make a strong showing in his race for re-election as alderman. This was important, because he now felt it necessary to resign as assemblyman, halt the criticism, but assure himself of full vindication by his ward. He did not want to give the appearance of resigning under fire. How could he resolve the problem of being in both camps?

THE HARMONY TICKET OF 1910

Cermak found his answer in a "harmony ticket." Both of the above factions and the only other important one (the Dunne-O'Connel group) were persuaded. There was always an undercurrent of approval for this kind of appeal among the rank and file, a feeling that Chicago and Cook County could be dominately Democratic if the factional tomahawks were only buried. As it was, the Republicans usually held the larger number of offices. This was the case in the city now, with Republican Fred A. Busse mayor. A mayoralty election was scheduled for 1911, and a successful campaign this year, 1910, would lay good groundwork for possible capture of the city hall. Many felt that a unit Democracy could control Chicago, with the result that there would be more "gravy" all around than under the present anarchic arrangements. This was believed despite the fact that each faction normally enjoyed patronage in one of the many local citadels of power—irrespective of the party in office—gained through bipartisan treaties with Republican factions. It was speculated that even that stronghold of Republicanism, the governorship, might be breached in 1912.

Cermak, because of reliable avenues of communication to two of the factions (in both of which he was organizationally a figure of prominence), was a useful person for the purposes of treaty making. His fitness was also greatly enhanced by his role as the battering ram of the United Societies. He was one of the chief instigators of the successful rapprochement, and functioned as one of the main arbitrators in the conclave which finally convened above Righeimer's Saloon and hammered out a slate acceptable to all factions. Later, he was one of the chief managers of the campaign. As a reward, no doubt, for his role in these negotiations, A.J. was given control of a "good" spot on the slate, clerk of the probate court. He named John A. Cervenka for the position.

The selection of Cervenka was in many ways a master stroke, and offers an enlightening glimpse into the deviousness of Cermak's political mind. Cervenka was a prominent and "respectable" Czech leader, head of the Pilsen Brewery in the Czech quarter, and recognized frequently as a Czech spokesman—for example, he had been a representative of the Czechs at the founding convention of the United Societies. Further, Cervenka had political ambitions. He had run for alderman in the Tenth Ward in 1901, and though supported by the Municipal Voters' League, had been defeated by the incumbent Novak, a Loeffler-Sabath-Harrison man. Cervenka considered that he had been tricked by "The Trinity." It was Cervenka who had nominated A.J. for secretary of the United Societies.

This was a rewarding situation for Cermak, and it illustrates some of the major features of the political deal. First, he paid off a political debt to Cervenka. Next, he was getting recognition for the Czechs in an important county office and at the same time satisfying those compatriots who wished to have ethnic candidates capable of evoking respect from the "Americans" and other groups. In supporting Cervenka, who had the greatest animosity for Sabath and Novak, he stood to gain a useful ally in a neighboring ward. Also, in a sense, he would be immobilizing Cervenka as a possible competitor by satisfying his desire for office. He might then count upon him as a subordinate ally, not as a possible contender for top leadership of the Czechs. Even if this objective could not be gained completely by Cervenka's gratitude if elected, during his four-year term Cermak could expect to grow in power and probably have an opportunity of gaining an office richer in pelf and prestige than that which Cervenka would enjoy. Although there was some element of risk in this, it was worth it if he could through Cervenka weaken Sabath in adjacent Czech territory. Evidently, A.J. felt rather confident that he could control Cervenka; in this, events were to prove him correct.

"Harmony" was repaid handsomely, as the unified ticket practically swept the county offices. A.J.'s man Cervenka was elected; he himself was re-elected to the council with practically no opposition, and at long last resigned from the assembly. He emerged from this campaign with a greater reputation for power and objectively greater power.

THE MAYORALTY ELECTION OF 1911

In 1911 a mayor was to be elected. Mayor Busse had been completely discredited as a result of the findings of extensive corruption in his administration, turned up by a city council committee under Charles E. Merriam. Alderman Merriam defeated J.R. Thompson, the Busse-Lorimer candidate, and Smulski, the Deneen representative, for the Republican nomination.[9]

The Democratic primary was to give Cermak much grief. The Harmony Ticket "was broken with an ax."[10] Each faction entered candidates and was determined to win. The Bull Moose rumblings had started and the previous Republican administration had been disgraced; all in all, it looked like a Democratic year. Harrison himself was a candidate; Sullivan entered Andrew Graham; and Dunne also was again a candidate. Dunne could be counted out by Cermak. He seemed least likely to win. The United Societies had supported Busse in his defeat of former mayor, former judge Dunne, in 1907. But here was the old Sullivan-Harrison dilemma. The power possibilities had to be accurately gauged if A.J. were to save himself from backing the wrong horse.

The difficulties of his choice are well indicated by a host of conflicting opinions as to his alignment in both the primary and the election. Harrison himself believes that A.J. was "friendly" to him. Sabath and others believe that he secretly supported the Sullivan candidate. Some members of the executive committee of the United Societies suspected the sincerity of A.J.'s support of Harrison.

[69]

Cermak's position was made even more uncomfortable in that Kostner, Czech leader being groomed by Harrison and Sabath to challenge him, had early announced support of Harrison. Under the circumstances, if he were to support Graham and Harrison were to win, assuredly Harrison patronage would go to Kostner and endanger Cermak's position as top Czech politician. In the light of this particular campaign, A.J.'s indecision and jockeying may seem strange, for Harrison won the primary, narrowly defeating Dunne but overwhelming Graham. In the long view Cermak's trepidation is more understandable. He recognized the enduring value of the Sullivan machine organization, in contrast to the personal following of Harrison. His estimate was eminently correct, for after this successful election Harrison was finished as a major force, while the Sullivan group continued in strength under different chiefs, ultimately being captured by Cermak. His dodging and equivocation here, then, are a classic illustration of political farsightedness—of a willingness to lose battles, if necessary, in order to win wars. To the Harrison faction (this far) went the engagements; but the Sullivan crowd and Cermak were to reap the ultimate plunder of victory.

A.J.'s doubts seemed to be settled by the primary. As between Harrison and Merriam, he could choose only the former. Certainly, Harrison was personally more palatable to A.J. than his aldermanic colleague Merriam, a University of Chicago professor of political science and foe of "corrupt special interests." To add further reason, the United Societies, after much debate, at last endorsed Harrison. Finally, the Bohemians had traditionally supported the Harrisons, father and son; and, of course, Kostner and Sabath were still strongly for Harrison.

Manifestly, from any point of view, it would have been impossible for Cermak to back Merriam openly. However, he might have done so in secret. This kind of subterranean knifing of one's party was the rule; and this election was no exception. Defeated Democrat chiefs Dunne and Sullivan assisted Merriam under cover; and two and a half of the three Republican groups gave Harrison *sub-rosa* support. The idea in each case was to capture the respective parties and gain revenge for earlier treachery.

Cermak was probably tempted to join in the sabotage of Harrison in order to please Sullivan, but it is doubtful that he did so. For he knew that if Harrison won, with all the attendant patronage of city hall, and his disloyalty were known, his fellow Czech, Kostner—Sabath's protégé—would be considered the Czech leader in the Harrison faction. With the patronage Sabath could obtain for Kostner in that event, Cermak's hold on the leadership of the Czechs would be in serious jeopardy. Not even Sullivan's good will was enough to counterbalance a risk of this kind.

Harrison won by a small margin. Professor Merriam claims, "We broke his hold on the . . . Bohemians especially."[11] But as far as Harrison was concerned, A.J. had delivered to the extent of deserving immediate patronage and an important place on the Harrison ticket of 1912.

Cermak emerged from this campaign in excellent position. On the one hand, he had played with the Sullivanites to the extent of creating suspicion of the locus of his loyalty. On the other hand, he was present in greater than life size on the victorious Harrison bandwagon. Nor could he find cause for unhappiness in the fact that the Irish (Sullivanites) were temporarily weakened in his party.

In 1912 he was returned by his ward to his third term in the city council. No major party candidate risked running against him, but nevertheless he succeeded in getting a large complimentary vote. The following comment indicates something about the state of his strength in his ward and, more important, how he was regarded by the press and probably his fellow politicians in terms of political strength. "His own record has made it advisable since then (1909) not to waste efforts in courting certain defeat, and no one has been found with the temerity to enter the lists against him."[12]

Cermak seemed to share this view. A statement of his radiates confidence.

I only hope my friends will not forget to vote for me. Even if I have no opponent, it will be nice to have a large complimentary vote. I had it last time, and although I have not sent out any letters or literature of any sort, I feel that I shall not be forgotten on election day.[13]

CHICAGO LEGISLATOR

During this period of party warfare, A.J. was functioning as one of the leaders of the city council. The consensus of all informants attests to the power and prominence of his position. Charles E. Merriam, an aldermanic colleague and an exceptionally reliable observer, was painfully aware of this. Cermak was a leader not only among the Democrats, but of the chamber per se. He worked very closely and well with the Republican administration of Mayor Busse. At times he was considered the administration's chief hatchet man in the council.

He once failed to function this way in connection with a $50,000 appropriation which Alderman Merriam had forced through the finance committee. This was to be used to investigate corruption in shale-rock purchase encountered by Merriam's committee on city expenditure. Merriam's fellow councilman from the Seventh Ward, Alderman Snow, was chairman of the finance committee. Because of fear of an adverse press, Merriam's request was allowed to be favorably reported by that committee. Merriam, however, learned that the scenario included a plan for Cermak to blast it out of existence on the floor. Merriam went to Cermak and said, "Why should a Democrat help a Republican administration? The papers are for it; the tax-payers are for it." A.J. made no reply. Alderman Merriam had no inkling whether or not he had succeeded in convincing the destroyer. Subsequently, when Merriam finished his advocacy of the proposal on the council floor, all eyes turned to Cermak, waiting the thunder. But none came. "He sat like a Sphinx. My appropriation was passed." Professor Merriam explained this strange switch as a product of Cermak's reluctance ever to be in the minority, plus his sensitivity to "what I had on politicians."

Cermak was, from the start, a man of power in the council, not only because of his cordial relations with the Republican mayor, nor because of his prestige among Czechs expanding now well beyond his ward, nor yet solely because of the United Societies threat. He also had personal qualities well adapted to council machinations. "To the city council Cermak brought a practical vision and a level headedness that at once made him a conspicuous member."[14] His committee assignments reflected his prestige. He was a member of the most strategic committee, finance. He was chairman of three leading committees: gas, oil, and electricity; schools; and elections.

The kind of role A.J. played in the finance committee may be inferred from the Merriam anecdote above. Since it was perhaps the most important committee, Cermak was faithful in attendance and prominent in its work. Not only did it control the purse strings, but it frequently functioned as a body supervising city administration and the administration of other council committees.

Of his other committees, the chairmanship of the elections committee was the most significant, for during this time the decennial redistricting of the wards was undertaken. Redistricting is crucial to the perpetuation of power of ward bosses. It does not require great imagination to have an idea of the tremendous pressures exercised upon the chairman of the committee responsible for this. The situation in Cermak's case was even more severe, for he was a man with one foot in each of two powerful Democratic factions and with a close attachment to the Republican group that was led by Busse.

To ease the pressure A.J. appointed subcommittees representing the three major areas of the city. Further, he made good use of delaying tactics to wear down critics. Begun in the winter of 1911, the job could not near completion until after the summer recess, A.J. announced in June. This would delay the new boundaries until probably after the fall primaries. A newspaper often friendly to A.J. charged that this move favored "reactionaries in both parties—the Sullivan and the Busse factions."

At the end of October Cermak's committee was still bogged down. The major obstacle was the question of whether or not, and how, the lines of the First Ward—stronghold of "Hinky-Dink" Kenna and his accomplice, "Bathhouse John" Coughlin—should be altered. Should the ward remain as it was, with a population of 40,000 as against the average of 62,000 for the other wards; or should it be extended to the south and the west?

By this time two plans had been worked out, but neither could gain a majority. One plan left the ward as it was and the other extended it. The one to maintain the status quo, not surprisingly, was the majority plan. Cermak pretended impartiality in public, attempting to give the impression of being interested only in forcing a plan to completion; but it is scarcely to be doubted that he was with the majority on the side of conserving for Kenna and Coughlin their rump fortress.[15] Apparently, his "efforts" to bring about an early solution could not be realized; for on October 30 he announced his intention to call a meeting of subcommittees for the next week, to set a date for a full committee hearing; this would definitely delay redistricting beyond even the general election date.

Nevertheless, Cermak was able to place his participation in the redistricting planning in a good light. He acted the role of one who was driving and cajoling the recalcitrants to a speedy and honest conclusion.

> I shall insist that they [the joint subcommittees] fix a date for the meeting of the entire committee so that a decision can be fought out there.
>
> If the committee cannot unite, I shall send the matter into the council with all the various maps and plans and urge that a non-partisan committee, selected by the mayor, be given charge of redistricting.[16]

He also chided those committee members who did not approve the majority plan, and those who would not support enlarging of the First Ward. However, he cast doubt upon the legality of the latter plan.

Although his words sounded reasonable enough to the average voter, Cermak's political maneuvering seems rather clearly implied. He was covering up his actual influence in favor of the plan largely retaining the status quo. If he could not succeed, the "non-partisan" committee to be appointed by Mayor Harrison could be so rigged that its recommendations would be acceptable to Cermak's allies, Kenna and Coughlin. Cermak's plan was pushed through, with the First Ward retained as a "rotten borough." During a later campaign Cermak referred to this redistricting as "admittedly a fair and just division," in spite of the gerrymander which increased the unrepresentative character of the First Ward.

A power in the council, Cermak still did not introduce a great quantity of legislation, nor were the committees he headed unusually productive. This does not mean that he did not work hard in committee or that his committees did not meet often. It takes fully as much effort to deny legislation an opportunity of reaching the floor as to produce it. Besides all his other activities his aldermanic job required much personal service to his constituents. Since he was both alderman and ward committeeman, the favors expected of him were doubled. It must also be remembered that the busy finance committee was a great drain on his time and energy.

The exception to the general rule of the unproductivity of his committees was the utilities committee. This unit included in its sphere of interest the supervision of the telephone franchise. In this committee Cermak made at least two strong stands against that potent utility company, one in a bill to abolish "nickel-first" telephones, another in a plan to reduce telephone rates. He also attacked another public utility, the surface lines, demanding better service for consumers.

One might almost have supposed that Cermak was conducting a crusade against the utility companies. This would be strange, for not many Chicago politicians braved the treasuries of the utilities. A closer look reveals that the gas company and the elevated lines were excluded from Cermak's attacks. These were Insull holdings. Insull was no mean foe. He was generous with money to both parties, or to some factions of both parties. Among the Democrats it was the Sullivan-Brennan faction with whom he dealt, for Edward F. Dunne was a confirmed supporter of municipal ownership of utilities and Harrison was outspokenly anti-Insull. In 1911 Harrison's chief campaign issue was cheap gas—and in the primary he was opposed by what Merriam called the Sullivan Gas organization. Even so, in the general election the Insull interests opposed Harrison and supported Merriam.

These factors may offer some explanation of the thinking of those who had accused Cermak of supporting the Sullivan candidate in the primary against Harrison, and also of the voting statistics among the Bohemians which caused Merriam to remark that Harrison's hold had been partially broken there. It is possible that Cermak had been pressured by Sullivan to desert Harrison in the primary and in the general election, for reasons factional on Sullivan's part, and also because of the Insull gas interests involved. If this is true, it must have made Cermak's problem in that mayoralty contest even more excruciating. His steering clear of attacks on the Insull interests while in the council tends at any rate to indicate some such situation behind his uncertainty in 1911, when he was ultimately kept out of the Sullivan-Insull group by the force of political circumstances. Like most other Chicago politicians, however, if he was unable positively to ally himself, he at least tried to make very certain of not arousing the enmity of the vast Insull exchequer. Although it was preferable not to cross swords with any utility giant, it was less risky to challenge the lesser ones.

It should be noted, too, that these touching stands on behalf of consumers were made toward the end of A.J.'s term; and it may at least be suspected that they were not unconnected with his candidacy for a new elective office, his first city-wide try: that of bailiff of the municipal court.

BELLIGERENT

BAILIFF:

FIRST

CITY-WIDE

OFFICE,

1912-18

IN THE spring of 1912, at the same time that he was being elected alderman for the fourth consecutive term, Cermak was also campaigning for the office of bailiff of the Municipal Court of Chicago. He was following the strategy of campaigning for increasingly influential offices at the same time that he guarded his achieved status by re-election to the office already held.

Cermak ran on the Harrison slate—the so-called Progressive Democratic Organization—which was as usual challenging the Regular Democratic ticket, Sullivan-Brennan. Although some have suspected that Cermak had made a deal with Sullivan at this time, Harrison was not among them; and during the outspoken primary campaign, Cermak certainly gave no cause for suspicion. He frequently stumped for himself and the entire Harrison Progressive Democratic ticket and with vigor.

As usual, A.J. had chosen a fortunate time for candidacy. It was a good Democratic year, the year of the Bull Moose, when the Republicans were badly divided locally and nationally. There were sweeping Democratic victories in Illinois and in Chicago. Cermak went into office with the tide, as did, among others, Edward F. Dunne for governor and Maclay Hoyne for state's attorney—neither was a Sullivan-Brennan man.

Cermak by now had one of the best Democratic wards, and by this time the Bohemian population had grown significantly. In 1910 it had reached 110,736. It was still at least fifth among the ethnic groups in numbers, but at the same time it was now large enough to merit consideration by political strategists.

A.J. gained his first city-wide office, for the first time reaching beyond his staunch Czech supporters, without any great change in his public personality. Francis X. Busch, prominent attorney and later A.J.'s corporation counsel, described the Cermak of those days as having "no manners, poise, or easy grace." Mr. Busch said:

> He was very careless in those early days. He appeared tough partially because he wanted to be a contrast to the Granger Farwell type of Dry. He didn't want to seem other than a rough, ordinary guy, speaking for the man on the street. The rougher he was, the more popular he was with his constituency.[1]

But if it was unnecessary to develop a new personality, new capacities had to be developed.

The office of bailiff was A.J.'s first experience as a public administrator or, for that matter, his first experience with relatively large-scale administration of any kind. In some ways the office of bailiff was a difficult place for a beginner to start learning the art of administration.

The bailiff's office had the usual difficulty of all police agencies in dealing with its clientele. The bailiff of the municipal court was responsible for the deputy bailiffs in each courtroom, and in the court generally, and for the maintenance of order in the court. But a greater responsibility was the serving of all the writs and processes and the handling and disposing of property as directed by the court. Cermak came to know very well the difficult position of himself and his office vis-à-vis the public. He once said that the problems of his office were "unbelievable," going on to illustrate with the statement that "500 suits [are] pending against the office, and complaints are numerous, regardless of how carefully affairs are conducted."

However, A.J. was not unsuccessful in this first attempt in administration. Although there occurred one major series of charges against him,[2] the press was generally favorable, and the judges of the court frequently spoke well of him. Toward the end of his term the chief justice praised him highly: "I have a high regard for Cermak's ability and honesty. He may be a wet politician, but he is a dry bailiff. He is a sober and two-fisted official."[3] A committee of judges was even more laudatory, avowing that Cermak had conducted the office

. . . in an aggressive, efficient manner . . . has apparently honestly, earnestly, and conscientiously endeavored to furnish efficient service. He personally is on the job each and every working day. He personally has shown an intimate knowledge and grasp of all the intricate details of the several departments of his office.[4]

Although A.J. was able to handle his new duties without being overwhelmed, he missed the rather continuous publicity which had been his in his role as alderman. Very early in his term, he began to attempt to remedy this situation. He issued reports of the accomplishments of the office, which were published in the press. The reports were largely meaningless, being mere statistical statements of the various kinds of writs served. He later improved the appeal of this type of report. During his campaign for sheriff, for example, his press announcements were in terms of the money his office had saved over the previous year.

Another move which was at least partially a public relations maneuver was his organization of the Bailiffs' Benevolent Association. All of his deputies were automatically members; dues were collected; and, in addition to benefits for members—such as burial and sick benefits—money was expended to help needy families. Cermak's office often had to execute evictions, and often immediate welfare services were not available. A.J. was already experienced in welfare work through his ward and precinct duties; now he came to the assistance of such unfortunates through his Bailiffs' Benevolent Association. Although the association was at one time attacked as purely a front for graft, some believed that it was actually functioning to alleviate distress. One editorial somewhat floridly described it as

. . . an organization which has done much efficient emergency charitable work. . . . It is a good and merciful thing to have back of the bailiff a substantial relief fund. The bailiff with a charity fund in hand is in pleasing contrast to the old day of the constable with writ and weapon.[5]

A.J. gave further evidence of his appreciation of the newsworthiness of innovation. In order to dispel the boredom of waiting jurors, he set up a well-equipped clubroom for them. One newspaper reacted this way: "If You Feel Clubby, Get on Jury Panel and Enjoy Good Time." Whether or not the jurymen became clubby, it was true that prior to that time no facilities were available for them; they had not even been able to leave the jury assignment room.

But A.J. had other problems than publicity and the administration of his office. There was little rest for Chicago politicians. Hardly had he settled in his new role than the 1914 election was at hand, bringing with it his familiar Harrison-Sullivan quandary. A.J. managed once again to keep in with both factions, supporting Sullivan (who, to the surprise of many, had at last succumbed to "public-officitis" and emerged from behind the scenes to become Democratic candidate for the United States Senate), but meanwhile working for the Harrison county slate. After the primary, "harmony" was somehow achieved again, and the campaign was largely a success. Although Sullivan narrowly lost his race to Lawrence Y. Sherman, there were important victories for both Harrison and Sullivan men; and Cermak's own man, Cervenka, endorsed by both factions, was also re-elected.

A.J.'s feat of retaining membership in both the Harrison and Sullivan factions has been described by Wendt and Kogan as a "neat bit of political legerdemain."[6] But he could not continue indefinitely with a foot in each camp. The time for decision approached with the coming mayoralty election.

THE MAYORALTY ELECTION OF 1915

As the 1915 election drew near, it did not appear to be a good Republican year. Although the Republicans held some powerful local offices, they were more divided than the Democrats. The Democrats had not only the President but also the governor of Illinois, one United States senator, important county offices, including the strategic state's attorney and county judge, and, of course, the incumbent mayor. And the national administration was still keeping the country out of the war.

Harrison entered the lists for his sixth term. Sullivan opposed him with Robert M. Sweitzer, a genial, open-mannered "regular," then holding the office of county clerk, important for patronage and control of election. The battle was very intense, with every pressure exerted. There were almost 50 per cent more votes cast than in the Republican primary. Sweitzer won by a huge majority, signifying the decay of the Harrison faction and the nearly total victory of Roger Sullivan. Harrison was deserted by many who had supported him in the past. One of the chief deserters was Cermak.

A.J. was loath to leave Harrison, whom he personally admired, and Harrison had felt his hold on A.J. becoming more and more tenuous, and admitted that "Tony was not completely loyal to me in my last election. He was in cahoots with Roger." Yet he pointed out that A.J. "still delivered his ward to me, *the only ward* to do so against Sweitzer." Harrison never confronted Cermak with any accusations. But political considerations came first with "Tony." Beyond all A.J.'s other political reasons for casting his lot with Sullivan was the fact that Sabath was closer to Harrison than was A.J. himself, so that he felt he had no real opportunities with Harrison.

The Republican primary was of great interest, for it marked the entrance into prominence of William Hale (Big Bill) Thompson. Thompson, who was wealthy and had wealthy friends, ran as a Lundin-Lorimer man. At the time a virtual political nobody, he became that faction's candidate because there seemed little chance of winning. It did not seem likely that he would win in the primary, where he was opposed by Harry Olson, chief justice of the municipal court. Olson, a Deneen Republican, was a judge of good reputation and had powerful friends among the "respectables," notably Victor F. Lawson, publisher of the *Chicago Daily News*. Thompson, beginning to show signs of his later potent demagoguery, defeated Olson by about 3,500 votes out of over 175,000 cast. But this resulted from more than demagoguery. As early as this, Thompson exhibited his tremendous influence among Chicago Negro voters. Without the overwhelming majority in the predominantly Negro Second Ward, he would have lost to Olson.

The general election began as a relatively quiet affair—for a Chicago mayoralty election. Thompson was not given much of a chance. But it soon became apparent that his money, his hold on the Negro voters, and his irrational platform appeals were making headway. Sweitzer became worried. But Sweitzer and Sullivan had more to fear than the efficacy of the Thompson campaign. As in the election of 1911, the various factions in both parties crossed party lines to help the opposition. Sullivan forces had supported the Republican candidate against Harrison in 1911. Now the Harrisonites, furious at defeat in the primary, backed Thompson.

There are some who believe that even Cermak scuttled Sweitzer in secret. Credence is sometimes given this hypothesis because it is well known that in Cermak's 1918 race for sheriff he was "knifed" by Sweitzer. However, it seems rather unlikely that he believed himself strong enough at this juncture to risk offending Sullivan. It is true that when A.J. was next an alderman (1919-22) he worked closely with Thompson, but one must note that at the time that relationship was not blatantly anti-Sullivan (by then, Brennan).

Whatever A.J.'s role in this election, Thompson defeated Sullivan's man, to the surprise of many. Thus began "Big Bill's" colorful career—which was to end sixteen years later in ignominious defeat at the hands of A.J. Cermak. But Cermak and Thompson were to cross swords long before 1931. Their first clash came very soon after Thompson's election.

THE WET PARADE

In October, 1915, Thompson without warning issued an order directing that the state Sunday saloon-closing laws be enforced. Thompson wrote that he had been informed that certain saloons were not obeying this law (which his corporation counsel had thoughtfully interpreted for him) and that since his oath of office required him to see that the laws were faithfully executed, he must order the saloons to comply with the law.

The mayor's message created a veritable explosion of wrath all over Chicago. And the bomb that exploded loudest was the collective might of the United Societies, with Cermak as vituperative spokesman. The Societies had been double-crossed, betrayed, A.J. bellowed. He produced a pledge signed by Thompson before the election. He asked the mayor: "Did you sign the pledge of the United Societies or did you not? Is your signature genuine or is it a forgery?" He greeted with derision Thompson's assertion that his signing the pledge was merely an expression of personal opinion. Slyly, he quizzed Thompson as to the real reasons for the closing order. Was it because of the fear of a grand jury action by the Drys? Was it because Deneen and others threatened indictment? Was it because of the most recent alibi—that Christian Science had compelled it? Thompson had given so many reasons—which was the actual one? A.J. ridiculed Thompson's assertion that he was merely enforcing a law. What about the gambling laws which were not being enforced? Would the mayor like some assistance there from deputy bailiffs, since apparently he hadn't enough police?

Thompson tried to reply, but given the majority attitude toward liquor, he was at a disadvantage. He tried to encourage action to have A.J. removed from his United Societies position, a suggestion to which A.J. responded with gleeful ridicule and sarcasm. To Thompson's recommendation that the municipal court judges force Cermak to leave his office, Chief Justice Olson replied that the court was not concerned with Cermak's politics; he was an independently elected officer and could be impeached only by the legislature.

There were many protest meetings and demonstrations, and the next major round between Cermak and Thompson came in connection with the protest parade scheduled by the Societies for Sunday, November 7, 1915. A.J. pretended amazement that Thompson was opposed to the parade. "Why should 'Brass Band Bill,' the 'King of Parades' object to such a demonstration? He loves parades." He went on to threaten: "If the Chief of Police refuses to grant a permit we will go to the City Council and obtain one. If he vetoes it we will pass it over his veto."[7] Thompson decided at last not to fight and issued a permit for the parade; but he refused to review it. Cermak said that this was an official insult from the city of Chicago, inasmuch as Thompson had reviewed the Dry parade.

Meanwhile Thompson continued his efforts to have Cermak removed by the judges. He wrote a letter to every judge, attacking not only Cermak but Chief Justice Olson as well. Olson called this "cheap politics," but said that the judges would consider the mayor's letter at the next meeting. Cermak's response was considerably more choleric: "I'll burn him up. He'll fly out of the City Hall. I've got some things on him I didn't intend to make public, but so long as he has attacked me again I'll use them ... I'll burn him up."[8]

Cermak was insistent that the investigation of Thompson's charges be made and that Thompson attend the meeting of the judges at which his charges were to be considered. Thompson, however, never appeared before the judges, although they twice postponed consideration of the matter and threatened to issue a capias to compel him to appear. In the end, the judges completely cleared Cermak and repeated Judge Olson's pronouncement that they had no power to remove him.

In the meantime the parade took place. It was a mammoth affair. There were perhaps not the expected 100,000, but a publication which was far from sympathetic estimated between 41,000 and 45,000; and the same journal estimated the number of spectators as between 500,000 and 750,000. A great many dignitaries were present on the reviewing stand. Although confirmed Drys depicted the marchers as "saloon-keepers, bartenders, beer-drinkers and ex-convicts," other Dry, more objective observers saw no evidence of saloon or brewery floats or of drunkenness, but an orderly march of ordinary people carrying such signs as "Foolish laws breed disrespect for all law"; "God put the Sun in Sunday"; "Why pick on Sunday the workingmen's holiday?"; "Morality is not created by law." At least a portion of the parade, however, made for Streeterville, an unincorporated area only a mile from city hall, where the sale of beer was never illegal.

There were noisy repercussions to the parade. Cermak was confident that it was a complete repudiation of Thompson and a great vindication of "personal liberty" and "home rule." Thompson, through his city attorney, announced that watchers had been assigned to compile a list of participants, and that those on the list would henceforth be *personae non gratae* in the city hall. Also ill advised was his allowing a spokesman to scold the foreign born among the Societies' ranks, in a statement which had an unmistakably condescending nativist, "know-nothing" tone.

The battle raged on for months. Cermak charged that Thompson's blacklist amounted to malfeasance in office and threatened grand-jury action and an investigation by the city council; Thompson accused Cermak and two Czech aldermen friends of attempting to influence the civil service commission in its contemplated disciplinary action against a Czech police captain who had allegedly failed to enforce Sunday closing—the wrangling seemed endless. But it was at length engulfed in the primaries of 1916. The Sunday-closing question became a myth after the primary, for Thompson could not long hold out under the pressure. Nobody was impeached; nobody was indicted—were there any results out of the six or seven months of shouting?

At the very least, Cermak emerged from this skirmish more than ever, and more strongly and widely defined, as the fearless champion of the Wets. He demonstrated that his Wetness was to the saturation point; that his courage in defending and extending the position of the liquor interests, the thirsty, and the foreign-born could not be questioned. Although he had been suspected in some quarters of looking favorably upon the election of Thompson, he had now made it clear in dramatic fashion that *anyone* who dared oppose the United Societies would be fought to the end, from his corner. And Thompson's reputation for Wetness was undoubtedly injured. Since in many other ways he was not regarded very highly by the puritanical Protestant elements, this was bound to harm him in the long run. He had crossed swords not only with Cermak but with the groups behind Cermak, for whom Thompsonism might ordinarily have had great appeal. This was a major misfortune for one who would make his mark as the exponent of the sky's-the-limit open town. And oddly enough, the man who forced him temporarily into the role of the blue-law advocate was to succeed, in the long run, in maintaining an aura of respectability sufficiently superior to Thompson's to cause his ultimate abdication.

There is little doubt that as the 1916 primaries approached Cermak was at a rising tide in power and prestige. The campaign against Thompsonism enhanced his position not only in the eyes of Chicago generally but among members of his own party. He had managed, too, to balance his patronage among all the factions. Thus it happened that in his own campaign for re-election as ward committeeman he had no opposition. The Harrisonites, although they were still bitter about his desertion of their 1915 candidate, could not oppose him as the Sullivanites had attempted to unseat Sabath as ward committeeman in 1914. The Harrison faction was quoted as saying that Cermak was going to allow each of his appointees to support his own faction. "We can't complain much; at least there is nothing we can do."[9] Not even Cermak's candidate for alderman, Joseph E. Novak, was opposed. One newspaper described Cermak as being "in peace and content." "The Harrison-Sabath people would rather he were actively in the fray for them, but Cermak sees no reason why he should excite himself."[10] Could any urban politician ask for more?

The flavor of this happy political situation is also indicated in the sporadic mention of his name as a mayoralty candidate for 1919. At a mass meeting in Pilsen Park he was introduced as "the next mayor of Chicago." The meeting was held under the auspices of the United Societies. Important among his fellow speakers were Maclay Hoyne—one of Harrison's top lieutenants—Alderman John Toman, and Otto Kerner. Conspicuously absent was Adolph J. Sabath.

Cermak's continued relationship with the Harrison group was fortunate for him, for Sullivan did not do very well in this primary, local or state, and came to near disaster in the general elections. It was, altogether, a poor Democratic year in Chicago, but A.J. himself remained undamaged. His ward was still firmly in his grasp, as was the United Societies. Fellow Czechs—most of them in Cermak's debt—were in the council and in other offices, and he himself had more than two years of office left, with the attendant patronage. He was firmly in the driver's seat, the reins in his grasp.

Suddenly, in the midst of this enviable political situation, the driver manifested an entirely uncharacteristic reluctance to drive.

In 1916, Cermak became ill, entered a hospital and underwent an operation for kidney stones. Following this operation, in the fall, he tendered his resignation from the county central committee. A few months later he issued a statement expressing his disenchantment with politics and desire to withdraw from the game. "The political game is not what it is cracked up to be. I have a valuable real estate business on the West Side and I shall give my time to that."[11]

He was forty-three years old. From the age of nineteen he had never been able to resist his attraction to the "game." Would he really withdraw now, when he had gained so much? In fact, he did not withdraw. But he did falter and lose ground. During the next two years he made some political miscalculations out of keeping with his usual shrewd, cautious pattern. Indeed, it sometimes appears as though he were seeking failure even while he continued to court success. This period of political clumsiness was marked throughout by the angry, explosive, vituperative behavior which was never strange to Cermak but which had heretofore been manifested at the right times, from a political point of view, and directed toward the right objects. The emotions now seemed to go out of control. Cermak, the man, rode roughly over Cermak, the politician.

An illustration of this phenomenon appeared in A.J.'s response to the Gemmill Investigation.

In June, 1917, Cermak was accused of graft, corruption, and misconduct of office. The charges were made by Municipal Judge Gemmill to a full meeting of the judges of the court. Prominent among Gemmill's accusations were: that the Bailiffs' Benevolent Association dues were exacted by duress and that the funds collected vanished as graft; that Judge Stelk—who had served in the past as A.J.'s attorney—was too friendly to Cermak; that there was "rottenness" in general among the judges.

The pandemonium was on. In the midst of charges and countercharges among the judges, someone telephoned Cermak, who dramatically appeared to confront his accuser. At last Gemmill agreed to withdraw his charges and said that he had not intended to imply that Cermak received either direct or indirect graft or that he countenanced graft. But A.J. was not satisfied. He insisted that since his name had been besmirched, a thorough investigation be made. He would either be vindicated and receive a public apology or would be impeached, "kicked out." He was upheld by Chief Justice Olson. The judges' committee on bailiffs immediately began to investigate. They summoned deputy bailiffs and set about questioning them.

There then followed six months of continued charges, counter-charges, insults, grand threats, counterthreats, hysteria, and much unjudicial behavior. Cermak's conduct was from the first violent and pugnacious. It often appeared that he was goading Gemmill. Within only a few days he had threatened the judge with libel suits, impeachment, and grand-jury action. Gemmill reinstated and extended his charges, so that they included padded payrolls, additional graft, and dishonest handling and sale of levied property. Although the judges, particularly Judge Stelk and Chief Justice Olson, also tangled with Gemmill, it was A.J.'s battle with him that remained central, and it was their exchanges that were aired most in hearing rooms and in the press.

The formal hearings, which began in October, were wild and disorderly. Cermak's tactics and behavior were of a piece with their character. He admitted to attempts to trap Gemmill by fake telephone calls, plants, and eavesdropping. It was alleged that he and his men trailed and intimidated witnesses. His men were ever present in the hearing room, in menacingly large numbers. A.J.'s personal behavior was menacing, often brutal, in the threats and innuendoes leveled against Gemmill, and in his attitude toward witnesses. A newspaper reported: "Cermak now sets record in noise as charges fly. Audience roars applause as municipal magistrates yell defiance in each other's faces."[12]

Altogether, 138 witnesses were heard. Gemmill himself—after repeatedly refusing to appear before the committee—finally appeared, balked at becoming a witness, and read off nine specific charges. Four concerned dishonest levies, care or disposal of property; three described improper conduct by deputy bailiffs; one was a charge that contributions to the Bailiffs' Benevolent Association were made under duress and that other forced political payments had occurred; and, finally, one charged Judge Stelk with interfering with an order of another judge through the bailiff's office.

The hearings, all grist for the tabloids' mill, did not end until late in November. On December 30, the committee made public its report to the entire body of judges, which accepted it without a dissenting vote. Cermak was unequivocally acquitted. It was the second such acquittal since the affair began, for in June a committee of judges had completely cleared A.J.; but Gemmill had insisted upon a new committee and further investigation, charging partiality and poor procedure.

The report praised the bailiff and the administration of his office in the highest terms. The judges then punished Gemmill for "unwarranted and false assertions reflecting upon the integrity of the officials of this court." By a vote of twenty to one he was given a public rebuke. So, to all appearances, the matter was at last closed; and Cermak, after six months of accusations, was finally vindicated.

But the old aphorism about smoke and fire is in this case almost irresistible, despite the complete exoneration. It is true that Judge Gemmill may have been motivated by a personal animosity toward Cermak—he had indicated dislike for A.J. prior to this time. Gemmill, a rather humorless Dry and an undeniably irascible individual, may well have been incensed by the spectacle of the wettest Wet imaginable holding a position as an official of the court. He may also have been seeking publicity for his next campaign. All the same, there were several allegations against Cermak which were not really disposed of adequately, even if they were never actually proved.

Bits of evidence brought out in testimony were either admitted by Cermak or Cermak witnesses or else not very persuasively denied. In connection with Gemmill's charges that deputy bailiffs were forced to join the Bailiffs' Benevolent Association and that moneys were taken from them in the form of initiation fees and dues, there was, for example, the case of ex-bailiff Szmergalski. Gemmill charged that this man had been ordered to pay ten dollars a month to the treasurer of the "Twelfth Ward Guards" and that he had done so for nineteen months. Both Cermak and Treasurer Joseph Novak denied this; but Szmergalski himself later testified to the effect that he *had* paid Novak $180 dues for the Guards, as well as money for Sweitzer's campaign in 1915 and $5.00 each for other campaigns. This was but one item of evidence pointing to the possibility that Judge Gemmill's accusations may not have been entirely groundless.

Although A.J. was finally cleared, one may hazard that six months of charges of graft and corruption made a more lasting impression on the minds of the electorate than the final pronouncement of innocence. Carter Harrison, speaking of this period of Cermak's career, was of the opinion that, "He did many risky things as bailiff." Less than a year after the Gemmill affair, A.J. suffered his first electoral defeat in his race for sheriff. The Gemmill matter cannot be interpreted as the sole or even the most important cause of his defeat, but it is likely that it contributed its bit.

One may legitimately wonder what Cermak hoped to gain from the investigation. He had an opportunity to avoid it at the beginning, when his accuser had been ready to withdraw his charges. Even supposing he felt confident of being cleared—considering his relationship with several of the judges and the certainty of a friendly state's attorney—why was he so anxious to take up the gauntlet? Possibly the answer lies in Senator Sorghum's dictum that "the politician who looks for a fight is the man who attracts attention." A.J. had not figured prominently in the news since his battle with Thompson, over a year before. Another primary was scheduled in the spring of 1918; and A.J.'s term of office ended in December, 1918. His recognition of the value of publicity—perhaps, too, his personal need of it—may have dictated his course.

However, in the progress of this case, he must have become uncomfortably aware of the other half of Senator Sorghum's pronouncement that "when you go after vindication there is great danger of prolonging a controversy which merely serves to remind people that you are under suspicion." It became evident before the end of the affair, when Cermak began to urge haste in winding up the proceedings, that he would have been happy to be rid of the once much-desired publicity. This did not, however, cause him to modify his public behavior, or to change tactics obviously not to his credit as an elected official in the public eye. His realization that the Gemmill affair might be doing him more harm than good must have come at a point when he was incapable of putting the brakes on his savage antics.

Cermak never repeated the kind of adventure represented in the Gemmill affair. Although other accusations came up in his career, he was never again faced with formal proceedings, and his entire response and technique with regard to such accusations underwent a great alteration. But this cool dealing came later. Now, having yelled and bullied and crashed his way through the many months of the Gemmill probe, he barrelled furiously on to further questionable political behavior.

THE CAMPAIGN FOR SHERIFF, 1918

The echoes of the Gemmill affair had scarcely died away when the United States entered World War I. It is only against the background of Chicago's attitudes and reactions to the war that the politics of the period can be understood. The war years were tense in most parts of the country, but the tension in Chicago, with its huge German-American population (many of them first generation) was even greater.

As in subsequent times, the middle west was the most isolationist section of the country, and Chicago was perhaps the center of neutrality sentiment in the early years of that war. Among other indications were resolutions by such an organization as the Chicago Federation of Labor, to the effect that the common people did not want war. Thompson capitalized upon this feeling and succeeded in welding a great number of German-Americans to him for many years. He gave some astonishing exhibitions in this line even after the United States had entered the war. The most discussed was probably his public reluctance to extend an invitation to Marshall Joffre and a French delegation. He soon earned the nickname of "Kaiser Bill."

But even Thompson and the huge German population could not stem the horrific spasm of patriotism that engulfed Chicago along with the nation. The American Protective League was organized; it lobbied, bullied, and threatened. Edward F. Dunne said it "goaded and insulted persons whose only offense was the possession of a German name." As everywhere in America, chasing the "Hun" became a favorite game. The entire battery of propaganda increased the atmosphere of hate with posters, street-corner speeches, atrocity fables. "Slackers" were sent white feathers. A Goethe monument was desecrated. The Bismarck Hotel changed its name to Hotel Randolph; the Kaiserhof became the nonoffensive Atlantic Hotel. Edgar Lee Masters wrote of this period, "Life in Chicago became a purgatory."

Cermak entered wholeheartedly into war work. He did not enlist, for he was now past forty. Nor was he in good health, although outwardly he was still a massive, powerful specimen. The kidney operation in 1916 was followed by a second operation for kidney stones in 1917. In 1918 he had a minor illness directly attributed to overwork in war activities.

He spoke everywhere. He was among the busiest of "Four-Minute Men." Theaters, picnics, but mostly street-corner gatherings, heard his voice. He addressed himself principally to the Czechs and other Slav groups in the entire area. He stressed the closeness of the heritage of Czechs and Slovaks, and emphasized the love and loyalty of both groups to the United States. The word "Czechoslovakia" was ever on his lips. And he was as blunt and outspoken concerning the war issue as he was in defending personal liberty. In his vocabulary "Hun" was an even greater favorite than "Czechoslovak." Nearly every political observer of the period noted Cermak's lack of discretion in this matter. Many tried to caution him, but he would have none of it.

A.J. did more than speak. He had perhaps the greatest number of war-organizational responsibilities among all Czechs. His leadership was recognized in the appointment to the chairmanship of Czech war activities for the whole country; he was also chairman of the Liberty Loan Committee of the Twelfth Ward. And he was president of the National Army Aid Association, a kind of U.S.O. organization which provided many facilities for soldiers. This was the first of many services Cermak performed for soldiers and veterans. These activities were eventually to reap him useful rewards.

It was in this sort of atmosphere that the 1918 primaries were held. Cermak's term of bailiff was ending, and he had cast his eyes on the office of sheriff of Cook County. In some ways this was the next logical step up for him. The office carried more patronage and considerably more prestige than that of bailiff. It may be speculated that his choice was conditioned by the fact that for many years this office was considered as traditionally belonging to the Germans. It is not unlikely that he estimated that 1918 would not be a good year for candidates with German names.

For the first time he was completely a Sullivan man; the period of transition stretching over long years had finally reached its culmination. Sullivan was opposed by the combined Harrison and Dunne groups, acting as the "Allied Democracy." In the primary the Czechs remained staunchly loyal to their leader, now also leader of Czech war activities. Cermak's former allies actively fought him this time, using every trick, even to the entry of another Anton J. Cermak in the Democratic primary for sheriff. Their efforts, however, were to no avail; Cermak was the victor. Then came the general election. His opponent was Charles W. Peters, a man of German antecedents. All stops were out. The full panoply of electoral "hoopla" was brought into play. Cermak ran largely on the basis of his record as bailiff, alderman, and legislator. He received considerable support from some segments of the press. One newspaper, praising his service as bailiff, declared that although there was no civil-service law, "Bailiff Cermak has maintained his own merit system, the effectiveness of which has been shown by the efficiency of the office."[13]

But his noisiest appeal was patriotic; that is to say, demagoguery. This campaign was synchronous with the Fourth Liberty Loan; so perhaps such a tactic seemed inevitable to him. Many recall his "vicious anti-German campaign." The advertisement he published in the Czech press is illustrative: "Czecho-Slovaks register. Germans still want to hold the Sheriff's office." Cermak was wrathful when Peters turned the use of this advertising against him. There was a terrible commotion in the headquarters of the United Societies one day as Cermak raged around waving a German language paper carrying *his* Czech advertisement translated into German. "I'm not," he said, "going to let that S.O.B. get away with it— posing as an American to the Americans and a German to the Germans!" Cervenka tried once more to get him to change his tactics, but he refused, "Why, you're not going to get any more German votes than I will," he raged at Cervenka.

Indorsements of every sort were sought. There were, not unexpectedly, great numbers by Czech organizations. Some Deneen Republicans, such as Chief Justice Olson, were also recruited. A large number of labor indorsements were secured, most important that of the Chicago Federation of Labor. There was support from a Negro nonpartisan group; a booster club of four hundred members was formed by city and county employees; soldiers in Verdun were allegedly writing letters home urging Cermak's election—the only groups, in fact, whose assistance was not sought were the Drys and the church leaders. They, however, willingly expressed their opinion of Cermak: a resounding negative.

Oddly enough, to the last group the United Societies may be added. The Societies did not oppose Cermak, but neither did he receive its indorsement. This was by his own wish. Although the Societies normally indorsed any member of its executive committee, Cermak believed that since there were so many Slavs running, it was better not to have the Societies indorse anyone. He succeded in making the arrangement with Peter Reinberg, an important German leader.

But all the electioneering efforts were in vain: Cermak lost. It was extremely close. Early official reports indicated that A.J. had won. Later count disclosed that he had lost by 3,083 votes of a total of over 250,000 votes.

The defeat was a tremendous blow to Cermak after eighteen years of uninterrupted successes. And it had come just when he seemed to be at the crest of the wave. Why had he lost? True, the brief Democratic tide was ebbing; but Democrats had won several local elections, and although J. Hamilton Lewis had been defeated by Medill McCormick for the Senate, he had carried Cook County by over 40,000 votes.

It may be that Cermak was overconfident. The long years of success had "fattened" him; his prominent role in war work, the anti-German feeling prevalent, and the fact that his opponent was of German descent, all caused him to exert less than maximum effort. (This election was the first and last time that Cermak campaigned for a new office so close to the end of the term of the current office. The habit he had formed up until now, and which he re-adopted after this defeat, always gave him two shots—one for the new and higher office and, in case of failure, a chance to seek re-election.)

How important his relaxed efforts were in his defeat is, however, conjectural. It is another cause which claims unanimous support. None of the many qualified persons questioned about this election failed to credit his anti-Hun activities as the major factor in his defeat. His rabid speeches had provoked the circulation of all sorts of canards about him. One of these had it that Cermak wore a belt made from the skin of a German soldier. The Germans actively opposed him, denouncing him in meeting after meeting; but many less vocal segments of voters, too, as well as individuals formerly loyal to him, were alienated.

Probably very important to his defeat, as well, was lack of assistance—in some cases actual opposition—from some Democrats. He sorely missed the usual Harrison support. There is no record of actual sabotage by the Harrisonites in the general election, but Adolph J. Sabath was very positive in stating that he had not supported Cermak in 1918. And there seems to be some evidence that Cermak was "knifed" by Sweitzer and his friends for allegedly deserting Sweitzer in 1915.

Last, this was A.J.'s first campaign in many years without United Societies' indorsement. In addition, he had been opposed by operators of Loop cabarets and saloons, having incurred their enmity a year and a half before by acting to stop entertainment and dancing in restaurants. These refused to post his literature, at the same time accepting the posters of other Democrats.

But, damaged as he was, nearly at the end of his term of office, for the first time in nineteen years defeated, shocked and depressed by this turn of events at a time when some had been touting him for mayor, he could still look to that steady factor in his progress: the Bohemians. He had not forgotten to insure it.

THE BOHEMIAN BAILIFF

During these six years of his first city-wide office, Cermak maintained his complex relationship with the Lawndale Czechs; and his influence among his countrymen spread far beyond the boundaries of Lawndale. Not in the slightest degree did he lose his consciousness of or pride in his origins.

The social relationships continued. Although he was very busy downtown, he did not neglect the Lawndale saloons and his drinking friends of many decades. Nor was he absent from many Saturday night affairs of *Ceske Beseda* of the Bohemian Charitable Organization. He took part with his compatriots in activities of every kind.

Not the least of these were the war activities mentioned above.

Although A.J. lost his campaign for sheriff, it is possible that his rabid behavior in reference to the war was pleasing to most of his constituency. The Czechs were deeply involved in the hope of the rebirth of an independent Czechoslovakia, and the Germans were all that stood in the way. Certainly they responded handsomely, these Czech followers, to the Cermak-led Liberty Loan and Red Cross drives. It was significant that the Czechs were led by Cermak in these activities not only in his ward or in his city but nationally. In the same context, he participated in activities which aided the Masaryk group and was one of the leading organizers in Chicago.

But his most pervasive and perhaps most significant relationships were in matters political. The Twelfth Ward Guards seem to have mushroomed everywhere in Chicago in this period, and Czechs other than the Guards also began to be conspicuous. The conspicuousness of their presence can in almost every case be attributed directly to Cermak.

In 1913 the new ward boundaries further reduced the diminishing German population of the Twelfth Ward. So Cermak discarded Alderman Schultz almost as easily as this is said. Although Schultz had already been nominated, Cermak ran Otto Kerner against him, and Kerner was the winner. From this point until the end of the system of two aldermen for each ward, Lawndale was to have two Czech representatives in the council. They might be Novak, Cepak, or someone else, but almost always they were "Cermak's." In addition, Cermak was influential in Cervenka's re-election as clerk of the probate court in 1914. He placed one man on the municipal-court bench, and Vopicka on the Harrison slate in 1912. Vopicka was also an officer of the Sabath bonding company, which received all the bailiffs' bonding business. Nor should it be overlooked that Cermak's good friend John A. Sokol was able to rent his warehouse to the bailiff's office.

Cermak's most important gain, however, was the election of John Toman as one of the aldermen from the adjacent Czech ward. This virtually ended the threat to Cermak's leadership of Kostner, the Harrison and Sabath man. Toman was usually at Cermak's beck and call. His position as chairman of the license committee was also very useful. Thus in 1917 this committee cooperated with Cermak in approving an ordinance vesting the

[96]

issuance of saloon licenses in a committee consisting of the chief of police, the corporation counsel, and the chairman of the license committee. This was intended to reduce the control of the police over the issuance and revocation of these licenses.

But the growing number of offices held by Czechs is only one criterion of Cermak's unabated feeling of ethnic identification. Another kind of demonstration is provided by the occasions of his coming to the aid of fellow countrymen in distress. There was the matter of his efforts to protect Captain Ptacek from disciplinary action by the civil service commission; it should also be noted that the commission accused Kerner and Toman of trying to protect Ptacek too.

The very fact of having a Czech police captain in his district was not unimportant to Cermak. In these matters and others, it can be seen that the identification and affiliation of Cermak with his people was continued through his term as bailiff and was as strong as it had been in the earlier periods.

POLITICAL
RECOVERY:
BOSS
OF
THE
COUNCIL,
1919-22

THE DEFEAT in 1918—though by so narrow a margin—might, it seems, have given A.J. an opportunity to reassess the allure and value of politics and to readjust his plans accordingly. The defeat brought to a climax a series of setbacks and misfortunes in Cermak's career dating from 1916. It seemed natural at this time to consider the possibility of giving up the satisfactions of a place in the public gaze. At least two alternatives existed: he could concentrate his energies upon his highly successful business enterprises; or he could continue to operate politically, but in the behind-the-scenes twilight zone.

But despite surface signs which appeared to urge and foretell such a choice, it seems clear that Cermak never contemplated these alternatives seriously. By January, 1919, while his contest for the sheriff's office was still pending, he announced himself a candidate for alderman. The decision had to be made some time before the announcement, in order to accomplish preliminary groundwork, so that the amount of time, if any, that A.J. could have put into soul searching was very brief indeed.

Given this unvanquishable drive for public office, the decision to attempt return to the city council was well taken. Cermak's strength in county-wide elections was not what he had believed. Best, then, for the outspoken anti-Hun to return to his home district, where the weaknesses of his losing campaign would not be an issue. Further, election to the office was all but assured in advance: ward committeemen seldom lost when running for alderman, almost never in a safe ward like Cermak's. He had little difficulty in arranging the nomination.

Some long-range and judicious political planning made this step possible. The alderman whose term was ending was a fellow Czech, Otto Kerner. Kerner, a successful lawyer, was reckoned by Merriam as one of the best Chicago aldermen, and a man of high integrity. His friendship with Cermak dated back to A.J.'s first campaign in 1902, when Kerner had represented him in a legal action to retain his name on the ballot. Cermak invited him to move to his ward, which Kerner ultimately did, although not in direct response to his invitation. A.J. obtained for him a position in the office of the corporation counsel, in Harrison's last administration, in 1911. When in 1913 redistricting had removed most of the ward's German population, Cermak persuaded Kerner to become a candidate for alderman against the German incumbent Schultz, although Schultz was already a candidate. Kerner was elected.

This event, plus the prior election of Cervenka, foreshadowed Cermak's future willingness, when political expediency directed, to nominate and support "decent," "respectable," and nonmachine-politician candidates—that is to say, persons not generally painted as bosses or tools of bosses. Always, however, from Cervenka to Henry Horner (who became "Cermak's governor"), he reckoned carefully in trying to ascertain how amenable they were to control. Nevertheless, as in the case of Kerner, he was willing to give them plenty of room to operate in most areas as respectably as they desired, even to the point of opposing their mentor! However, for some period of Kerner's incumbency, the other alderman from A.J.'s ward was Novak, the same man whom Chief Justice Olson had labeled "Cermak's alderman" during the Gemmill hearings. In other words, A.J. could afford to have one alderman who was well regarded by the forces for good government.

It was Kerner, then, whose term expired in 1919, and A.J. had little difficulty in causing him to step down. Some accounts allege that Kerner voluntarily withdrew, advising Cermak to run, because it was essential that A.J. not drop from the public view. Judge Kerner himself did not offer such an explanation.[1]

It surprised no one that A.J. had an easy victory in the primary. For the general election he was also in a good position. In addition to the huge edge he had against any opponent by virtue of his position as ward committeeman, he received the indorsement of the Chicago Federation of Labor, and, wonders of wonders, that impregnable fortress of respectability, the Municipal Voters' League! The League praised Cermak's energy and his stand for economy and balanced budgets. Still A.J. was faced by a real threat in this campaign. His Republican opponent, a Czech compatriot, ran a good race. The Cermak majority, though not really narrow, was smaller than in earlier ward races, and was a far cry indeed from the two elections which had not even been contested. There was a feeling on the part of many Lawndalites that "Tony's been in long enough. Let's give someone else a chance."[2]

Nevertheless, A.J. was the winner, once again demonstrating his dominance of the ward. There is some probability that defeat in his ward at this juncture would either have finished A.J. as a political power or else have caused him to adopt a less conspicuous role. This election to his fourth term as alderman ended the downswing crisis period of his political career. The challenge overcome. he had little difficulty in winning re-election, in 1921, to a fifth term.

THE WAR AND THE IMPACT OF THOMPSONISM

Much had happened in and to Chicago since Cermak's first terms in the council. His behavior in 1919-22 can best be understood in the light of the extremely important developments that had taken place. Thompsonism and the first World War were two separate cataclysms, but they coincided in time, and each made worse the effect of the other on the state of public morality and the tone of politics in Chicago. During the earlier years when Cermak was alderman, and in his first years as bailiff, although politics in the opprobrious or spoils sense was by no means absent from Chicago, the city and county administrations were at a relatively high level. From the nineties, when the Municipal Voters' League had largely rid the council of the "Gray Wolves," until 1915, many observers have said that the Chicago City Council was the best local legislative body in the country. Also, during most of this period, Chicago enjoyed the administration of high-caliber mayors like Edward F. Dunne and Carter Harrison.

But in 1915, Lundin and Thompson took over the crumbling Lorimer spoils machine, defeated Olson in the primary, and beat Sweitzer for the office of mayor—with Harrison, defeated by Sullivan candidate Sweitzer, turning his organization to the defeat of Sullivan's man. Thompson's vicious campaign against Sweitzer, including anti-Germanism, anti-Catholicism, and general scurrilousness, heralded the dawning of a new and more vulgar era in Chicago politics. Charles E. Merriam described the descent of Thompsonism in this way:

> With the War, calamity descended upon the city.... The spoils system swept over the city like a noxious blight, and the city hall became a symbol for corruption and incompetence ... the civic idealism of the community was for the moment put to the rout. The Council was wrecked, the administrative services looted, the election machinery captured, and vicious hands reached out for the schools and the courts. The prejudices and passions and greed of the city were thoroughly exploited to the accompaniment of a rich pyrotechnic display of the inevitable type.[3]

This was the era when the "Big Fix" was born, as Thompson ruled from 1915 to 1923, and again from 1927 to 1931. Civic plunder was organized on a scale never before seen in Chicago, or perhaps anywhere else. It included the whole gamut of crooked politics used anywhere in the country, as well as some new schemes for the enrichment of the insiders. Most important in this period was the organization and sale of "protection" for a long catalogue of illegal activities. Protection had always been a purchasable commodity; but now, with the advent of Prohibition, more was needed, and more was made available.

Rarely had there been such a combination of agencies and influences so highly organized in an effort to dominate government in any area, with the purpose of securing and selling immunity from law. Thompson and his cohorts were undoubtedly not the whole cause, perhaps only a symbol or a manifestation of a tremendous moral reversion in the wake of the war; but there can be little doubt that the not-very-well-hidden cynicism and the crude demagoguery of Thompson *et al.* made a still better climate for the flourishing of moral retrogression.

Playing a major role in all these developments was the Eighteenth Amendment, pushed upon an unsuspecting country by a highly organized minority. The temporary wartime Prohibition became a part of the Constitution. To Chicago this was almost unbelievable. During the period now under consideration the city twice clearly indicated its attitude on the subject. In 1919 when the issue of Wet and Dry appeared on the ballot, the vote was 406,190 Wet and 147,179 Dry; in 1922 the vote was 500,757 Wet and 110,707 Dry. Thus on the basis of official election returns during Cermak's first year as alderman in this period, Chicago was Wet almost three to one; while in his last year as alderman, Wet sentiment was about five to one.

It is therefore cause for little wonder that protection for the manufacture, distribution, and sale of "booze" became highly organized and worth millions of dollars: as Al Capone used to say, it was merely a matter of supplying a highly prized commodity to thirsty Chicagoans. And if protection for bootleggers in opposition to federal law was a practical necessity, then in the same terms, why not for other kinds of proscribed activities such as gambling, prostitution, burglary, strong-arming, and racketeering? Once the law-enforcement machinery was purchased, how could the beneficiaries complain if the purchasers branched out from bootlegging pure and simple? Even had they seriously wanted to object, they were, by taking payoffs, accessories to every other kind of crime.

There can be little doubt that the ambivalent attitude toward the enforcement of Prohibition was a major contributing factor to the general decline of morality in the Age of Whoopee. The "noble experiment" is now quite generally used as an illustration of the sociological dictum that laws are not made simply by enacting a statute, especially when the law runs counter to mores and customs. In other cases besides that of Prohibition laws, custom sometimes repeals the acts of legislatures. This was exactly what, in his own way, Cermak contended in his stand against the Sunday-closing law.

The identical phenomenon could be seen at work during this period in connection with several other areas of legislation then coming into existence in answer to the needs of an expanding urban civilization. With the large numbers of motorcars recently in circulation many new laws concerning automobiles had to be passed. Similarly, with a tremendous upsurge in building, new building codes became necessary; and with the growth of a self-conscious labor movement, many new laws governing labor relations were entered on the books. In these matters, as with liquor and gambling and perhaps prostitution, a kind of double standard of morality existed. Most communities and "good citizens" were against sin, bootlegging, gambling, prostitution, reckless or drunken driving, poorly constructed buildings, and vicious practices with regard to labor. But individuals in their roles as drinkers, poker players, stag-party participants, automobile drivers, home-builders, or employers, had quite other attitudes. When acting in these roles, rather than as bulwarks of the community, they were not seriously opposed to buying beverages from a bootlegger or frequenting a speakeasy; they were not really incensed at the book-maker with whom they placed a bet, nor by the atmosphere of the country club with its slot machines and poker parties; they were broad-minded about "going down the line" or sowing wild oats with professional ladies of the evening; they were offended if stopped for speeding or for driving after drinking; they saw nothing very outrageous about cutting corners in the quality of building materials or in the provision of inadequate fire-protection features in new structures; and they were not highly upset when police took a firm hand with striking workmen who were probably agitators or Red Bolsheviks, or anarchists, anyway.

When this kind of dual standard exists—one for the community as a whole and one for the individual—it is almost inevitable that a system of protection is organized. In this way individuals can have their cake and eat it. They may as members of civic groups view crime and corruption with dismay; while as individuals they are assured of a liquor supply, need not be concerned with traffic violations, have ample opportunities to gamble, may build unsafe buildings and sell faulty materials, and in general not feel their rugged individuality hampered or restricted by law. For in each of these cases, if the "fix" is organized, immunity can be bought.

In this first period of Thompsonism, the control of liquor was highly centralized under the aegis of the political machine; and for a time the greater violence of the William Dever era (1923-27) and Thompson's third term (1927-31) was averted. The flow of liquor into the city, its manufacture locally, the distribution in the Loop and in outlying wards, as well as the organization of vice in general was under the control of Big Jim Colosimo. He ruled from his headquarters at Twenty-Second Street (later to be named Cermak Road) and Wabash Avenue until, in May, 1920, he was murdered and the syndicate taken over by Johnny Torrio.

Another important landmark of this period was the notorious Landis award. Chicago builders and building-trades unions had been engaging in great disputes during the postwar building boom. Ultimately the disputes were brought before Federal Judge Kenesaw Mountain Landis.[4] His decision was a major victory for the employers. He decreed a 12½ per cent hourly reduction of wages; compulsory arbitration; the end of sympathy strikes; and a revision of laws concerning the regulation and restriction of materials for building. The association of contractors proposed to use the award as a tool in their union-busting campaign between 1919 and 1923. They proposed to deal only with unions that agreed to abide by the Landis award. To support them the Association of Commerce organized the Citizens Committee to enforce the Landis Award. Leading business "respectables" became members under the leadership of Thomas E. Donnelley and James A. Patton. Huge sums were raised for the purpose of "keeping the workers in their place." Thompson's chief of police, and his ally, State's Attorney Crowe, stood for law enforcement vigorously, thereby helping the cause of the Landis-award group.

Another notable event of this period was the arrival en masse of the Negro in Chicago. The need for labor, coinciding with the end of immigration during the war, contributed to the rapid acceleration of an earlier, steadier growth in numbers. Many tens of thousands of Negroes arrived in Chicago from 1914 to 1919. In 1919 a terrible race riot, with forty dead and hundreds wounded, capped the immigration. But not even this event could check the flowing tide, as the effects of the new restrictive national immigration policy were felt in the continued need for more cheap labor. All during this period and beyond it the Negroes came, contributing tremendously to the strength of the Thompson machine.

POLITICS, 1919-23

Although Cermak's election saw the organization of the city council by a Democratic majority, the political trend in 1919 was definitely Republican. Despite his rapacious regime, Thompson was re-elected in 1919. Thus Cermak was forced to work during his entire second period in the council with Thompson, his arch-enemy of 1915-16.

The 1920 Primaries

The Democratic primaries were as usual fought between the Sullivanites and the now quite weak remnants of the Harrison and Dunne factions. The Sullivan regulars won most of the contests in which they made major efforts. The Sullivan-Brennan organization demonstrated its ever-increasing power by nominating Michael L. Igoe for state's attorney over Maclay Hoyne, who was running for his third term. This was accomplished in spite of the usual support of Harrison candidates by the local Hearst newspapers. This office was considered in many ways more strategic for a local machine than that of governor or senator.

By this time Cermak had completely identified himself with the Sullivan-Brennan group—he knew well enough when to desert a sinking ship. For his complete transfer of allegiance he was to receive his reward by becoming the Brennan candidate for president of the county board in 1922. In this period Cermak became chairman of the Sullivan-Brennan Cook County Democratic Committee and a member of the influential managing committee.

Much vigor and venom were shown in the Republican primary, as local Republicans smelled the exhilarating odor of power and pelf. A full county slate was entered by Thompson-Lundin; it was opposed by Deneen and other factions. The campaigning was bitter. Robert E. Crowe, Thompson-Lundin candidate for state's attorney, exemplified the tone and the intensity of the electioneering as he violently denounced the League of Nations and international bankers and used railroad time tables to look up the train he would use to send Victor Lawson, publisher of the *Chicago*

Daily News, to the penitentiary in Joliet. Thompson-Lundin won a notable victory, nominating their candidates for governor, state's attorney, and other county offices.

Republican Intraparty Strife

The great Republican landslide which placed Harding and "normalcy" in the presidency carried the entire Republican state and local tickets into office. The avalanche was complete—it looked as though the local Democracy would be buried by the victorious Republicans for a long time.

But this was not to be. Almost immediately the victors began to quarrel over the spoils and also quickly overreached themselves. The first manifestation came in the judicial elections of 1921. The respective county central committees nominate the slate for judges of the Circuit Court of Cook County. Usually the Chicago Bar Association makes recommendations to each central committee, and often there is a single coalition ticket nominated by both central committees.

Thompson-Lundin-Crowe would have none of this. Even a great admirer admits: "They proposed to dictate the ticket and then elect it."[5] Crowe told sitting judges they had better begin hunting for new office space. The overconfident spokesmen believed that they were entitled to the "political 'edge' if politics was to be played about the courts."[6] And politics there was, for the circuit judges appointed the South Park commission, which planned to spend about thirty million dollars during the coming years. For other reasons too, protection among them, it was well to have a cooperative judiciary. The Thompson crowd listened to no recommendations of bar or press. They felt certain that they had the organization to ensure victory for any kind of slate in the normally light voting of the special judicial election. Only four sitting judges were included on their ticket. Unceremoniously dismissed were Republican jurists of high repute, most of them Deneen men.

The Democrats made a wise move. They nominated a coalition ticket which included all of the Republican judges who had been jettisoned by Thompson. A tremendous campaign was undertaken to save the judiciary from the unappeasable appetite of Thompson-

Lundin-Crowe. Instead of the expected small vote, a large number turned up at the polls and elected the Democratic-sponsored coalition ticket by more than three to two.[7]

Cermak was one of the leaders among the men masterminding this coup. Much credit redounded to him and the other Democratic leaders who had "saved the judiciary." One of the judges elected on this coalition ticket has said that this move resulted in "tremendous strength" for Cermak.[8]

Still stunned by their overwhelming defeat on the heels of their 1920 landslide, the Republicans launched into intraparty strife with a vengeance. Thompson's corporation counsel, State Senator Samuel A. Ettelson (an ex-Insull lawyer), introduced Thompson's transportation bill in the legislature. This bill included provisions for a five-cent fare on the non-Insull surface lines. Great was the dismay when, despite Thompson's presence on the senate rostrum and the ubiquity of the "Big Bill" hats worn by the legislators, the measure was defeated. Similarly beaten was a Lundin tax bill which would have weakened the control of the Barretts (Thompson allies) over Cook County tax machinery. Although it was defeated, this move attempting to tread upon the Barretts' toes was not soon forgotten by the Barretts nor by their friend and ex-law partner, State's Attorney Crowe. Shocked and disillusioned, Thompson-Lundin friend Governor Small decided to veto the appropriation of Attorney General Brundage (then a factional rival) on the closing day of the session. Brundage replied by indicting Small for embezzlement of state funds during Small's term as state treasurer. Brundage also instigated a civil suit for recovery of the money.

Also in 1921, Crowe broke with Thompson, allegedly over law enforcement but probably because of the disastrous judicial election. Crowe wanted no part of a weakened Thompson. To conduct his raids, Crowe had to utilize a detail of Chicago police. Thompson's chief of police assigned to Crowe as head of this detail Ben Newmark, whom Stuart described as "then not notorious, but regarded as a racketeer by those 'in the know.' "[9]

Another blow descended upon Thompson as a court decision found invalid the primary law under which the 1920 ward committeemen had been elected. In this election Thompson, Lundin, and Crowe had elected 34 of 35 Republican ward committeemen.

The effect of this decision was to return to office the ward committeemen of 1916, largely Deneen men.

Cermak and the Democrats, holding no state and few local offices, could only watch with glee their spoils enemies destroying each other. They waited until public wrath should chase the Republicans out and allow the plums of office to be gathered easily. In the meantime they made whatever bipartisan alliances were feasible in order to gather such crumbs of patronage as were available. By virtue of their victory in the 1921 judicial elections, they received some spoils. Because of their support of several Deneen judges, a cordial relationship with that faction was assured. This relationship was to be useful to Cermak in his next office as county board president. As for Cermak himself, he made his peace with Thompson of necessity, and while maintaining full stature in his party, was able to enjoy more gravy than most of his Democratic colleagues.

LEADER OF THE CITY COUNCIL

During this period of violent Republican intraparty strife, Cermak was the leader of the Democratic members of the city council. Strangely, even during this period of great Republican successes, the Democrats were greatly in the majority in the council; thus, A.J. was the majority leader. This leadership was formalized by his position as chairman of the committee on committees. His position of power was further strengthened by chairmanship of the revenues committee, of the railroads committee, of the railway-terminals commission and several other strategic committees. Again, we see him in the unique position of being a leader of the city council under a Republican mayor.

But his situation vis-à-vis Thompson in this period was somewhat different from his relationship to Busse in 1909-12. In the earlier period he had been a much less important party leader and was by no means the most important alderman. Also, in those former times the two major parties were in more competitive circumstances than in 1919-22. In this period Cermak was the majority leader at a time when the Democrats were at a low point in voting strength and control of government, while except for the council the Republicans were generally powerful.

Faced with the prospect of a spoils Republican machine in control, what strategy might be adopted by Democratic leaders? There was great danger that the party holding the mayor's office and the spoils might eat into the vitals of the Democratic organization. Undoubtedly Brennan and Cermak squirmed in this dilemma. But one thing they could do. They could attempt to go along with Thompson in exchange for some crumbs, and wait for the propitious time.

For the kind of bipartisan dealing which was now needed Cermak was well equipped. It was no doubt in part this aptitude which gained him his place of eminence in the council and made it possible for him to emerge from a state of declining power and influence into an almost immediate assumption of council leadership. That he did immediately grasp such leadership is agreed upon by all observers—"Within two months he ran the city council."[10] His aldermanic colleague, Republican Charles S. Eaton, commenting upon A.J.'s ascendancy, attributes it not only to his particular facility in bipartisan leadership but to "native political acumen and aggressiveness": "I'd frequently ask myself how far he would go if only he were educated. Tony was way over them all. In mental equipment he was above four-fifths of them. The opposition used to call him 'Foxy Tony.' "[11]

A.J. and a group of cronies, including Aldermen Bowler, Arvey, and McDonough, were in the habit of meeting in a side room off the offices of the transportation committee. It was well known that this group "ran the show."[12] A.J. sealed his position of dominance through a tremendous quantity of work. He is remembered as the "hardest worker in the council."[13] His habits are well illustrated by his behavior on the regularly occurring aldermanic junkets taken by council committees to investigate the ways other municipalities were solving problems faced by Chicago. While the other aldermen took full advantage of the opportunities for paid recreation, Cermak's sole concern was to acquire information useful to the work of the council—and to himself as a figure of authority. The Pullman-car crap and poker games, jokes, and barbershop harmony with which the majority of "frivolous fools" diverted themselves did not attract A.J.[14] He generally spent his time in pumping whatever technical experts were present on the trip. Very rarely did he join his colleagues in partying or doing the town. He was unmovable in convening daily committee meetings, which he insisted be held in the morning, in order that the afternoons be left free for investigating the matters for which the trip had been projected. It may be imagined how enthusiastically this *Diktat* was received by aldermen who had spent the night in celebration. A.J., having methodically collected great amounts of data, was wont to greet his heavy-headed colleagues with an impressive flow of information and statistics. The degree of his influence in committee and general council deliberations was thus greatly increased. His fellow councilmen could scarcely oppose to his mass of documented research a menu from a Greenwich Village speakeasy!

Cermak's departures from the orthodox behavior of aldermen did not add to his popularity among them. But "they had to respect and kow-tow" to him. Among other reasons, they feared the power of his United Societies position. "They didn't want to get in a row with the 'damned Bohunk.' They knew he could get the money to have them beaten." This is not to say that his leadership was entirely unopposed, for he had continuing problems with the Anti-Saloon League and with the organization he referred to as the "damned Municipal Voters' League."[15] He had to contend with a small but restive clique of west-side Democrats led by his Czech rival Kostner; and he was ferociously opposed by Republican trade-union leader Oscar Nelson.

His leadership was most frequently exercised away from the floor of the council rather than in the battle of debate. He carefully prepared the way by shrewd manipulation of patronage or by threats; and his pervasive control of the committee network, where the bulk of legislative work was conducted, was also a useful tool. But if unable to achieve his goals by wire-pulling and pre-debate tactics, he was not loath to launch into open warfare. On these occasions he perambulated up and down the aisles of the council chamber, lining up votes. "Tony was at home in the council. He shouted and waved his arms. His language was crude and he mixed his words. But he was vigorous as he walked about, and attracted attention." In spite of his lack of rhetorical polish it was impossible not to be impressed by the exhibition of naked force displayed in this "huge, powerful, broad from side-to-side and deep from front to rear" figure.[16] The council could not disregard him, and most often it did his bidding.

His tactics and personal qualities were even more effective in committees. Although mostly concerned with matters in the purview of his own committee, he made constant appearances and introduced many ordinances in other committees. He appeared to consider the entire realm of municipal problems his personal concern. He was completely autocratic in the committees he headed, and in his attitude toward both members and witnesses or experts who testified. There was little appreciable difference in his conduct with a Dry such as Farwell and the ladies who testified against saloons or vice. His was a far cry from the manner of a chivalrous, dandyish J. Hamilton Lewis. "He was always full of his own convictions. He behaved as though anyone in his right mind would know that he was right."[17] Met by opposition, he shouted and pounded the table, flayed his arm, shook his fists. "Some were afraid he'd crack them one. No one wanted to tangle with him."

The manipulatory devices employed by A.J. served him well in putting across some of his own pet schemes. Among these was the effort to bring about reorganization of the police department. In this effort, as in many of his council activities, was revealed one of his major objectives: to build up the power of the council so as to keep it from succumbing to Thompson. For even though Thompson seemed unable to control it, his personal popularity with the aldermen, his ruthlessness, and his great resources of patronage were a constant source of danger here to Brennan, to Cermak, and to the entire out-party. In order to achieve his objectives, Cermak had to go along with Thompson. "Tony was a real Thompson man at this time, partly because he needed patronage, and also in order to keep the independence of the council. He never clashed openly with Thompson in the council."[18]

For his efforts with regard to police reorganization, A.J. was well prepared. Alderman Eaton said, "He knew more about police captains' activities and operations than anyone I've ever talked to."[19] He was always intensely interested in police problems, his familiarity with them going back to his first political appointment as bailiff in the justice-of-peace court. With the advent of Prohibition he realized that police activities would become even more important to anyone with his liquor views. His intention to effect a reorganization of the police department was taken in opposition to the wishes of Thompson's chief of police and, by inference, to those of Thompson. But in this case placating Thompson became secondary, and Cermak fought for his program. "He knew it was a gigantic thing and liable to incur much opposition, but he knew it was important and was ready to tackle it. He knew it would meet great public approval."[20] In bringing about the enactment of the reorganization, he overcame all obstacles.

His plan for reorganization showed one major emphasis: the goal of reducing some of the control of the mayor and chief of police and increasing the autonomy of police captains. His reason for this, in addition to the desire to strip Thompson of some of his authority over the police, was conditioned by his frequently stated belief that the job of the police was "to catch thieves and murderers, not to reform people." He was obviously acting on the fear that, with the coming of Prohibition, Thompson might again attempt to win the Drys through a rigorous enforcement of Prohibition laws. Autonomous police captains might be more amenable to influences aimed in the opposite direction.

Cermak himself wrote the first draft of the ordinance. It curtailed the power of top management, as it had been intended to do, and many of its provisions still exist today.

LEGISLATIVE ACCOMPLISHMENTS AND APPEALS

All written accounts and interviews agree that Cermak's major accomplishment in the council was his role in the furthering of the Chicago City Plan. This plan is justly famous. It included the reclaiming of portions of Lake Michigan and many miles of the lake front, hundreds of miles of street extension and widening, reorganization of rail passenger and freight terminals, and provision for the building of adequate harbor facilities. The Chicago Plan was described by the Regional Survey of New York in this way: "In this century and on this continent Burnham's plan of Chicago stands as a great presentation of a grand architectural conception of city building."[21] The partial product of this plan, Chicago's magnificent front-yard façade, was a gigantic achievement of many men, covering several decades. The dozens of miles of broad boulevards linking Lincoln and Jackson parks; the series of lovely man-made lagoons; and the indisputably magnificent skyline (truly visible, according to some critics,[22] only to incoming boats) are civic accomplishments which are a source of great pride to Chicagoans.

During these three years in the Council Cermak is unanimously credited with having furthered many of the projects included in the Chicago Plan. One Republican commented that "much, if not most, of the credit for the fact that the work of carrying out of the plans is already well under way must be credited to him."[23] There is little doubt that without his assistance the very large number of ordinances for specific projects could not have succeeded in getting through the council. A.J., of course, had both his ears to the ground in these cases. In most instances the voters enthusiastically approved the measures when they were presented in referenda.[24] At the same time, many powerful influences offered resistance or created special problems, so that the complexities of the planning were enormous.

Another of A.J.'s major council interests was revenue. Here, for the first time in his career, he became the great spokesman for economy—a role which was to be of great importance in his political future. When A.J. assumed leadership of the council, Chicago finances were in a poor way. Four years of Thompsonism had been nearly fatal to the exchequer. Within a year of the advent of Prohibition, there occurred the serious decrease in revenue which Cermak had always anticipated and worried over—that due to the loss of revenue from saloon licenses.

Cermak's solution was simple, but ingenious. New sources of revenue had to be found; but this was not an easy matter, for the municipality had little freedom of action in this area because of the strictures of the legislature. Cermak hit upon an extended scheme of licensing—a "voluntary" scheme, since the city had no legal authority to impose such fees. Some observers regard this licensing plan as his most outstanding legislative feat in this period.[25] He personally prevailed upon some score of businessmen and professions to pay annual license fees, when they were under no legal obligation to do so. A more painless way of getting out of the difficulty and solving the problem could scarcely have been devised. Taxes were not raised—and could not have been, unless the legislature could have been persuaded to raise the city's taxing limit. Under Cermak's scheme cooperation from the legislature did not have to be implored. At one point, however, the aid of the legislature was sought successfully in an effort to broaden A.J.'s licensing ideas. From this endeavor resulted the city vehicle tax.

Cermak not only initiated this novel system, he also administered it. He had set up a bureau of licenses, to all intents and purposes autonomous of the mayor and other executive agents, directly under Cermak's control. Formerly licensing had been carried on by the police. Here again Cermak sheared Thompson of some of his power. A.J. boasted of and referred to the bureau, accurately, as "my License Bureau." But Thompson could not very well complain. Cermak was bringing in revenues otherwise unavailable.

His hovering pride in the license bureau did not interfere with his more general interest in all fiscal matters and in economy. His unhappiness with the city's financial plight was so great that he even suggested a reorganization of some of the council committees, especially the finance committee. Apparently, his greatest fear was that the finance committee was again going to attempt to get higher taxes.

> The Finance Committee has gotten into a rut. It needs new blood. Some other method of supplying funds must be found instead of always crying for an increased tax-rate. Tax bills are high enough. The public is entitled to a new deal and I'm going to use every effort to get it for them.[26]

How strenuously A.J. always tried to avoid raising taxes! A more calculated appeal to voters could scarcely be devised.

But A.J.'s interests were, as usual, catholic and far-ranging, encompassing matters outside those of major legislative concern. He was the "compleat" city father. Nothing from tag days for the poor or for policemen's widows to the question of the diet of prisoners was outside his ken. He identified himself with all local problems and expressed himself not merely as an alderman from one ward but as a representative of the collective public weal. He took upon himself the mantle of civic representativeness for all the world as though he were already the elected mayor. And, in fact, his attitudes upon the most diverse questions were attentively reported day by day in the press, as though it shared his view of himself as the tribune of the people.

The Eighteenth Amendment was proclaimed in January, 1919, before Cermak's return to the council, and went into effect one year later. However, the Illinois Prohibition laws became operative in July, 1919.

Cermak and the United Societies remained confused and ambivalent towards the law until about the middle of 1920. However, they announced their intention to maintain the organization and to fight "the old women of both sexes in an effort to retain for the country some semblance of liberty and self-government."[27] And Cermak, covering their confusion, trumpeted with great bravado: "Chicago may be dry for two months, but not for any longer."[28]

But by early July, 1919, he was complaining about policemen "sleuthing" for beer in saloons. He said that the beer supply had all but vanished since the previous December. Even

... the final big night's celebration was a near-beer affair all the way through. There wasn't a beer jag in town.... When the police begin to act as stool-pigeons for the Anti-Saloon League, and spend their time in saloons that haven't had any real beer for five days, trying to smell 2¾ per cent beer, with the amount of crime that is outside for them to work on, I think it's time to let the people of Chicago know some things.[29]

Cermak and the Wets were particularly bitter, for they had spent a great deal of money and energy in a Wet-Dry referendum just that spring. To the proposition: "Shall Chicago Become Anti-Saloon Territory?" the city returned a resounding negative. Three quarters of those voting on the measure voted against it. Little wonder that Cermak and the United Societies were angry and disconsolate. They did not know how to proceed, although innumerable meetings were held and many avenues of attack considered. Early in 1920 the path the Wets might take and the tactics they might use began to be seen more clearly. Their plan was to try to effect a modification of the Volstead Acts to allow the manufacture and sale of light wines and beer. They planned to support only such delegates to the national conventions as supported their new program. These plans were announced at a meeting called by

Cermak, at which he threw down the gauntlet to William Jennings Bryan and other Dry Democrats. He announced support of Edward J. Edwards of New Jersey in the Illinois presidential primary. Cermak issued what was to be in rough outline the policy of the Wets for years to come.

We propose to elect national convention delegates, Democrat and Republican, who are wets. We will concentrate on the nomination and election of members of Congress next November who will favor a light wines and beer amendment to the prohibition enforcement act.... It is getting so that the government must take early action to save the people from themselves. There are large numbers of people slowly killing themselves through the manufacture of home-made concoctions. Let us have light wines and beer. Nobody ever got drunk on either. Besides, the people want it. This is heralded as a free country. I sometimes wonder if it is.[30]

Cermak carried his idea for beer and wine to a meeting of the Chicago delegation to the Democratic national convention. He did not have much success here, nor did Governor Edwards' candidacy get very far.

In 1921, however, he was responsible for the passage of a remarkable resolution by the council. It called upon the various state and federal officials to take steps to bring about a wine-and-beer amendment. The vote was 52 to 6. And later he pushed through a measure which caused the city to send a plea to all cities over 25,000 in population for the wine and beer amendment. After passing the measure, he bitterly denounced the Drys.

The people who are opposing allowing the public to express itself are the same ones who are trying to limit Chicago's representation in the General Assembly. They are the same folks who would saddle two-thirds of the taxes on the people of Chicago without giving them proper representation.... The city lost ... 33 per cent of the total cost of running the city government at the time the dry law was passed.[31]

The council's attitude on Prohibition was dramatically demonstrated when all but nine members left the chamber during a criticism of a Cermak Wet suggestion by one of the few Dry aldermen. With this kind of support in the council, Cermak's struggle was facilitated.

A.J. next lined up the council to oppose any expenditure of city funds to enforce the prohibition law. He took the position that, since it was a federal law, the federal government alone should enforce it. Besides, he charged, federal agents allowed liquor to enter the city with their full knowledge. The following year he dragooned the council into a similar economy measure as he led opposition to a plan to set up a special branch of the municipal court to try violations of the Prohibition law. "Let the federal government pay for the presentation of its cases."[32] The council responded to his prodding with record enthusiasm as the measure was defeated. Only four votes were recorded in favor of it. Cermak gave tongue to a new war cry: "Prohibition does not prohibit; it poisons."

Thompson, although he was later to campaign as the Wettest of the Wets, still retained at this time some of the ambivalence toward the Drys which he had exhibited in 1915. Without council approval, Thompson had set up the office of a law-enforcement commissioner to administer federal and state Prohibition laws. He appointed clergyman John Henry Williamson to the position and paid his $10,000 salary from the mayor's contingent funds.

Cermak attacked the office as illegal because it had not been provided for in the budget. He accused Reverend Williamson of violating the law each time "the overlord of the Mayor's cabinet" collected his salary. Cermak flaunted his indifference to the Drys and to Reverend Williamson as a serious threat. "Let the enforcer take notes. Let him preach against me next Sunday. I'll be here to answer him."[33]

His struggle against Prohibition was not limited to activities in the council, where he was powerful and where his Wet views were so completely supported. His attacks elsewhere were frequent and vigorous, providing almost daily fodder for the newspapers, especially for the *Chicago Tribune,* which was also rabidly anti-Volstead Act. He addressed large numbers of meetings on his favorite topic, appearing before audiences of all kinds—from the high-status City Club to a local chapter of the American Association of Engineers. Often these meetings were set up as debates, and they were almost always given before relatively Dry, and therefore hostile, audiences (A.J.'s United Societies constituency did not require debates on the subject). In the course of these speeches, statements, and debates, the main outlines of Cermak's latest Wet line began to emerge. Here is a synthetic version of this line, in Cermak's own words, digested from several sources.

Prohibition has not prohibited. They're still making beer and wines.... Advocates of prohibition argued that the law would make the police force unnecessary. They said that the $7,000,00 saloon license revenue would not be needed. Do you know the police force has been increased every year since this law went into effect?... There have been great increases in cases of drunkenness in the Municipal Court.... The city and county jails are overcrowded.... The penitentiaries have the largest number of prisoners in their history.... Chief Fitzmorris needs 1,000 more policemen.... Burglary insurance companies have paid out more than three times the amount in claims in 1921 than paid in 1914.... It is not a question of saloons or no saloons. If they [the voters] should declare for wines and beers then it would be up to the legislature to decide whether beer or wine should be sold through saloons... or in some other way.... Let's go to the people and see what they want....

The South never has respected the amendment proclaiming the Negro equal. More than 83,000 stills have been confiscated in the South. Why should the South tell us to respect the 18th Amendment?

His council activities and appearances before other groups were supplemented by other political activities. He insisted that Prohibition be the issue in the 1922 primaries. "This is a burning question. It will continue to burn. We'll get action in April."[34]

A.J. thus helped assure Prohibition as the chief issue in the 1922 general elections, although when his candidate was attacked on the basis of his Wetness he became very indignant. His indignation was a little difficult to justify, since he all but singlehandedly provoked the issue. The method used was to sponsor an immense petition campaign to place the Wet question on the ballot in November. Public-policy questions to appear on the ballot in Illinois require the signature of 10 per cent of the voters in the most recent general election. In this case the requirement was roughly 300,000 signatures. The campaign was begun in January, 1921, and Cermak was deeply involved in its management, simultaneously with his other Wet activities. As a part of this endeavor, A.J. became instrumental in organizing the Anti-Prohibition League of Illinois.

The petition had a stormy career, running through the primary campaign and well into the general-election campaigns. Under Cermak's leadership great sums of money were expended in extensive newspaper and other publicity. Every few days he issued bulletins of the progress of the signature collection. He charged his enemies of the Anti-Saloon League with starting a phony petition to sabotage the true will of the people, and attacked Senator Volstead, who was reported to have made light of the Cermak plans. A.J. denied that Congress alone could amend the prohibition law. "It is not for Congress to decide. Congress is not above the people."[35]

His rage against the Anti-Saloon League's opposition to the petition is interesting evidence of political "double-think." In 1917 when the Anti-Saloon League had sponsored a Dry petition, Cermak had led the opposition. This had included court proceedings and had delayed the appearance of the question on the ballot until 1919 (of course, this petition had been started before Prohibition). When in 1919 the issue did appear on the ballot, we have seen how successfully A.J. mobilized the Wets to vote down the plan to create antisaloon areas in Illinois. The whole situation offers a classic example of the thinking of both rabid Wets and extreme Drys. For both, all other issues of public policy were habitually subordinated to the question of whether, how much, and when individuals might drink. Of course, in the case of the 1922 petition, the question was the reversal of the Anti-Saloon League petition. It now was: "Shall the existing state and federal prohibitory laws be so modified as to permit the manufacture, sale, and transportation of beer (containing less than 4 per cent by volume of alcohol) and light wines for home consumption?"[36]

By July the success of the petition was assured. Cermak announced that over 500,000 signatures had been collected. At the end of August a triumphant series of celebrations was planned for the end of the petition campaign and the ceremonial submission of the petition. A huge rally was held in Chicago with many imported national Wet leaders participating, among them Al Smith. The petitions were to be carried to Springfield by a cavalcade of one hundred automobiles. Cermak's work was crowned with the glory of victory. The voters approved his initiative measure by the resounding vote of 81.9 per cent.

Although the United Societies was no longer a powerful agency after Prohibition, Cermak continued as secretary. In its declining days he even managed to have an old friend and Twelfth Ward supporter, Michael Zimmer, elected as its president.

THE LEADER OF THE COUNCIL AS CZECH

During this period Cermak continued to act and to be recognized as leader of the Czechs. The threat to his power in his ward implied by the aldermanic election of 1919 quickly evaporated. In the 1920 aldermanic elections he felt it unnecessary to select a candidate, so certain was he of his control over whichever of ten pretenders might be successful. Among the candidates were Alderman Novak, A.J.'s secretary Henry Sonnenschein, and Joseph Cepak. All were Czechs. One newspaper not friendly to Cermak emphasized his strength in his ward at this time as follows: "Alderman A. J. Cermak is Democratic committeeman . . . and if he said the word probably could settle the trouble."[37]

These terms, he had several Czech colleagues in the council. Troublesome Kostner was among them, but his threat to Cermak had been nearly liquidated by the weakening of the Harrison faction. Kostner's Czech colleague from the Thirty-Fourth Ward, John Toman, could usually be relied upon by Cermak.

A.J. continued to reside in Lawndale, and his many business interests were still located there. Through the agency of membership in a growing number of Czech organizations the frequency of his face-to-face contact with community members was undiminished. He became even more involved than hitherto in Sokol affairs. His trip to Prague in 1921 as representative to the international gymnastic meet provides an index to his prestige in this group. He continued to sponsor outings and picnics in Pilsen Park. In 1922 he organized a semiprofessional baseball team and built a stadium for it in the center of the Czech community. The "Cermak Indians" became a source of community pride.

His position of chief prominence among his people was clearly recognized in 1921 when he received an invitation from the Czechs to visit Czechoslovakia in order to advise their infant government. During this three-month trip, he was diligent in keeping the home front informed about his activities in the old country; his letters published in the press stressed the relative good fortune of the people of the United States.

Well before the end of his term in 1923, A.J. was faced with the problem of deciding whether to continue consolidating his current position or to attempt to reach for greater prestige and more responsibility. For him the choice was not close; in the most realistic sense, there was probably no question of a choice. Hardly had the year 1922 begun when he became a candidate for president of the Board of Commissioners of Cook County. Apparently, he had had enough of the council. As he had told Cervenka in 1915, he was "going on the county." He badly wanted to be the "Mayor of Cook County."

· 8 ·

"MR. PRESIDENT"

WHEN, at the end of 1921, A.J. decided to become candidate for president of the Board of Commissioners of Cook County, he had little difficulty in getting "slated," despite his 1918 defeat. His prominence in the City Council could not be overlooked nor denied; the Czechoslovaks demanded recognition; and A.J. was still the symbol of Wetness. A.J. ran as a Regular. But he was no longer "doing Roger's bidding," for Sullivan had died in 1920.

Sullivan's crown was immediately claimed by George E. Brennan, his erstwhile chief lieutenant. Even before Sullivan's death the Regulars were often called the Sullivan-Brennan faction. Sullivan had built up the Regular machine over nearly a generation. He had been opposed during this time by the factions of Carter H. Harrison and Edward F. Dunne. Sullivan was usually more powerful when his enemies were out of office, but even when they held the mayoralty or governorship his organization had to be considered. While Harrison was mayor, Sullivan usually controlled the state machine; and even during the time Harrison was mayor (1911-15) and Dunne was governor (1912-16), he was able to maintain himself, because in those days Dunne and Harrison did not work together. After 1916 Sullivan all but reigned supreme in the Democratic party, although a Harrison man was state's attorney until 1920. Upon Sullivan's death, Cermak's name was mentioned, among others, as a possible contender for the throne of boss. But A.J. did not yet feel prepared to take on the Irish.

The names of Brennan and Cermak are always linked in the reminiscences of Chicago politicians. Both came from the Braidwood mines. Brennan taught in the elementary school after having lost a leg in a mining accident. The school was the same that A.J. attended as a boy. But the legends that Brennan was A.J.'s teacher and that Brennan advised A.J. to seek fame and fortune through the ranks of the Bohemians and later slated him for his first nomination do not seem to be based on fact. It is a fact, however, that while A.J. was in the legislature Brennan was in Springfield as an employee of the state Democratic committee, and that the two men saw one another. Undoubtedly in the two decades from 1900 to 1922, as Democratic leaders their paths necessarily crossed often, but there is little evidence that Brennan displayed any of the paternal, kindly interest in his "Bohunk" Braidwood associate which is implied by the legends. Quite to the contrary, many have stated that Cermak on his part hated Brennan,[1] and there are grounds for believing that the feeling was mutual.[2] There was, besides, the factor of Cermak's having been largely a Harrison follower for the first fifteen years of his career. Nevertheless, from 1915—that is, from the virtual demise of Harrison—Cermak was with Brennan.[3]

Brennan was an accomplished performer in the jungle of Chicago partisan politics. His methods and attitudes were similar to those of Sullivan. Both were powerful men, masters of the bipartisan deal, but personally acceptable in some of Chicago's most fashionable drawing rooms. Both were backroom bosses, each restricting personal office-seeking to United States senatorships. Both lost in these contests. Like Sullivan, Brennan maintained strong ties with the utilities, Insull referring to him accurately enough as "my friend." Merriam described Brennan as "likable," "genial," "suave and forceful," "full of chuckling humor and equally full of guile and intrigue," "strong in personal contacts . . . with his infectious chuckle and his apparently universal benevolence"[4]—a man, in short, with very few personality traits in common with A.J., who was to succeed him.

Brennan placed his abilities to the test in the primary of 1921, entering a full slate of candidates for county offices. A.J. was one of its most prominent members.[5] The challenge was not accepted by either Dunne-O'Connell or Harrison, and nearly went by default altogether. Quite late a Citizens' Democratic ticket was entered by a group of relatively unimportant Democratic office-holders.

Brennan made valid his assertion of leadership by a clean sweep. There were charges of fraud by the defeated, and a recount was begun. Although, as usual, considerable evidence of irregularities was turned up, none of the major candidates was endangered. Cermak was not one of those affected by the charges of irregularity. Within a week his opponent, Daniel F. Ryan, incumbent president of the county board, admitted losing by "a substantial majority" and pledged his support for the general election.[6]

THE GENERAL ELECTION

The Republican factions split the various offices in their primary. The nominee against Cermak was Charles S. Peterson, a Brundage man. The contrast between the two candidates was immense. Peterson was not a "politician," but a wealthy north-sider, who had never held elective office. He appeared to be the kind of "clean" businessman Cermak liked to use on citizens' advisory boards. He was a sort of 1920 Martin Kennelly or perhaps a local Wendell Willkie. Although he lacked powerful machine support, the Drys, the churches, and many "respectables" were expected to support him. The *Chicago Tribune*, not friendly to Cermak except as he stood against Prohibition, described the Democratic candidate in this way:

Cermak has been a professional politician for years. In the state legislature and in the city council he has been a man of considerable force. He usually fared well with all measures he has sponsored. He has been successful in ward and sectional politics, and a power in organization matters.... Cermak is prominent in Democratic affairs, largely because of his leadership among those of Bohemian birth and descent. Behind Cermak are believed to be all the forces of the Democratic organization, considerable wet strength, the entire Bohemian vote.[7]

The two rivals promised a campaign that would permit them to remain friends after the election. The sweetness and light did not last long. It would have been strange and wonderful if it had, since A.J. was facing a Dry.

Cermak's platform was heavily weighted with items that might have come from the report of a little Hoover Commission. He promised "judicious expenditures," "intelligent and humane" administration, "economical purchase," good appointments, and "reduction of the cost of government."[8] He also promised "expansion and upbuilding," "construction," and "care and maintenace."[9] But much of this was smoke screen. The real issue was Cermak's Wetness. At times he appeared to complain of this, remarking that his opponents focused their attacks upon his liquor record instead of taking up the matter of his record as a public official. But in general he was not unduly perturbed by the presence of this issue. Certainly he himself scarcely ever passed up an opportunity to speak of it. By this time, not only had he been for twenty years the Wettest of the personal-liberty advocates, but during this very campaign he was directing signature-collection activities for the petition to place the Wet-Dry question on the fall ballot.

The referendum itself, since it was to be purely advisory, might not have injected the beer-and-wine question into the whole race. Cermak's candidacy for an important office assured this result. He who had been " 'the works' of the United Societies . . . the political fighting organization of the wets . . . brought down upon his head all the bitterness and invective at the command of the Anti-Saloon League."[10] But it was not Cermak's "head" alone that was affected. The liquor issue permeated the entire election. The Democrats did not mind this, but the Republicans were not at all pleased by such a development. They did not care to take a stand on the question, and they were very discomfited that the Drys should have helped push to the forefront this "false issue . . . to even up old scores."[11]

A.J.'s enemies were not in a joking mood. Their attack was bare-knuckled. The pledge cards which they circulated made it abundantly clear that they considered the election very important and that they regarded Cermak as their chief target. The pledge cards of the Anti-Saloon League of Illinois included the following: "I realize that if we are to have honest government the people who want it must vote. I also realize that Cermak's wet candidacy makes a special crisis this fall."[12] Important in the Anti-Saloon League's plans for resolving the "crisis" was support of Cermak's opponent Peterson.

A.J. responded to his attackers with vigor. He defended his record as a public official ceaselessly. He charged the Anti-Saloon League with being responsible not only for Prohibition and the increased crime, disease, and insanity that he said had resulted from it, but also with attempts to limit permanently Cook County's representation in the legislature.

Just four days before the election, Prohibition agents conducted a mass raid on saloons in Cermak's ward. The choice of this locality at this time was no accident, nor was the statement, published in several newspapers, that "Alderman Cermak's saloon ... was not searched by the agents, although saloons in the near vicinity were raided."[13] A.J. was livid. He denounced this latest "roorback" and explained that he was not and never had been "interested in a saloon or in the manufacture or sale of alcoholic liquors."[14] However, it was not clear whether the Anti-Saloon League or some west-side Republicans were responsible for instigating the raids and the subsequent reference to "Cermak's saloon."

Although the campaign seemed to be less a matter of Democrats against Republicans and Cermak against Peterson than Anti-Saloon League versus Cermak, Cermak still devoted attention to Peterson himself. In addition to charging that Peterson had no experience as a public official, Cermak denounced him as a hypocrite. This tactic was a favorite Cermak device until his death. It consisted in extravagantly accusing any opponent who was suspected of being politically Dry of being privately Wet. In this case Cermak charged that Peterson was known to serve and drink liquor in his home, and that he had, moreover, "one of the most thrilling cellars in Chicago."[15]

Although A.J. did not altogether restrict himself to the liquor issue, he was most at home and at his best in this area. He was quite willing to make his stand before groups generally believed to be Dry. He did not equivocate on these occasions, and often made positive impressions by virtue of his frankness. For example,

Cermak's stock, it was conceded in all headquarters, has gone up several notches in the last week. Since his speeches before the women's clubs . . . while he stands for light wines and beer, the women have seen him, listened to him, and found he didn't have a pair of horns or snort fire.[16]

A.J. received favorable treatment from the newspapers, especially the two Hearst organs. The *Chicago Evening American* indorsed him in an editorial as "the logical man" and "an official who SAVES money."[17] The *Herald and Examiner,* continually friendly in its columns, referred to A.J. as a "booster for all clean sports" and the "father of the City Athletic Commission."[18] The *Chicago Tribune,* although in the past antagonistic about Cermak's alleged superiority to law in his United Societies capacity, because of its own opposition to Prohibition was sympathetic in its reports.

It is scarcely surprising that various Czech groups expressed their devotion and loyalty. The Irish-American Society of Cook County volunteered its support. The Poles were forthright and unambiguous in their backing, reflecting A.J.'s assiduous work to win the allegiance of this very numerous Slavic group. The Polish Fellowship League of Illinois (including nearly every Polish organization in the state) informed A.J. that it was unanimously in favor of his candidacy and pledged "whole-hearted support."[19]

In this campaign A.J. continued to make use of appeals to devotees of sports and athletics. He spoke to sports clubs and presented trophies; he was active in attempting to pass a bill in Springfield to legalize professional boxing in Illinois. The activities of the "Cermak Indians" also received useful publicity at this time, as well as A.J.'s feats in his speedboat. Combining the appeal of benefactor-to-children and patron-of-sports, he sponsored a free wild-west show in his ball park, with plenty to eat and free tickets to Cubs Park. He arranged automobile transportation for youngsters and gave them a day in the country; he sponsored a free "Tennis Week"; and he admitted children without charge to see the "Cermak Indians" in action.

Cermak was elected, as were most Democratic candidates. He had not, however, led the ticket as many had predicted he would by virtue of his central position on the Wet-Dry issue. As a matter of fact, he won by a rather narrow margin of 20,000 votes out of over 700,000 cast. It is true that all the results were close, the leading candidate, Sweitzer, having a margin of only some 76,000. But

Cermak, defeated once for a county office, had proved his ability to win such a position. Brennan had proved his claim to leadership of Cook County Democracy. Although the Republicans lost most positions by small margins and were able to salvage a few offices, this election warned that, whatever the security of national Republicanism and "normalcy," Cook County was growing restive under the Thompson-Crowe-Lundin-Small brand of Republicanism.

WINNING CONTROL OF THE BOARD

Cermak was "mayor of Cook County," but what, if any, good would it do for him? For he began his term in the unfavorable position of a minority executive. Of the fifteen commissioners, eight were Republicans.[20] As usual, the predominantly Republican districts outside Chicago elected Republicans to all five of their seats, while three more Republicans were elected in the city of Chicago. Uppermost in Cermak's mind, and generally discussed by politicians, was the question of whether the Republican majority would govern, or whether Cermak would somehow be able to gain control commensurate with his headship. Some were of the opinion that A.J.'s problem would be fairly simple for a master bipartisan dealer, especially since the eight Republicans were factionally divided. The cleavages were particularly deep, inasmuch as the jockeying for the 1923 mayoralty election was already in full swing.

In this atmosphere of doubt Cermak was inaugurated. His inaugural address clearly underlined his own unease about his minority situation.

> Enlightened public opinion, it seems to me, demands that we shall ignore personal and partisan considerations in the discharge of our public duties. . . . The success or failure of our future service to the people will, in a large measure, depend upon whether or not we divide upon party lines or resolve to act as a unit, irrespective of partisan considerations, to give the people all they are entitled to have from us. . . . We ought to understand that the people are interested solely in the results which we may obtain in their behalf, and not in our partisan, political or personal obligations.[21]

But the all-out appeal for nonpartisan unity was not to be heeded. Despite factionalism, the Republican majority of one proceeded to organize the board to insure Republican control. The first resolution introduced by Cermak's righthand man Emmett Whealan was for the continued use of the rules of the preceding year, when the board had been controlled by Democrats. The measure was defeated eight to seven. A Deneen Republican then introduced a resolution to adopt the rules used by the last Republican administration. This was passd by a vote of eight to seven. The adoption of these rules involved nearly absolute Republican domination of the board. For example, six of the seven standing committees were given Republican chairmen; the seventh (public service), receiving a Democratic chairman, was unimportant since it operated almost exclusively through subcommittees. Of thirteen subcommittees, Republicans headed seven. Republicans dominated every committee by at least a two-to-one ratio, but in the two most important ones, rules and finance, control was increased to five to one. The subcommittees of the public service committee were similarly packed. Although the Republicans generously allowed the Democrats six of thirteen subcommittee chairmanships, they actually retained full control of nine of the thirteen subcommittees. Cermak fought valiantly, submitting an alternate list of committees, largely the obverse of the Republican one. As the Republican list had been approved eight to seven, so Cermak's list was defeated by a corresponding vote. Fortunately for Cermak these rules and these committees were approved for only one year. Perhaps this was why he did not veto the measure. And perhaps, too, he had some scheme calculated to divert the Republican steamroller.

In most of the early weeks the results continued to be expressed in terms of eight-to-seven party cleavage with tiresome regularity. But A.J. and his Democratic colleagues never gave way without a battle and some attempts at retaliation. Riding the crest, the Republicans succeeded in electing a Republican, Oscar Wolff, as coroner to replace incumbent Peter Hoffman, who had been elected sheriff. The very next motion by A.J.'s alter ego, Whealan, was a resolution to take action against Sheriff Peters to recover certain fees (Peters was the man who had defeated Cermak for sheriff in the election of 1918). The attempted retaliatory act died in committee as did every single Democratic action of those early months.

A.J. suffered greatly during this frustrating time, and frequently gave vent to his feelings in angry outbursts. The meetings of the board were often shouting, noisy affairs. But soon A.J. managed to concoct some kind of answer to the Republican majority. In a surprise move, in his capacity as president of the Board of Forest Preserve Commissioners, he placed all forest preserve jobs under civil service. The Republicans were helpless, for Cermak had complete control of the Civil Service Commission (in whose appointment the board did not share), and to override the veto of the president of the Forest Preserve Board required unanimous vote of all commissioners. A.J. let it be known that he was going to demand strict enforcement of civil-service regulations, but, tongue in cheek, he added also that he would treat the Republicans fairly if they would treat him fairly.[22]

The Republicans were enraged, but there was nothing they could do. Worse was yet to come. In the spring of 1923 Republican Commissioner Murray told his colleagues he would henceforth "be with Cermak."[23] One can readily imagine the agonized Republican outcries against this treason.

Many theories were advanced as to the method of buying Murray. Two of these are most persuasive. The first explains Murray's action as the fruits of a standard bipartisan deal. Murray was regarded in many quarters as a Brundage man, and Brundage had one of the strongest Republican candidates in the 1923 mayoralty primary. Cermak was rumored to have coveted the Democratic nomination for mayor, but was passed over. Therefore, it was believed, Brundage had persuaded Murray to cast his lot on the board with Cermak, in exchange for Cermak's support of the Brundage mayoralty candidate. This explanation received some corroboration in the fact that Charles S. Peterson (A.J.'s erstwhile opponent for president), also a Brundage man, later also joined A.J. in controlling the board.[24] However, Peterson's action may have been taken quite independently of a Cermak-Brundage deal. Peterson may very conceivably have joined the Cermak bandwagon when it was seen that A.J.'s control was absolute. The crucial transfer was Murray's. After that became a *fait accompli,* Cermak had the invaluable margin of the single vote upon which the Republicans had hitherto banked.

The other explanation of the capture of Murray is that it was a simple, unadorned little spoils scheme. Murray—an early specimen of the wild advertising merchants of the Madman Muntz variety—was recently bankrupt and in a tight financial corner. It was arranged that a company which he organized for this purpose was to receive whatever contracts for county employees' uniforms were available. If this version is true, the price was small: Murray received less than pottage.[25]

The complete change in power alignment was startlingly demonstrated in March, 1923. Only a few days before, A.J. had been battling fruitlessly against the Republicans' move to have appointed a legal adviser—a position which, naturally, they intended to see filled by one of their own men. After the power shift, not only was the Republican choice for legal adviser deserted but Cermak appointed two attorneys of his own choice. There were no dissenting votes.[26]

These appointments merely foreshadowed the completely supine position the Republicans were to take for the rest of this term (to December, 1926) and, in general, until the end of the Cermak regime in 1931. The Republicans were able to take some rearguard action, aided by the fortuitous death of Commissioner Daniel Ryan. Until the qualification of Daniel Ryan, Jr., late in 1923, even with Murray's vote the voting alignment was seven-to-seven. However, during this hiatus period A.J. was usually able to get his way. The Republicans knew that he would have full control in a short time and wished to avoid incurring his enmity, so that they could remain in line for at least a few crumbs of patronage. In the meantime, Cermak had some patronage leverage which in most cases was sufficient to dragoon the Republicans. His capture of the forest-preserves patronage through the placement of hitherto exempt positions under civil service was his most important tool here. He announced to his colleagues that despite civil service he favored equal distribution of patronage. However, as in the case of George Orwell's *Animal Farm,* where all animals were equal but pigs were more equal than other animals, Cermak's notion of equality was ninety-two jobs for Democrats and eighty for Republicans.

The Republicans made their last determined stand in September, 1923. Cermak appointed his good friend Frank Venecek (whom he had first appointed assistant county agent, then county agent) superintendent of Oak Forest Institutions. Although Murray was with him, the vote on the appointment resulted in a seven-to-seven deadlock. Cermak withdrew the appointment, only to resubmit it a week later. Within the week he succeeded in causing a unique reversal in the evaluation of Venecek's qualifications. The appointment was unanimously approved.

Cermak assumed full control in December, 1923. The personnel of the board was again complete, and Murray's purchased allegiance gave A.J. the necessary precarious majority. Using this he caused the board to be reorganized on December 4, 1923. His revenge was complete. He arranged for complete freedom of appointments for himself of all positions under the jurisdiction of the board, and in addition pre-empted the useful patronage job of custodian of the county building. Currently, this appointment was controlled by Republican Sheriff Hoffman. Democrats headed all committees except one, and this was given to Commissioner Peterson, suspected of being loyal to Cermak anyway.

But the completeness of the Cermak counterrevolution was best displayed in the new rules, which he dictated and which were adopted. These rules, unlike the rules the Republicans had imposed, were adopted for three years—until the end of the term of the current board. All possible avenues of Republican attack were now closed. Cermak was pitiless. Flushed with the fullness of victory, on the day the rules were adopted he arrogantly gaveled down a Republican resolution for efficiency—"There is going to be efficiency, but it will be Democratic efficiency."[27]

His domination was to continue through his entire office, although Murray died late in this term. By that time the power alignment of county Republicans had changed, Brundage's man losing the mayoralty and Crowe having been re-elected state's attorney. John A. Pelka, Slav and Crowe-Barrett man, was elected to fill Murray's office;[28] Frank J. Kriz, a Czech, filled another vacancy, becoming one of Cermak's men;[29] and A.J.'s dominance remained undisturbed.

SURVIVAL

AND

SUCCESS

IN

COOK

COUNTY

POLITICS,

1923-28

THERE is little question in the minds of A.J.'s associates of this period that as the 1923 election drew near he dreamed of becoming a candidate for mayor. It was, however, a dream which had to be deferred. The times were against him. Another type of candidate was deemed more likely to succeed.

Although Brennan had succeeded in his first election as boss, Sullivan's mantle was still somewhat new. He was far from being in absolute control of the party. If he could elect a mayor—a feat his predecessor never accomplished—his future could all but be assured. But it was more than ever imperative that a Democratic mayor be elected. The continuance in power of the Republicans was dangerous to the conservation of his manpower and, ultimately, to his control and authority. With a Republican city administration, the Democratic majority in the council had constantly to trade across the lines, as Cermak's experience and technique had made clear. These facts made untenable the acceptance of a Thompson overture for continuing the bipartisan status quo by nominating a weak Democratic candidate.

Who, then, should the Democrats nominate at this critical time?

Sweitzer, genial, potent in county elections, had been routed in
two previous mayoralty tries. Someone other than a regular politician type was needed. This requirement would have been one
strike against A.J. even if Brennan ever seriously considered it.
And this seems extremely doubtful, in spite of A.J.'s embryonic
expectations. Brennan and the Irish were by no means eager to
honor a "Bohunk." Nor was their reluctance altogether a product
of ethnic prejudice. The Democratic Irish politicians of the 1920's
could not conceive that a Czech, especially a non-Catholic Czech,
had the slightest chance of being elected to the most coveted local
office.

But there were other factors working against Cermak's chances
in 1923. The juggernaut of irresponsible, demagogic Thompsonism had continued unabated for nearly a decade. The word
"Chicago" was becoming synonymous with lawlessness, violence,
and corruption. The people, it was supposed, were aroused now
by the results of an open town. Brennan felt that he could not
outbid Thompson at this time for the support of the "antisocial"
elements. His only chance of success, then, lay in finding a candidate of high reputation, in contrast to Thompson. It was not
known until quite late that Thompson would not seek a third
term. His attempt to persuade Brennan to nominate a weak
candidate in return for ample *quid pro quo* was a last-ditch
measure. When the plan did not succeed, "Big Bill" withdrew
from the campaign.

Before this, however, many leaders of respectable, independent
elements, determined to end the rapacity of Thompsonism, had
requested Brennan to nominate a "good" candidate who might
defeat Thompson if he decided to run. The support of persons
like Mrs. Kellogg Fairbank, Charles E. Merriam, Harold Ickes,
and a number of important civic organizations was an advantage
not to be taken lightly. Fortunately for him, these persons and
agencies were receptive to the candidate Brennan finally settled
upon, William E. Dever.

Dever seemed like a godsend to a boss in Brennan's predicament.
A self-made man of good reputation, as alderman and judge he
had had many years of political experience. He was Irish-Catholic
and had close ties with Harrison and Dunne. Greatly desiring to

elect a mayor, Brennan felt that it was worth much to avoid a primary struggle with other factions, even in their very weakened situation. Would Dunne, O'Connell, and Harrison go along?

They would—and almost eagerly. Out of office for years, they saw here what seemed to them an opportunity to repair waning fortunes. They all had faith in Dever's loyalty and in his respectability, and both Brennan and Dever assured them that there were no strings attached. So Dever was slated, and everyone was satisfied—except Cermak. His enthusiasm for Dever was not conspicuous. Although Dever was not a fanatic Dry, neither was he an outspoken Wet; and it is not too much to imagine that A.J. might even have preferred the Wet open-town status quo of Thompson—if the nomination could not be his own. But he was in no position to battle the Irish in the party as yet. His chagrin had to be swallowed. Brennan, however—perhaps intending to mollify Cermak—slated and nominated John A. Cervenka for one of the only two other city offices being contested, city treasurer. Faced by a Brundage-sponsored Republican, Arthur C. Leuder, Dever won the mayoralty by a wide margin. Cervenka was also elected handily.

It soon developed that, despite earlier avowals, there were indeed strings to Brennan's selection of Dever. Brennan emerged as the controller of patronage for the Dever administration, and Harrison and Dunne-O'Connell were left high, dry, and fuming.[1] Brennan had apparently not been precisely foolhardy. He was able to receive sufficient prior commitments from his mayor to make it very unlikely that Dever could build up a rival machine. What harm could Dever do, even though he appointed a highly competent cabinet, having ceded control of patronage?

These calculations, however, went slightly awry. Although Dever had often stated that he did not believe in Prohibition, he did think that law should be enforced. He was unable to watch with equanimity the collusion of police, grafters, and gangsters. Breweries were still in operation; speakeasies were endemic; and gang wars became commonplace as the struggle for control went on. Dever became angrier and angrier at the spectacle. The more incensed he became the Drier he became—or at least more and more of the opinion that, personal liberty or no personal liberty, something had to be done about the situation existing in Chicago. Soon he was to take energetic steps to remedy this state of affairs— steps which were to have serious consequences for his own career and for Cermak.

THE ELECTIONS OF 1924

In the midst of Mayor Dever's disturbance and close upon the heels of Cermak's disappointed hopes came the elections of 1924. Cermak had just finished the coup d'état which gave him complete control of the county board; and it was just over a year since the Cermak-led beer-wine referendum had overwhelmingly illustrated Wet sentiment. In view of A.J.'s still rankling reaction to being passed over for the mayorality candidate and of Dever's increasingly Dry symptoms, many thought that A.J. might cause a showdown in the primaries, especially since Brennan was sticking fast to Dever despite his dehydration.

Cermak gave early indications of making just such a stand. He insisted that the Wet-Dry issue be prominent in the primary and he did all he could to secure the nomination of Wet candidates. When the organization agreed upon Judge Norman L. Jones— relatively Dry—as gubernatorial candidate, he warned that his ward would not support anyone who did not agree with the results of the 1922 referendum.

But he could not risk the fight which many expected, in spite of his warnings. Judge Jones won the gubernatorial primary, and A.J.'s ward delivered for him. Although he showed his coolness to Brennan-Dever ("Dever Ditches County Wets"[2]), he remained loyal to the party. His rationalization of party discipline deserves quotation *in extenso*.

As a Democrat and as a member of this organization, I want to say that I am for the Democratic state ticket, as endorsed by the pre-primary convention and by the county committee. I am for it in its entirety.

It is true that I was not entirely satisfied when the ticket was named, but I made the objections I had at that time within the organization and as a member of the organization. I had hoped that the candidates would stand for some of the same things in which I am greatly interested—personal liberty among them.

I believe there is something in the theory that the election campaign and not the primary campaign is the right time to make that sort of declaration.

At any rate when the organization had acted I accepted its verdict and I will pledge myself that every man on the state ticket will receive 95 per cent of the Democratic vote cast in my ward.

I am a candidate for delegate to the national convention. . . . I am going to New York in the hope that the national convention will nominate someone like the great governor of the state of New York, Al Smith.[3]

Bitterly disappointed in the local Democratic candidates in 1923 and 1924, A.J. apparently was hoping to salvage something for the Wets in national politics. Here too he was doomed to disappointment. Although the Illinois Democratic delegation (led by Brennan) worked for Smith, John W. Davis—an un-Smithlike figure—was ultimately the choice of the national convention.

Cermak's pessimism about the Democratic local, state, and national tickets was justified by events, although there is no way to determine whether unequivocally Wet platforms or candidates would have been more successful. At any rate, 1924 continued the recent dreary succession of Republican landslides. President Coolidge carried the state by over 800,000; Len Small, in spite of embezzlement charges, won by nearly 350,000; Deneen easily defeated A. A. Sprague for senator; and State's Attorney Crowe was re-elected by nearly 300,000, again defeating Michael L. Igoe. The Republicans made a clean sweep of nearly all local offices, defeating among others P. A. Nash, later destined to become senior partner of the Kelly-Nash machine. The fact that this could be done, in view of the near anarchy among local Republicans, is a good index to the strength of the Republicans nationally and locally at this time. Local Democracy, although relatively well united, receded from its important gains of 1922, perhaps reflecting some criticism of local leadership. On the other hand, this kind of result was quite typical of Illinois in presidential years. Until the end of the long Republican tide in 1932, local Democrats characteristically had greater success in nonpresidential years, when they did not bear, as it were, the onus of a chronic national out-party.

But for Cermak there was an additional factor to be included in this analysis: the failure of his party at all levels to declare openly for an end to Prohibition. History was to vindicate Cermak in his position—a position for which he was the most vocal, and fairly lonely, representative at this time.

TWILIGHT ZONE

Although Cermak was in full control of the county board, exercising greater executive power than any predecessor through imaginative manipulation of legal prerogatives as well as shrewd political moves, his general political situation was again ambiguous. There was some similarity between the present state of affairs and his period of declining fortunes in 1916-19. There was, however, this significant difference: he was now in possession of one of the choicest local political offices.

But his relations with the organization had become more and more strained. He was for a period stripped of his chairmanship of the county committee, and his relations with Brennan and Dever were distant. There can be little doubt that A.J. was not a member of the Brennan ruling clique. He was not in the same position vis-à-vis Brennan as he had been to Sullivan and Harrison in the previous decades. But he had nowhere else to go. Cermak's only alternative was a clear break with Brennan, which would involve a struggle for which he was as yet unprepared. The coolness of the relationship often came to light in public differences with Dever over law enforcement. Dever insisted on attempting to halt the ever rising tide of gangsterism; Cermak's objections, frequently vocal, were to the methods used to accomplish this end.

Once more A.J. cast himself in the role of champion of personal liberty, against a mayor bent on law enforcement; but this time the entire setting was different and Cermak's tactics were completely changed. He who had so blatantly challenged Thompson a decade before was almost incredibly restrained in his complaints against fellow-Democrat Dever: no personal attacks, no vivid harangues in the press. Besides his approaches through moderate requests, he tried to checkmate Dever's zeal through operations in the City Council. He directed an attempt to have an ordinance enacted which aimed at curtailing the mayor's power to revoke licenses. Dever threatened to veto what was described as Cermak's fight against "Police Action in Booze Raids" and his support of the "Plan for Curb on Mayor."[4] But even in action of this kind, the most significant aspect of A.J.'s behavior was caution, moderation, and circumspection. One might have believed that the old Cermak was no more.

A reminder of the Cermak of yore was given during the aldermanic election of 1925 when the loud, vituperative side of his
political character once more emerged. But the reason for this
can also be seen as a manifestation of a somewhat weakened political position. Again A.J. was being seriously challenged in his own
ward. This time his adversary was Rudolph Mulac, a Republican
Czech, who attempted to capture the seat of Cermak's man Cepak
in what was by this time the Twenty-Second Ward. This was really
serious. Rebuffs for nomination, embarrassments caused by the
Irish leadership—these were as nothing compared to being attacked
at the seat of power, the ward—and by a fellow Czech. Mulac at
this time was a West Park commissioner, by appointment of Governor Small. This challenge seemed to indicate that Cermak's
former *modus vivendi* with Small's friend Thompson had come to
an end. Cermak was able to defeat this challenge and maintain
his stronghold inviolate. But it required considerable effort and
a violent election.

Despite Dever's efforts, gang war continued in Chicago. In the
fall of 1924 Dean O'Bannion, a leading beer overlord, was assassi-
nated. Al Capone's allies, the Genna brothers, were suspected; and
O'Bannion's henchmen conducted a major commando-type military retaliatory operation in Genna-Capone territory. Within four
months four of seven Genna brothers were killed. As in all such
tribal feuds, the killers were never apprehended.

During this period one observer notes that there were fifteen
breweries in operation in Chicago and an estimated 15,000 to
20,000 retail outlets of miscellaneous categories.[5] The brewery
belonging to Lake and Druggan was enjoined from further operation. The court order was defied. Finally Lake and Druggan were
sentenced by a federal judge to serve sentences of a year in prison
for contempt of court. It did not surprise most Chicagoans that
Sheriff Hoffman saw to it that his "guests" lived in great comfort:
"This was to be expected."[6] What was slightly more irregular
was the fact that these two prisoners spent so little time in prison.
Sensational newspaper stories described their sorties to visit dent-
ists, doctors, and lavish lake-front apartments. Druggan made
ninety such excursions during his year of imprisonment, allegedly
at the price of one thousand dollars a month.[7]

Even for Chicago this was too much. Sheriff Hoffman, for a generation a powerful Republican leader in the country towns, was tried and convicted of contempt of court. He served thirty days in jail and paid a fine of $2,500. To all intents and purposes this ended his office-holding career. There was more to come. Johnny Torrio, heir to Big Jim Colosimo as head of the syndicate, was also indicted, and convicted of operating a brewery. Before he began to serve his sentence he was cut down by machine-gun fire, though he survived the attack.

During all this time it was an open secret that the gunmen were on good terms with policemen, Prohibition agents, and above all, with politicians. Diamond Jim Esposito was a Deneen ward committeeman, and all the others had close political alliances. Politicians were prominent at all gangster ceremonial occasions— at banquets, weddings, christenings, wakes, not to except the frequent flower-choked funerals. Sometimes they were pallbearers.

This was more than Dever could stomach. He had already been trying to stamp out crime, but he was bitterly aware that cooperation from most of the police force was perfunctory. They made raids, all right; but as Cermak frequently pointed out—and with justice—it was almost always the small fry who were raided. The big boys, the syndicate operators, were seldom annoyed. When they encountered difficulties at rare intervals, it was usually from a federal authority. Nevertheless, Dever valiantly intensified his campaign, and he began to meet with greater success after the attack on Torrio. Torrio, though he barely escaped with his life, departed from the scene. His domain fell to Al Capone, like Torrio an alumnus of a New York mob; both had been imported to Chicago by Colosimo. But Capone had earlier established headquarters in Cicero, and although he ascended the throne vacated by Torrio, there seemed little reason for moving his headquarters into Chicago now that Dever was increasing the "heat."

This is the basis for frequent charges of Cermak's understanding with Capone. Since Capone's fortress was a county town, in the area of supervision of the county board, many observers have *ipso facto* assumed that Cermak was responsible for the unchecked sway of Capone's Cicero rule.

It certainly cannot be denied that Cicero was Caponetown. And there was scarcely any illicit activity that could not be found there and in nearby Stickney—from drinking and gambling of every sort to prostitution—and all of these on a far grander scale than had ever been known in Chicago itself, or perhaps anywhere in the country. And there were the attendant circumstances of protection. By midsummer of 1924, according to the figures of government investigators, Torrio and Capone were each pocketing $100,000 a week.[8]

Although it is true that Capone was not disturbed in his Cicero domain, before or after the exit of Torrio, it must be remembered that Cermak and the county board had few, if any, law-enforcement powers. Whatever such powers they could have claimed would have been for unincorporated areas, and Cicero was a town of considerable population with its own government. Cook County government was proliferated among dozens of independently elected officials. At least two of these had greater law-enforcing responsibilities and authority than did Cermak and the county board. These were the state's attorney and the sheriff. It is of course a fact that A.J. customarily had the most cordial relationship with the state's attorney. In this case the man in question was Crowe, who was a personal friend of many years' standing. Furthermore, for several years in the twenties Cermak (with Brennan) and Crowe had a smoothly working bipartisan arrangement. It is therefore conceivable that some pressure could have been brought by Cermak upon Crowe to clean out Cicero. Cermak's administration was full of incidents where he used the board's fiscal authority to demand certain kinds of action from other independent officers. However, it is at best a very tenuous conjecture to propose that Cermak could have dragooned Crowe successfully. Crowe was in this period at the height of his power as an official and as a Republican boss. His first term as state's attorney had been commended by a whole host of respectables, including the Chicago Crime Commission (headed by the crusading Frank J. Loesch, erstwhile counsel for the Pennsylvania Railroad, and later member of the Wickersham Commission on Law Enforcement). But even supposing that A.J. had cared to try forcing Crowe's hand in this matter, Crowe's relationship with Brennan from 1923 on was so close that it is doubtful that Cermak could have accomplished much—except his own political doom. This is precisely what happened to Dever. As to the sheriff, A.J.'s relationship with Hoffman was extremely stormy during most of his term, with frequent clashes resulting from the battle for patronage.

In sum, Cermak's direct responsibility and authority for crime prevention in the county was at best negligible, and on balance he had very few extralegal devices available to this end. The judgment, held by many, that Cermak deserved the full onus of the lawlessness in Cook County appears to be ill founded. It is germane to the point that Dever—a relatively honest and high-caliber public official, enjoying immensely greater executive power and immeasurably greater control over police—did not succeed in his attempt to combat crime within the city of Chicago.

This is not to say, however, that Cermak strongly opposed the open towns in the county or even the Capone regime. Certainly he would have been somewhat out of character had he gone on record as opposing the Wet element in the situation. Further, he agreed with the Dry advocates that gangsterism and the general crime wave were inextricably linked. Only he differed as to the solution. Whereas the Drys harangued about venal politicians and police, Cermak laid the blame for everything on the Volstead Act. Since he never attacked violators of prohibition acts, he consistently refrained from taking action against the unfortunate by-products of these laws.

Two additional factors of importance in the crime problem were the courts and the pardon power of the governor. The lavish use of pardons by Small had provoked opponents in the 1924 elections to write a song entitled "Oh Pardon Me." The courts were frequently accused of dealing leniently with indicted gangsters. It was no accident that Capone was finally jailed by a federal court. Again, critics point to the control that politicians wielded over judges. In Cermak's case they charge that a Cermak judge allowed the Capone dog track to operate under injunction. This judge was Harry Fisher, undoubtedly a close Cermak associate. But judges can only sentence if cases have been properly prepared and presented by the prosecutor. It is simplicity itself so to arrange things that a judge has little choice but to find for the defendant. Improper warrants, illegal search, and extortion of confession are but a few of the loopholes cooperative prosecutors may leave for clever defense counsel. The *nolle prosequi* is even more useful.

The constant linking of his name to gangsters was, however, disquieting for Cermak. In the long run his continuing Wetness—despite besmirching—was to pay greater political dividends than Dever earned in assuming a Dry position as the result of the scandal of gangsterism. But in the period from 1923 to 1926 the bad press Cermak received as a result of this situation added considerably to the unease he was already suffering because of his uncertain political position. This sort of anxiety was one of the prices he had to pay for holding office instead of being a back-room boss. By contrast, Brennan, with Dever fronting for him, had a much easier time.

This period of A.J.'s career, with its adverse publicity as well as the inchoate nature of his relationship with the organization, bore a marked resemblance to the earlier period of the Gemmill hearings. To make the similarity still greater, he now fell seriously ill. On August 15 he left his desk, not to return for two months. The return was only temporary. It was necessary for him to spend several months of the winter in Florida to complete his convalescence. Again his malady was internal, diagnosed as influenzal infection of the bowels, and colitis. Colitis is now generally regarded in medicine as a psychosomatic dysfunction. It is probably not coincidence that both these periods of serious illness occurred at times when A.J.'s political fortunes were relatively low. From this point on Cermak's maladies were to be of a similar nature until, indeed, the colitis condition—and not, as most suppose, an assassin's bullet—was to cost him his life.[9] Now, as the end of his term approached, A.J. was a man physically ill and with considerable doubts concerning his political power and prestige.

THE ELECTIONS OF 1926

While other candidates were announcing themselves for the 1926 elections, Cermak used his illness as an excuse to avoid committing himself for re-election. His coy behavior lent color to the rumors of another schism, as in 1923, between him and the organization. Some believed that A.J.'s reluctance was a sign that he intended to enter the mayoralty campaign in 1927, a move that might "precipitate the biggest Democratic fight over the mayoralty since the old Harrison days," as one of the shrewdest political writers predicted.[10] At last, however, A.J. returned from his recuperative trip and announced his candidacy. Apparently another *modus vivendi* with Brennan had been reached. Although A.J. was not of the inner circle, he was active in the preparation of the organization slate. Moreover, Brennan and Michael Igoe, chairman of the platform committee, went along this time with A.J.'s demand for a "flatly wet platform."[11]

The puny remnants of the Dunne-O'Connell and Harrison factions, rallied under the banner of the "Democracy of Illinois," presented no real threat to the organization in the primary. The Brennan-Cermak forces, moreover, had made a host of bipartisan deals with the Republican Crowe-Barrett-Thompson-Brundage faction, which faced the Deneen-Small-Lundin Republicans in the primary. These bipartisan arrangements were not a new departure for the parties concerned. There already existed a shared control between Brennan and Crowe-Barrett in the sanitary district, on the South Park Board, and in Cermak's county board. To the tune of charges of bipartisan dealing and fraud, the combined Crowe-Barrett-Thompson-Brundage-Brennan-Cermak forces scored great victories in the primaries, leaving the local Republican opposition and the remnants of the Democratic dissidents demoralized and all but destroyed. Now the victorious Republican faction went on to face the victorious Democratic faction in the election, for which bipartisan deals had also been made.

A.J.'s Republican opponent, Boutell, was alleged to be one of the persons in the bipartisan agreement scheduled to "get the ax." Boutell was in other ways a not very formidable opponent.

A.J. was fortunate in the minor-league status of his opponent, but he was even luckier that the center of publicity during the summer preceding the election was the manifold corruption in the Republican primary. For it was now that Cermak, for the first time since the Gemmill hearings in 1917, faced serious charges of complicity in graft. The charges under other circumstances might have exploded like a bombshell. Now they scarcely competed with the more titillating items available: the violence in the primary, the gangland-style murder of one of Crowe's assistant prosecutors, and so on.[12] Nevertheless, the charges were made, and they had to be met.

The accusations were to the effect that the county board had been purchasing land through middlemen rather than from the original owners. The Citizens Association, which brought the charges, accused the county board of having thus wasted over a million dollars in purchases of forest-preserve lands.

Cermak's reaction to these charges by an organization of important business leaders and respectables was in every way different from his replies to attacks from professional Drys and from political opponents. His vitriol and rage were replaced by an attitude of sweet reasonableness and cooperation. This technique became the prototype of his replies to attacks from such quarters in the years to come. Ninety per cent, he asserted, of all real-estate transactions of the forest preserve had been carried on without the use of middlemen. He denied that money had been wasted; on the contrary, he pointed out, the value of forest-preserve lands had increased by $25,000,000. He invited the Citizens Association to inspect all records of the forest preserve, offered full access to all materials, and his full cooperation. Further, he pointed to the distinguished list of citizens whom he had named to membership on the forest-preserve advisory committee.

The charges were never proved. Although they undoubtedly did some damage, it was not sufficient to defeat Cermak, who won by a greater margin than many of his colleagues. The bipartisan combine delivered nearly all the offices which had been contracted. Unfortunately for Cermak, a reversal occurred in the composition of the county board, where A.J. now faced the prospect of four years of office, with eleven Republican members on the board of fifteen. There appears to be some ground for suspicion that Brennan had been involved in another deal calculated to weaken his Czech colleague.

Analysis of Cermak's votes shows nothing remarkable so far as the Chicago strength is concerned. What was unusual was his performance in the county districts outside of Chicago. He defeated Boutell in the traditionally Republican country towns as well as in the city, while these same areas were returning Republicans to

all five of their seats on the county board. There was nothing accidental in this result. Rather, it was due to a long period of conscious effort, planning, and arduous political activity. For many
colleagues and observers, the Democratizing of the country towns
was considered Cermak's chief accomplishment as a political organizer.[13] Cermak, realizing how frequently the Republicanism of
the country towns denied many county offices to the Democrats
despite leads built up in the city proper, believed that a substantial
alteration of party strength in the country towns might change
Cook County from normally Republican to normally Democratic.
By 1930 A.J. was to see this conjecture justified.

His method was simple. He relied chiefly upon that well tested
political currency: jobs. He made no fetish of party regularity in
patronage policy, and Republican leaders frequently were appointed by him to the best patronage jobs within his province.
The motive for these appointments was of course not altruistic,
nor were they made purely on the grounds of special qualifications.
The *quid pro quo* were votes and control of what had hitherto
been town and precinct Republican organizations.

This tactic was not reserved for Republican leaders. A systematic drive went forward to recruit Republican precinct workers
in the country districts. The Democrats had only skeleton party
organization in these areas, if they had any. The situation was
analogous to that of the Republican party in the deep South when
that party is out of national power. Few votes were cast for Democrats in general elections. Cermak did not try to build up the
shadow Democrats who held party positions in the country towns.
Instead, he began to recruit those Republicans who had run
second in the elections of local Republican precinct leaders. Most
frequently these men had gained 30 to 40 per cent of the votes in
a given constituency.

Instead of giving recognition to the nominal local Democratic
worker—in repayment for the small handful of votes he had been
able to corral—Cermak gave the runner-up Republicans jobs and
thereby made Democrats of them. As in the case of city precinct
captains, these newly created Democrats were often able to carry
with them a substantial portion of their local following. In most
cases the jobs Cermak used were forest-preserve positions, although

he had nominally placed them under civil service early in his first term.[14]

Cermak's administration received further vindication in the approval by large majorities of bond issues for a new county jail and for roads and bridges.

Boss Brennan, who had emerged from the shadows to run for senator, reaped scant personal benefit from his bipartisan arrangements. Like Boss Roger Sullivan, he made a good fight, but he lost by over 67,000 votes.

THE POLITICS OF 1927

From some points of view the benefits of A.J.'s *rapprochement* with Brennan and Dever seemed to have been canceled by the results of the election. For although A.J. had little difficulty in winning re-election, the ratio of eleven Republicans to four Democrats on the county board was obviously not a very welcome development, even for such a master bipartisan dealer as Cermak. Since the Democratic majority had now disappeared, A.J. would have to be still more resourceful to maintain control.

There was some feeling that the Brennan inner circle had not been anxious to fortify Cermak's position. These suspicions were related to the 1927 mayoralty campaign, which was beginning even as the 1926 elections were taking place. It had not been forgotten that there had been two earlier booms for Cermak for mayor on a frankly Wet platform and that for several years following the election of Dever in 1923 the relationship between Cermak and Brennan and his Irish circle had not been cordial. The movement to nominate Cermak in place of Dever never got very far, although it was well known that Dever had lost much of his popularity because of strict enforcement of the liquor laws. Brennan decided to go along with Dever. It is doubtful that A.J. was ever seriously considered by him as a replacement.

The situation now, however, was somewhat different from 1922-23. At that time, Thompson having withdrawn and Crowe being estranged from Thompson, it had not been difficult to reach an understanding with Crowe and others of his faction. It was well known that Brundage's man Leuder had not had the support of several Republican factions. As a result of the organization of

Crowe-Barrett-Thompson-Brundage and their relatively great success in the most recent elections, Crowe ostensibly ended his dealings with Brennan. Some believed that this was partially due to the failure of the bipartisan combine to elect Crowe's man Savage as county judge.[15] For whatever considerations, Crowe did not keep Thompson in exile after the 1926 elections, as many had expected, but publicly supported him for mayor. By December 10, 1926, the Thompson campaign, with Crowe as full partner, was under way.

What was Cermak's move now? Again denied the mayoralty nomination and being somewhat isolated from the ruling group in his party, A.J. had to shift for himself.

Whereas Brennan and Crowe seemed to have parted company because of the mayoral realignments, Cermak openly moved even closer to Crowe and the other Republicans. He had little choice if he wanted to maintain control of the county board against an eleven-to-four majority. Of course, the Republican majority was one vote short of being able to override A.J.'s veto, and by this time he had so arranged things that most appointments did not require the confirmation of the board. And although his party was greatly in the minority, it was recognized that for a variety of other reasons A.J. maintained a "powerful grip" over county business.[16] Nevertheless, in the matter of the budget for the county board, in forest-preserve matters, and in other details, a united Republican bloc could have greatly hampered him; and in his inaugural speech he made an eloquent plea for nonpartisan administration.

But he did not rely exclusively on his powers of rhetoric. He took steps to consolidate his relationship with Crowe and other Republicans toward the end of maintaining his control. William Busse, one of the few non-Crowe-Barrett-Thompson-Brundage men elected to the board in 1926, believed that Cermak had little serious difficulty in accomplishing this. He claimed that A.J. succeeded because he had Crowe and other Republican leaders "in his lap."[17] Cermak took early steps to insure keeping these gentlemen there. P. J. Carr, sheriff-elect, one of the most popular Democratic vote getters and highly placed in the Brennan inner circle, died shortly after the election. A.J. was instrumental in the county board's action to select a successor who would hold office until the next general election in 1928. The board elected Charles E. Graydon, who had been an unsuccessful Crowe candidate for sanitary trustee in the 1926 election.

Thus, Cermak cooperation enabled Crowe to annex the office of sheriff after the electorate had placed a Brennan man in the office—in conformity with the Crowe-Barrett-Thompson-Brundage-Brennan agreement. Graydon took over the office from Sheriff Hoffman, who still held it even after having been found guilty of contempt of court. However, the scandals of the privileges Hoffman had granted bootlegger prisoners had removed his name from the Republican slate. Hoffman was one of three very powerful Republican country-town leaders. Where would Hoffman go now? Who would take care of him?

Cermak came to the rescue. Hoffman was appointed to a $10,000 forest-preserve position. With Crowe and Hoffman thus in his debt, A.J. had little difficulty in continuing control of the county board. John F. Delaney, a close associate of those days, said that A.J.'s control was even greater in the second term than in the first.[18]

Despite Cermak's resentment against Brennan-Dever, there was no open break. A.J. did not choose to risk a frontal assault on Brennan as the results of the Democratic mayoralty primary made clear: Dever was nominated without any organized opposition.

However, the antipathy toward Dever seems to have come through in the Republican primary. Not only did Cermak's ward and adjacent areas under his influence—all generally predominantly Democratic—enter the Republican primary, but they also gave "Big Bill" Thompson considerable majorities over his Deneen opponent Litsinger. With this useful assistance, Thompson won the nomination easily. Doubtless, Thompson's personal popularity was a factor in his success in these Democratic wards, but this, even taking into account the added factor that the Democratic primary was virtually uncontested, does not altogether explain the heavy votes in the areas in question.

Thompson and Dever, then, faced one another in the general election for mayor. The mayoralty campaign, often called the America First campaign, was perhaps even more wild and irresponsible than the primary and general elections of 1926.[19] The basest kind of appeals were made and the most irresponsible charges. Thompson was most guilty, but some of the supporters of Dever, "the best mayor Chicago ever had," were not far behind in their efforts to gain victory for "Dever and Decency." Dever's Catholicism played a role, as did the Ku Klux Klan. Business groups lined up on either side, Insull, of course, with Thompson. Thompson's hold on the Negro voters was dramatized by frantic Dever supporters in a cry against "Africa First." Thompson, amazingly enough, attempted to make use of his record, particularly as a builder. His complete arsenal of demagoguery was mobilized against Dever, who, in spite of Brennan's hovering presence, had had a generally creditable administration. In order to drag the "America First" panoply into a local election, the Thompson forces concocted the school-histories issue. This began by denouncing the superintendent of schools as the imported tool of Dever, Merriam, and other reformers who were by definition internationalists; went on to find that the history texts used in the public schools were "tainted by treason"; and at length reached its goal of using Thompson's favorite issue, that of the menace of King George, which Thompson had been furbishing for presentation since 1918-20.

The primary issue in the campaign—at least from Cermak's point of view—was enforcement or nonenforcement of the liquor law. Many persons, notably Cermak, believed that Dever had retreated from his Wet position of 1923. Thompson stated that he was "wetter than the Atlantic Ocean," promised to "open up 10,000 new places, and take the police away from the task of frisking hip pockets and inspecting refrigerators."[20]

The Dever forces were unable to match Thompson; but they tried. In addition to the "Africa First" whispering campaign, a reply in kind, they attempted to use legal tactics against the irresponsible Thompson. The end of the Brennan-Crowe alliance, to all appearances, was dramatically illustrated in petitions to curtail Crowe's jurisdiction over the election, and that of the sheriff and coroner, both Republicans. Thompson replied with charges that this was a Democratic plot to steal the election. Thompson and Crowe were in turn charged with having gangster alliances, and the case of the gang murder of Crowe's deputy McSwiggin was repeatedly utilized. As election day neared, violence grew more imminent, with rumors that the police were to be armed with rifles and machine guns for the day. Republican Sheriff Graydon requested state troops from the governor to patrol the precincts. Violence reached the surface at last in the explosion over the shooting of Vincent (Schemer) Drucci by a policeman in an arrest made on the eve of election. Drucci, in league with Thompson, died after being shunted by police from hospital to hospital. The Thompson forces, now incensed, admittedly recruited the Capone gang.[21] The next day the polling places decided the contest, not without violence.[22]

Anti-Dever sentiment was indicated in the results of the general election more clearly than in the primary. Thompson defeated Dever by about 83,000 votes, despite over 50,000 votes for Robertson, the Lundin independent. Anti-Dever feeling was highlighted by the fact that the defeated Democratic candidates for city clerk and city treasurer each polled higher totals than the head of the ticket.

Cermak's secret opposition to Dever is strongly indicated by election results in his particular spheres of influence. In the ward that he himself "owned"—one of the best Democratic wards—Dever polled a majority scarcely larger than that which had been delivered to Thompson in the primary. In those wards subject to Cermak's influence and control, such as Toman's, Rosenberg's, and Sabath's, the showing for Dever was also conspicuously poor. There were majorities of less than 3,000 in the first two. The knifing in the last was most apparent; in Sabath's ward Dever won by only 172 votes. The sacrifice of Dever was not restricted to A.J. and his allies, as Thompson's comfortable victory reveals. Nevertheless, when one compares the totals Cermak was to roll up for himself in these four wards in the very next mayoralty election—32,000 more than Dever gained—it seems fairly clear that greater efforts on his part in Dever's behalf might have made some difference here. The voting for Cermak's man Szymczak in this election also appears to supply corroboration for the secret anti-Dever vote. Szymczak received over 2,000 votes more than Dever in Cermak's ward; in Sabath's, well over 3,000 more; and in Toman's, 1,000 more.

Although some observers, among them Professor Merriam, intimate that Brennan himself took the lead in the double-crossing of Dever,[23] analysis in retrospect of twenty-five years seems clearly to indicate that the credit—if that is the appropriate word—for the knifing of Dever and the consequent aid in the election of Thompson must be given to Cermak and other similarly single-minded adherents of "personal liberty." This was a demonstration of Brennan's much less than perfect command of local Democracy. Not only was Dever characterized by the Cermak element as a traitor to personal liberty, but there is adequate evidence to show that the subsurface resentment against the long domination of the party by the Irish was rapidly bubbling to the surface.

Thus Cermak was greatly instrumental in the election of the man whom he was to defeat four years hence. This event solidified his already very close lines of contact with Crowe and Thompson, and served to enhance his prestige with non-Irish elements of the party and with those Irish who were for a variety of reasons opposed to the heavy-handed Brennan hegemony. The election of Thompson left Cermak more than ever the symbol of a new dissident Democratic force which was frequently reported on the point of rebellion. Brennan, whose man had lost, who was constrained to surrender the city-hall patronage, also had to try to mollify this group. It is certain that his control over local Democracy, never really complete, became weaker from this point on, even though neither Cermak nor anyone else risked an attempt to unseat him.

There is little doubt that by the summer of 1927 Cermak believed that he was stronger than ever in the party. He held what now was among the party's most lucrative patronage positions; he was supported by loyal Czech and other non-Irish elements; he faced a now much less potent Brennanite force; and he enjoyed the best kind of relations with the Republican "ins." With several more years of his term left, this seemed a psychological time to attempt another important promotion. The election for governor was the following year; and Republican Governor Small, who had had a very turbulent and malodorous administration, was not at this time close to Thompson-Crowe. Also, it was almost certain that the Democratic nominee for president would be Al Smith, running on a platform of modification of Volsteadism. What could be more logical for Cermak than to assume that the most fitting man to head the Democratic state ticket should be himself? No one challenged his Wetness; and his admiration for Smith, whom he had supported in the 1924 convention, was also generally known. Why not Smith and Cermak in 1928? There is no question that A.J.'s sights were set upon this next target very early—perhaps as soon as it was clear that he could not have the 1927 mayoralty nomination. There may have been some foundation to the rumor that Brennan had given A.J. some assurances of the gubernatorial nomination, even as he refused sanction to him for the mayoralty candidacy.

"CERMAK FOR GOVERNOR"

The shouts attendant upon the mayoralty election had barely died away when newspapers friendly to A.J. began to carry the headlines, "Cermak to run for governor."[24] The boom was on.

For many months A.J. refused to admit that he sought the nomination, but many statements he made left little doubt that he considered himself available. One such remark showed a glimmering of resentment about his unsuccessful attempt to replace Dever as mayoral candidate. "The governor, because of his power, can do more to nullify the prohibition acts than can the mayor. The people of this state voted overwhelmingly for light wines and beer. Their wishes should be granted."[25]

From this date to February, 1928, when the slates were finally completed, most informed political opinion, as reflected by political journalists, editorials, and politicians, considered the nomination as all but assured for Cermak. He was generally considered the best available running mate for Al Smith, who was expected to be the presidential candidate. Not only was he a "liberal," but he also had many downstate friends, was a proved vote getter, and was, moreover, a non-Catholic.[26]

The boom rolled on, although the normally friendly *Herald and Examiner* told A.J. in an editorial that he did not have a chance of being elected in such a prosperous year. It said, "Tony, we fear you are being kidded by experts."[27] In spite of this, his own ward organization's annual "Cermak Day" was used as an occasion for the launching of the unofficial Cermak-for-governor campaign. The onset of his serious illness in September did not dim the ardor of his backers. The efficacy of his intensive organizational work in the country towns was again demonstrated, as one hundred country-town precinct captains indorsed his candidacy. By mid-October, it was believed that Cermak had been virtually agreed upon. The party chieftains were reported to have ordered him south so that he might get in physical condition for the campaign. Cermak left for Hot Springs, evidently sharing the general view. Only the *Journal* was more cautious in its attitude; and its caution was justified, for the decision still had not been reached by December when Cermak was being described as "every man's choice."[28] The speakers at the party meeting taking place at the time of this pronouncement included many important Brennan associates, such as M. L. Igoe and T. J. Crowe.

Cermak returned to Chicago at the end of the year for a few days; then, apparently still confident, returned to continue his recuperation. But by the end of January rumors reached him that this nomination also might elude him. He was now being mentioned as a candidate for senator. His reaction made it plain that he had no notion of withdrawing his name from consideration as a gubernatorial candidate.

> I am not a candidate for U.S. Senator!
> At no time have I ever given any consideration to this office, or even thought of it, nor would I seek the nomination for it.
> Many of my friends throughout the city and state have mentioned my name in connection with a campaign for governor. . . . I have not been seeking the office, nor have I made any statements pro or con on the matter of seeking this nomination. I am in the hands of my friends, and if they seek to make me governor of the state of Illinois—it is up to them.[29]

A.J.'s disclaimer did not last long. A week later he telephoned the county organization which was busily engaged in finishing its slate making. He brought to a halt the proceedings to endorse Floyd E. Thompson for governor. He returned to Chicago immediately to attempt to save the nomination which he had claimed he had not sought. In an interview on the train he declared that he was acting purely on principle. "The time has come for a showdown on issues. It might as well be done now."[30] He insisted that the issues which the party must take before the voters must be considered by the local organization.

A.J. now had a somewhat different account to offer regarding his attitude toward the nomination for governor:

The situation before I left appeared to be well known. I betray no secret, when I say that at least four of the outstanding men on the county slate came to me and urged me to stand for governor.

They made it plain their own candidacies hinged on my decision. I said I would be glad to make the fight if it were the wish of the county committee and the leaders generally. I was assured it was their wish and so I agreed to make the race for the nomination and election....I have no quarrel with anyone, but I'm going to stand by my promise. I'm ready to go before the county and state committees and state my position. I've got to stand on the principles for which I've always stood. My liberal views are well known.[31]

Upon his arrival in Chicago he announced that he would definitely enter the primary for governor. He would do this in order to enhance Smith's chances for the presidential nomination. He did not hide his belief that Judge Thompson had not been friendly to Smith's candidacy in 1924.

Brennan convened the county managing committee in order to reach a decision on the Cermak-Thompson nomination. There were rather widely held beliefs that Brennan would be unable to prevent a rift in the ranks of the faithful. Thompson's supporters—meaning those closest to Brennan—had apparently already made their decision, while A.J. seemed adamant.

Even before the meeting was convened Cermak knew that the committee was set to indorse Thompson. He said he would attend the meeting anyway but would not attempt to press his candidacy in a prearranged situation. He maintained stoutly that he was still a candidate.

In the first session of the county managing committee meeting he refused to withdraw. In the second session he challenged the authority of the committee to indorse Thompson, on grounds that the committee was improperly constituted.

But he did not have a chance. Brennan had arranged things too well in his absence. There were thirty-two votes for Thompson and only eight for Cermak. In the afternoon session several important leaders, such as Sweitzer and Dever's former corporation counsel, Busch, had made speeches for A.J. However, they "were forced to vote for Judge Thompson,"[32] along with many others. Among these were Barth Collins, Edmund J. Mulcahy, attorney for the county board; other Cermak appointees; and County Commissioner Frank J. Wilson. One can imagine the degree of Brennan pressure necessary to persuade such men to vote against their patronage chief.

Cermak's rage was undisguised. Not only did he announce that he would not be forced out of the race, but he threatened to call a meeting of the county central committee—of which he was chairman—in an effort to checkmate the decision of the Brennan-operated county managing committee. The county central committee's membership was legally fixed; and although many individuals were members of that body as well as the managing committee, Cermak insisted that he could get a majority of the central committee to indorse him. Perhaps the Brennanites believed there was something to this Cermak threat, or perhaps they only wanted to evade an open schism with A.J. even after they had neatly tricked him. At any rate, they attempted to dissuade A.J. from his intention in a caucus lasting far into the morning hours.

They evidently did not understand the depths of Cermak's disappointment, anger, and hate. Several of his colleagues testify to his passionate reaction. Many report actual tears of anger and frustration. As he left the hotel, he is reported to have uttered a malediction which was at once a threat and a vow: "I'll —— the Irish some day!"[33]

A.J. never called a meeting of the county central committee to challenge Brennan's authority. However, he gave the Brennanites several bad days by refusing to withdraw. Enormous pressure was put upon him to withdraw and accept the indorsement for senator, and many long conferences were reported in the Hotel Sherman headquarters. On February 16 Cermak announced that he would not oppose Thompson in the primary because his wife was seriously ill and because his own physicians and his family were against his entering into such an activity. The same factors also militated against the senatorial nomination, but to a lesser degree, since no primary battle was envisaged for that office.

Despite his own poor health, the illness of his wife, and the severe rebuff he had been dealt, A.J. finally agreed to allow himself to be drafted for the senatorial campaign. He accepted only because of a unanimous vote by the county central committee. His lassitude was dramatized by his absence from the "draft" meeting. His acceptance was based, he said, on a desire to maintain party harmony, and because of the men who had accepted positions on the county ticket upon the understanding that he was to have been the candidate for governor.

THE 1928 SENATORIAL CAMPAIGN

Outmaneuvered by Brennan, Cermak became a candidate for an office he never sought and did not contemplate with relish. His interests were almost entirely local and state. He rarely made statements about national issues, with of course the important exception of Prohibition, and never about international matters, except those relating to Czechs. In his campaign the latter was completely neglected.

He obviously entertained some doubts as to his qualifications for the Senate and for the social life of Washington. Further, Illinois seldom elected a Democratic senator; the last had been in 1912. Bosses Sullivan and Brennan had failed in attempts to become senators. Mostly, however, Cermak was unenthusiastic because even in the event of election he feared that the loss of local patronage might place him on the political shelf.[34] An unsuccessful campaign would merely be an unrewarding strain on his health and resources, since his term of office had two more years to run.

Nevertheless, he threw himself into the campaign with vigor and continued to be unceasingly active for over eight months—from March to the election in November. This activity seems somewhat strange, since the Brennanites had no organized opposition in the primary; a possible Dunne-O'Connell-Harrison ticket never materialized. His zealous application, beginning with the first days of March when he "nailed the Wet plank in his platform," is even more surprising in view of the severe illness he had suffered the past autumn and winter, and in view of the fact that his wife was so seriously ill that at one point he had to rush to her bedside in Florida. The reason, apart from whatever personal psychological factors might have operated to make him drive himself, can be found in Cermak's dedication to the Wet issue. Cermak's own Wet position had been taken by the county Democratic ticket. This was demonstrated by statements of Brennan and O'Brien to the effect that Cermak was to be kept busily on the stump for the three days prior to the primary. Thus, his interest in repeal of Volsteadism; what appears to be a genuine concern with the nomination of Al Smith for president; and the interests of the local candidates, all served to embroil him more deeply in the pre-primary campaign than would at first appear to be warranted. Because neither he nor the local ticket had organized opposition, from the very first all ammunition was aimed at the prospective Republican foes in the fall election. Cermak and the entire Brennan ticket were nominated by large votes.

The intensive campaign for the general election did not begin until June, the month of the national convention. From that date, ailing though he was, A.J. toured up, down, and all around the state in an intensive campaign. There were speeches several times a week, and in the later stages several times a day. No audience was neglected: labor, farmers, ethnic organizations, business. Now and then A.J. made brief excursions into denouncing the corruption of the Republican national administration and praising Democratic contributions in Congress, and made a comment here and there about the tariff—but about 95 per cent of his time and effort went into attacks on Prohibition.

As had been his habit from the start of "the noble experiment," the elements stressed in his denunciations of Prohibition were almost identical with the ones the Dry forces had used against the saloon evil. That is to say, in almost no speech did he omit cataloguing the evil effects of the Eighteenth Amendment and the Volstead Act. "Prohibition does not prohibit!" he cried; then, often in great detail and with extensive use of statistics, he would describe its responsibility for the increase in crime (it gave bootleggers, gangsters, and hijackers a profession); poverty (losses in taxes and employment); disease (caused by dangerous moonshine); insanity, divorce, immorality, and disrespect for law.

He was as blunt and outspoken as usual, and he carried the

attack to the enemy. This was made easier for him in this case, not only because of the paramountcy of the liquor issue, but because both important Republican contenders before the primary, Otis F. Glenn and Frank L. Smith (running on a "vindication platform"), were supported by his erstwhile Anti-Saloon League foes. With the Anti-Saloon League committed to his defeat, A.J. could hardly have waged a restrained campaign even if his general compulsions would have otherwise allowed it.

His approach within his own party was not unlike his tactics with the opposition. In the Democratic national convention he again demonstrated that he was far in the van of all the Chicago "dripping-wet" Democrats. The Illinois delegation was conceded to be the most ardently Wet of all state representations, and A.J. was the Wettest of the Illinoisians. Although one of Brennan's close friends, M. L. Igoe, was elected as the Illinois representative for the national platform committee, it was A.J.'s Wet planks which were presented to the Illinois delegation for later presentation to the national platform committee. At first glance the Cermak proposal was milder than one might have expected. It pledged enforcement of all laws "without discrimination" and "with equal zeal" but denounced resort to "crime and lawlessness" by government agencies and officials under pretense of law enforcement; "To compel obedience to law by crime and violence is anarchy."

We ... reaffirm our unswerving belief in the constitutional guarantees which in the past made this nation the symbol of human liberty and individual security. Among these guarantees we recognize the right of the citizens to petition Congress for redress of oppressive laws or constitutional provisions, and to advocate the modification and repeal of same, leaving the people the ultimate verdict thereon.[35]

The reason for these weasel words rather than the usual Cermak trumpeting may be found in the rather strong Prohibitionist tendencies of many of the southern delegations. It had been those forces which had stood in the way of Cermak's Wet proposals in 1920 and in 1924 and which had passed over the candidates Cermak had supported, Edwards in 1920 and Smith in 1924. The Smith managers were trying to avoid a major fight on the Wet issue, which they believed might cause the loss of the nomination to the "Happy Warrior." Brennan was one of Smith's close friends and undoubtedly caused Cermak to modify his Wet plank. Brennan believed, however, that the wording of A.J.'s proposal concurred with Smith's views and would not offend the southern delegates.

But even this compromise was not sufficient for Smith's managers, and Brennan went along with them. The next day the Illinois delegation refused to instruct Igoe to present the Cermak plank to the platform committee with the formal backing of the Illinois delegation. Cermak was furious. He finally agreed, reluctantly, to the suggestion of Melvin A. Traylor, president of the First National Bank of Chicago, to have the plank presented without formal sanction. Although A.J. finally acquiesced (he was always deferential to bankers), he did so without enthusiasm.

> Personally I am in favor of the repeal of the Eighteenth Amendment. We should not "pussy-foot" on this. Show your colors. I would rather be defeated than to try to fool the people that my views are different now from what they were during the last twenty-five years.[36]

When the convention at length accepted a relatively Dry plank, A.J. and close friend McDonough were reported as roaring in protest and fighting to the last. In contrast, Brennan expressed satisfaction with the convention's stand because "Smith is his own platform; people don't read platforms."[37]

But A.J.'s Wet sentiments were not muffled in Illinois as they had been in Houston. Home again, he attacked the Anti-Saloon League with vigor and venom. Congressmen, senators, federal judges he accused of hypocrisy for sentencing individuals who possessed a pint, while they themselves "sat in open cabarets, drinking champagne and whiskey."[38]

Cermak's opponent Glenn was largely spared until late in the campaign. A.J. first trained his heavy guns upon Glenn after becoming aware of rumors allegedly circulated by Glenn's headquarters to the effect that A.J. did not really desire to be elected. Cermak denied this, and then went to work on Mr. Glenn. Admitting his early reluctance to run because he had wished to continue his important work on the county board, A.J. averred that now his "heart and soul" were in the contest because he felt that it was his duty to help Smith and to work against Prohibition. He was devoting every minute to the campaign that could be spared from his county duties, and what was more, he was financing his own campaign.

Why was his opponent, Glenn, so reluctant, asked A.J., to reveal his position on Prohibition? Because he was a tool of the Anti-Saloon League and because for him the senatorship was only a job; whereas for Cermak it was an "opportunity to aid in restoring of the liberties of the American people."[39] Glenn, he said, was a hypocrite: he talked Dry in rural areas, but in the cities "he probably will seize an empty beer stein and declare, 'Boys, I'll never take it from you, because it is empty.' And he won't endeavor to legally bring it back to you."[40]

Whenever his tirades against the hypocrisy of Glenn palled, A.J. attacked presidential candidate Herbert Hoover and other captives of the Anti-Saloon League. If Hoover were elected, he charged, there would be a great increase in all sorts of blue laws limiting personal liberty on Sunday, and also attempts to regulate the sale and use of tobacco.

As the campaign approached the climax the battle was carried more than ever to Glenn. Cermak challenged him again and again to a public debate on the issues. Glenn demurred, offering one excuse after another. No debate ever took place. Toward the very end A.J. brought out his lowest attacks. He demanded to know whether or not Glenn had been an inmate of an institution for reasons of acute alcoholism, on three separate occasions (Glenn admitted having been in the institution, but said that it was because of a "breakdown"). He charged that Glenn was ineligible for office because he had received a fee from the executive department while he had been a state senator.

But A.J.'s energetic campaign went for no immediate avail. He was overwhelmed by the Hoover landslide. Still he ran a very handsome race. He ran ahead of both Smith and Judge Thompson in total votes. In Cook County he polled 133,000 more votes than Smith and almost 95,000 more than Thompson. Whereas Smith, with the almost religious fervor of the Democratic organization behind him, lost Cook County by 95,000, Cermak carried it by over 40,000. Cermak also won in Chicago by 77,000, while Smith lost by 21,000. Smith carried eleven counties and A.J. fourteen.

Anyone who could run ahead of Al Smith in Cook County was

a man to be reckoned with. Immediately another mayoralty boom for Cermak was on. Most politicians believed that A.J. had gained much, despite defeat. In addition to the prestige of a good vote, it was believed that he had "polished himself up" for the 1931 mayoralty.

THE LOCAL ELECTIONS OF 1928

As has been stated, the Brennan Democrats had had no organized opposition. As usual, the Republican preprimary and primary battles were bloody. This primary is usually called the "Pineapple Primary."[41] The results of this great uprising against America First demagoguery were to influence heavily the course of local politics for many years.

As it was a presidential year, delegates to the national conventions were included in the contests, as well as a governor, a senator, congressmen, legislators, a state's attorney, and many other strategic county offices. In addition, there was a large city bond issue at stake, "full of fat pickings for the faithful, a clever mixture of the City Plan and the Gang Plan."[42]

The old Crowe-Barrett-Thompson-Brundage combine entered a full slate including alliances with state and national candidates (Brundage by now was not a very important factor). Everything seemed to point to a complete sweep for the gentlemen conquistadors. By all odds they seemed to possess the strongest machine in the history of the state. Thompson's victory in 1927 following the general success in 1926 appeared to have made them unbeatable. After Thompson won the 1927 primary, he had entered a non-aggression status-quo pact with Deneen; thus it was thought that harmony would prevail among the Republicans. But Crowe-Thompson were not satisfied to allow Deneen the handful of offices he now controlled. So powerful did they feel that they decided to destroy Deneen completely. This assured a primary battle. Of course, Crowe ran for re-election. Also on their slate was Frank L. Smith for senator and Small for governor. Thus Small and Smith headed the state slate with Thompson a dominant factor in every phase. Smith had been denied his seat in the Senate; Small had had a $600,000 judgment returned against him for interest money due the state; Thompson's expert-fee case was pending; and Crowe still smarted from the charges of fraud in the 1926 election as well as charges of crime and gangster connections, symbolized by the McSwiggen case. In spite of all this, the combine was confident that few would be courageous enough to oppose them with energy.

> The chill, brutal facts were available. . . . The Thompson-Crowe . . . merger had attained . . . a control of Cook County offices which almost passed belief. They held a voting majority in, or ruled by threats of defeat "next time" all the police power, all the machinery of prosecution, a string of judges, both municipal and state . . . members of taxing bodies.[43]

If they could succeed in this primary, their power in city, county, and state would be all but complete. There would no longer be factionalism in the Republican party. Then they would be able to out-Brennan Brennan and liquidate whatever bipartisan alliances remained, and perhaps liquidate the Brennan machine as well. In national elections Illinois and Cook County for ten years had been normally and heavily Republican. This factor almost insured victory for those who succeeded in the Republican primaries, especially in a presidential year such as this.

The opposition to the Thompson-Crowe-Small-Smith forces formed slowly. Luckily, dissident downstate elements succeeded in uniting behind candidates for senator, governor, and attorney general rather than giving the entrenched forces the benefit of divided opposition. Deneen, in reply to Crowe-Thompson's shattering of the status quo agreement, entered a full county slate and joined forces with the anti-Smith-Small downstate groups. To oppose Crowe, Judge John A. Swanson, a Scandinavian jurist of high reputation, was selected.

Still the outlook for Thompson-Crowe *et al.* was bright. Thompson and Barrett, recently elected, were at the zenith of power. Vindictive Crowe was generally feared. Some labor elements were on their side, while business, professional, and civic groups were reluctant to stand up to the frightening vested group. The Chicago Crime Commission and another civic antivice group, the Committee of Fifteen, timidly expressed support for Crowe. Four thousand members of the Chicago Bar Association, doubtless bearing in mind the state's attorney's useful *nolle prosequi* powers, loaned their names to Crowe's renomination. The steamroller went on to the tune of America First, out-with-international-bankers, down-with-Hoover, and draft-Coolidge. Thompson harangued unceasingly, often with the Chicago Police Octette in tow. Its favorite selection was "Big Bill the Builder." Corporation Counsel Ettelson often joined Thompson's favorite musical group as it rendered his favorite number. Adding to the air of confidence, Deneen's chief lieutenant and best vote getter, Haas, died shortly before the primary, leaving a clear field for the Crowe-Thompson candidate, County Commissioner John W. Jaranowski.

With every trend in favor of Crowe-Thompson, a sudden series of events occurred which quickly and radically altered the situation. First, "Diamond Jim" Esposito, alleged gangster and loyal Deneen cohort, was found murdered with fifty-eight bullets in his body. About a week later the homes of Senator Deneen and Judge Swanson were bombed. No one was injured, but the bombs were real "pineapples," not giant firecrackers.

The bombings roused Chicago's citizenry. Crowe and Thompson were denounced. Crowe made matters worse by accusing Deneen and Swanson of causing their own houses to be bombed in order to elicit sympathy. Thompson injudiciously echoed his ally. The arrogance of this attitude set off a local counterrevolution. A citizens' committee was organized and became very active in spite of threats against the chairman. It tried to get bomb insurance for its meetings and continued to fight. The Bar Association, which had hitherto been cowed to impotence, finally conducted a poll of its membership and announced the result—five to one against Crowe. The Crime Commission and its leaders, Frank J. Loesch and Henry B. Chamberlin, at last brought to an end its role of Trilby to Crowe's Svengali and endorsed Swanson.

Nearly all the newspapers opened a great barrage against the entrenched group. The suits against Small and Thompson were recalled; Smith's ousting from the Senate was blazingly publicized; and the relations of Small, Smith, and Thompson to Insull were given great coverage. The "Traction Trio" was accused of trying to steal Chicago streets.

Crowe and Thompson met the attacks with acrid slander, but the newspapers were unfriendly, and the Deneen forces were fighting back. Litsinger, an important Deneen man, angered by typical

Thompson canards, began to reply in kind; he described "Big Bill" as having the "hide of a rhinocerous and the brain of a baboon." Lundin, who had finally been successfully isolated by his one-time creature, Thompson, reminded audiences of his prophecy of 1927: that if Thompson were re-elected Chicago's reputation would be blemished beyond all repair.

As the seriousness of the counterblows was realized, Crowe-Thompson became panicky. Their countercharges grew even more irresponsible and they complained about unfair attacks. Thompson threatened to resign if Crowe were defeated. "Your mayor does not have to be abused and perhaps indicted. He will not spend half his time defending himself against his state's attorney. He ate regular before mayor and he will eat regular again."[44]

While charges against Thompson and his buffoonery were general, the accusations of collusion with gangsters against both Thompson and Crowe were still more outspoken. The Thompson-Crowe enemies had plenty of ammunition for these salvos. The gangsterism that had erupted in Chicago synchronously with Prohibition had become even more aggravated during Crowe's regime; and in the year since Thompson's re-election, gang wars were epidemic. Even the Capone gang had moved boldly into Chicago and opened headquarters near the city hall.

The relation of Crowe-Thompson to gangland was evidently well known to politically sophisticated Chicagoans. This was aptly demonstrated by Frank J. Loesch, lawyer for the Pennsylvania Railroad and president of the Chicago Crime Commission, which had supported Crowe until February. When Loesch and the Crime Commission finally decided to abandon Crowe, Loesch went to Capone in order to seek his cooperation for a clean election. According to Mr. Loesch, Capone, surrounded by large photographs of Washington, Lincoln, and "Big Bill," agreed to help. Mr. Loesch was grateful, for he realized that "Capone ran the city."[45] Capone told Loesch that he could not guarantee results in the entire city but within his domain he would "have the cops send over the squad cars the night before election and jug all the hoodlums and keep 'em in the cooler until the polls close."[46]

The story may be apocryphal, but Mr. Loesch, one of the most respected pillars of respectable society, told it on many public occasions. Thompson-publicist Stuart believes that it is "greatly exaggerated with reference to Capone's control over police."[47]

Capone was much disappointed if he had expected that anyone officially connected with Mayor Thompson was going to give him real aid in taking over the North Side. Capone at that time undoubtedly was much dissatisfied with the treatment he had received under the Thompson administration. Moreover, Thompson by that time was "too hot."[48]

Protected by gunmen, aroused Chicagoans again exercised their prerogatives as citizens. What to many seemed a miracle occurred: the most powerful political machine was put to rout by a last-minute burst of indignation by relatively unorganized forces. Swanson defeated Crowe by 201,207; Small lost Chicago by 254,772 and the state by 439,793; Smith lost the state by 243,459 and Cook County by 123,585. The remainder of Deneen's county slate was also victorious by great margins. Graydon, Crowe-Cermak interim sheriff, was also buried in the avalanche. The Crowe-Thompson organization was able to salvage only a handful of nominations, and the huge city bond issue was also swamped. Dissident forces captured four fifths of the national convention delegates and the state Republican committee. The Crowe-Thompson forces managed to retain control of the county committee, but Thompson himself was defeated for ward committeeman.

As usual, the election was full of violence, bloodshed, and fraud. It was said that "every horse voted."[49] A Negro opposing Crowe henchman Eller for ward committeeman was murdered, and many ward workers were intimidated and kidnapped. Another special grand jury, complete with special prosecutors, was convened. Loesch, Charles Center Case, and Francis X. Busch were appointed members of the *ad hoc* prosecuting staff. Cermak and the county board reluctantly appropriated money for the proceedings.

What was the position of the Brennanites during this violent Republican struggle? Not having any opposition, what little pre-primary campaigning was undertaken by them was aimed at probable opponents in the general election. But were they only by-standers to the bitter Republican battle? Professor Merriam thought not. He was of the opinion that Brennan had an agreement with Crowe-Thompson to aid them in destroying the opposition.[50] One cannot dismiss lightly the opinion of such an eminent on-the-spot observer. But if he is indeed correct, the motivation of Brennan and Cermak is not easy to understand. If the Thompson-Crowe gang should succeed, would it not have been then in a position to destroy its former bipartisan pals? Besides, to a considerable extent, Thompson and Crowe appealed to the same Wet groups upon whom Brennan and Cermak relied. Of course, it may be conjectured that Brennan, believing (as everyone else did at the beginning) that Thompson and Crowe were invincible, felt he must work with them. Although he and Crowe had parted company when Thompson ran in 1927, they still had certain bipartisan arrangements. In a presidential year the Republicans were destined to win most state and county offices. In such a situation it is possible that the Brennan forces might have taken the position that it is better to be with the winners, even though ultimately they might weaken their own organization. In any case, in this primary bipartisanism never became a major issue as it had in 1926; and it is difficult to find offices where either Brennan or Crowe-Thompson nominated sitting ducks for either side to topple in November. The Democratic nominees for state's attorney and for sheriff were not important vote getters, it is true; but at the same time, neither was the Crowe candidate for sheriff. From the point of view of Thompson and Crowe, it also seems doubtful that they would have sought Brennan support.[51] At the start, their power and confidence was such that it is unlikely they believed they needed such assistance. They were infinitely more powerful than they had been in 1926. And being sure of winning the primary and then certain of Republican victory in the fall, why should they have felt compelled to give away gratuities?

Cermak had no major role in determining the Brennan strategy. All the same, controlling as he did the county board only through Crowe's agreement, he gave a slight indication of his sympathies by appointing the wife of a Crowe commissioner as interim county recorder.[52] Also, as has been indicated, the county board was less than enthusiastic about appropriating funds for the investigation of alleged Crowe-Thompson violence during the primary. And in discussing this period with the writer, neither Mr. Crowe nor any Thompson admirer ever complained of Cermak's attitude in this crucial event which all but permanently shattered what had been a high-riding machine.[53]

In November the Hoover landslide carried with it the entire Republican state ticket and a major share of the pivotal county offices, but without any bipartisan overtones. It is important for future developments to note that the victorious Republicans were mostly Deneen men, including Swanson, state's attorney, and Elmore, sanitary trustee. The Democrats (no longer Brennanites, for Brennan had died in August) retained control of the sanitary district. Two Democrats, Clayton F. Smith for recorder and Dr. Bundesen for coroner, polled overwhelmingly the largest number of votes, much larger than those of any Republican.

Immediately, vigorous booms for mayor were launched for both of them—and for Cermak. Whatever degree of aid he had given defeated and discredited Crowe and discredited Thompson, he succeeded in evading becoming tarred by the same murky brush used against them. Nor was he attacked on these grounds in the vindictive judicial election of 1929, when he was so outspokenly opposed to Thompson and cohorts.

· 10 ·

CAPTURING

COUNTY

LEADERSHIP

THE 1928 Republican landslide again demonstrated the stalwart Republicanism of Illinois and Cook County and the continuing Republicanism of the nation. A Dry Republican President and Congress presaged no change in Prohibition legislation. All state offices, the legislature, both United States senators, both congress-men-at-large, and most downstate congressmen were also Dry Republicans. Locally the more respectable Deneen Republicans had captured more offices than they had controlled in many years, including the important office of state's attorney. Further, they had, in cooperation with the 1928 downstate victors, wrested the state Republican organization from the domination of Small, Smith, Thompson, and their ilk. On the surface, then, in Chicago and Cook County the Democrats now saw the Deneen element, relatively Dryer and more respectable, as their most powerful opponent.

But in many ways this was a mirage. In spite of the disastrous losses in 1928, Thompson was still in possession of the chief local prize (and his term had still over two years to run); Barrett was still boss of the taxing machinery; and most important, this group still controlled the formal local Republican machinery.

The Democrats, holding no state offices and having no city patronage, were in control of more local offices than any Republican faction. But their situation, nevertheless, seemed dark. It was generally expected that this normally minority party, whose traditional strength vis-à-vis the Republicans had been a relatively greater unity, was about to burst asunder in an orgy of factionalism. George Brennan died in August, 1928, and there appeared no one to accede to the throne with as little dissension as had accompanied Brennan's succession to Sullivan. The day following the 1928 election, discussion of the expected fragmentization became public.

In the beginning the discussion found four centers of power among the Brennan ranks: (1) the South Park Board faction led by M. L. Igoe and Edward J. Kelly, (2) the sanitary district group under the leadership of T. J. Crowe and Martin J. O'Brien, (3) the remnants of the Dunne-O'Connell-Harrison factions, and (4) a westside county board group dominated by Cermak and including Congressman James T. Igoe.[1]

However, within a short period it was evident that the contending groups were, in fact, only two. The Dunne-O'Connell-Harrison faction, which had been largely moribund since 1916, had ventured to oppose the organization in 1926—only to suffer ignominious defeat. It had been unable to enter a slate in 1928. Besides, Cermak had already all but insured its adherence to his banner. In September, one month after Brennan's death, Cermak was host at a dinner given by him to celebrate the return of Harrison, Dunne, and O'Connell to the organization, apparently the Cermak wing.[2]

Cermak's earlier position of prominence in the Harrison faction should not be forgotten, nor Carter Harrison's unqualified endorsement of Cermak's 1922 and 1926 campaigns. After the return of Harrison, Dunne, and O'Connell, they took the stump for Cermak in the senatorial campaign. Dunne publicly acclaimed him as "a stalwart champion who has been sounding the bugle of personal liberty for twenty years."[3] In addition to winning over these Brennan foes, Cermak began detaching many erstwhile Brennan henchmen, cutting deep into the inbred Irish inner circle.

Fearing Cermak's strength the other two groups, the South Park and sanitary district, quickly fused. They realized that each was too weak to attempt to withstand the Cermak *putsch*. Without exception this aggregate which now attempted to deny Cermak's accession was composed of the Irish who had under Brennan's headship dictated the program of local Democracy. Martin J. O'Brien was chairman of the managing committee of the Cook County Democratic organization, the body through which all of Brennan's decisions had been legitimized. T. J. (Tim) Crowe, secretary of the managing committee, had been for the six years preceding head of the sanitary district and Brennan's spoils agent for the bounty which had been split with Robert E. Crowe. Edward J. Kelly and M. L. Igoe who had been Brennan's men, sharing control of the South Park Board with Crowe, were also intimate Brennan allies. Kelly was also chief engineer of the sanitary district. Igoe had dragooned the Brennan-controlled minority membership in the state house of representatives, had twice been unsuccessful Brennan candidate for state's attorney and had been Brennan's choice for the Illinois member of the platform committee of the national convention.

There were several others who were considered among the Brennan heirs. Alderman John S. Clark, long-time chairman of the council finance committee and frequently mentioned as a 1931 mayoralty candidate, was a leading Cermak opponent. Joseph Gill, Brennan's brother-in-law, and Alderman A. J. Horan, a protégé of T. J. Crowe, were other important members of this caucus. It was against this group that Cermak had to contend in his effort to become the boss. He had long prepared himself for the ensuing struggle; nevertheless great and bitter battles were involved. His adversaries had the great advantage of being the "ins" and, much more important, of being heirs to a tradition of Irish domination of local Democracy.

The struggle for control began in a subterranean fashion immediately upon Brennan's death. It burst into full flame after the November elections of 1928. Nearly all journalists, as well as serious observers of the caliber of Merriam and Gosnell seem to imply that Cermak simply "took over" after Brennan died. One example of this oversimplification is offered.

A. J. Cermak became the Democratic leader. . . . Cermak was president of the County Board, president of the Forest Preserves, dictator to the Demo-

cratic minority in the General Assembly, influential in the Thompson administration.... And he was ambitious for more power.[4]

In reality, despite frequent journalistic bulletins, Cermak's
domination did not become complete until December, 1930, a
period of two years. The process began in August, 1928; and
although he made continuous and increasing gains, the last important revolt was not crushed until it was clear that he intended
to take for himself the 1931 mayoralty nomination. An analysis
of the complex Cermak thrust for control throws into bold relief
the techniques and the persons through which a local political
leader reaps the harvest of over a quarter of a century's labor in
the vineyard of political manipulation.

What were his assets for the ensuing struggle? In the first place,
among powerful local Democrats he was one of the more important
public figures. This he owed to his long and uninterrupted office
holding and his penchant for generally favorable publicity. In contrast, most leaders of the opposition wing—such as T. J. Crowe,
O'Brien, Gill, or even Clark—were relatively obscure figures to the
average Chicagoan. Cermak's name was by now well known; he
was a big man in his community. Thus he could with greater
success speak to the rank and file of the voters and to Democrats
via the newspapers. Moreover, since his tenure as president of the
county board, he had attained a reputation as a relatively able
public official—this in spite of a few damaging attacks by civic
organizations. None of his opponents could match the stature of
his office or his public reputation, except perhaps Clark.

He had the greatest patronage office then under Democratic control, while his opponents had relatively little patronage.[5] Several
of the Irish who would probably have joined the opposition owed
their offices either to Cermak appointments or to Cermak's support
of their request for nomination. They had to weigh their moves
cautiously, and few were willing to climb onto the anti-Cermak
bandwagon unequivocally. In the case of these men, the O'Brien-
Crowe-Clark forces had to do without considerable patronage
which they might otherwise have enjoyed.

In addition, we must not forget the Czech core of Cermak power.
This was firmly anchored in his ward, in the fealty of the adjacent
Czech ward of compatriot ward committeeman Alderman John

Toman, and in considerable influence in the neighboring ward of ward committeeman Congressman Adolph J. Sabath.[6] Cermak's power also extended to other contiguous Czech areas on the near southwest side including the country towns and suburbs in that part of the county, and to the Fifteenth Ward, whose committeeman was his faithful county board associate, Emmett Whealan.

Whealan, long Cermak's trusted henchman on the county board,[7] symbolized the goodly number of Irish ward leaders who were either indebted to A.J. or who required his support or sponsorship. Because of his long important patronage power, because of his commanding influence among the Czechs, because of his power as leader of the United Societies and the Wets, the aggregate number of such persons was great, although they were by no means all Irish. The situation of Congressman James T. Igoe was similar to Whealan's, and he was on Cermak's side from the first. For a variety of complex reasons—in most cases existing patronage or promised patronage, as well as general dissatisfaction with the policies of the Brennan-type ruling clique—Cermak early annexed the support of several other Irish ward leaders. Most of these were not among the most prominent, but in the aggregate they represented a not inconsiderable force. Among these may be included Alderman Joseph B. McDonough, Edward J. Mulcahy, Barth Collins, Boetius H. Sullivan, and Thomas J. Courtney.[8]

There were others too among the Irish whose support Cermak could probably rely upon as soon as he could demonstrate that he had a reasonably good chance of coming out on top. There had been several such who had supported his 1928 gubernatorial candidacy up to the last moment before the Brennan steamroller flattened Cermak's hopes. County Clerk Sweitzer, who controlled the order in which candidates' names appeared on the ballot, was one of these. Dever's corporation counsel, Francis X. Busch, a ward committeeman and influential among "respectables" and in financial circles, was another.

A few other Irish who by inclination would have been in the forefront of the anti-Cermak forces were fairly neutralized by virtue of holding Cermak appointments. Joseph Gill (for a time) and James C. Denvir were included in this group. Gill was, as noted, Brennan's brother-in-law, and was comptroller of the forest preserves. Denvir was chairman of the county Civil Service commission. All in all, Cermak had considerable avenues of control and influence in the Irish camp. This tended to disperse his opponents, whereas he was able to maintain a high degree of unity among his supporters.

Cermak had other important sources of support. M. J. Szymczak, young Polish leader, was one of the most important of these non-Irish politicians. Cermak had for years been grooming him to woo the support of his large ethnic group. In 1928 Szymczak had been elected clerk of the superior court after gaining the nomination for city treasurer in 1927, although he lost along with Dever. Both nominations had been received through Cermak's efforts. From the north-side Germans Cermak had the support of another young man, State Senator Charles H. Weber. Quite soon he annexed the support of west-side Jewish leaders Moe Rosenberg and Jacob Arvey, respectively committeeman and alderman of the Twenty-Fourth Ward.

To a large extent he could now rely upon his appointees, the men who had tried in vain to support him for the gubernatorial nomination in 1928 until frightened away by Brennan. Of considerable value was the loyalty of many country-town committeemen whose good will Cermak had been courting assiduously. Helpful in the work was John F. Delaney, committeeman from Maywood, who had been in charge of Cermak public relations (and ghostwriting) during most of his term as president of the county board.

A less tangible asset, but nonetheless important, was Cermak's reputation as a winner. For two decades in control of one of the most reliable Democratic wards, holding continuous office, he had won all but two of a large number of elections. He had never lost a primary. One loss was by an extremely slim vote, whereas the loss of the senatorial contest, especially in view of his reluctance to run, was generally considered a victory. Most believed that, while no Democrat could have won in 1928, few could have run ahead of Al Smith. Everyone loves a winner and none more than politicians—especially if the winner is on their side. In contrast, among his chief opponents, Igoe had lost three elections, O'Brien had lost in 1926, and T. J. Crowe in 1928.

These were the chief sources of Cermak's strength against the entrenched but divided Irish. Before analyzing his technique for achieving victory it would be useful to take a brief backward glance at the genesis of A.J.'s power vis-à-vis the Irish.

In every organization there are dissidents, and the Cook County Democracy was no exception. Each of the groups among Cermak's followers and some of his Irish supporters fall into this category. Cermak, by virtue of his office, experience, and skill, was able to unite these dissidents against the power holders. For years now other ethnic groups besides the Czechs had been dissatisfied with the distribution of party spoils. Chief among these were the Poles and the Jews, with the Germans not far behind. There was much to justify these attitudes. Not only had top party leadership been exclusively Irish since 1915 (and a generation before that in the Hopkins-Sullivan regime, not to mention Dunne-O'Connell) but at least thirty-three of the fifty city ward committeemen in 1926 had been Irish.[9] A similar disproportion held true in the case of the more desirable—indeed all—patronage positions,[10] and, what was even more irritating, in the process of slate construction. Wooddy's analysis of the 1926 Brennan county slate revealed twenty-five Irish candidates of a total of forty-two.[11] Moreover, with few exceptions the important offices were reserved for the Irish. This situation was not restricted to this one campaign. The dissatisfaction of these ethnic components of the party found ample justification in their relative voting strength as compared to the Irish. All of the above except the Czechs were much more numerous than the privileged Irish. The Poles were more than double and the Germans and Jews almost reached this figure.[12] These numerically superior groups, receiving only the crumbs of the good things of political spoils, had become more and more restive. They clustered around Cermak, who symbolized both their fears and aggressions and their hope.

Just as A.J.'s break from the Harrison faction had been a gradual weaning, so was the development of his dissatisfaction with what he considered Irish selfishness. It reached its climax in his passionate vow following the loss of the gubernatorial endorsement, but it had been long abrewing. The situation in 1928 may be traced from 1922, after he became president of the county board and a really important person in the party. We have seen his sometime threats to bolt the party and witnessed his chagrin at being passed over in 1923 for the mayoralty. Most of Dever's administration marked a period of ever growing coolness toward Brennan and the Irish, aggravated by their "pussyfooting" on matters affecting "personal liberty." The abortive Cermak-for-mayor booms in 1922 and 1926 were reflections of Cermak's discontent.

During this period, although never giving A.J. the things he felt entitled to, Brennan had grudgingly recognized the growing importance of his formidable Czech ally and rival. The nomination and election of Cervenka as city treasurer in 1923 may be considered such recognition. At the same time one may see in this a desire to build Cervenka up to rival the ambitious Cermak. However this may be, a considerable number of medium prestige positions were given to Cermak's men during Dever's regime.[13] None of these was of the first rank, commensurate with Cermak's power. There was some low-level patronage from other Brennan officeholders, and Cermak had of course reciprocated by appointing large numbers of Brennan men in his jurisdiction. Many, such as the position of Brennan's brother-in-law Gill, were the best jobs Cermak controlled. In general, the patronage he received from Robert E. Crowe and other Republican allies compared favorably with what he was able to get from his own party.

Cermak was becoming less and less patient with these tactics. The crisis was reached when the nomination for governor was denied him.[14] It is impossible to assess the psychic cost of swallowing his hurt and anger and professing party loyalty by accepting the senatorial nomination. A most critical illness lasting from January to May, 1929, was probably not unassociated with these events.[15]

Even before this he was not a well man. Serious illness had not been absent for long ever since 1915. And by now he was in his middle fifties. How long could he afford to wait for the big prize which he had so abundantly demonstrated he deserved? When would he ever be in a better position than he was in 1927, having just won for the second time his important office—and by such a large majority? Did he not deserve the nomination simply as reward? Had he not faithfully delivered his ward and given his influence in other areas to Sullivan and Brennan for over twelve years?

It is doubtful that Cermak could have postponed a final reckoning with Brennan much longer—at any rate not without the most serious psychic and physical consequences. This was clearly indicated by ever more insistent demands on Brennan. In the caucuses to nominate the judicial slate in the summer of 1927, for instance, after having agreed to run for the senate, Cermak demanded both judicial vacancies. He succeeded in enforcing his demand even though one of the vacancies was earnestly desired by M. L. Igoe, one of Brennan's closest henchmen.[16]

This was the situation in the summer of 1927, with Cermak reaching the breaking point in his animosity toward Brennan and the Irish, and they being forced to meet some of his demands (although not his most insistent ones) for recognition. Nevertheless, Cermak never joined head-on battle with Brennan.

When the Democratic leader died in August, 1928, Cermak immediately began to rally his forces even while he conducted his senatorial campaign. Quickly he brought about the support of the Brennan-hating faction, headed by Dunne, O'Connell, and Harrison. Almost as soon, he entered into a working alliance with a far more important group, certain Jewish leaders. At this time the most important center of Jewish power in the party had its locus in the Twenty-fourth Ward (North Lawndale), a territory adjacent to Cermak's bailiwick in South Lawndale. The power wielders for a generation had been the Rosenbergs, Michael and Moe. Michael had been a trustee of the sanitary district until his death early in 1928 and had also been ward committeeman. Upon his death his brother Moe succeeded him. The alderman from the Twenty-fourth was young and ambitious Jacob Arvey. All these men had important connections with the whole of the Jewish community spread out over many sections of Chicago. They included close ties with the chieftains of what formerly had been the Ghetto, the Humboldt Park area, the Albany Park district, and the Hyde Park territory where resided Horner, the Lindheimers, and Barnet Hodes (but also M. L. Igoe and William O'Connell). Cermak had ties of considerable cordiality and of long standing with the Rosenbergs and Arvey. Arvey had been an important Cermak aid in controlling the city council in 1919-22, while propinquity made many contacts with the Rosenbergs a necessity. But perhaps more important was their common anti-Irish feeling. Like Cermak, Arvey and the Rosenbergs smarted under what they felt were continual blows to their prestige and inadequate recognition by the Irish leadership. It was not necessary to convince the Jewish leaders that they could not expect a sudden reversal in the policy of the Irish. In contrast, the relationship between Jews and Czechs in Chicago had always been most amicable. Until recently and perhaps even today, the Czechs boast of the Jewish Sabaths as among their leading citizens.[17] The fact that Cermak's adjutant and personal secretary for twenty years, Henry Sonnenschein, was also Jewish did not lessen the favorable attitude toward Cermak. But important as these considerations were, the Rosenberg-Arvey alliance with Cermak was founded upon a substantial economic basis. During the notorious investigation of Rosenberg's income in 1934, Rosenberg revealed that he and his brother had had the closest working arrangement with Cermak since Cermak's days of city council leadership in 1919-22. "Rosenberg said Cermak had always been influential with the utility companies and in fact, had got Rosenberg his first business with them."[18] In another report Moe Rosenberg explained the long relationship of the Rosenbergs and Cermak in this way. "He used to do a lot of things for Mike [Michael Rosenberg] when he was in the city council. He helped get a lot of this utility business."[19]

Because of these pervasive ties, upon Brennan's death A.J. first "went to the Jews—the Rosenbergs."[20] A pact was sealed with Rosenberg, involving his support—moral, political, and financial— in an effort to capture the party leadership. Rosenberg's admission of this treaty was implicit in his considerably oversimplified explanation of the capture of the party leadership.

After George Brennan died there was not much left of the Democratic party and we got together and reorganized the Democratic party, Cermak and myself. And when we reorganized it and took the party over, there was a deficit of about $200,000 in bills payable.[21]

The corroboration—of persons close to the leadership of both factions—of Rosenberg's statement anent the party's financial situation and his and Cermak's solution of the problem is persuasive evidence of the truth of Rosenberg's confessions.[22] Many other observers stated that very important in Cermak's accession was his financial position vis-à-vis the opposition.[23]

But if Rosenberg's political and financial assistance was invaluable, Cermak's early agreement with Irish leader P. A. (Pat) Nash was equally critical. He was among the first and the most important of the Irish whom Cermak was to woo successfully. Nash was ward committeeman of the Twenty-eighth Ward, in the heart of the O'Brien-Clark-Crowe territory of the west-side Irish. The recruitment of Nash was made relatively early because Nash had made a serious break with Brennan in 1923 after Brennan's election.[24] Being considerably older than the rest of the Irish leadership, he had been a very important member of the Irish branch of the Democratic party since the days of Hopkins and Sullivan. However, this strength was left well camouflaged, then and subsequently, when he became the senior partner of the Kelly-Nash alliance.[25] Although usually in the background, Nash's great power and political skill gave him a considerable reputation among local politicians as "the great harmonizer." He had been one of the three highly strategic county reviewers from 1918 to 1924 but had been defeated for re-election in 1924. That was his last essay for public office, although he retained the powerful office of ward committeeman. In addition, Nash was another "fat cat." So profitable was his sewer-contracting business that in 1925 his name was included in the list of the ten Chicagoans having the highest incomes.[26] It was well known in Chicago that Nash Brothers did more sewer-contracting business than any other firm. During his term as reviewer, Nash had had much contact with leading businessmen, who were—then as now—interested in the friendship of tax officials. In the conduct of his sewer business he had also had innumerable contacts with every local government. It was in this context that he had become friendly with Edward J. Kelly, chief engineer of the sanitary district and president of the South Park Board.

This was the caliber of one of Cermak's early Irish allies in his *putsch* for leadership of the party. Many of the lesser-fry Irish chieftains not only were reluctant to support the "Bohunk" in beating the Irish for the boss-ship but also were afraid of retaliation at the hands of the Irish leadership in case the Cermak attempt failed. With Nash openly in Cermak's camp these fears were decreased. The great importance of landing Nash is recognized by every politician interviewed, pro-Cermak and anti-Cermak. Henry Sonnenschein, Cermak's secretary, said that "Nash instigated the movement to Cermak."[27] James C. Denvir, defender of the Brennan heirs, charged that "Nash delivered the Irish."[28] Although most of these manipulations were very secret, late in 1928 all newspaper reports describe Nash as a Cermak follower.[29]

The recruiting of Nash had other than psychological values. Also important was his wealth. Many have said that Cermak "bought the organization." According to the Rosenberg confession, Rosenberg gave Cermak $30,000 in 1929 in order to help liquidate the debts of the Democratic organization. Whether Cermak settled these debts at fifty cents or thirty cents on the dollar, there still remained a gap of from $30,000 to $60,000. Although Cermak by this time was quite prosperous, there is every reason to believe that he did not relish disbursing his own money for political purposes. There seems little doubt that some of the remaining money came from Nash. Besides money Nash also had that best of all political currencies, jobs. This patronage, on his own payroll and upon those of some political friends, was useful, especially when added to the great patronage controlled by Cermak. Mr. Denvir stressed the fact of so many politicians on Cermak's and Nash's payroll as one of the most important elements of Cermak's success.[30]

The situation in broad outline in the fall of 1928 before the general election found Cermak—already in alliance with Rosenberg, Nash, and a great number of lesser cohorts, with money and jobs—facing the Brennan heirs, who held the managing committee of the party, controlled by Martin J. O'Brien, chairman, and T. J. Crowe, secretary.

The managing committee was formerly the real heart of the local Democracy. It was through this body that Sullivan and Brennan had ruled. Its membership was not legally fixed but was appointed by the party chieftains. It included ward committeemen as well as other leaders who were important to the faction controlling the managing committee. Cermak had long been a member of this body, but it had merely functioned as a Brennan rubber stamp. It was under the authority of this committee that all important party decisions were ratified and announced. It was here that slates were made and political fortunes created or destroyed.

By contrast, the Democratic central committee (of which, fiction said, the managing committee was the executive body) of which Cermak was chairman, had relatively little power beyond certain legal functions such as nominating judges of the circuit court. It was for this reason that Cermak had been allowed to keep this position—one of considerable honorific value—during the period when his influence with Brennan was at a low ebb. The membership of this body by law included each of the now fifty ward committeemen and those from the country towns. Thus there was considerable overlapping of membership in the two party organs.

Despite the more strategic position of the managing committee, active support of the majority of the ward committeemen insured control of the party and of every organ of the party. Cermak's logical move, then, was to demonstrate such support. The vehicle for this demonstration was the famous round-robin letter. Cermak, with yeoman assistance from Rosenberg and other allies, circulated this epistle among all the ward committeemen.[31]

In effect, the signers of the letter declared their support for Cermak as the successor to Brennan. According to one informant, the round robin was a skillful and completely unexpected coup. "Before T. J. Crowe, O'Brien, Clark, and the rest woke up, Cermak had a majority."[32] All informants agree that great pressure was exercised in order to obtain signatures. Many committeemen allegedly signed because of fear—fear of loss of jobs held either by them or by friends and relatives. Others signed because they were promised nominations or appointments. Rosenberg's revelations leave little doubt that some money also exchanged hands. Finally it is alleged by a Cermak foe that several signatures were forged.[33]

With this telling stroke added to the other positive items in the Cermak column, the already less powerful opposition became even more weakened. Gradually, more and more ward chieftains and office holders were detached from what was then known as the "Sherman Hotel crowd." Although rumors of the secret struggle were rife, the press did not report these early machinations, possibly because of interest in the fall elections; but by December, 1928, many conflicting stories were published referring to the rift.[34] By November the schism was so deep that Cermak did not appear in the Sherman Hotel headquarters once the election had taken place.[35] As soon as the election was over, some hasty political reporters were writing that "Cermak Ranks New Chief of Democracy."[36]

The same kind of headline was written a month later: "Democrats Hail Cermak as New Chief."[37] This headline was based upon an important coup but hardly signified complete victory. Cermak had merely demonstrated temporary ascendancy over the Brennan heirs by convening in *Pat Nash's office* (rather than in the headquarters of the organization) a caucus of most of the newly elected Democratic officials. The caucus considered the distribution of newly gained patronage and decided that ward committeemen would be recognized directly by officeholders in filling positions. This plan was in opposition to that of Martin J. O'Brien and T. J. Crowe, who wanted a patronage subcommittee of the managing committee to supervise the distribution.[38] The response of these leaders to Cermak, rather than to the managing committee, marked the formation of two groups out of what had been the Brennan machine.[39] However, the attendance of these leaders in some cases did not signify bolting the managing committee. John S. Clark continued for a long time as part of the high command of the Brennan heirs, although he participated in the Cermak-Nash caucus. Sheriff Traeger and Recorder Clayton F. Smith, also present, did not as yet completely desert O'Brien and Crowe. The same is true of Sweitzer, who during this struggle was something of a chameleon.[40] Other newly elected officials who did not attend telephoned to say that they wished to be considered "in the caucus," but they had no intention of bolting the managing committee.[41]

Nevertheless, the caucus demonstrated great Cermak strength.

Whether an attempt will be made to unseat O'Brien-Crowe depends upon their attitude and conduct toward the new program. Cermak told his followers he entertains no desire to have the managing committee placed in the hands of new officers. He explained that he had long fought against Brennan's so-called one man rule of the party and that he was against allowing the organization to come under the domination of a few men.[42]

Though T. J. Crowe and O'Brien were out of office, their adherents, Clayton F. Smith, John Conroy, and John Traeger, had been elected as recorder, assessor, and sheriff, respectively.

What else did the Sherman Hotel crowd possess? One cannot overestimate the power of the desire to retain Irish dominance, which was strengthened by virtue of being in control of the managing committee. It was easier to guard an entrenched position than to take it by force as Cermak was constrained to do. Finally the Sherman Hotel group had a certain amount of sentiment on its side in the form of Brennan's deathbed testimonial. According to Joseph Gill, his brother-in-law, as he was dying he declared his will for the Democratic organization and asked Gill to convey his message. According to Gill, Brennan's dying desire was that Michael L. Igoe be elected national committeeman and Martin J. O'Brien remain chairman of the managing committee.[43]

Needless to say, whatever the sentiments of the nearly two thirds of the ward committeemen who were Irish, Cermak did not honor the testament. What was more embarrassing, neither could one of the designees, M. L. Igoe. Igoe was at this time minority leader in the legislature, and he was one of the five commissioners of the South Park Board. Edward J. Kelly was the other Democratic commissioner. Although the Republicans were in the majority, the Democrats shared control by virtue of a bipartisan arrangement with Thompson-Crowe-Barrett Republicans. The Democrats' share was so great that Kelly was president and Igoe auditor.[44] But Igoe's term as commissioner was to end in February, 1929, and he would face re-election by the judges of the circuit court. The nominations of the Democratic judges are made by the central committee of which Cermak was and had been chairman. Several Democratic judges owed their positions to Cermak. It seemed doubtful that Igoe could be re-elected if Cermak chose to exercise a veto through "his" judges. (It should be remembered that among these judges were such dependable Cermak supporters as Fisher and Kerner.) Thus, Igoe, whom many expected to be the real leader of the Brennan heirs, was for a time neutralized in the face of many rumors that he would be "traded off" by Cermak.

Although A.J. denied these rumors,[45] Igoe's strength for some time was not openly opposed to Cermak, although eventually he was to be troublesome. Cermak did not wish to drive the Irish out of the party. All he wanted was that they submit. Since Igoe for the time being was quiescent, he was allowed to become national committeeman, as Brennan had requested. It is doubtful that Cermak would have agreed to this had he felt secure in his control.[46]

Kelly, Igoe's colleague on the park board, was also checkmated in his desire to join the Cermak opposition.[47] His close ties with Pat Nash were instrumental in this, as well as fears for his reelection when his term expired.

In similar ways other Irish leaders were either neutralized or recruited to the Cermak camp. This was not restricted to his own party; he also dealt with Republicans. But he began blazing new paths in bipartisan arrangements. The old Brennan deals were amalgamated although, as we have seen, Cermak, independently of Brennan, had had long and cordial relationship with Robert E. Crowe and satisfactory dealings with Thompson. But Crowe had lost for state's attorney, and the new incumbent, Swanson, was a Deneen man. Since 1908 Cermak had made it his business to be on the best terms with the chief county law-enforcement and prosecuting officer. A.J. had a healthy respect for indictments and grand jury investigations.

Besides, he read the election returns well. Not only had Crowe lost, but his ally "King Len" had been thrown out of the governor's chair; and Deneenites had captured most of the county offices won by Republicans. Wisely, Cermak decided to deal with the faction which controlled the state's attorney's office (against the wishes of the Sherman Hotel group), even though the Crowe-Thompson-Barrett crowd still controlled the local Republican organization and Thompson still held the city hall.

And so he dealt with the Deneen faction's local chieftain, newly elected State's Attorney Swanson. The deal had two parts; organization of both the South Park Board and the sanitary district by combination of Democratic and Deneen commissioners and trustees. The Sherman Hotel group desired that these bodies be controlled as they had been before, by coalition with the other major Republican faction. But Cermak was adamant and had his way because of his control over the judges who held Igoe's job in escrow. Thus the sanitary district, which now had only seven trustees—three Democrats, three Crowe-Thompson-Barrett Republicans, and one Deneen Republican—was organized, and the Deneen trustee, Elmore, was elected president. In exchange, the Deneen judges joined the Democrats in re-electing Igoe.[48]

Although this deal assured Cermak that "Swanson was in his pocket,"[49] there was considerable bitterness among the Sherman Hotel crowd. They charged that Cermak had paid too much to Swanson-Deneen in the way of patronage and in the person of the presidency of the drainage board. It was alleged that in making the deal Cermak had double-crossed trustee Harry A. Berger, to whom he had promised the presidency of the district.[50] This charge was never made public, but the deal for the division of patronage was. Trustee Ross Woodhull admitted to a state senate investigating committee that Deneen forces were given the presidency, the chairmanship of two important committees, and 40 per cent of all patronage.[51]

An element in Cermak's successful coup with respect to the park board and the sanitary district was the fortuitous—for Cermak—outbreak of the notorious "whoopee" scandal which involved the previous administration of the sanitary district. This was precipitated by the action of civic groups as soon as the election placed the new state's attorney in office. As a result, indictments were returned against eleven persons—trustees and top officials.[52] The state senate also conducted an investigation. The most flagrant instances of graft, mismanagement, payroll padding, illegal favors, and nepotism were found. Among those indicted were T. J. Crowe (who had been president of the district, but had failed to be re-elected in 1928); James Whalen and John J. Touhy, trustees; and Edward J. Kelly, chief engineer.[53]

T. J. Crowe was in the very top of the Sherman Hotel command; Whalen and Touhy were not far behind him in stature. All three were ward committeemen. The importance of Kelly has already been indicated. The quality of the exposures, the amount of civic wrath engendered, the prospect of facing indictments demanded by a reform state's attorney who was "in Cermak's pocket"—all of these threw not only the defendants but their friends in the Sherman Hotel into something of a panic.

There is little doubt that Cermak used this misfortune of his opponents to good advantage. Some informants who must remain anonymous stated that Cermak offered the defendants immunity if they agreed to go along. But the history of the case by itself gives concrete assurance that a deal had been made. Analysis reveals that Cermak was the only person at this time who was in a position to arrange the deal, because of his relationship with Swanson, and with Judge Fisher, who both as chief justice of the criminal court and as a trial judge became deeply involved in the developments.[54] The indictment against Kelly was quashed early in the case, and the prosecutor never attempted new indictments. After much delay and trickery, and Judge Fisher's insistence upon sitting in the case (against the opposition of the prosecution on the ground that Fisher's friendship with the defendants was prejudicial), sentences were returned on February 5, 1932.[55] Touhy and Whalen were among the three acquitted.[56] It was no coincidence that T. J. Crowe was among those found guilty. He and another trustee were given sentences of one to five years. Apparently Cermak was less confident of Crowe than of Kelly, Whalen, or Touhy. However, Crowe was probably never intended to go to prison, for none of the convicted persons spent a single day in jail.[57] It is not unlikely that Cermak wanted the pending sentence only as a threat. The preparation of Crowe's appeal was allowed to take sixteen months.[58]

Because of the many delays, the sanitary-district case hung like a pall over the Irish elements of the party for several years. It was not until December, 1932, that Whalen and Touhy were acquitted. Crowe's appeal was still pending when he died. There can be no doubt that the freedom of action of the Sherman Hotel group vis-à-vis Cermak was circumscribed by these facts. But before it was over, Cermak's control had been consolidated so tightly that they could not overturn it, except upon his death.

Throughout the entire period of this struggle accusations were made and rumors emerged in the newspapers, all purporting to show that Cermak was manipulating every string to capture the party. Cermak regularly replied to these charged with innocent disclaimers—except for occasional Freudian slips. In December he was busy denying "trading off Igoe." He also denied using "Swanson's name as a bludgeon" to this end or to the end of effecting a sanitary-district agreement with Deneen, or, finally, toward a Cermak-Deneen reorganization of the county board.[59] In the early days of the battle he was in the habit of denying any knowledge of any deals with Deneen-Swanson, on the one hand, but of reiterating from time to time that such combinations were "beneficial to the rank and file of the party."[60]

However, there is reason to believe that the Sherman Hotel group was not idle during the period that Cermak was plotting its demise. It too made threats to those of its followers who seemed to be changing their loyalty. It too attempted to use bipartisan arrangements to stymie Cermak. One such attempt went to the core of Cermak's strength, the county board. During December, 1928, and January, 1929, there seemed to be a campaign to organize the county board against Cermak. Cermak made this charge in public, and inasmuch as he was not interested in driving any Democrats out of the party, it is doubtful that he would have made such a statement unless there was some truth in it. He made it plain that the plot was organized by anti-Cermak Democrats and anti-Deneen Republicans.[61]

This charge was repeated several times and reporters wrote of it as fact rather than innuendo. Charles V. Barrett of the Crowe-Barrett-Thompson-Brundage organization was at one time reported as one of the instigators. He attempted to woo the support of the county commissioners by offering them preferred positions on the ballot when they were to run for renomination in the spring of 1930.[62] Barrett's (and the Sherman Hotel boys') plans did not succeed.[63] Nor were A.J.'s enemies even able to maintain what strength they possessed. Almost daily reports indicated more and more Irish leaders attending one or another Cermak caucus. Everyone who saw the handwriting on the wall discarded Irish solidarity for more practical considerations.

With everything going well for Cermak, and much headway made toward party control, he was stricken by illness and confined to his room. The attack occurred on January 25, 1929, in A.J.'s hotel room. In spite of it, he attempted that night to preside over a meeting of the county board. There he again collapsed. The diagnosis was the same as in 1925-26: colitis and gastric complications.[64] Three physicians announced that no operation was planned for the time being. It was stated that he had been "suffering from melancholia" ever since the death of his wife on November 24, 1928. Not to be regarded as a coincidence, in view of his emotional state, the making of his will was announced on the same day he collapsed.

Mrs. Cermak's death had not been a sudden one. It was preceded by months of serious illness. A.J.'s entire arduous senatorial campaign had been conducted with the knowledge of this illness on his mind. When the campaign ended, he turned all his energies toward wresting the leadership of the party from the Sherman Hotel boys. In the midst of this struggle, Mrs. Cermak's death occurred, but the demands of A.J.'s career were still present. When the funeral was over, more taxing work, including his duties as county board president, remained. Then came physical collapse.

He was bedridden but did not cease his work until February 6, 1929, when, accompanied by a daughter and a granddaughter, he went to Florida to recuperate. Newspapers on February 13, 1929, carried accounts denying reports of the day before which had described another attack. The attacks *per se* were not denied but it was claimed that the reports had been exaggerated.[65]

But there is no doubt that his illness was most serious. He did not get back to his desk in Chicago until May 5, 1929.[66] This single siege had lasted for nearly three and one-half months. For a man who lived politics every day of his life, that was severe punishment. Moreover, A.J.'s enforced exile from the political battle-front was especially intolerable at this time, for the battle against Brennan's boys was far from won in January. Cermak was terribly worried about what was going on in Chicago during his absence. He kept in close touch with his Chicago assistants, particularly Henry Sonnenschein, and undoubtedly son-in-law Graham as well. Daily reports were made to him, sick as he was. Of special concern to him were rumors circulated by the opposition that he intended to capture the party by any means he could. Doubtless this was true, but Cermak was not anxious to have it publicized. He wired his denial.

At the present time any ambition or aspiration to leadership of my party in Cook County is most distant in my thoughts.

My chief concern is the condition of my health, and next to that, carrying through of a plan of retrenchment and economy in administration of county affairs by which the apparently unavoidable deficit...may be kept as low as possible.

I have not inspired, or considered any move such as has been attributed to me in recent newspaper articles—the seeking of party leadership—and I cannot too strongly condemn any attempt to create dissension in the party by spreading of such misinformation.[67]

But the rumors persisted in Chicago. Boetius H. Sullivan, of Cermak's group, announced that a split was to occur by virtue of the quarrel between Cermak and Brennan's friends. Most Democrats agree that a schism was approaching. M. J. O'Brien admitted that "A lot of the fellows believe there will be a split."[68] There were more than rumors. Cermak's power was challenged in the newly inaugurated city council in April. The Sherman Hotel boys, in combination with non-Deneen Republicans, captured the committee on committees and deposed Cermak's good Czech friend Toman from an important chairmanship.[69] Evidently the Irish were not yet ready to surrender. A.J.'s comment from Florida was: "So they want a fight. I will be back in Chicago next week; I am ready for whatever they want."[70]

His return did not result in an open clash, however. In July Cermak and O'Brien worked together in planning the slate for the following April primaries. But the lull was temporary. The squabbling began again in August, as the party started discussions of the November judicial elections. Again A.J. and O'Brien were at odds.

THE JUDICIAL ELECTION OF 1929

Cermak understood very well the importance of this first election in which his leadership was being tested. It is likely that failure at this point would have allowed the former Brennan heirs to recapture the party machinery. Rosenberg's confessions are replete with references to the importance attached to winning:[71] "I was building up Cermak at that time. It was his first fight as leader of the party and, as Cermak became leader, that made me so much stronger. We were looking to put Cermak in the Mayor's chair, which we did."[72]

The judicial election concerned only twenty places on the superior court and two vacancies on the circuit court. Seventeen incumbents were running for re-election for the superior court positions.

Cermak and O'Brien differed as to plans for the election. O'Brien wanted to continue earlier coalitions with the Crowe-Thompson-Barrett Republicans, while Cermak at this time was opposed to coalition. He declared publicly that coalition was not the best way to find judicial candidates of the highest caliber and integrity; actually, his objections to coalition with Crowe-Thompson-Barrett were based on his fears that this faction and Irish anti-Cermak Democrats would work together to try to reduce his own power.

In the course of this quarrel, Cermak succeeded in capturing all the party machinery. The first portion of the contest concerned the respective authority of the two local Democratic administrative organs: the managing committee, headed by O'Brien; and the central committee, of which Cermak was chairman. Legally, Cermak's committee was the one that was allowed to nominate the judicial candidates for his party. However, precedent was on the side of the O'Brien forces, for Brennan had virtually dictated judicial nominations since 1921. But now Cermak insisted upon invoking his legal prerogatives. Not only did he convene the nominating convention, he also had himself empowered by the convention to appoint two advisory committees to help select judicial candidates.[73]

Although both the advisory committees were well packed with Cermak men, one of the committees began to cause A.J. great anxiety by conferring with the Crowe-Thompson-Barrett Republicans.[74] A.J.'s fear of the Irish-led opposition now moved him to strip it of its control of the managing committee. He called a meeting of the county central committee. The meeting adopted a resolution setting up a committee to recommend new machinery for the conduct of the party. The party reorganization was completed by October. Cermak retained his position as chairman of the county central committee and Clayton F. Smith became the new chairman of the reconstituted managing committee. The career of O'Brien's managing committee came to an end.

Meanwhile, A.J. had slightly altered his anticoalition stand, saying that if there were to be coalition, the Deneen faction had to be allowed to enter into it. In that case the Democrats should receive eleven of the twenty-two positions and the two Republican factions should divide the remaining half.[75] In the end, A.J. went ahead and pushed through the nomination for all seventeen sitting judges, Democrats and Republicans; but, declining coalition with Crowe-Barrett-Thompson-Brundage (C-B-T-B),[76] he nominated two of his men and one Deneen man for the three vacant positions on the superior court bench. Three of these sitting Republican judges were Deneen men, among them Cermak's old nemesis of 1916, Judge Gemmill. Cermak's motto: "You don't keep books in politics" was here clearly illustrated. The pact with Deneen was made explicit by nominating one Democrat and one Deneen Republican for the two circuit court vacancies to be filled. The C-B-T-B faction also placed the non-Deneen Republicans on its slate. Since Illinois law did not permit candidates to run on two tickets, these judges had to decide on which slate they would remain. Ultimately, they remained upon the Cermak slate, to A.J.'s great disappointment. He seemed to hope that somehow he could get rid of the C-B-T-B judges and then divide their vacancies with Deneen. But that was not to be.

The C-B-T-B Republicans invented an unusual technique. The so-called city-hall element entered only a truncated ticket of five candidates, while an avowedly Brundage-sponsored "People's Ticket Against Coalition" entered a slate of twelve candidates. As A.J. tirelessly charged in the campaign, although Brundage professed aloofness from the city-hall gang, in reality his ticket and the city-hall ticket were complementary.

Regardless of the behind-the-scenes jockeying for power that was responsible for the Cermak slate, it was generally conceded that his slate was definitely superior to that of the Republicans. He had approval of most of his candidates by the Chicago Bar Association, and the support of an independent committee of "respectables."[77] With this as a start, plus the scandalous public record of C-B-T-B, it was not surprising that Cermak's appeals to the better elements were successful in this campaign, notwithstanding the opposition of the Better Government Association (whose two chief officers had been important Anti-Saloon League officials) abetted by members of the Protestant clergy.

The Cermak ticket scored a signal victory, completely overwhelming the C-B-T-B ticket. The magnitude of the victory is more impressive still, considering that C-B-T-B had been very successful in the alderman elections held in February of that year.

But once more A.J. paid for political victory with his health. He did not suffer a complete collapse as he had on the last occasion, but it was necessary for him to make two recuperative trips. One was made immediately after the election. The second, more protracted one, did not end until just before the 1930 primary election. He was trying to gather together all the strength of his powerful but ailing body for the first full county election of his reign.

THE ELECTIONS OF 1930

In retrospect it is easy to be a shrewd political analyst. Contemporaries have a much more difficult time. The political situation in 1930 is an excellent case in point. From a later vantage point, a discernible Democratic trend away from the Harding, Coolidge, and Hoover landslides might easily be identified. But in the summer and fall of 1929, and even in the winter and spring of 1929-30, the rapid shift away from the Republicans does not appear to have been generally discerned by contemporary observers.[78] Although the stock-market collapse of 1929 had caused serious traumas in the nation, such generalized economic results as mass unemployment and danger of starvation were not so clearly seen. This must be borne in mind in considering the 1930 elections in Chicago.

If the 1929 judicial campaign was an important one for Cermak, the 1930 elections were infinitely more so. In the case of the former, one can make a case for the view that Cermak was in luck, that his great victory was at least in part due to C-B-T-B mismanagement in not agreeing to the kind of coalition which Cermak might have found acceptable. Also, in 1930 the prize was much greater: most important county offices (including Cermak's own); five sanitary-district trustees; several circuit judges; fifteen municipal judges; the chief justice, clerk, and bailiff of the municipal court; several state offices and a very large state legislature ticket; and finally, all members of Congress (including two Congressmen-at-large) and a United States senator.

A.J. could not begin intensive work on the campaign until after the judicial election in November, after which he took his short recuperative trip. However, even during that early period conversations about the slate were being conducted. The search for top man on the ticket was ended by slating J. Hamilton Lewis for the senate. Lewis was perhaps not quite the man Cermak would have chosen ideally; but he was, after all, indebted to the Dunne-O'Connell-Harrison wing.[79]

Since this was Cermak's first major election, and since his victory over the Brennan heirs was far from absolute, making the slate was full of the most delicate problems. On the one hand, Cermak had to have a good ticket and a balanced one; on the other hand, it had to be so designed that the Irish opposition could not make a comeback. At the same time Cermak had to be careful not to push his opponents into entering an organized opposition Democratic slate.

One of the big question marks was Cermak's intentions regarding his own office as president of the county board. From mid-January until March, he declared that he would not seek re-election because his health did not permit it—his physicians had advised against it, and his family was also opposed. He spoke of getting an "even better vote-getter" than himself to replace him, although he made it clear that he did not intend to relinquish party leadership. The possibility that he would not run caused enormous consternation among the Cermak forces. His absence would weaken the whole slate; and it was also feared that the Brennan boys would be able to nominate one of their own clique to the county board presidency. A.J. was urged and pressured from many sides to reconsider, beginning in January with a delegation of "prominent citizens and professional men—mostly Democratic, but some Republicans."[80] Finally, Rosenberg, Nash *et al.* prevailed upon him to agree to be a candidate at least through the primary.[81] This decision, together with his return from his Florida recuperative trip, stopped a minor splurge of would-be candidates who had announced themselves against Cermak-chosen nominees.[82]

Thus, Cermak allowed himself to be drafted, although this time it was not a case of playing a coy, hard-to-get game, but a real choice between health and politics. Once committed, he made the gamble on his health without reservations. For he did not withdraw after the primary, and to the primary itself he directed the maximum of effort. Although he had eliminated an opposing primary ticket, he wished among other things to replace certain ward committeemen whom he distrusted. Therefore, he ordered a full primary campaign and expressed a desire for a record-breaking vote.

Here again we have Rosenberg's testimony to give some indication that considerable money was spent in this campaign. Rosenberg's admitted contribution directly to Cermak was only $20,000, but more was given to other chieftains.[83] There is no doubt that there were many other sources of income as well.

Since the Cermak slate was unopposed, the Democratic primary campaign was aimed at the prospective foes for November. Cermak's favorite charge against the Republicans at this time was that they were withholding tax bills until after the primary. This matter was close to A.J.'s heart, since the county board was in difficult straits.

But his most wicked barbs were still reserved for his old Dry enemies, in the persons of the officials of the Better Government Association and the candidates they supported. The wildest of his many encounters with these enemies occurred in the halls of the staid City Club. The very fact that A.J. would venture into such a den of Republicanism, there to face the attacks of candidates of the Business Men's Republican Organization, is indicative of his political courage—or of his insensitivity. Even on this alien terrain he showed Cermaklike lack of tact. Of his long-time Anti-Saloon League foe, E. J. Davis, who was sitting nearly at his elbow, he said: "He is in nothing better than a racket."[84] Similar remarks followed; and the meeting adjourned with shouts of "Liar!" "Throw 'em out the window!" and "Down with 'em!"[85] When Davis offered to make public his books and bank accounts and challenged Cermak to do the same thing, A.J. replied with a grin: "The government is examining my books right now."[86]

Most of the campaign, although strenuous, was not so violent as this. Cermak felt that the efforts made in the primary were well rewarded by the "unprecedented primary vote."[87] He believed this augured well for the fall. The Republicans, who spent huge sums, polled a combined vote much smaller than they had polled in 1928, while the Democrats polled 50,000 more than in 1928.

Cermak's slate was broken in only one instance. Edward J. Barrett defeated Cermak's candidate M. C. Zacharias for state treasurer.[88] Comparison of the 1926 slate—the last Brennan slate for the same offices—with this first Cermak slate, provides a telling difference in ethnic composition. Although A.J. had to be careful not to drive the Irish into an open revolt, the number of Irish names on the 1930 ballot was in somewhat different proportion than in 1926, when of the forty-two most important offices on the ballot twenty-five had been filled by Brennan with Irish names. On this slate, in addition to Zacharias, such names as Coliani, Myer, Friedman, Kaspar, and Walkowiak appeared prominently. The shift is most clearly seen in the nominees for justice of the municipal court. In 1926, of twelve nominated by Brennan, eight were Irish.[89] In 1930, of fourteen nominations for the same offices, only five were Irish.[90]

An unusually large number of changes occurred in the personnel of the ward committeemen between 1928 and 1930. The 1930 list shows ten new names.[91] Here one finds in three instances Irish names replaced, in one case by a Pole, in another by a Czech. At least two committeemen extremely unfriendly to Cermak were defeated, and he was directly responsible for electing at least six of the new committeemen—Kaindl, Jensen, Zintak, Weber, T. J. Bowler, and Voss.

In the Republican senatorial primary, Deneen's opponent was Mrs. Ruth Hanna McCormick, daughter of the famous Republican national boss and wife of the late Senator Medill McCormick. She defeated Deneen by a huge vote and led the city-hall forces (now Thompson, Harding, and Snow) to victory in most of the other offices.[92]

The general-election campaign got off to a slow start—except for that of the senatorial candidates. In Chicago "Big Bill" held the center of the stage as he bellowed against the city's financial groups that were insisting he reduce the city budget. Later, he began a typical Thompson tirade against Mrs. McCormick and the *Tribune*. Now that Deneen had been defeated, Thompson's anti-*Tribune* bias easily overcame any party loyalty he might have had. This bias was increased by Mrs. McCormick's statement that she had won the nomination without Thompson's help. To the consternation of his chief lieutenants, Harding and Snow, Thompson's continued diatribes against Mrs. McCormick were gradually putting "Big Bill" in the camp of the Democratic candidate, Lewis, and thereby injuring the whole Republican ticket. These men and other Republicans never forgave Thompson for this. Some explain his behavior as motivated by his appetite for re-election in 1931. It is supposed that he did not want to be attached to a loser, and Mrs. McCormick, handicapped by revelations of her huge primary expenditures and by her sex, did not seem to have much chance of winning.[93]

In addition to Thompson's antics, the election campaign was somewhat further handicapped by another major crime show. On June 9, 1930, Jake Lingle, police reporter for the *Tribune*, was killed; the celebrated Lingle case occupied the press and the city for over a month.[94] Then, on July 14, Jake Zuta, a well-known gangster, was machine-gunned while in the custody of police, by fellow gangsters in downtown Chicago.[95] The Lingle and Zuta cases resulted in the convening of a special grand jury for the consideration, once again, of crime and politics.

Under the circumstances, the political campaigning was delayed. It was just as well for Cermak. An advisory committee Cermak had appointed in 1929 to study county road construction made its report in July. It reported that inefficient construction had cost the county $1,677,000 since 1927.[96] The release of the report at this time was not good news for Cermak and gave additional reason for delaying the campaign.

As a result of these factors the local campaign did not really begin until as late as October 26—except for the Wet phase. Cermak announced his party's issues as prosperity, Prohibition, and taxation. It surprised no one that he blamed the lack of prosperity, as well as high taxes, upon Prohibition—and that he blamed the Republicans for all three.[97] Nor was it surprising that Prohibition practically monopolized the field of oratory.

Since March signatures had been collected for the referendum petitions, and Cermak had made several addresses. He was extremely disturbed when he learned that certain Republicans also wanted to circulate petitions for repeal. He stated from the first that "the issue is a Democratic one and we won't submit to its being carried off by outsiders."[98]

So central was the issue made that Cermak announced: "We're going to denounce and read out of the party any of our candidates who want to run as drys."[99] He castigated the Republican candidates who did not respect the overwhelming Illinois preference for Wetness. They were, he said, creatures of the Anti-Saloon League, as was the national Republican organization. Since this was so, he charged that the local Republicans who were sailing under Wet colors were insincere, and that the Wet petition they were circulating was a hoax.[100]

He was able to devote very little time to his personal campaign. The few speeches he made emphasized the record of tax savings made by the county board and by generally increased efficiency in county administration.[101] However, he relied, in addition to his general prominence, upon many impressive indorsements, particularly for the public-welfare accomplishments of his board.[102] As usual, he had strong backing from veterans' groups.[103]

Cermak and the Democrats won by a nearly complete landslide. Not only was almost the entire ticket elected, but the majorities were huge.[104] The Democrats elected a senator, a congressman-at-large, and the majority of district congressmen.[105] In the county the victories were even more sweeping. Every office for which a single official was elected was won. And in every collegial body a great majority was gained. Of fourteen associate justices of the municipal court, ten Democrats were elected. A Democrat defeated the incumbent chief justice of the municipal court, who had served for twenty-four years. Democrats were elected as clerk and bailiff of this court.[106] Cermak was re-elected to his third term as president of the county board. His majority was one of the largest gained by any of the candidates.[107]

All of the ten county commissioners elected from Chicago were Democrats; three of the five county town commissioners were Democrats.[108] All five members of the sanitary board elected were also Democrats. A clean sweep was made of five vacancies on the circuit bench and one on the superior bench.[109] Sizable gains were made in the legislature.[110]

This was the greatest Democratic victory in Illinois in a generation, and perhaps the greatest since the Civil War. To complete Cermak's triumph, all of the Wet issues were overwhelmingly approved, in Chicago, in the county and in the entire state.[111] And, to cap the climax, in spite of the disclosures pertaining to waste and irregularities in county road building, almost $5,000,000 in bonds for county purposes was approved. Cermak had proved himself handsomely.[112]

But even in the midst of his triumph, his old foes attempted insurrection. The Democrats had elected five sanitary trustees in November, giving them eight of the nine trustees. The lone Republican was Elmore of the Deneen faction, who had been elected president of the district in 1928 through a Cermak-Swanson deal. M. L. Igoe, Brennan's national committeeman designee, and John S. Clark attempted to wrest control of the district from Cermak. They made a vigorous fight but lost. They controlled four of the Democratic members, and Cermak the other four. Deneenite Elmore sided with Cermak's men, and the revolt died as Cermak's designee, T. J. Bowler, was elected president. A.J. appeared to have written finis to the Brennan boys, and to be at last the acknowledged boss of local Democracy.

Nevertheless, the Irish were to make one more attempt to send "the Bohunk" back to Lawndale. This attempt came about as Cermak reached for the star of the mayoralty.

THE

1931

MAYORALTY

ELECTION

As soon as the dust settled on the astounding Cermak-led Democratic victories of 1930, the task of selecting a new mayor was hard upon Chicago. As the almost indiscernible postelection lull settled upon the city, it might have been prognosticated that the pending election of a mayor would end as a hectic affair.

"Big Bill" Thompson was approaching the close of his third four-year term—twelve years of hysteria, vulgar vaudeville tactics, and unmitigated rabble-rousing perhaps unsurpassed in urban politics. The twilight of his career coincided with a great crisis in the life of the city. The crisis was compounded of a near bankrupt city treasury, the economic disruptions of the depression, and a mammoth crime problem.

THE MAYORALTY PRIMARY OF 1931

The Choice of the Democratic Candidate.

Few could have doubted that Cermak intended becoming a candidate, given his earlier ambitions in this direction and the magnitude of the November, 1930, triumphs.[1] Cermak was undoubtedly strong enough to take the nomination, but he had the added problem of winning the election. He would jeopardize victory if he could not retain party unity. He finally succeeded in this effort, and once again "demonstrated at once his ambition and his adroitness by sidetracking a long list of democratic 'availables' and securing united party support for his own nomination."[2]

It required two months of constant negotiations of the most delicate sort to bring this about. Conferences with other would-be candidates, with leaders of the still ambitious ex-Brennanites, and with leaders of civic reform and "silk-stocking" elements were held daily. In these discussions Cermak proved himself highly skilled in the art of group diplomacy, in having his will prevail in a great variety of contacts. In almost every case the conferees supported candidates other than Cermak. Yet without exception he succeeded in winning them to his point of view: Cermak for mayor.

Relatively speaking he had much less difficulty with "the forces for good" than with the irreconcilable Irish. For two years Cermak had made every effort to retain the support of the Irish, while at the same time fortifying his own leadership. In repeated skirmishes with the ex-leadership, Cermak, after emerging victorious, never exacted vengeance. Thus, although T. J. Crowe and M. J. O'Brien were unseated from control of the party managing committee, both retained their ward committeemanships. (A few less important Irish ward leaders were purged.) John S. Clark, one of the top ex-Brennan boys, remained chairman of the council finance committee and was chairman of the managing committee's executive committee. Gill and Horan were nominated and elected to their highest offices in 1930. But to M. L. Igoe, Cermak made the greatest concessions. Igoe, originally considered the logical successor of Brennan, was temporarily neutralized by Cermak, who had him elected national committeeman in accordance with Brennan's alleged political will, and also arranged his re-election to the lucrative position as South Park Commissioner.[3] Further, Igoe not only was permitted re-election as state representative but was also allowed to continue as Democratic floor leader. Nevertheless, in the negotiations for the mayoralty candidacy Igoe proved to be perhaps the most stubborn stumbling block.

He was by no means the only one among the Irish who had the mayoralty bug. The day after the November, 1930, election, numerous trial balloons were released. On November 5, 1930, Cermak, Igoe, Clayton F. Smith, and Herman C. Bundesen were

reported as leading contenders for the Democratic nomination.[4]
There was even talk about a renaissance of the Dunne-O'Connell
and Harrison factions because of Lewis' great victory in the senatorial race.

The preliminary skirmishes between Cermak and the Irish took
place during a party junket to Hot Springs a few days afterward.
Almost two weeks later, Cermak, in reply to a reporter's question,
gave a partial list of possible candidates. He was less coy than in
1927; now his name, like Abou Ben Adhem's, led all the rest.[5]
In addition to the persons mentioned above, Cermak listed Pat
Nash, Sweitzer, Judges John S. Sullivan, Denis E. Sullivan,
Michael L. McKinley, John P. McGoorty, and banker Melvin
Traylor. In the meantime, patronage difficulties also acted as a
wedge between Cermak and the Igoe-Clark opposition, helping
to muddy the already confused mayoralty picture.

It has been an open secret that the relations between Cermak and Igoe
have been a bit strained since the Hot Springs, Arkansas, powwow, when the
first call to discuss patronage precipitated a wordy battle in which a dozen or
more leaders became involved.[6]

After the return to Chicago it had appeared that "harmony" had
been restored, but this "harmony" was only on the surface. Since
the return to Chicago, Cermak's conferences had been largely with
his own cohorts such as Nash and Roger Sullivan's son, but "The
spectre of mayoralty ambitions hovered around the background.
It cast the largest shadow over the meetings which resulted in the
organization of the Sanitary District with Trustee Thomas J.
Bowler in the president's chair."[7]

Apparently the failure of their sanitary district *putsch* convinced
Igoe and Clark that they could not match strength with Cermak,
and toward mid-December they appeared to be more conciliatory.
But also important in this new attitude was the position of powerful banking and business groups.

The "others" have become an important factor in the situation, not being
politicians but an element identified with the financial and commercial leadership of Democratic leaning and capable of enrolling the kind of support
that stood back of Col. A. A. Sprague until he withdrew his name from
consideration.[8]

Colonel Sprague was by no means the only "silk stocking" whom

Cermak had to discourage and at the same time recruit in his behalf. Many other outstanding businessmen wanted to be mayor, and things looked promising inasmuch as Thompson seemed likely to be the Republican nominee. Cermak's powers of dissuasion were considerable. There is no doubt that he pointed out the dangers of facing Thompson calumny to would-be candidates. But he also used other and more negotiable instruments of persuasion. Thus, Colonel Sprague was promised a desirable cabinet position.[9] It is also alleged that he agreed to name Francis X. Busch as corporation counsel and in general to appoint good qualified heads of departments.[10]

While it gradually became clear that A.J. was making himself acceptable to business leadership, the Irish contingent did not give up. Meetings and caucuses continued to be held in an effort to come to an agreement.[11] Now Clark was the ace-in-the-hole.[12] By this time Cermak was impatient, and petitions were in circulation asking him to be a candidate.[13] However, he still wanted a united party, and he still continued the palavers. He had little to lose by continuing the talks and attempting to convince the Irish that they should become reconciled to his candidacy. He was certain of the support of a preponderant number of Democratic ward leaders.[14]

At this time it was estimated that Cermak could have got the votes of forty committeemen, while Clark could at best count upon only fifteen. Moreover, before Clark entered the picture it was believed that "Cermak had made substantial progress in ironing out dissension" and that "Igoe and Alderman Michael Kenna have been won over."[15] But it required another week before the Clark candidacy was scotched. Again the dynamics of the deal were not revealed in the press. Mr. Clark, however, declared that he had been offered $250,000 to withdraw—not by Cermak but by the men who were interested in Cermak's nomination.[16] Also in the deal was the promise to have the indictment against T. J. Crowe and the others involved in the sanitary-district scandal nol-prossed. Mr. Clark did not specify what happened to the offer, but he did say that that night "the organization candidate was sold out in a hotel room."[17]

By December 18 the word was out that "it was all set for Cermak." What relief A.J. experienced! This news meant, in the words of an able observer, "elimination of the factor that appeared most threatening to Cermak—the possibility of meeting a candidate of Irish extraction closely identified with the late Mayor Dever's regime in the primary."[18]

On December 24 Cermak received a handsome Christmas present—the unanimous indorsement of the county managing committee.[19] Also indorsed were Alderman Edward J. Kaindl for city treasurer, Major Peter J. Brady for city clerk, Judge Francis B. Allegretti for the superior court, and Alexander L. Smietanka for the municipal court.[20]

A few days later, Cermak had been unanimously endorsed by the Cook County Democratic members of the state legislature and had prevailed upon them to support his designees for legislative floor leaders: Igoe for the House, and Courtney for the Senate.

Results of the Primaries

Thompson's opposition within his party was irreconcilable. A portion of former Thompson allies, led by Snow and George E. Harding, supported Municipal Judge John H. Lyle; the Deneen forces supported former Alderman Arthur F. Albert. Both the *Tribune* and the *Daily News* were rabidly anti-Thompson, but they too divided forces, the *News* supporting Albert, the *Tribune* backing Judge Lyle.

The Republican primary was an incredibly vulgar freak show, consisting largely of exchanges of insults between Thompson and his two rivals, and Thompson and the *Tribune*. Thompson, of course, outdid his enemies in this sort of contest. When the insults were ended and the votes counted, it seemed that the electoral success was in direct ratio to the skill in invective. Thompson won, defeating Lyle by nearly 70,000 votes, and Albert was far behind.[21] As in several previous essays, Thompson owed his victory to a divided opposition.

Although Cermak was unopposed in the primary, a great effort was made to roll up a large primary vote. The efforts were crowned with success, as Cermak received a vote of 234,258.[22] This was nearly 56,000 votes greater than the votes for Dever in the practically uncontested primary of 1923. All other members of Cermak's slate won by majorities of at least three to one.

After the primary, a single weak link developed in the united Democratic front, the appearance of an "independent" candidate, Dr. Bundesen, the coroner. Although A.J. gave the impression that an independent candidate was of no consequence, in reality great activity began to head off the Bundesen candidacy. In a conference with political and businessmen allies, A.J. said frankly, "Bundesen wants to be health commissioner, and I'll give it to him," adding: "I think he'll withdraw."[23] The next day Bundesen's headquarters was dismantled.[24] Five minor candidates also filed, but the election commissioners (Cermak-controlled) adjudged all petitions as illegally filed.[25] Thus, every early effort to divide Cermak's supporters and thereby conquer was unsuccessful. The campaign settled down to a short, vicious contest between the two major contenders.

THE MAYORALTY CAMPAIGN

On the eve of A.J.'s fight for the biggest prize, the odds were tremendously in his favor. By clever manipulation he had for all practical purposes eliminated all opposition in his party. He had, in the words of Irish leader Clayton F. Smith, Cermak-backed chairman of the party managing committee, "the Democratic party united and enthusiastically behind the candidacy."[26] And he was more determined to win this election than any in his long career: "I've got every dime I could beg or borrow on this campaign," he confided to one of his assistants.[27]

In contrast to Cermak, Thompson headed a crumbling, shadow organization, demoralized by the prospect of defeat and weakened by desertions. Ending twelve years of administrative and political buffoonery, having just emerged from a cutthroat primary, he had to run against the onus of frequent disclosures of every form of corruption and of crime and lawlessness. His was also the onus of a far from popular national Republican administration, whose continued support of the "noble experiment" was not exactly popular in Chicago. He carried, as well, the handicap of long association with Len Small. And finally, the depression weighed heavily upon Chicago, and the wheels of political fortune had made it a Republican depression. Before the campaign, city employees had had payless paydays (in contrast to the county employees for whom

Cermak had been able to borrow money from friendly bankers), and unemployment, evictions, and soup kitchens had become commonplace. One observer noted that "no Republican who ever lived could have carried Chicago that year. The city was bankrupt."[28]

One of the few civic groups to stand with Thompson was Cermak's ancient foe, the Better Government Association, which stomached without criticism the typical Thompson antics. The Association itself, however, was at this time directed by the prejudices of its leadership. Most clear-cut among these prejudices—in addition to Dryness—was a fundamentalist, Puritan, quasi-"Know-Nothing" animus. It was therefore not surprising that the Better Government Association chose white Protestant Thompson—only a sometime and very weak Dry—over foreign-born, "liberal" Cermak.[29]

Deserted by almost all his supporters, except the Negroes, Thompson fought back with the ferocity and the ethics of an animal at bay, launching into "a campaign of vilification and quarter truths."[30] Unsuccessful in his early attempts to divide Cermak's supporters by having other candidates entered, he now tried to cause rifts among the various Cermak backers—the ethnic groups, the business groups, certain religious groups, and newspapers. Ethnic, religious, racial, and economic prejudices were all invoked to a degree probably never equalled in an American campaign.

Tony, Tony, where's your pushcart at? Can you imagine a World's Fair Mayor with a name like that?

I won't take a back seat from that Bohunk—Chairmock, Chermack or whatever his name is.

Calls himself a "Master Executive"... you Negroes know what a *master* is... who kicked all the Negro caddies off the golf courses?

The Master clubbed the Irish... the Poles... off the ticket... first time in my life I ever saw the Irish lay down without a fight.... Vote for me... jobs for Poles... jobs for Negroes... jobs for the Irish... you can call the City Hall the Capitol of Poland....

I built the schools, the playgrounds, kept the water pure, reduced the price of the kiddies' milk... the Chicago skyline... that's my skyline.

Saving Tony... saved six millions out of a $10,000 salary... built the county jail without a boiler... grafts on coal and paving... *Chicago Tribune* called him a horse-thief, now they say elect a thief.

Tony, the Jew-hater, supported by Rosenwald, the faker-philanthropist,

[205]

trying to hedge his way out of hell with his benefactions ... Tony, the tool of the loop millionaires, reduced their taxes by his reassessment, in league with the International Bankers trying to get us into the League and send our boys to die in some European boundary dispute ... Tony, the German-hater, called the German-Americans Huns.

The Tribune, greatest curse Chicago ever had, sold out to King George to get 1,200 square miles of Canadian land ... lies about me dribbling with idiot pictures ... can you believe their type? Wrote my obituary when they thought I was dying ... wouldn't they like to know how I got it?—called me an international figure always on the front seat of the great American band-wagon (not the garbage wagon like Tony) ... now look how they lie about me.[31]

Thompson continued such diatribes against "the dictator" and "the Master" after coupling "Tony, the Master," and "Silas, the grafter."[32]

There is a vast literature on strategy in campaigning, and there are many monographs on particular campaigns. Unfortunately, not many definite answers have been found concerning the utility or effectiveness of campaigns. Among professional politicians and among many scientific observers the tacit assumption traditionally has been that campaigns were influential, if not determinative, in elections. That is to say, the particular kind of campaign, the organization, the strategy used, were closely related to success or failure at the polls.

However, the widely acclaimed study by Paul F. Lazarsfeld and associates indicates that the effectiveness of campaigns may be largely a myth.[33] It was discovered that long-term social, political, and economic trends were more determinative of the intention of voters than a short campaign—irrespective of the quality of the strategy used. It was suggested that the true functions of campaigns were to reinforce the intentions of the confirmed party-column voters and to energize the lethargic. Relatively few conversions were made; however, where a change of voting intentions did occur, it was found that campaign propaganda was instrumental.

It must be remembered nevertheless that the Lazarsfeld study, even were it definitive—and it is not—was not concerned with a local, urban election. More important, however, is that Cermak, his cohorts, and the opposition all acted on the assumption that the campaign—and a particular kind of campaign—was of the highest importance for winning the election. Thus, although the relative influence of the campaign of 1931 cannot be assessed, its analysis provides an index to the political behavior of the many groups and individuals involved, and of A.J. himself, in what he regarded as the crowning effort of his career.

The organization for an election campaign is not unlike the organization of a military campaign. In each case there are forces of cadre or regulars, a hierarchy of command, special and general staffs, and a whole series of auxiliary units. This pattern was faithfully followed in the 1931 campaign.

The Democratic Regulars

The Regulars were made up of the normal party organization. In this echelon the Democratic party was organized into a unified, smoothly working machine, with A.J. and his associates firmly at the helm. All of the party decision-making machinery was in their hands, and the overwhelming majority of the ward committeemen were loyal. Beyond them there was a larger body of efficient precinct captains and other workers. Because of the large patronage available, because of a fair and effective method of its distribution on the basis of party work, and because great care was taken that party funds regularly reached these lower levels, the loyalty of most of these persons was assured.

The Irish regulars of the old Brennan faction were "in," and on the surface solidly and enthusiastically supported the Czech candidate. Such former foes as Igoe, Clark, and even Martin J. O'Brien played important roles in the campaign.

Because of Cermak's past record of favorable contacts with Jewish leaders, it came as no surprise that he had their complete, openly avowed, and enthusiastic support. This group included Adolph J. and Joseph Sabath.[34] Probate Judge Henry Horner was treasurer of Cermak's campaign, and one of his closest campaign advisers.[35] Also deeply involved was B. F. Lindheimer, recently appointed as a South Park Commissioner through Cermak influence. The most important Jewish organizational leaders, Arvey

[207]

and Rosenberg, were, as has been mentioned, committed to Cermak for mayor, and extremely active.

Although in Chicago before the present Democratic era Italians were in the main Republicans, and although Thompson had given generous appointments to Italian leaders, A.J. had long since started to cultivate the Italian vote by the tested device of placing persons with Italian names on the ballot and appointing them to patronage positions. As a result, by 1931 there were a number of Italian leaders in the Democratic party, the majority of them Cermak creations, and vigorously on his side.[36] Polish Democratic leaders also flocked to his colors.[37] A.J. had stayed on good terms with the relatively few German leaders among local Democracy, and in many instances was responsible for the creation of new German leadership on whose loyalty he could depend. In this campaign the support of these leaders was very important, since Thompson had always enjoyed great popularity among German voters.[38] Even among the Scandinavians and the Negroes—among whom to speak of Democratic leaders was at that time almost a contradiction in terms—A.J. had managed to lay a little groundwork, so that by 1931 what fledgling Democratic leadership existed in these groups was in his pocket—if not, indeed, his own creation.[39]

It is scarcely necessary to say that every Democratic Czech leader was unequivocally behind Cermak. A.J. had made nearly every one of them, and even the exceptions required his continued support, A. J. Sabath and Cervenka being cases in point. Of the others, all foursquare behind A.J., the names are by now familiar: Sonnenschein, Vopicka, Denemark, Venecek, Police Captain Ptacek, John O. Hruby (elected to the state assembly in 1930, when son-in-law Graham became a state senator), Cepak ("Cermak's walking-stick"), Bicek, Triner, and Toman. All had prospered in the past from A.J.'s benefactions; most would continue to do so as long as he was alive. Most of them confined their activities in the campaign to work among the Czechs; however, Triner acted as general purchasing agent for campaign materials.

A.J. had a large number of supporters, of course, who do not fall into any of the Democratic categories just mentioned, and numbers of Democratic individuals contributed heavily to his campaign, within as well as without the party. Important among these were Mayor Harrison, Francis X. Busch, Barrett O'Hara, J. Hamilton Lewis, and Bundesen.

Thompson's Organization

Thompson's forces presented a strong contrast to Cermak's. The once conquering machine was rusty and lacked many of its most important parts. Thompson was not supported by the Deneen faction which had backed Albert for the mayoralty. He was also opposed by State's Attorney Swanson. Lyle, who had been the candidate of all the anti-Thompson forces not members of the Deneen group, was tacitly for Cermak. Thompson's old friend Robert E. Crowe did not openly desert him, but his support was hardly more than nominal.[40] In 1934 when Crowe (along with Harold Ickes) was read out of the party, he charged that the majority of the Republican county committee had knifed Thompson and supported A.J.[41] Barrett, who had wanted to be the mayoral candidate but was frightened off by "Big Bill," deserted and supported Cermak.[42] Corporation counsel and ex-Insull attorney Ettelson also decamped.[43] Perhaps the most serious loss was George Harding, one of Thompson's oldest and richest supporters, who had parted with "Big Bill" when the latter insisted on supporting Lewis in 1930. "Big Bill's" first boss and early mentor, Lundin, not only did not support him, but avidly opposed his former pupil. Lundin lieutenant Dr. J. Dill Robertson, who had run against Thompson in 1927, was even more vehement in his anti-Thompsonism. He tried to get the rock-ribbed Republican Hamilton Club to indorse Cermak.[44]

Thus, Thompson could rely only upon what was left of his tottering machine, the city patronage employees, and a portion of the Republican ward committeemen and office holders. Among important factional leaders only Len Small was in his corner; but Small was out of office and had to make restitution of $600,000 to the state of Illinois; and few thought he would ever be an important figure again.

An amazing number of the party chieftains who deserted Thompson publicly indorsed Cermak and the tacit support of more was generally acknowledged. During the campaign such reports as these were common: "More G.O.P.'s Back Cermak";[45]

"Three Lyle Chiefs Back Cermak; Whole Organization for Democrats."[46] The organized support of the Deneen (Albert) and Lyle groups was observable as early as March.[47] Thompson's council leaders, Alderman Oscar Nelson, L. B. Anderson, and Cronson were on Rosenberg's list. It is worth noting that Anderson was a Negro and Cronson represented a ward with a large Negro population. An attempt was obviously being made to cut into even this last solid Thompson block of voters.

The wealthy and influential Republican respectables who supported Cermak will be described presently. Suffice to mention the Cermak-for-mayor Republican Club, whose board of directors sounded like a cross between the Blue Book and a roster of the directors of Chicago's richest corporations. Its honorary chairman was Franklin McVeagh, who had been in Taft's cabinet.[48]

Support of Auxiliary Groups

Business groups. Cermak's manifold appeals to the business elements in the past were handsomely rewarded in this campaign. Business leadership was almost unanimously in his corner. The then president of the Chicago Association of Commerce, Robert Isham Randolph, indorsed Cermak, as did several former presidents. Sewell Avery, president of Montgomery Ward, and William G. Dawes were Cermak backers. Silas Strawn, ex-president of the Industrial Club and the Commercial Club, was a Cermak booster, and typical of some of the tremendously powerful persons in this category. Like the others, he was not only a power in the business groups but a society leader and a leader in civic and professional groups.

Also supporting Cermak were Frank J. Loesch, Thomas E. Donnelley, George Getz, Robert J. Dunham, Julius Rosenwald, Harry Eugene Kelly, D. F. Kelly (president of the Fair), and Edward Hurley. Melvin Traylor, president of the First National Bank, was one of the strongest backers, and in 1932 became Cermak's choice for favorite son in the national convention. Loesch, counsel for the Pennsylvania Railroad and president of the Chicago Crime Commission, was also a past president of the Union League Club as well as the Chicago Bar Association. The support of these men and the groups they represented was channeled through a network of Cermak-for-mayor businessmen's committees. Characteristic of the kind of support given by these committees were the activities of the most important among them, the Businessmen's Committee for Cermak.

This committee was the over-all campaign unit representing businessmen and appealing to business groups and the general citizenry. Its membership included persons from both parties. Its president was Colonel A. A. Sprague, and it was he who represented the business community on Cermak's campaign high command and who was the chief liaison officer with this powerful economic class. Sprague was eminently fitted for this job. He was wealthy, indubitably a "silk stocking," a leader in veterans' affairs, and a dabbler in politics. It was now well understood that he would have one of Cermak's chief cabinet posts, commissioner of public works.

The secretary of the committee was Benjamin F. Lindheimer, a representative of business groups other than those with which Sprague was associated. Lindheimer was also a rich businessman, although not a socialite except in Jewish society. He was a close friend of Horner, with closer ties to party politics than Sprague had.[49]

Sprague and Lindheimer ran an efficient committee. They had dozens of businessmen as members and what appeared to be unlimited funds. Such an ambitious program of broadcasting was used—daily, for several weeks—that they required a director for radio campaign activities. There were full campaign addresses by business leaders. These addresses comprised the "Cermak Prosperity Parade." There were spot announcements. The committee sponsored many meetings and made business speakers available for still others. It had a high voltage newspaper campaign, with large numbers of half- and full-page advertisements.[50]

Although Thompson, with his own wealth and "good family," had a history of friendly ties with some business leaders, many of them had by 1931 deserted him. Aside from the other factors influencing these people, Thompson's personal flamboyance and clowning had done much to alienate them. Moreover, not only had Thompson not recognized business interests through appointments as A.J. had, but he had never used advisory committees to give these powerful persons a feeling of participation.

[211]

Labor groups. In this campaign A.J. enjoyed substantial labor support, but it did not begin to compare with the near unanimity of business groups. Cermak's chief labor lieutenant was Martin P. Durkin, then vice president of the Chicago Building Trades Council, in 1953 to become the first Eisenhower Secretary of Labor.[51] The fact that A.J.'s labor support was less than it had been in other elections was not so much a result of his unceasing promises of a "business government," "economy," "efficiency," and abolition of "unnecessary jobs," although these were programs not popular with organized labor. Nor was it a product of his close association with big business leaders, although this situation, also, could not have endeared him to many men with caps. It was a result of Thompson's own relatively favorable relationship with organized labor.

In general, clowning, "plain-folks" "Big Bill" was close to union leaders. One of his sometime cronies was Alderman Oscar F. Nelson, for long years the vice president of the Chicago Federation of Labor. It may have been owing to Nelson's influence that the Chicago Federation was on Thompson's side in this election.[52] James C. Petrillo, ubiquitous leader of the Musicians Union, had also had a long association with Thompson. A long and rather impressive list of other Thompson labor-leader friends is found among the roster of members of the Thompson-founded and Thompson-dominated Fish-Fry Club.[53]

The underworld. During Cermak's tenure as county president, his enemies made continuous charges about A.J.'s close contacts with the underworld; and although no evidence was ever offered to substantiate these, the whispers continued during Cermak's tenure as mayor. Thompson, whose group had a long record of Capone affiliation, attempted during the mayoralty campaign to turn these charges upon Cermak. In the minds of rabid Drys, the fact of Cermak's Wetness and the support of the organized Wets were sufficient proof of underworld connections.

For obvious reasons it is not possible to determine accurately the political sympathies of the underworld. It appears unlikely, however, that Cermak could have enjoyed widespread hoodlum support in 1931. His diatribes against them during the campaign, including such specific items as his warning to ward bosses that he would not countenance any deals with the underworld,[54] must have made some impression, to say nothing of his close association with avowed foes of gangland. The fact that persons like Loesch, Brunker, and Harry Eugene Kelly were involved in A.J.'s campaign undoubtedly would have cooled gangland's attitude toward him, even assuming their desire to be with a probable winner, now that these and other reformers had proceeded, in the words of an enemy, "to anoint Cermak, garb him in the robes of 'reform' and put a halo on his head."[55]

That Thompson enjoyed underworld aid and favor is supported by more evidence. In his twelve years as mayor, he had not yet got around to honoring his many pledges to drive out crime, although he had the police power—which Cermak as county-board president lacked—as well as close political ties with State's Attorney Crowe. It is notorious that the Capone headquarters moved back to within the shadow of the city hall upon Thompson's reelection in 1927. The McSwiggin case and the Lingle escapade uncovered other ties between Thompson and the underworld. Capone associate Serritella was a Thompson ward committeeman and a member of Thompson's cabinet. Thompson's admirer, Stuart, admitted that the Capone gang had been recruited by Thompson during the 1927 election and that "Schemer" Drucci had been in the Republican camp, as well as Marty Guilfoyle, gang boss of the northwest side.[56] Summing up the crime situation during Thompson's reign, Charles E. Merriam remarked: "Your own common sense will tell you that Chicago is in the grip of criminal gangs and racketeers."[57]

Ethnic groups. In this election, as always, the support of ethnic groups was urgently sought by both candidates. Support of the various ethnic political leaders, discussed earlier, was translated into the support of the voters in these groups to varying degrees. The backing of ethnic leaders and groups not primarily political was indicated in the campaign in the usual ways: banquets, meetings, and receptions where the candidates were honored; formation of supporting ethnic clubs composed of nonprofessional politicians; and the indorsing of candidates by outstanding nonpolitician members of the various communities.

There were fewest such manifestations for Cermak (but none

for Thompson) from the Poles, perhaps because they were considered to be one of the most deliverable of groups, one in which ethnic ward leaders and the church exercised a high degree of control. Thus, Polish support for Cermak can be roughly adduced from the support given him by the important Polish political leaders. Both A.J. and Thompson had good relations among the German community; but Cermak attracted greater numbers of prominent individuals, such as Oscar Mayer, William Rothman, Ernest J. Kreutgen, and Ernst Buehler. A.J. also received indorsements from many prominent Jews—Julius Rosenwald; New York's Dr. Stephen S. Wise; bankers Lawrence F. Stern, Alfred K. Stern, and Oscar G. Foreman; and many others. Numbers of Jewish auxiliary campaign groups supported him. Although Thompson was supported by the Progressive Jewish Businessmen's Association for William Hale Thompson for Mayor, this group gathered to itself no individuals of the prominence of A.J.'s backers.

The Negro community, however, remained overwhelmingly with Thompson, its loyalty manifested by large numbers of meetings and by the support of the chief Negro newspaper, the *Chicago Defender*. Thompson attempted also to capitalize on Cermak's defeat of the Irish within his party; and it is true that the only known "Democratic club for Thompson" during this campaign was one formed among the Irish. But this single indication of Irish nonpolitical support did not match A.J.'s impressive list of indorsements by prominent Irish, as well as by various Irish-American, clubs.[58]

Women's groups. In the United Societies days, Cermak had been considered the chief *bête noir* of women leaders such as Mrs. Merriam, Mrs. Bowen, Miss Vittum, Miss Addams, and other fighters against the "dance hall evil." But as county president, Cermak got to be on very good terms with the same ladies. Many of them were appointed to citizens' committees and gradually changed their opinions of A.J., so that by the time of the mayoralty campaign former female enemies had become political friends. A.J. capped his improving relations with women—especially "silk-stocking" ones—by nominating and electing one of their members, Amelia Sears, to the county board in 1930.

Thompson, after the years of clowning and open town, had become an even less desirable figure to women voters than A.J. had been. He had a women's organization working in his behalf in this campaign but did not have the assistance of the outstanding women leaders.[59]

The most important Chicago women's groups in political affairs were the Women's City Club, the Illinois League of Women Voters, and the Chicago Women's Clubs. Although each acted in an investigative and educational capacity only, the leaders of these clubs were women of prestige and of considerable political experience. A.J. had tremendous support from these women, not in their official capacities as officers of the women's clubs but rather in *ad hoc* campaign committees.

There were many Democratic, Republican, and independent women's organizations and committees working for A.J. in this campaign. The caliber of their leadership and prestige can be indicated by some typical figures: Mrs. Kellogg Fairbank, leader of society, prominent in civic groups, and former Democratic national committeewoman; Jane Addams; Mrs. Joseph T. Bowen (Louise De Koven), former Republican national committeewoman; Mrs. Elizabeth Conkey, Democratic national committeewoman.[60]

The "silk stockings." In Chicago political vernacular, this term refers to the highly placed, socially prominent, presumably independent voters. Often "silk stockings" are prominent on the periphery of the two great parties, in civic groups, in business groups, and in women's clubs. Therefore, many leaders of this element have been mentioned. There were also specialized independents who could not be classed in any of the above groups but who exercised influence in political affairs and whose support was an asset. Such persons were Dr. Graham Taylor, Harriet Vittum, Jessie Binford, and Wilfred S. Reynolds. These individuals represented many others who were favorably impressed by A.J.'s work in the field of public welfare.

More important, however, was the active support of men like Charles E. Merriam and Harold Ickes. They were experienced in campaigning, had the respect of large numbers of independents, and were the backbone of the campaign aimed at the independent voters. Merriam and Ickes were impressed by the danger of continued Thompsonism. The day after Thompson announced his candidacy, Merriam and Ickes sought Cermak out and personally offered their unsolicited support. Cermak offered no commitments, nor were any demanded.[61] The attitude of these two men was symbolic of that of the great majority of independents of this class, who believed that A.J., whatever his faults, was better than Thompson.

Civic organizations. Chicago is honeycombed with myriad civic agencies of every description. These usually cooperate with the newspapers rather than with the parties but can be very influential in elections when aroused, and at other times they carry much weight in determination of public policy. They are nominally nonpartisan but, inasmuch as their memberships are largely from the upper economic strata, they tend to be heavily Republican in both local and national politics.

The overwhelming support given to Cermak by large numbers of leaders of these organizations has already been indicated. Even the Municipal Voters' League—to which A.J. used to refer most often as "the damned Municipal Voters' League"—had its secretary indorse him. He used the League's 1921 assessment of him as one of the chief indorsements of his record.[62] The Bureau of Public Efficiency, which had protested some of A.J.'s actions as county president, showed its friendship through the backing of Rosenwald, its founder and financer. The Citizens Association issued a statement completely indorsing Cermak's purchases of forest-preserve land since 1926. In sum, one can say that A.J. had the support of the leadership of every civic organization except one—the Better Government Association.

The press. The utility of newspaper support is a commonplace of American politics. In recent years there has been a tendency to belittle the influence of the press on elections, but it can be said with some certainty that in 1931, when the use of the radio in politics was in its infancy, it played a major role.[63]

Gosnell found that in Chicago neighborhoods where certain newspapers were read the response of the voters was correlated to the political attitudes of the newspapers. One reason he adduced for the inefficacy of the press in some elections was the fact that the metropolitan dailies did not reach the homes of some of the submerged groups.[64] But A.J. was particularly strong in these submerged groups. Therefore, if he received strong support from the metropolitan press, it would assist him in those areas where he was least strong.

Chicago had a large and vital foreign-language press. There were a dozen dailies whose circulation was over 20,000. The total circulation for all foreign dailies was over 400,000, and for the weeklies, over 600,000. In this election, following the lead of their subscribers, most foreign-language journals were in Cermak's camp—even such a normally Republican organ as the *Greek Star*. The Negro press continued to back Thompson; and he was also supported by *L'Italia*.

But, for Cermak especially, the attitude of the metropolitan dailies was of much greater significance. The major dailies in Chicago in 1931 were the *Tribune* (circulation 470,000); *Daily News* (390,000); and the two Hearst organs, the *American* (450,-000) and the *Herald and Examiner* (280,000).[65]

Perhaps fortunately for the community, in most cases these journals were not united in policies. In the 1931 election the *Tribune* was vigorously anti-Thompson from preprimary days. This was merely a continuation of the old *Tribune*-Thompson quarrel, which had been preceded by *Tribune*-Lorimer antipathy.[66] The *Tribune* made good use of its facilities in attempting to defeat Thompson. It ran 275 column inches of editorials and 617 column inches of cartoons intended to discredit Thompson.[67]

When Thompson faced Cermak in the general election, the *Tribune* continued its battle to end Thompson's career. Cermak received *Tribune* backing in twenty-two marked ballots, in 297 column inches of cartoons, and in 106 inches of editorials.[68]

The *Daily News* was traditionally Dry and was considered to enjoy the greatest prestige among business, professional, and independent elements. The *News*, unlike the *Tribune*, had rarely been friendly to Cermak. It could hardly have been, with its unequivocal support of the "noble experiment." However, its animosity toward Thompson was even greater. As in the case of the *Tribune*, the anti-Thompson crusade of the *News* was carried to the general election, making A.J. a generous gift of unexpected backing, although the support was less pro-Cermak than anti-Thompson.

The two Hearst organs had been friendly toward both candidates although much closer to Thompson. However, they did not relish backing a loser. To escape the dilemma, they pretended neutrality in this election. However, their pro-Thompson bias could not be hidden. Thus, a mild indorsement of Thompson was made by the *American*,[69] and the *Herald and Examiner* published twenty-five column inches of anti-Cermak cartoons.[70]

Cermak was thus the beneficiary of the support of the two dailies which overtly took sides and was secretly opposed by the two other major organs. Unquestionably, his was the bulk of newspaper backing.

Issues and Appeals: Campaign Propaganda

Campaigns have always been largely propaganda duels, and often the side which is more skillful in the manipulation of symbols defeats a party which has more solid assets. The many victories of "Big Bill" were clear manifestations of this phenomenon on the local scene. The basic postulates of the art of propaganda were constantly in evidence in the campaign of 1931.

General appeals. The propaganda drive was undertaken simultaneously on two levels. The first of these consisted in attempts to appeal to the generality of voters, the citizens of Chicago seen as an undifferentiated mass, not as a collection of smaller units of political opinion. These appeals were chosen on what may be called the "against sin" criterion. That is to say, the appeals were limited to "issues" to which no decent, God-fearing person could object. On the American urban scene the most foolproof appeals in this category include lower taxes, elimination of waste and graft, economy and efficiency, a crusade against crime, and the promise of an effective and nonpolitical school system. In Chicago, a "liberal" policy toward liquor can be considered as belonging to this classification.

Every one of these clichés was used by Cermak with nearly equal emphasis and intensity. Given the record of his opponent, this was perhaps inevitable. But all of these, and a few others, were wrapped in a general package which might most aptly be described as "salvaging Chicago's reputation." Thompson's behavior and his record, plus the important objective fact that Chicago did indeed enjoy world-wide notoriety, made an ideal target for this attack. What were the chief components of this poor reputation? They were lawlessness, vice, crime, and gangster domination; greater unemployment than in most other principal cities; graft and corruption of staggering proportions; high taxes; and a politically captive school board. A.J. called constant attention to these sad facts and their consequence: voters refusing to approve bond issues; the federal and other governments' refusals to appropriate funds to participate in the scheduled world's fair; strangers fearing to come to Chicago because of the gangsters, the city thereby losing the lucrative convention business; industries deserting Chicago, and the remaining industries becoming stagnant and frightened because of high taxes.

Because of the critical situation of the city, resulting from Thompson's iniquities, the rescue of the civic reputation was formulated as a great crusade to which all good persons—fathers, mothers, and taxpayers—were bound to contribute. And time after time, speakers and newspapers telescoped all of the issues into one: "The real issue before the people of Chicago now is the elimination of Thompsonism and everything connected with it."[71]

But anti-Thompsonism and saving the city were subdivided into several discrete appeals, each closely related to the over-all issue, reputation. The first of these was crime. A.J. was vehement in his attacks upon crime and backed his position by having introduced anticriminal legislation in the state assembly. The issue of crime—which he charged was caused by Thompsonism—was cleverly joined to other "against-sin" appeals. Crime helped cause the city's poor reputation; it helped cause unemployment and unfavorable business conditions; and crime in turn came about in part because policemen were harrowing citizens by attempting to enforce Prohibition.

The next major general issue or appeal was what may be called the fiscal issue, also closely united to the restoration of the city's reputation. A new mayor would be a sign of the city's rejuvenation, which would cause a rebirth of confidence in the city and in the government of the city. The confidence of citizens, of Chicago businesses, and of outlanders would cause the return of prosperity through a great increase in building and in manufacturing. Thus, prosperity would return and unemployment be ended.[72]

Cermak would end the crushing burden of taxation. He would because he had proved that he could: had he not performed this feat as county president? While the tax rate of other local governments had risen greatly, he not only had maintained the county's tax rate constant but had even lowered it. He would be able to accomplish this because he was an able administrator, as his record plainly showed. His first act would be to place the city's finances on a sound business basis. (Sometimes his first act was going to be to study unemployment, or to reorganize the police.) Next he would cause retrenchments and economies by eliminating graft. Then he would cause major reorganizations which would effect even more economies. As proof that Cermak was qualified to make good his promises, he and other speakers constantly referred to his record. A.J. regularly taunted Thompson about his reluctance to compare their records.

Last of the general issues was Prohibition. Of all the appeals, this one was least used with the mass of citizenry. A great many speeches contained no mention whatever of the matter; and when it was considered, the tone was a good deal more moderate than in former times. There were no attacks on "Dry Cossacks." Could this be A. J. Cermak, erstwhile leader of the United Societies, implacable enemy of the Anti-Saloon League? Even the Better Government Association, now affiliated with Thompson, was conspicuously ignored by Cermak.

There were good reasons for this restraint. Everyone knew A.J.'s position in this matter. Thompson was not a particularly good target for this appeal. He, too, was Wet enough, though a bit erratic in his attitude. But the most important reason for the lack of emphasis on Wetness was the fact that an extremely important group of Cermak backers in this campaign—large numbers of the business, independent, women, civic, and "silk stocking" elements—were Drys. Many of these persons unquestionably had to overcome considerable aversion in order to bring themselves to support Cermak. It was not wise to aggravate this condition. This is not to say that A.J. ever compromised his position on Prohibition. Nevertheless, the relative emphasis given the issue in this campaign was slight by former standards.

Selected parochial appeals and issues. The campaign could not be confined to appeals to the mass of citizens. The citizens of American urban areas—or so the politicians reckon—are seldom so civic-minded that they can be expected to respond to such general appeals alone. In unique or crisis situations there may be exceptions. When the large majority senses that the civic rot is so severe as to threaten not only complete governmental dysfunction but also the fabric of day-to-day primary relationships, then the public may act. Knowing this, politicians playing Cassandra have often tried to simulate crises. Thompson was the most skilled wolf crier in Chicago history, as he evoked the image of King George and battalions of Redcoats surrounding Chicago aided by a fifth column of international bankers.

But since such simulated crises do not usually succeed in arousing the majority of the voters, the general appeals are reinforced by an intricate network of appeals to special interests—to what may be called parochial groups. A.J. was a past master at this fractional approach. Although this election *was* one of those rare crisis occasions, these discrete groups were not neglected. However, since Cermak's role in this campaign was that of the leader of "the forces of good," his appeals to special interests were much less high-pressured than were Thompson's. Thompson really could not discuss the issues; therefore, he went after the parochial voter with bare hands.

The appeals to these groups can be classified in three categories. The first is an attempt to win loyalty and support by direct appeal to the self-interest of a given unit. This is usually rational, at least in part. Promises of jobs, or higher wages, or lower taxes illustrate this class. The second category of appeal is simply the recognition of the existence of a group as a group, or the recognition of the importance of a given interest. (Conversely, this may take the form of ignoring certain groups.) The appeal of "recognition" is the most favored one in the case of ethnic groups.

This recognition may consist of naming a park or a street after an ethnic hero. But a much more decisive sign of recognition is appointive or elective office. The traditional loyalties of ethnic groups to parties is often explained in these terms. Thus, the fact that the Democrats in Chicago elected a Bohemian as alderman in the 1890's is often cited as the reason for the party affiliation of the majority of Czechs. Similarly, the fact that the Republicans elected a Pole as state treasurer in 1906 is the explanation given for the large Republican bloc among Chicago Poles prior to 1931. The clearest illustration in this category was the nearly religious adherence of Negroes to the G.O.P. up to the present Democratic era. In Chicago they remained loyal to the disreputable Thompson machine until the very end, not only because of traditional historic bonds but because Thompson recognized them by relatively large numbers of appointments.

Although one may be impatient at the shortsightedness of this attitude upon the part of such groups, one has to understand and sympathize with the deep-seated emotional desires of submerged groups and out-groups for representation. The appointment or election of one of "our boys" gives a tremendous vicarious ego satisfaction to every member of the community. As one observer has put it: "To be recognized and represented by a crook is better than not to be recognized or represented from one point of view."[73] The classic appeal to ethnic groups has been of this kind. Once an ethnic representative is appointed or elected to office he often becomes a leader of his people, and he or other leaders have to be constantly recognized or rewarded.

The third category of special appeals is the use of indorsements by outstanding individuals of a group, or by organized groups themselves. The reasoning here seems to be that if one prominent Italian or one Italian club approves of a candidate, it will tend to make all Italians flock to the candidate's colors. Or, at any rate, large numbers of indorsements will create an illusion of victory and will motivate the undecided to get on the bandwagon.

Appeals to ethnic groups. Cermak used each of these three categories of appeals in attempting to win the support of ethnic groups. Appeals to rational self-interest were least emphasized. Unlike Thompson, A.J. did not make wholesale promises of jobs. He did not promise to make the city hall the "capital of Poland." He did not have to. He had proved himself in this respect to all ethnic groups. He had always distributed jobs to every nationality group. All these individuals had to do was to be good Democrats—that is, good Cermak Democrats. The closest attempt at the use of the rational appeal to self-interest came in calling attention to his position as a Wet and his role in the passage of the bill repealing the state Prohibition law.

This reliance upon his past performance is clearly indicated in Cermak's many speeches to ethnic groups, unique in the absence of parochial appeals. Indeed, the speeches to these groups differed little from addresses to downtown civic organizations. Although he was flanked by illustrious ethnic sons in every appearance before these groups, A.J. never referred to his sponsorship of these individuals for office, apparently feeling it unnecessary.

Thompson used the whole gamut of appeals to direct interest. A handbill, so worded as to make it appear to have been issued by Cermak forces, listed an impressive number of jobs given by Thompson to Negroes. Cermak's headquarters denounced the handbill as a forgery.[74] The handbill was designed to serve a double purpose: to put the onus of race prejudice upon A.J., at the same time reminding Negroes that "Big Bill" was a benefactor.

The "recognition" appeal was also tacit rather than made explicit by Cermak's own words. He never publicly promised recognition of any kind nor called attention to his record of recognition. But the very fact of the intensive campaign units made up of ethnic leaders was at the same time an indication of recognition and clear evidence of the desire for the support of these groups. In this category of recognition, Cermak did not have to boast. All any group needed to do was to consider the large number of offices which had accrued to their sons through Cermak's efforts, that is, all except the Irish. These officials of every group demonstrated A.J.'s belief in dividing the spoils. But Cermak's forbearance did not restrict his supporters. There were many kudos given to his "friendship for all races." Here is a typical accolade by an ethnic leader: "The public career of A. J. Cermak has been notable for many things, but one of his finest traits has been his fairness to every race, and his recognition of all our citizens in the matter of public offices."[75] A.J.'s friends did not have to search backward through his history for evidence. In this election there were contests for five offices. The five Democratic candidates were ethnically divided as follows: one Czech, one Pole, one Irishman, one Italian, and one with a German name (Kaindl) representing a Polish constituency. As for the use of the third category of appeals, indorsement, A.J. was more than richly supplied.

Cermak's appeals to ethnic groups were sharpened and made real by the introduction of what was called a racial issue into the campaign. Thompson's ravings on this subject were foul, bigoted, and self-contradictory. On the one hand he attacked Cermak because he was foreign-born ("Tony, Tony, where's your pushcart at? Can you imagine a World's Fair Mayor with a name like that?") On the other, he made blatant and crude accusations of ethnic bias on Cermak's part. Cermak was a "Jew hater"; he "kicked the Irish out of the party"; he also disliked Negroes, Germans, Poles, Scandinavians, and all the rest. Thompson loved them all—although he poked fun at Cermak and vulgarly rebuked him because Cermak's father had not fought with Farragut as Thompson's parent had. Balder appeals to antiforeignness and ethnic prejudice have rarely appeared in the history of American politics.

Thompson's most underhanded appeals were intended to discredit Cermak with the Negroes, the Irish, and the Jews. In addition to the forged anti-Negro document purporting to have emanated from Cermak's headquarters, Thompson made much use in speeches to Negroes of Cermak's campaign title, the "Master Executive." "You Negroes know what a Master is. If Thompson isn't elected you'll have to enter the World's Fair by a back gate."

The basis of Thompson's insistence that Cermak hated the Irish was simply that Cermak had taken the mayoralty nomination. "He is big enough to say to an Irish Democrat, 'You get out. I'm going to run for mayor.' "[76] Thompson pressed this ridiculous charge in every way, for he rightly suspected that, although A.J. had succeeded in retaining the overt support of Irish leaders, there was considerable animosity toward him in the ranks of the unseated Brennanites and other Irish. The active support of Cermak by Irish leaders, however, did much to contradict Thompson's accusations. Although A.J. himself denied them in an unusually temperate manner, Clark, Igoe, and others regularly took the rostrum on A.J.'s behalf, to attack Thompson's pleas for intolerance.

Thompson's other major effort along the lines of *divide et impera* was aimed at the Jews. Leading Jewish figures were lampooned and derided. Judge Horner was a favorite target; even more abused was Thompson's old enemy Julius Rosenwald, a "faker-philanthropist" who was supporting and financing the "Jew hater" Cermak. Thompson frequently repeated charges that Cermak was one of the organizers of a "restricted" subdivision, and that Graham, his son-in-law, was an officer of the corporation. He found a Jewish cat's-paw to take up and elaborate this charge: a Jewish Thompson-for-mayor club.[77]

But these hysterical attacks availed little. Cermak's long history of friendship with Jews, personal and political, was too well known; and the continuing public support of the overwhelming bulk of the leadership of the Jewish community—politicians and nonpoliticians, German Jews and Polish Jews—was more than a match for the anti-Semitic charges. The slanders about the restricted housing corporation were met head-on at a gathering of three thousand Jewish women in Rosenberg's ward, where every prominent Jewish leader appeared to give the lie to the anti-Semitic charges. The last prop was pulled from beneath the story by the revelation that Congressman Sabath (a bona fide Jew) was also a member of the accused real estate corporation.[78]

Appeals of this kind on Thompson's part carried an inbuilt doom, in any case. Because, in spite of his expressions of love for all "races," his nativist, Americanist bias could not be hidden. Neither he nor his high-pressure publicists seemed to realize that many members of other ethnic groups were foreign-born, just as Cermak was; and that Thompson's assaults upon A.J.'s background were understood as assaults upon them as well. They and their leaders reacted accordingly. This kind of statement, from a German leader, was a typical response:

> In this campaign there has appeared a ribald song deriding the name of the Democratic nominee. . . .
>
> To solicit any man's support on a basis of deliberate stirring of dormant racial, religious or any other prejudice, is vicious and un-American. And such appeal will be resented by the voters and reflected in an overwhelming victory for A. J. Cermak.[79]

In the early stages of the campaign, A.J. left his defense on this front entirely to others. Clothed in his new public dignity and restraint, he continued to ignore, or comment upon only in passing, Thompson's ugliest attacks. Not until the last week of the campaign did he allow the dam to burst. Even then, although he could not refrain from mentioning Thompson's vicious tirades in every speech of that final week, his replies were not in kind.

> ... he finds fault with my name. That's the same name I've always had, it has been honored by the people of Chicago and Cook County during my public career and I say I wouldn't trade it for all the mayor's jobs in the world.
>
> Of course we couldn't all come over on the Mayflower—or maybe the boat would have sunk. But I got here as soon as I could, and I never wanted to go back, because to me it is a great privilege to be an American citizen.[80]

Appeals to religious groups. Usually organized religions do not engage in active campaigning except insofar as certain ethnic groups tend to be members of a given religion. Thus, native Americans and Scandinavians tend to be Protestant (included, of course, is the Negro community); the Irish, the Italians, and the Poles are overwhelmingly Catholic; and the Germans and Czechs are divided between the two branches of Christianity. Among some ethnic groups clergymen take considerable roles of political leadership. In Chicago, Irish Catholic and Polish Catholic priests have sometimes preached political sermons and have urged votes for particular candidates.

Among the Protestant churches political activity is perhaps no more frequent, but it is quite openly avowed. In Chicago during this period, the chief political action group for organized Protestants and for Protestant clergy was the Better Government Association. The B.G.A. and many independent Protestant ministers were squarely behind Thompson. However, theirs was not the entire voice of Chicago Protestantism. An assembly of Congregationalist ministers, after being urged to follow the B.G.A. line, had this to say: "The interests of Chicago could be better served by voting for the present opponent of William Hale Thompson than by supporting an independent candidate."[81] The basis of this left-handed "indorsement" was given by one of the clergymen. "In my opinion Cermak is bad. But Thompson is worse."[82]

We have here a clear indication of the great distrust with which the Protestant clergy regarded Cermak. Recognizing fully the character of Thompson, some persisted in the support of "Big Bill," while others gave lukewarm approval to Cermak. The lack of rapprochement between A.J. and this group was largely due to his unabashed Wetness.

Cermak made no special religious appeals or appeals to churchmen or church members, except insofar as the anticrime appeals and the restoration of Chicago's reputation may have appealed to moral church affiliates. It is certain that they were not primarily aimed at this clientele. It is doubtful, in any case, that any moral appeals of such a confirmed Wet would be believed by the Protestant groups. However, Cermak had good organizational contacts with the Catholic hierarchy through his support by Catholic ethnic groups. All politicians, particularly on the ward level, make sustained efforts to remain on the best of terms with churchmen in their constituencies. Cermak had always followed this line, although he refused to compromise his Wetness. Among Czech clergymen this was not a great disadvantage. The leading Czech Protestant minister, the Reverend Vanek, was on the best terms with A.J. This was also true with respect to the Catholics, and by no means restricted to Czech Catholics. For many years Cermak had numbered among his friends the prominent Irish prelate, Reverend Frawley. His good relations with the Catholic church were furthered by the fact that his wife had been a devout Catholic and that all his daughters were educated as Catholics and were practicing Catholics.

Although Cermak made no religious appeals, Thompson did. In the first place, a considerable part of his campaigning in the Negro wards was conducted in churches. This was a product of the fact that the Negro churches were even more active in politics than other Protestant groups.[83] Since more than half of the Negro voters were church members (and about one quarter of these attended church regularly), it is clear that religious appeals here would be expedient.[84]

Late in the campaign, Thompson also attempted to arouse religious prejudice against Cermak. A.J. warned the voters that campaign documents alleging Cermak's anti-Catholic bias would be distributed. His headquarters announced that 200,000 bills were to be distributed in front of churches. A later report indicated that the bills had been distributed on Easter Sunday; Protestant churches had also been included in the distribution. For the Protestants, a different set of inflammatory charges was made against Cermak.[85]

Although it is known that the "church vote" is largely a chimera, in a bitter contest such as this no organized groups are neglected.

Appeals to business groups, civic organizations, newspapers, and "silk stockings." In general, the leadership of each of these groups comes from the same social and economic stratum. There were minor variations among the appeals to these groups, but on the whole the similarities were much greater than the differences. In brief, the broadest specific appeals to these groups were identical with what has been described as the anti-Thompson issue—the appeal also made to the generality of citizens. To all these groups the pledges of lower taxes, economy, and efficiency in administration were compelling. This was also true of the anticrime appeal and the appeal of the restoration of Chicago's reputation. These appeals were efficacious with this audience owing to the presence among them of aims and desires based almost equally upon economic and noneconomic considerations. The economic considerations were not general and unsophisticated, as with the mass of the voters, but were more particularly defined in the case of this group. Many of this class of supporters had investments in the impending World's Fair, and there were real fears that the unfavorable international press caused by the Thompson regime would jeopardize the success of these investments. The same bad press was also causing deleterious effects upon the value of city securities in which many of these persons had considerable holdings. One pro-Thompson observer notes the importance of this factor in this way:

Cermak knew the power of big money. He built himself in with the bankers. Undoubtedly he told them if elected mayor he would follow their recommendations with reference to the city's financial and revenue policies. The bankers were loaded with city paper. He would continue to stand with the big interests in reference to tax matters. He would work with big business in putting the city and other governments on what the money interests might regard as a sounder basis. He promised retrenchments, a business administration; on the other hand he would run the politics, the patronage, and of course the police department.... The bankers accepted Cermak. He kept faith with them. The newspapers? Cermak wisely had kept on friendly terms with all newspapers. It was not hard to do. With most of them it was anyone to beat Thompson. Cermak placated newspaper friends of Colonel A. A. Sprague, much favored for mayor in certain quarters, by promising that if elected he would appoint Sprague as commissioner of public works with a free hand. And he promised to start his administration with Francis X. Busch as corporation counsel. Busch had strong friends in the anti-Thompson newspaper offices.[86]

We have seen the tremendous support A.J. received from these groups and have alluded to the recognition extended to them. Sprague, Busch, Sexton, Collins, Lindheimer, and others would not only recognize these groups, but act as their representatives in the city government. In addition, it was promised that the many citizens' advisory committees which Cermak had appointed as county board president would be continued, and it was implied that they would exercise great powers. This not only satisfied the desire for representation but also gave to many considerable ego titillation; they had the satisfaction of being city fathers without becoming soiled by politics.

Perhaps this ego flattery was more important for some of the "silk stockings" and the independents than for the other groups, although the independents particularly were offered more solid recognition. Cermak offered Merriam his choice of any cabinet position or a place on the school board.[87] However, these groups were more attracted by the restoration-of-reputation appeal, even though they were by no means unaffected by the economic pledge. This was well understood by Cermak, as his many speeches to this clientele clearly illustrates.[88]

At the City Club he called attention to Thompson's vicious campaign tactics; presented his stock economic issues; promised to appoint men and women "of high character and demonstrated devotion to civic welfare"; promised to restore the city's reputation and to drive out crime, to restore confidence and deal energetically with unemployment; and again pledged "hearty cooperation with every agency."[89] He further promised an effective administration of the merit system through appointment of a civil service commission "of forceful, capable and honest men, who will be free from every form of political interference."[90] Finally, he renewed his pledge to fight for consolidation of the crazy quilt of local governments.

Indeed, in speeches to these groups Cermak did sound as if he had been baptized with civic holy water. Whether or not he truly enjoyed this new role, it can be said that he did not blanch at appearing before these unfamiliar audiences upon whose delicate ears "hundert" or "Tivo'li" doubtless fell jarringly. His opponent completely ignored this clientele. On the single occasion that the rival candidates were scheduled to share the same platform—before a University of Chicago audience—Thompson thought better of it and did not make an appearance.

Strategy and Techniques in the Campaign

The issues and appeals chosen for the campaign were a product of the conscious and unconscious application of certain arts and techniques distilled from mature political experience. The war cries used, the sequence of events, and the media and materials employed were designed for many specific uses. Although Thompson's flamboyance and his easily assailable record made certain portions of Cermak's platform inevitable, questions of emphasis and choices nevertheless had to be faced and solved. This is indicated in the early search for useful slogans upon which to base the Cermak campaign. Quite early there emerged two guiding mottoes, "Chicago Needs a Mayor," and "Redeem Chicago." These slogans were fortified by other statements from Cermak's headquarters illustrating that campaign strategy was being consciously planned. It was announced early and repeated often that A.J. would conduct a dignified campaign based entirely on problems of direct local concern. He would ignore personal and partisan attacks, as befitted a "Master Executive."[91] This was a frank bid for independent and Republican votes.

The images of the candidates. In every campaign elaborate pains are taken to depict candidates as attractive human beings. The efforts to humanize Dewey, Taft, and others who were conspicuously lacking the "human touch" are well known. This same type of effort is not neglected even in the case of candidates more fortunately endowed. Thus, Earl Warren was usually photographed with his attractive family; the plain-as-an-old-shoe family life of the Trumans was stressed; Franklin Roosevelt was portrayed as a gay, optimistic, courageous fighter for the underdog; Eisenhower became a modern Cincinnatus; and "Big Bill" was not only a builder but the protector of the kiddies' milk supply and the stalwart defender of Chicago against British imperialism and the cabals of the international bankers.

The picture of the candidate is an important item among the arts and techniques of campaigning, for a candidate is not only an abstract bundle of issues, he is also a personality who embodies a whole pattern of ideas and ways of dealing with public problems. It is inevitable that the very choice and manipulation of issues will construct an image of the candidate. However, the issues themselves are often chosen in the light of what best suits the picture of the candidate which has been decided upon as the one to be sold to the electorate. And many other devices besides the issues are used to complete this portrait. A faulty portrait may be a serious handicap in a campaign; therefore, major attempts are made to destroy the public portraits of opposing candidates. Many have called attention to the damage done to Willkie's chances when the Roosevelt managers attacked his public image—the homespun self-made man—as the "barefoot boy from Wall Street."

A. J. Cermak was not a man with an overabundant supply of personal glamor, the human touch, or even ordinary personal warmth. To supply this missing element, his family was brought into the picture. His young granddaughter Vivian Graham, eleven or twelve at this time, was among the most frequent campaign speakers. Five-year-old Mary Ellen Jirka also asked for votes for her grandfather. These attempts, however, were relatively minor touches. The major emphasis was upon Cermak the public man. A.J. was painted as a serious, capable, solid, successful public administrator and businessman of long and uninterrupted success. The portrayal was reminiscent of the "Great Engineer" portrait drawn of Hoover in 1928. The entire project was oriented around the phrase, "The Master Executive." But there were at least two other facets to the complete role: A.J. the humanitarian and A.J. the tolerant, courageous defender of personal liberty.

Cermak attempted by every public act and utterance to be completely faithful to the role he was playing. The hallmark of his performance was personal dignity. Throughout, he eschewed personal attacks on Thompson, though he called attention to

Thompson's diatribes, and single-mindedly insisted on issues, and the candidates' records.[92] He insisted he was cognizant of the serious problems faced by the city and of the heavy responsibilities of the office he sought. "I have," he would say—referring to Thompson's clownish trick of symbolizing his opponents as various animals—"no jackasses, no elephants, no rats."

While A.J. devoted his efforts to acting in conformity with the portrait decided upon, the definition of the virtuous qualities of the "Master Public Executive" was also being made by other spokesmen. Party leaders and leaders of every auxiliary campaign unit took part in this selling program. To women leaders A.J. was a "competent executive, with a sense of responsibility toward his job and experiences to fit him for the office," and he was also "honest, intelligent, forceful." To political supporters he was "tolerant," "humanitarian," "businesslike," "forthright," and "vigorous."

Thompson was portrayed as the reverse of the "Master Executive"—a buffoon, irresponsible, incapable, surrounded by grafters and gangsters. The bulk of this portrayal, in line with Cermak's new-found dignity, was left to other Cermak speakers, particularly such irreproachable persons as Merriam, Loesch, Mrs. Fairbank, and Sprague. The anti-Thompson press was extremely helpful in detailing the negative Thompson portrayal. Thompson retaliated. Since "Big Bill" had virtually no formal issues, a good deal of his efforts went into the attempt to destroy the public image of Cermak. Cermak was a greedy swine; he was "Dictator Tony," in command of the county, the forest preserve, and the Democratic party; he was a tool of King George, of Silas Strawn and the international bankers; he hated all ethnic groups; he was an enemy of the Catholics and of Protestant morality; and he was a grafter and an incompetent official.

The illusion of victory. This time-honored technique was used with the greatest regularity by the Cermak forces, beginning at the preprimary stage. During the postprimary campaign, never a day passed that Cermak and his associates did not boast that there was no doubt about victory. As the campaign progressed, A.J.'s public certainty appeared to grow. By March 27 victory was assured, and by March 30 he predicted a "sweeping plurality." "There is no

longer any doubt. . . . We have the campaign won." On election eve
his confidence seemed to reach its peak.

We have won our battle. All that remains to do is to clean up the field of
battle and make the defeat of the enemy a rout. The result is certain. . . . But
we must make our victory . . . impressive. Every 10,000 votes we add to our
plurality will count. . . . Our fight is now to swell that majority.[93]

The use of campaign media. A wide choice of media is available
to campaign managers. In this campaign every old medium was
used, and some innovations were employed by both sides. Extensive use was made of the written word through the metropolitan
press and the ethnic press, in news columns, editorials, and paid
advertisements. We have seen that A.J. enjoyed the greater part
of newspaper support. Nevertheless, there were many and expensive paid advertisements. Most of these were placed in the name of
the several auxiliary campaign committees.

In addition, there were marked ballots, auto stickers, cartoons,
and badges. Nor was the photograph neglected. The face of the
"Master Public Executive" confronted Chicagoans from billboards, small cards, throwaways, and the many thousands of posters
displayed in business establishments and homes. The function of
the pictures and badges was patently nonrational, merely another
device to create the illusion of victory. There were also more
formal campaign pamphlets describing the achievements and personalities of the candidates. Cermak's headquarters issued a whole
series dealing with his savings and humanitarian activities on the
county board. The most impressive and expensive pamphlet was
From Illinois Mine Boy to Chief Executive, distributed in one
million copies.[94] Thompson had at least three major pamphlets:
The Tribune Shadow; Thompsonism; and the *Annual Report* of
the board of education.

But human contact is far more emotion-provoking than the
written word or the photograph. This accounts for the great use
of rallies. Both sides realized that no substitute for the rally as a
creator of enthusiasm had been invented. The political meeting
has the advantage of enabling favorable interaction between cam-
paigner and audience; moreover, there is the well-tested contagion
of enthusiasm among the members of the audience. There were
rallies of every size and including every kind of audience. There

were huge city-wide affairs at the Stadium and Coliseum; large downtown meetings at theaters and hotel ballrooms; large regional meetings at such places as the huge Aragon ballroom; and smaller meetings in every ward.

The candidates were indefatigable; some days four or five meetings were addressed. There is no doubt that Thompson was superior to Cermak in his rally performances. Few politicians have been so entertaining that they could charge admission for their political speeches. Thompson did just that. Cermak's efforts at dignity, on the other hand, hampered what little native capacity (at its best before small west-side meetings of Czech or Polish audiences) he had along these lines. All the same, he persevered. No attempt was made to hide him, to have him conduct a Coolidge campaign of silence or a Harding front-porch campaign. But good use was made of the more successful orators in his stable, notably, J. Hamilton Lewis.

Radio was still relatively new as a campaign device, having been first used extensively for this purpose only as recently as 1924. Although neither Thompson nor Cermak was expert at the fireside chat, both sides made much use of radio. Even in the uncontested primary campaign Cermak made twelve radio speeches. During the campaign proper he broadcasted nearly every night, and many of his noonday Loop speeches were also broadcast. There was, besides, the "Cermak Prosperity Parade" sponsored by the Sprague businessmen's committee, which went on daily for two weeks. Thompson spoke over four local stations for sixteen nights, fifteen minutes on each, using an aggregate of sixteen hours of radio time in two weeks. Cermak used the radio finally to make his round-up reply to Thompson's abuses. The speech was given at 11:00 P.M. on election eve, so that Thompson would have no opportunity to reply.

Both candidates pioneered in the use of the film as a campaign medium. Here Thompson had an edge on A.J. He had the support of the Motion Picture Operators Union, which showed Thompson à la Will Rogers on many a streetcorner.

The Serritella Scandal

It is the opinion of some observers that about a week or two before the election day A.J.'s campaign had grown stale and that

Thompson was gaining.[95] At this juncture, the state's attorney's police raided the offices of Thompson's city sealer, Daniel Serritella. Serritella was a ward committeeman, state senator, president of the Newsboys' Union and frequently described as an associate of Capone.[96]

The state's attorney was that same Swanson with whom A.J. had been on such good terms since their joint efforts in organizing the sanitary district in 1928. Swanson, a stalwart Deneen lieutenant, had been elected in 1928 after defeating Thompson's partner Crowe in the "Pineapple Primary"—in the course of which his own home was one of those bombed. The attacks during the recent primary did not do anything to cause a rapprochement between Thompson and Swanson or any other Deneen man. Indeed, it was freely stated that Swanson was supporting Cermak in exchange for Cermak support of Swanson's re-election in 1932.

Serritella and assistants were arrested, and records were impounded. A grand jury returned indictments—of conspiracy to defraud the citizens—against Serritella and his chief deputy. The allegation was that in return for political contributions merchants were allowed to use short weights and measures. The state's attorney's office released a statement charging that $54,000,000 were lost by citizens due to Serritella's protection of cheating merchants.

Considering the economic situation, the $54,000,000 swindle was like a bombshell. Whatever final spurt Thompson was believed to have made was stopped in its tracks. The newspaper poll taken the week of the election gave some indication of the eventual results: Cermak 33,494; Thompson 18,270.[97]

Results of the Election

Cermak won an overwhelming victory.[98] He polled 671,189 votes to Thompson's 476,922, a majority of 194,267.[99] This was, up to this time, the greatest majority ever polled in a Chicago mayoralty election—50,000 greater than had been Thompson's over Sweitzer in 1915; nearly 250,000 greater than the Dever votes in 1927; and more than three times as great as Dever's majority in 1923. It was also by far the largest vote of any Chicago mayoralty election. Of the registered voters, 82 per cent voted; 40.5 per cent of the votes were cast by women. Cermak carried forty-five of fifty wards. Of the five wards Thompson won, three constituted the Black Belt, and the other two also had large Negro groups. It is evident that this anchor of Thompson strength had supported him to the end.[100] Of the two other wards which were lost, the "bloody Twentieth" was lost by less than a thousand votes; and the Twenty-eighth by only 305. However, Cermak won four wards by under a thousand votes each. All the others ranged from comfortable to huge majorities. His home territory responded splendidly. Cermak totaled 57,054 votes in his own wards and the adjacent ones led by Sabath, Toman, and Rosenberg.[101] In these wards Thompson had only 15,195 votes. Therefore, Cermak's home territory was able to neutralize the advantage Thompson had acquired in the Negro areas. Thus, Cermak's huge majority was rolled up in the forty-one other wards which were exclusively neither Thompson nor Cermak territory. He carried every north-side and northwest-side ward. From this it is apparent that he won the bulk of the German, Scandinavian, and Polish votes. The Jews also responded handsomely.

But what about the Irish? It is clear that Thompson fell heir to a sizable vote from the Irish and from wards controlled by Irish leaders.[102] Although most of the Irish leaders delivered their wards to the Czech candidate,[103] only one of the wards delivering best for Cermak had an Irish boss; and this boss was A.J.'s old friend, McDonough.[104] Of the four wards which Cermak carried by less than a thousand votes, all had Irish bosses: Igoe, Moran, Walsh, and Touhy. Not surprisingly, Igoe's was the best example. This ward was won by Cermak by only 187 votes, whereas Dever had carried it by nearly 3,000 votes in his disastrous 1927 campaign. (It had also given Lyle a comfortable plurality over Thompson in the 1931 primary.) Since in every other ward but one Cermak had exceeded Dever's 1927 vote, it seems probable that Igoe had executed a mild double cross.[105]

Of the wards in which Cermak's majority was relatively small (no more than seven to five), the overwhelming number were controlled by Irish bosses: Whalen, Powers, O'Toole, Layden, Noonan, Brady, Bowler, Clark, Kelly, T. J. Crowe, Gill, and Donahue. Only three wards controlled by non-Irish leaders belong to this category: those of Kohl, Jensen, and Pryzbylo. Of these,

Kohl was a T. J. Crowe-Clark man.[106] It should be noted, however, that the wards of these Irish leaders had either been carried by Thompson in 1927 or, in those cases where Dever had won, had given Dever a smaller vote than was given to Cermak. Some of them had also given Thompson some of his greatest pluralities in the 1931 primary.[107] But strangely enough, the Nineteenth Ward of City Clerk-elect Brady had been the banner Lyle ward in the primary. In sum, it seems quite likely that the Irish ward leaders had not exercised all their muscle in order to increase the majority of the Czech candidate.[108] It is clear that the Irish ward leaders were far from reconciled to Czech domination—and the most unreconciled was Igoe.

But Irish recalcitrants notwithstanding, the great coalition, composed of the Democratic machine, the dissident Republicans, the independents, the ethnic groups, and others described above, had been too much for Thompson. Also influential in the victory were the absence of an independent candidate and the effects of the depression. A. J. Cermak was now mayor—World's Fair mayor, and acknowledged boss of Chicago and Cook County Democracy.[109]

· 12 ·

DEPRESSION
EXECUTIVE:
THE
POLITICAL
ADMINISTRATOR

CERMAK became Chicago's thirty-eighth mayor, the first who was foreign-born, and the first of non-Celtic or non-Anglo-Saxon origin. It was difficult for him to believe that he had won. His characteristic caution would not permit him to accept his victory even when reports indicated that he was running 200,000 votes ahead. His headquarters was in a jubilant, shouting mood; but Cermak was a study in contrast. As he was hugged, slapped on the back, congratulated, his manner was serious, and his face showed strain and fatigue. "The quietest person there . . . was the mayor-elect." After making a short radio statement, A.J. slipped out of the headquarters by a side exit. Reporters asked him if he intended to attend the organization's victory celebration. "Oh, no," he replied. "I'm going home and to bed."

Cermak did not gloat over his defeated foe. His words of thanks to the electorate and his entire demeanor showed that he was cognizant of the heavy task he was about to shoulder. There was seemingly no elation, and certainly no horseplay, in his reactions. He did not yell hoarsely as he is often quoted: "Who's got the pushcart now? I've always kept it handy to push Big Bill into the lake." The only note of triumph which crept into his behavior was in his comment upon seeing his name over the mayor's office for the first time. "That's the name my opponent didn't like. But it's there, and the majority of the people seem to like it." Indeed, there did seem to be general satisfaction with the results of the election, which had been of great national and international interest. From all over Europe as well as from every corner of this country congratulations poured in to Chicago and the new mayor.

Cermak lost no time in assuming office. In the past a good deal of formality had accompanied the changes of administration—and also delay. Usually the change required two weeks; the previous record had been six days. Cermak was officially mayor within forty-eight hours. It is probable that the quantity and speed of his activities have had few parallels in urban government.

This is a summary log of his first day in office: (1) took oath of office and had his hand accepted by the city council, (2) signed an order dismissing 2,200 temporary city employees, (3) made a personal survey of city finances, (4) presided over meetings of the county board and the city council: at 3 P.M. he resigned as county president and at 4:20 P.M. he convened the council, (5) ordered the school board to submit reports of its temporary employees and a copy of the payroll, (6) placed highest-ranking civil servants in charge of each department and instructed them not to sign pay warrants for those persons who had not been working, (7) made several cabinet appointments, (8) resigned as chairman of the county central committee and succeeded in having his designee for successor approved.

This was to be only a normal workday while he was mayor. Everyone who observed him in this office comments upon his almost unbelievable application to his duties. Sixteen-hour days were far from uncommon for him. Often he made a dozen speeches in a day in his efforts to save the city government from floundering on the rocks of total insolvency. He received endless callers, questioners, petitioners, informants; he held innumerable conferences with political aides and administrative heads of departments. His desire to have his own finger on every pulse, his basic belief that after all there was no one as trustworthy as he himself, and his insatiable demand for information made it mandatory for him to keep his doors open to all callers. The unceasing activity, the feverish excitement of his office is caught in this statement by the late Professor Leonard D. White, describing his first glimpse of Mayor Cermak.

I was ushered into his office by Corporation Counsel Frank Busch. Busch had a key to a private entrance—a private escape hatch; we didn't go through the main reception room. The room was jammed. Men stood layers deep in front and to the sides and behind Cermak. Several were talking and attempting to have him sign papers. Busch interrupted the proceedings and introduced me. The hardest and coldest look that's ever been directed at me emanated from his eyes. "I'm glad to see you," he said, shook hands, and turned back to the chattering audience.[1]

Cermak's inaugural address was a full statement of the major municipal problems and of his plans for solution.[2] The problem of "first importance" was the financial condition of the city: high taxes, high cost of administration, and the depleted condition of the treasury. This situation was to be remedied "by the elimination of incompetence, waste and unnecessary duplication of services, and the application of modern methods in ordinary use in well-ordered private businesses." In order to achieve economy the Mayor called upon the council for cooperation and asked it to approve the appointment of a mayor's advisory commission whose functions would include "a thoroughgoing study of every department of the city government with the definite objective in view of making practical, constructive recommendations." Cermak outlined a partial framework of reference for the advisory commission which read like the recommendations of a little Hoover Commission.

The commission members included many who had had experience on other Cermak committees, especially on the Cook County Commission on Public Finance and Economy.[3] He deliberately appointed some of the same persons who also served on the latter commission so that effective liaison could be maintained. (The county commission's duty was to recommend consolidations among the various local governments, while the mayor's commission was restricted solely to city matters.)

The speech, except for its promises of administrative reform, was hollow. No mention was made of that economic disaster much greater than high taxes and municipal waste: the depression. The problem of supplying relief to the unemployed was to loom as one of the most crucial of Cermak's mayoralty, yet not a single reference was made to it. Nor was there a statement of what steps would be taken to prop up the dangerous fiscal situation of the city. Reorganization was certainly important, but some funds were initially required to pay city employees. Within a few months this problem would also haunt the Mayor; yet there was no reference to it in the inaugural address.

Many qualified observers have allowed themselves to be less than objective in assessing Cermak because of a firm belief that he was the archetype of grafter—"Ten-percent Tony." But if Cermak was actually as avaricious as his worst critics would have us believe—and the evidence is far from conclusive—this factor alone is not a sufficient measure of his effectiveness as an executive. Let us therefore observe Mayor Cermak in action in the complex problems that confronted him.

THE DEPRESSION IN CHICAGO

The keynote to an understanding of politics and administration in Chicago from 1931 to 1933 is that outstanding economic fact: the depression. Chicago was one of the hardest hit of all major cities as, in general, urban areas suffered much more than rural communities. By October, 1932, the general estimate of Chicago unemployed was approximately 750,000 (of the national total of eight million), while only 800,000 were still employed. Of this number, a large percentage worked only part time. By this time $1,500,000 was the weekly cost of relief. To indicate in part the seriousness of the situation in Chicago as compared to the rest of the country: by October, 1932, Illinois had received $14,000,000 in federal loans for relief, while the total of such loans to all the states was only $28,000,000. The bulk of the federal money was used in Chicago, where there were 145,000 families receiving public assistance. "Rents declined more drastically than in any other large city except Detroit. By 1935 rents were only one-half of what they had been between 1923-25."[4] But cold statistics are unequal to depicting the feeling of terror and lostness which gripped not only Chicago but the entire nation.

Chicago, crossroads of the continent, in addition to its own impoverished, was host to tens of thousands who left homes in search of that will-o'-the-wisp, a job. Hundreds of thousands lived in the ugly shadow of starvation, cold, nakedness. The voluntary charities were unable to meet the unprecedented demands after the early stages, and the state and local governments were slow to act. There was no precedent to guide them. The voluntary agencies made dauntless attempts to function by means of tried methods, such as fund drives. Public bodies passed bond issues, tried a variety of tax measures, diverted funds from permanent improvements, and sought loans from the state and federal governments. None of these measures was successful. The private fund raising was handicapped because many former donors were now unable to give; the public efforts were scattered, unintegrated, and nearly always a matter of last minute spasms. Bonds were floated or a new tax was enacted or a loan negotiated on the eve of closing the relief stations. In brief, it was a haphazard, unimaginative attempt, constantly handicapped by a reluctance for government to subsidize able-bodied men and by the refusal of many rugged individualists to believe that jobs could not be found if only the individual were willing to work.

Such economic hardships created discontent all over the world. In some places governments fell; in some American cities important changes were made. But Chicago remained unaltered in major ways. The social and economic philosophy of its business and political leaders militated against any basic change. Violence, however, was not totally absent in the response of the masses to severe economic deprivation. The persons in need of assistance came to organize themselves and made demands upon the authorities, including Cermak. The Chicago Workers Committee on Unemployment, the Workers League of America, and numbers of Unemployed Councils took the lead in negotiating for proper, or increased, relief. They held demonstrations in front of relief stations, which were guarded by police. Frequently riots ensued; persons were wounded; on one occasion a demonstrator was fatally wounded by the police, and Cermak's life was threatened by alleged Communists. Sometimes protest parades were held. For each a police permit was required. The police and the Mayor were often reluctant to grant them, fearing activities of agitators.

More often than not permits were ultimately granted upon threats by the unemployed of marching in defiance of the police.

By the summer of 1931, there were evictions by the thousands in Chicago for nonpayment of rent. Often the dispossessed had no place to go and were reluctant to leave their dwellings. After a time, the Unemployed Councils began a policy of restoring evicted tenants to their flats without benefit of court process. Often police were summoned to halt the extralegal proceedings, and riots would result.

The depression affected every economic stratum. In September, 1932, by Cermak's own statement, of the city's 228 banks only 51 were still open. Thousands of businesses failed. Professional men and Ph.D.'s were eager to find menial employment. Public employees were not paid regularly and faced extraordinary hardships.

Cermak's entire term as mayor was spent in the ever deepening shoals of the economic crisis. It overshadowed every decision, every governmental activity. It was a keenly felt guest in every social encounter. Although the subject was omitted from his inaugural address, it is certain that the special crisis of the times was never absent from Cermak's consciousness. It pervaded his entire administration.

THE MASTER PUBLIC EXECUTIVE AS THE COMPLEAT LORD MAYOR

Although most of Cermak's energies were directed toward fiscal problems, the office of Mayor of Chicago demands fulfilment of a great many more diverse roles than that of chief finance officer.

> The Mayor of Chicago is the City's most impressive show piece; he is its chief personnel agent; he is its city manager; he is its chief lawmaker, its chief financier, its diplomat, its leader, all in one; or he should be, if he did all that is expected of him. Which of these roles he will play and which the city will best enjoy depends upon the man and the occasion.[5]

Cermak's performance in the complex roles of this office has been ignored or dismissed by otherwise competent observers, chiefly owing to their belief that he was "the biggest crook of the lot," or "the most ruthless and acquisitive man in Chicago politics," or "a spoils politician," or simply that he came under that wonderfully all-inclusive anathema, "Boss." These descriptions are fairly accurate. And yet they do not describe his actual performance as mayor. It was a performance that fulfilled to a considerable extent Merriam's theoretical requirements that the mayor be one who "will provide an element of leadership for the city, a form of leadership in which will be fused the elements of political organization, legislative dominance and administrative supremacy."[6]

During Cermak's tenure as mayor, the spirit of "the fifth floor," the mayor's office, pervaded the city hall to a much greater extent than had been usual. Whatever Cermak lacked in magnetism he made up for in power, dominance, and decisiveness. Everyone knew who made the decisions, and everyone knew that what Cermak demanded done was done. More than most other Chicago mayors Cermak knew, in the words of his successor, "what was going on in the city hall,"[7] and every other center of political power might have been added as well. No Chicago mayor surpassed him in detailed knowledge of the intricacies of administration, including operation at the lowest ministerial level. He was completely familiar with the jobs not only of cabinet officers but of the cop on his beat, of the building inspector, of the garage mechanic, and of the clerical employee.

In every administrative organization there is a vast amount of unorganized or organized inertia, and sometimes sabotage, on the part of the permanent bureaucracy against the temporary political administrator. Several Chicago mayors have paid dearly because of this phenomenon. Dever was virtually forced to be a one-termer as his subordinates wilfully overexceeded his instructions to control the liquor traffic. Kennelly, another reform mayor (1947-55), was subjected to the same treatment in the course of his efforts to place a few obstacles in the path of some ward bosses and some policemen who desired to "make a buck." Undoubtedly the Irish Kennelly, who was known to be honest, was more admired by the average cop or city employee than that "— — Bohunk," who was generally believed to be "in it only for himself." Nevertheless, during Cermak's term, fear prevented the destruction of administrative policy at the lower levels: "The s.o.b. would crucify me!"

Cermak played the complicated administrative instrument like an agile "pianist playing six keyboards at one time."[8] He realized full well that his power was not limited by his legal authority. He did not hesitate to use his prestige, his patronage, and his complete control of the party to effect his desires. He manifested an interest in and capacity for large and complex policy problems, as well as an ability to meet the incessant demands of the supervision of a large and complex administrative service. There can be no doubt that he had a highly developed feel for administration and an unparalleled energy and will to see that what he desired came to pass. "He had a great faculty for getting at the heart of problems in major and minor things. He saturated himself through the ears rather than through books."[9]

A.J. showed a considerable shrewdness in judging men. He made few mistakes in his appointments; and when he did make a mistake, he proceeded to rectify his error without sentimentality. He made it his business to *know* men; therefore, he constructed a considerable espionage system which reported directly to him. It was common gossip that the Mayor employed the services of numbers of stool pigeons. As soon as he took office, he brought Cervenka over from the county because of his desire "to have definite knowledge of the condition in every department of the city hall from trusted sources."[10] He was not averse to having persons under surveillance, or to having wires tapped or letters opened. He made it his business to have information concerning the weaknesses and foibles of administrative and political lieutenants; and he took pains to learn the identities of their enemies.

Perhaps most significant, Cermak had the ability to grasp and interpret the spirit of the city and of its large and powerful political opinions. He had a highly developed sensitivity to the existing equilibrium of social, political, and economic forces at any given time. He had an intuitive feeling for the traditions and aspirations of the city and its complex groupings. It is difficult to say whether this was learned in a conscious manner—at least in part this was probably true—or whether his own hopes and fears and aspirations fortuitously coincided with the psychic needs of the majority of Chicagoans of this time.

It is not enough to say that he knew what the people wanted—although this was surely true—and that he symbolized in his every action these desires. He was "right"[11] in his battle for free-flowing alcohol and in his canonization of his definition of personal liberty in the variety of guises through which this appeal appeared;

he was "right" in his demands for home rule and in championing Chicago against downstate and other foes and detractors; he was "right" in his sensitivity to the deep-felt antagonism of non-Irish Democrats to the monopoly of party power by the Irish; he was "right" in becoming a great Chicago booster when the world's fair demanded a fearless mayor to redeem the city from Thompsonism; he was "right" in recognizing the power and influence of the wealthy and the independents; he was "right" in recognizing that reform and reorganization of governments were desired by the majority; he was "right" in his relative steadfastness toward retrenchment; he was "right" in quick recognition of the dangers to the status quo inherent in the mass poverty of the depression; he was "right" in his belief that only the federal government had the resources to meet the crises of the depression and that the time for direct federal aid to municipalities had arrived; he was "right" in recognizing that the dispossessed had a claim on government, that work relief was superior to the dole, and that cash relief was preferable to assistance in goods. It is unlikely that all of these "right" guesses were a product of conscious and objective analysis of existing situations and the assessment of the political possibilities of each.

Cermak's batting average on right guesses was not built up by means of evading a stand. Apparently he was unacquainted with that most useful modern parry, "no comment." The closest he came to this were times when, in search of a proper decision (the feel of the city's pulse), he would say that his mind was open and that he was amenable to any practical suggestion. Even in these cases, however, when once he decided what the city wanted, he acted with vigor and without pussyfooting.

Anton J. Cermak was a real mayor—spoils politician and believer in honest (and perhaps not-so-honest) graft though he undoubtedly was. His short record in office is compared favorably by competent observers with the best of any other mayor in the city's history. And much was expected of him as he assumed office—particularly by good-government forces and experts in administration. One observer noted that Cermak had a "firm grasp of the situation, both the party organization and public opinion" and that his "practical sense" would force him to give a good account of himself. Cermak realized that he had to deliver. There is ample evidence to support the view that, apart from his keen understanding of political realities, he desired above all else to be a " 'real World's Fair mayor' in the best sense of these words,"[12] and to "make a name for his kids."[13]

CERMAK TACKLES THE FISCAL PROBLEM

Given the general economic chaos, it is not strange that the most pressing and continuing problems of Mayor Cermak were in the fiscal area. But this was only partially due to the depression. By 1929 most local governments were in a deep financial morass, resulting in good part from archaic governmental and revenue systems and an impossible tax mechanism.[14] For these reasons, the very existence and solvency of the Chicago area governments—unlike the governments of other cities also hard hit by the depression—were threatened. Because of the favoritism-ridden, politically corrupt, and anarchic tax system, a reassessment of all Cook County property was started in 1928 and was still uncompleted when the depression set in.[15] Cermak had been one of the early supporters of reassessment, but neither he nor the other proponents anticipated that it would take so many years. As a result, governments in Cook County, the county and the city proper, notably, had had such depleted revenues since 1929 that their fiscal existence was hand to mouth. As of May 1, 1931, according to Cermak, there were $670,000,000 in unpaid taxes. By June, 1930, only 80 per cent of the 1928 taxes had been collected, only 60 per cent of the 1929 taxes, and only 50 per cent of the 1930 taxes. Some of the nonpayment of taxes was a product of the depression, but this was further aggravated by a "tax strike" of real-estate owners. The "strike"—caused allegedly because of discrepancies between taxes on real property and personal property—was to be one of Cermak's chief headaches. In this context, however, it merely points up an additional cause for the unprecedentedly low municipal revenues.

The fiscal chaos, however, antedated the depression, the havoc caused by the reassessment, and even the raids on the city treasury in the years of Thompsonism. Much of this was due to inadequate municipal fiscal powers granted by a jealous legislature—more Chicago-downstate rivalry. As a result there was a host of hand-tying, minute regulations by the legislature: debt and tax limits, precise defining of the use of corporate funds by division into special funds, hundreds of regulations concerning the minutiae of appropriations and budget matters.

Because of the pervasive and heavy-handed control by the state, all manner of devices and subterfuges have had to be used in order to find funds to operate the local governments. The most notable device—indeed giving Chicago its fame in public finance circles—was the tax-anticipation warrant.

The tax-anticipation warrant is a form of script issued by the municipality to bankers in exchange for cash, to employees in payment of work, and to merchants in payment of deliveries to the city. Its security consists of taxes to be collected in the future, that is, of anticipated taxes.[16]

The revenue was always mortgaged before being collected, and less revenues were available since these warrants usually circulated for considerably less than par value. By the time Cermak assumed office Chicago had a backlog of almost a century of tax-anticipation warrants. In the last years of Thompson's reign, since normal collections had been reduced by virtue of the reassessment, an even larger resort to scrip had been made. Not only was it used to operate the machinery of government, but because Thompson refused to make any retrenchments in the face of reduced income, it was used in great quantities to extract cash from many special-purpose funds. In these cases these warrants were used as I.O.U.'s, which not only resulted in a depleted general corporate fund but also impoverished special funds whose assets now were largely tax-anticipation warrants. By June, 1931, the city of Chicago and the board of education had a total of $173,768,277 in outstanding warrants (for the years 1928 to 1931 inclusive), which had accrued annual interest of nearly $9,000,000.[17]

At the time Cermak took office the end of this sleight-of-hand financing was almost reached. Even tax-warrant manipulations were impossible. With the city practically denuded of cash, there were such huge amounts of the warrants outstanding that bankers and other usual customers were unwilling to invest in them any longer. Since this source of cash was closed the older issues of the warrants could not be redeemed when they matured, which caused a further depreciation of the market for new issues of the scrip. The city was broke.

Being broke had many unpleasant consequences.[18] Throughout Cermak's term there was a danger that city bonds and other "full faith and credit" obligations would be defaulted. As Cermak said, if this occurred, "it would take twenty-five years at least to rehabilitate the city's credit and make possible the city's selling its bonds or tax warrants in the future."[19] On June 3, 1931, he told the legislature that "we have no cash at the present time" to meet $2,900,000 interest on city obligations and $460,000 on similar board of education paper due on July 1, 1931. There were other debts, too. On June 3, 1931, the city owed $4,500,000 in unpaid bills, and the board of education a like amount; the city also owed $6,500,000 in judgments on which interest was accruing.

The semimonthly payroll became a regular occasion of crisis, by far the most harassing. During his entire term Cermak was always scurrying from Springfield to Washington, to local bankers, and to New York financiers to find funds to pay city employees. He was for most of the period in a kind of frenzy resembling that of a rat in a maze, ever seeking for the solution to the puzzle, while each successive escape hatch turned into the entry way to another part of the maze. During this period of less than two years Cermak was ill several times, at least twice seriously so. He carried the heavy load of local and state party leadership in a period that was very critical not only for his own leadership but for the success of his party.

Cermak drove himself and his associates without surcease, trying to keep the machinery of government going, to rectify the decades-old archaic fiscal and administrative practices, to reduce drastically municipal expenditures, and to dragoon other local governments, over which he had no legal control, to do the same. Many of these activities were manifestly outside the normal, legal scope of a mayor's obligations or prerogatives; others were obligations he might easily have dodged. But he made no attempt to evade responsibilities not formally his. The times were not normal, and in some ways neither was the Mayor. He tried every known method of solving the financial muddle.

CERMAK AND THE BANKERS AND FINANCIAL LEADERS

In the light of Cermak's long and generally pleasant association with bankers and controlling economic groups, it is not surprising that he turned to them first and continuously in his great dilemma. The mayor's advisory commission he appointed in his inaugural messages (hereafter referred to as the Avery Commission, after its chairman, Sewell Avery) was composed of many of the leaders of the local finance and business elite. This commission was most particularly interested in causing economy in the city government. But Cermak used with even greater effect the Citizens' Committee on Public Expenditures (called the Sargent Committee, after its general chairman, who was chairman of the board of the North-western Railroad). This body was perhaps even more representative of the city's economic rulers. It is impossible to overestimate the pervading influence of these groups upon Cermak's attempts to save the local governments from collapse.

Some have charged that Cermak was actually a captive and minion of the economically powerful.[20] More than once members of the city council complained at the high-handed demands of the bankers, and Cermak often admitted that certain policies were pursued because the bankers "have us over a barrel." And he was usually right, for the bankers were actually the only potentially consistent source of funds. Indeed, even had Cermak followed nearly every demand of the bankers, one may well ask what alternative there was.

However, it is not possible to conclude that Cermak was merely a "lackey of LaSalle Street." He was too thoroughly at home in the intricate field of public finance to be led by the nose. Intimate associates, themselves well versed in fiscal matters, attest to A.J.'s qualifications in this realm—corporation counsels Busch and Sexton, and Szymczak, who has been a governor of the Federal Reserve system for more than two decades.[21] An experienced reporter stated that the bankers were "astounded" by Cermak's familiarity with city finances, and that "Cermak talked such good sense that the bankers listened."[22] Mr. Busch, who was counsel for the Avery Commission, is firm in his assertion that in reality Cermak was in full control of that body's proceedings and its findings.[24] Whether or not this is so, there is good reason to suppose that, as with other groups that he impressed, A.J. was able to assert himself with the bankers. His was hardly a hat-in-hand personality.

In one form or another, he was in continuous contact with the economic powers that be. Immediately after his inauguration he asked the "helpful" bankers to supply him with three of their best men. These men were to be used to conduct a thorough investigation of the city's financial plight as well as the system and practices of the comptroller. This kind of assistance was sought for every fiscal matter. Whenever new legislation was required it was either proposed by the economic lords or had to be cleared with them. And they also pressed Cermak to great efforts to pilot bills to successful passage. The bankers were on the spot when federal aid was invoked and in negotiations with out-of-Chicago banking agencies.

But the most direct and continuing contact with this group resulted from attempts to bring them to loan the city money. As early as May, 1931, Cermak announced that banks would be willing to loan money if certain pending legislation (reform of the tax machinery) were passed.

His countless conferences with bankers and other financial leaders were to cease only with his death. Less than a month before the shooting, he announced that one of his citizens' committees had sold $5,500,000 worth of warrants but that, again, immediate cash was needed for payrolls. Needless to say, he was negotiating for a loan. He was still trying to find money for payrolls in conferences with James A. Farley at Miami Beach the day Zangara's bullet found him.

THE MAYOR AND THE FISCAL POLICY IN THE LEGISLATURE

All of Cermak's attempts to get loans from bankers were *ad hoc* proceedings. To cause any important improvement, legislative action was necessary, indeed the bankers insisted on several items of legislation as a requisite for considering any loans.

From the first it was apparent that the bankers and Cermak's advisory committees would insist upon the destruction of the inefficient and often venal county tax machinery, replacing it with a single consolidated body. This was no small project. The three-man board of review was Republican-controlled and the five-member board of assessors had a Democratic majority. Most of the members had been recently elected. There were also thirty Republican township assessors to round out the patronage picture. The problem was not only to persuade a Republican-controlled legislature to abolish mostly Republican offices; Democrats also had a vested interest, and both parties had profited greatly from the historic tax fix. But the bankers insisted that this regime be ended, on the theory that the current nonpayment of taxes was largely caused by uncertain, unequal, and grossly dishonest assessments.

It is doubtful that Cermak was heartily in favor of the scheme. In 1930 he had helped elect four members to the tax boards, and it was quite likely that in 1934 he would gain a majority of both boards. But he was a political realist; the local governments were bankrupt and the bankers insisted. Not only did he indorse the so-called Cermak bill but, after hours of heated debate, he forced an indorsement out of his organization.

But the reform of the tax machinery would not of itself supply the immediately needed revenues. A.J. supported among several other proposals a personal property tax with teeth and an extension of the city's licensing power. He himself led the lobby. But although he cajoled, threatened, and drew the most dire pictures of the consequences if his plans were not approved, every important proposal was defeated.

As nothing of real help to Chicago was accomplished by the legislature, Governor Emmerson appointed the Governor's Tax Conference and charged it to recommend a program of fiscal relief for Chicago. The Tax Conference recommended: a new county tax administration similar to the one defeated in the regular session; a 20 per cent tobacco tax; a state income tax; and some less important items. To act upon these matters a special session of the legislature was called.

For this session Cermak was much better prepared. There had been time to plan the strategy and to organize support. The Republican Governor was cooperative; all the metropolitan papers supported the recommendations, as did nearly the entire business, banking, and good-government fraternity. This was true of every measure save the state income tax, although lack of enthusiasm for it was not made public. Cermak himself was not in favor of the income-tax measure and did not conceal his discontent when it was passed. His criticism was based on the fact that the bulk of such a tax would be paid in Cook County, but that the metropolitan area would only receive half of that total. "Just the old story, I guess— put the burden on Chicago and Cook County," he mourned. However, the Illinois income tax was challenged in the courts and never went into effect.

The legislative battle soon became embroiled not only with the Chicago-downstate rivalry but also with M. L. Igoe's determination to get the gubernatorial nomination in spite of Boss Cermak's coolness to his ambition. The tax conference scheme called for the appointment of the new tax officials by the county board, but early in the session Cermak conceded that the downstaters would never accept such a degree of home rule. After many suggested compromises on this measure, the Kelly plan (named after D. F. Kelly, president of a large State Street store) finally met with considerable favor. Under this compromise the governor and the president of the county board each appointed one member of the board of appeals, and they jointly appointed the lone assessor. The old boards would be abolished, but the thirty township assessors would be retained as deputies. However, the first appointees would serve only until November, 1934, thereafter to be elective.

The Igoe revolt was now in full progress; Igoe called the Kelly plan "the most violent assault on home-rule for Chicago ever attempted."[24] His actions were generally conceded to be at least partially motivated by personal political interests. But Cermak and others realized that the opposition was aiming at Cermak's prestige.

Cermak at first had not appeared overly fond of the Kelly scheme. But he was caught in a maelstrom which carried him hither and yon. Despite many public shifts, he fought a rearguard action to see the program passed; eventually, it was. Cermak now began to insist upon other legislation for immediate relief. Again the legislature was unresponsive, and Cermak unleashed continuous blasts against it. He had begun, in his extremity, to let loose angry tirades at one uncooperative group after another, even such friends as the bankers and the schoolteachers. When he learned that the legislature was planning to adjourn until after the primaries (a period of nearly two months), his anger was enormous. "I'll close public buildings and public institutions until they give us relief."[25] But all of Cermak's threats were for nought. Politicians want to be at the grass roots at election time. The legislature adjourned. Whereupon Cermak advised its members that they "may go to hell"—a piece of advice understandably resented, and answered by various assemblymen, althought not quite in kind.[26]

Now that Springfield had not given the needed relief, other things had to be done—certainly Cermak never contemplated closing the public services. Although new legislative proposals were planned from the moment of the adjournment of the assembly, Cermak could not put off dealing with the fiscal problems for the duration of the primary—or for any amount of time. He now redoubled his efforts along nonlegislative lines, with special emphasis on attacking the tax strikers and those who were challenging the validity of assessments in the courts. Immediately after the adjournment he gave a new, and probably unprecedented, twist to these efforts. He personally telephoned those persons who owed over $20,000 in taxes and begged that they pay what they considered to be a fair share of their indebtedness. He directed Comptroller Szymczak to call many others. He told a group of teachers that if this did not succeed, he would give them the list of names, so that they might second his plea.

This kind of appeal was used in every possible manner—in the press, on the radio—and to every conceivable group. It was almost always coupled with the plight of the impoverished teachers and the hope of returning prosperity: "If only the people who are holding back could be made to see what great benefits will accrue all the way around if taxes are paid promptly."[27] Frequently the appeals to good citizenship were united with the most slashing attacks on the leaders of the tax strike. Cermak attacked them as "tax dodgers" and as profiteering from the donations of misguided home owners. "They are collecting money under false pretenses." This is but a mild sample of his regular unrestrained attacks on this body of erstwhile supporters, the sacrosanct real-estate taxpayers. Thus, in his distress Cermak turned on still another group which he had long cultivated. He discharged a Republican lawyer, president of the elite Hamilton Club, who had been employed as an expert by the city, because his firm represented the Association of Real Estate Taxpayers. "His position is absolutely inconsistent. Here we find him in this building saying, 'Give me $100 a day,' and over there he says, 'Don't pay your taxes.' "[28]

All during this period, while the litigation over the legality of the assessments went on, the Mayor gave no quarter in his enmity to the strikers, threatening the leaders with everything from grand-jury action to removing police protection from them. He was particularly incensed when he was approached by the tax dodgers to settle for 50 per cent of the taxes owed. "I'll close the city hall first!"

When at last the Supreme Court definitively broke the backbone of the strike, A.J. moved again in the direction of cajolery. After all, it must often have been difficult for him to attack the very groups whose good will he had so assiduously cultivated. Thus, it is not strange that from time to time he tried to mitigate the harsh tactics to which necessity forced him, by making some conciliatory gestures. He sponsored a bill to allow individuals to file petitions requesting an extension of time to pay delinquent taxes. This was aimed at home owners and was calculated to protect them from forced sale for delinquent taxes. But before this could be enacted, Cermak arranged for a short extension of tax payments through his control of the Democratic party.

Again, as a part of his great campaign of solicitude for the teachers, he wrote a letter to County Judge Jarecki requesting a moratorium on the taxes they owed. Whether or not it was legal, he asked for this tax holiday on grounds of justice and equity. He further attempted his traditional policy of compassion for the little fellow. Although he fought passionately for the vigorous enforcement of the personal-property tax, he always made clear he did not include ordinary folk among those who should pay the tax. The law was not intended to tax such persons' radios, pianos, and "jalopy" automobiles. At the end of 1932, when the reformed tax administration was operating, Cermak vigorously assaulted it—and an old friend, now County Assessor Jacobs—for the low assessment of Gold Coast residents in contrast to persons of moderate means. "The people of Chicago have long been patient with such discriminations and they will not tolerate them further."

But these makeshifts could not be substituted for legislative action. After the primary election the legislature reconvened but was occupied mostly with matters of public assistance, an area in which Cermak was also vitally interested. Fiscal matters had to wait for the regular 1933 session. By the summer of 1932, A.J. was fully committed to the sales tax. Where was the little fellow now?

> Like nearly everything else, methods of raising revenue for the maintenance of government are undergoing a change. For generations these revenues were obtained principally from real estate and other tangibles.
>
> Prohibition, with its loss of excise revenue to local, state, and national governments... brought about an increase in rates to the point where now... the levies are virtually confiscatory.
>
> The sales tax is the best substitute yet proposed.... That kind of tax is least felt by the taxpayers, while at the same time providing funds with which to maintain... necessary services.[29]

It appears that to A.J. a sales tax was not a real tax. In one breath he said "taxes cannot be increased"; "taxes must be lowered," while in the next he was urging the sales tax.

> All taxes are obnoxious and it would be a utopian situation if the public could be given a moratorium on taxes....
>
> The least painful tax, and the one most certain of collection is the sales tax, and when the new Legislature is inaugurated January 4, bills will be introduced to put it into effect. There has been opposition to such a tax in the present Legislature, but we are confronted with a situation, not a theory.[30]

By December Cermak's legal advisers were drafting the necessary legislation, and Cermak continued his program of public education calculated to make the bitter pill easier to swallow. Cermak's pressure for this measure was crude but relentless. A portion of the proceeds of the tax was to go for public assistance, and there is no doubt that situation was critical. He constantly threatened that he would ask Governor Horner for the militia if his demands were rejected. Cermak left for his fatal meeting with Roosevelt before final action on the measure. By then Cermak, the boss of Illinois, had a Democratic governor and a Democratic legislature, with his son-in-law president of the upper chamber. No legislation which he honestly demanded could have been denied.

Zangara's bullet prevented Cermak from knowing that his bill had passed and that the militia did not have to be called. Whatever the justice of the tax, it proved to be a very lucrative source of revenue.[31]

The struggle to receive proper fiscal authority from the legislature was protracted and was not completely won during Cermak's lifetime; the continuing hunt for loans from banks was also often unsuccessful. The question of borrowing money from the state government never really arose, except as the state played a role in public assistance. For these reasons, Cermak turned to Washington, beginning a trend which grew to full flower during the New Deal. But even Cermak was not quick to take this action. The tradition of American urban politics did not include reliance on the federal government.

It was not until a year after Cermak became mayor—by which time the depression was well along and the municipal finances were still in an impossible condition—that appeal to Washington was first made. Cermak vigorously urged a federal "prosperity loan" to turn the tide of the depression. "I honestly believe it would act like a miracle cure and that we would see material benefits within sixty days. Surely there can be no question but what the government must lead the way back to normalcy."[32] This was an unusual view for a laissez-faire businessman-politician. Cermak was one of the first old-line politicos who learned quickly from objective necessity. He did not remain idle and merely wait for the inexorable laws of Smithian economics to operate while men starved. Although all of his training pointed to a wholehearted acceptance of the American rugged individualist businessman's mystique, he was able to recognize the crisis nature of the situation. Perhaps he would not have fitted too badly into the first Roosevelt cabinet—an appointment that was bruited about before his death.

Here is Cermak's version of pseudo-Keynesian economics.

The first thing that must be done is re-establish public confidence and initiative by a program of building, construction and public improvement. The minute the prosperity loan program is passed, you will find persons bringing their money out of safety deposit boxes, vaults—yes, and even cigar boxes, sugar bowls and from under mattresses.

It would bring a return to sane values and restore the buying power of the nation. All the people need is an example and they will do the rest.[33]

Soon he made more direct demands. Not only did he want money for public assistance, but he also began action to receive Reconstruction Finance Corporation loans. Cermak organized an elaborate lobby to go to Washington to get the loans. He kept the telephone wires to Washington hot. All Illinois congressmen were pressured. The delegation he was to lead in the assault on Washington was chosen, and held conferences on strategy.

Despite all the efforts, the trip was useless. The R.F.C. refused to make a loan directly to the city, and the local bankers would not act for the city. Upon his return Cermak gave a characteristic account of all the — — persons who had refused his pleas. "Chicago was treated the way Congress is treating the rest of the country. They don't care what happens to the country." He called Congress a "font of bolshevism."

They are fiddling as Rome burns. They are more interested in their party's control of the country than in the welfare of the people.... Secretary of the Treasury Mills told us they could do nothing for us, but would be glad to talk to us socially. I wonder if they think that all we have to do is to go to Washington to talk to them socially.[34]

But this initial setback did not stop the Mayor. He went back to the well again and again. A month later he instructed the comptroller to request a $20,000,000 loan from the R.F.C., and in September he went to Washington again for a loan. By this time Chicago had received two loans from the R.F.C. In November Cermak repeated the same journey for the same purpose, and once again he succeeded in receiving a small loan. He continued to invoke federal aid regularly until his death. This was one of the chief items on his agenda for conversations with Farley and Roosevelt in Miami Beach.

ADMINISTRATIVE ECONOMIES

Finally in the category of attempts Cermak made toward the solution of the fiscal ills of the city were his activities as chief administrator of the municipality. Perhaps it is for his record in this field that Cermak is best remembered—admiringly by some, with distaste and revulsion by many. Public officials who attempt to curtail the costs of government call down upon their heads the imprecations of those affected. The payrollers who are fired or whose salaries are reduced, the officials whose positions are abolished, and the businessmen whose municipal contracts bring smaller returns do not normally look with love upon the instigator of such movements.

When Cermak entered office he was deeply committed to a program of economy and retrenchment. His record as a tax-reducing official was dear to him, as was the support of business groups and taxpayers who demanded lower cost of government. His campaign as a "Master Public Executive" demanded drastic delivery. The citizens' committees he appointed continually pressed him to effect greater and greater reductions. Finally, the objective fiscal fact of a near-empty treasury allowed little alternative.

He started auspiciously enough by discharging more than two thousand temporary employees on his first day in office. But this action was not quite what it seemed, for most of these employees were replaced by "deserving Democrats"—at least for a short time. No significant retrenchments occurred the first few months. It was not until the legislature adjourned its regular session in June, without enacting legislation necessary to rescue Chicago's crumbling financial structure, that Cermak began to act vigorously. But from this point on he was remorseless in his attempts to curtail expenditures. No sentiment for old-time employees, for the lame or the halt—everyone who was not necessary had to go. So relentless was this crusade that Cermak's reputation for ruthlessness was considerably enhanced. Every sort of scheme was utilized to save payroll expenses: mass layoffs, staggered time, payless vacations, the abolition of sick leaves and of the five-day week.

Of course, there was opposition from persons affected. A.J. showed no mercy for the enemies of economy, were they aldermen, judges, or employees under his direct jurisdiction. The municipal court judges refused to accept a pay cut and Cermak lashed them as follows: "The fourteen day wage cut goes for everybody, and they might as well take it graciously as have it forced upon them. . . . I am sure they will listen to reason. . . . But if they don't, they'll get the slash anyway."[35] Alderman Clark, who had stated that Cermak's plan for a 15 per cent reduction in costs would impair services, was addressed thus: "We are going straight ahead. . . . If Alderman Clark wants to throw sand on the track, he won't get very far."

Heads continued to roll. By the middle of August, 1,085 people had been discharged at an annual saving of $2,483,041. Many of these were Thompson men, but Cermak was not replacing them.[36] Even these measures, however, were not enough. As preliminary discussion of the 1932 budget began, Cermak's advisory committee recommended a 20 per cent reduction, 10 per cent in salaries, and Cermak defended the suggestion.

But every now and then the spoils politician in A.J. emerged, and he publicly differed with his efficiency expert, Jacobs, or his advisory committee. There can be no doubt that the reduction of patronage must have cut him deeply, although he seemed to manifest an almost sadistic delight in playing the role of a politician Paul Bunyan. When it was recommended that forty-one of fifty ward superintendents—generally reckoned as the most political and useless jobs—be eliminated, Cermak called them "indispensable" and the action "false economy." He took a similar defensive position relative to the police department.

However, he generally supported Jacobs' recommendations for the new budget against attacks by aldermen. "The city council is impaired. Of course we can't cut the fire and police. . . . Surely the unemployment situation is bad enough, but industry has had to do it, and we are the last, but it must come." He added, "Criticism of Mr. Jacobs is unfair, and it won't stop our efforts."[37]

In spite of much grousing, the finance committee of the city council acted favorably on most of the economy and reorganization recommendations. But when the legislature adjourned without enacting other "must" bills, the really serious economy attempts began, "probably the most searching retrenchment program ever attempted by local governments."[38] Thousands were to be laid off. Purely skeleton forces would be retained except in the police and fire departments. The schools might have to close for three months. Cermak submitted an ordinance calling for dismissal of 2,470 additional employees and the virtual curtailment of some services. He warned that this was only a start. Two to four thousand more would have to go.

Protests were furious. The chief of police called it a "calamity"; an opposition alderman predicted the "breakdown of local governments ... loss of life in riots and epidemics." Department heads screamed dire warnings: Chicago would have an inadequate water supply for fire fighting. The finance committee voted to defer action on the wholesale layoff. One alderman voiced the attitude of many: "These citizens' committees are welcome to give us their sincere suggestions, but they have no right to come in and bulldoze and browbeat elected officials."

Momentarily stymied, Cermak tried another tactic. He requested authority from the council to "eliminate all unnecessary employees." If it was not granted, then he would use his general powers of supervision. He seemed willing to compromise—the 2,470 figure was only a target—but he was prepared to act on his own. "I've given the aldermen nine weeks. ... If they do not give me the authority, I'll use the power I have."[39] Cermak's dare was accepted, and the requested authority was denied to him.

The mass dismissals were carried out: 1,492 employees were discharged as soon as the primary ended. In addition, a very drastically reduced budget was submitted to the council and quickly approved by the finance committee. Salaries were to be cut by 21 per cent; sick leaves and vacations were to be eliminated; all employees were to be laid off for one month; all monthly employees were to be docked four days a month; and maintenance of all motor vehicles was abolished. Cermak made a few minor concessions, but the budget was tentatively accepted. All city employees lost seventy-eight days' pay and sick leave. This included the mayor but—not surprisingly—not the aldermen. There were only three negative votes as the galleries cheered. Later the council accepted the budget definitely. The unprecedented budget was $13,000,000 under the total for 1931. A large proportion of the reduction was at the expense of employees. Many other types of appropriations were cut, but interestingly enough the appropriations for several council committees headed by good Cermak friends were increased enormously. Cermak was shrewd enough to reduce the appropriation for the mayor's office slightly, but Brady, Szymczak, and Kaindl were given more funds. As the election of 1932 approached, A.J. gave some evidence that the defense of retrenchment had become wearying. He complained to his old friends of the Chicago Association of Commerce:

> In normal times it would be comparatively easy to succeed in honest efforts to readjust the city's finances. It would require courage to eliminate payrollers but it could be done.
>
> In these days, however, every employee severed from the payrolls becomes a charge upon charity, and a bitter enemy of the mayor. Were it not for the support of fair-minded citizens, the job would be impossible.[40]

His unhappiness was understandable. In his year and a half in office he had reduced expenditures by $19,000,000, and the end was not yet in sight. As the 1933 budget preparations began, he announced still further reductions. The citizens' committees were still pressing; and even more important, the banks were promising a loan conditional on a low budget.

Most of the above economy efforts had been directed toward personnel. Mayor Cermak did not restrict himself to these items. With his characteristic interest in detail, he constantly sought to save even insignificant sums. Nothing was too minute to escape his attention. Time after time he warned the police to enforce licensing regulations vigorously; the repair of police department vehicles was ordered reduced, and the number of drivers available to fire officials was cut down. Cermak ordered a "suppression" of the use of city telephone by employees, had 242 removed, and gave up his own official private line. He ordered a reduction in the use of the city automobiles, and warned employees they had better learn to walk. At one point he was so desperate that he began negotiating for the sale of the municipal water works to a private corporation, although he changed his mind about this. He became furious with the Material Service Corporation because it increased its prices to the city. "If Illinois concerns are going to 'gyp' the city, we'll simply go elsewhere for our material." The firm referred to was one allegedly close to Cermak; but he lashed out at it as he had at other erstwhile friends in the course of the battle to keep the crippled city going.

The continued bad temper the Mayor displayed during his short term in office had sufficient objective causes. Had he not tried his best with bankers, with the legislature, and with Congress? Had he not taken such politically reprehensible actions as discharging large numbers of employees? Had he not tried to be a "real world's fair mayor"? And what was there to show for it? Shortly before his death, the city was three and one-half months behind in salaries (although this was better than other local governments) and the city's bills were nine months in arrears.

Cermak demonstrated considerable understanding of public finance and the impossible money problems facing the city. Although he invented few of the treatments, he accepted a large proportion of the advice of what to him and many others seemed the most responsible and best-qualified persons: the bankers, the big businessmen, and the good-government elements. In attempting to put these recommendations into operation he exhibited the most tireless and determined leadership. At times he was unwise, nearly always a Cassandra, and frequently ill-tempered and abusive. He may have lost some supporters in the process, but he probably would not have succeeded to the extent that he did if he had employed more restrained tactics. The reductions in employees caused deep resentment in his organization, and the reduction in salary of some of his lieutenants and the elimination of some of their sinecures was never forgiven. In the sense in which the word leadership is often used—with moral overtones—he was not a leader in this entire enterprise. But the line which divides the leader from the driver is a nice question in social analysis.

ADMINISTRATIVE REORGANIZATION

The notion of reorganization in the minds of citizens' groups, and in Cermak's mind, was even more inexorably tied up with economy than was the case with former President Hoover in his work with the commissions which bore his name. As with Hoover, so with Cermak and his citizen advisers: efficiency was verbalized as an objective, but to all intents and purposes it was used merely as a euphemistic synonym for economy. In other words, it was the cost and not the quality of service which was the prime target. Or, alternatively, there was a semimagical belief that if government costs were cut, efficiency would automatically result.

With this philosophy of administration, Cermak's advisory commission—to which former Cook County efficiency expert Jacobs was attached—began to work. The commission worked rather sporadically, but Jacobs was on the job full time. Most early efforts went into plans for a central purchasing agency; the first reports were submitted at the end of 1931.⁴¹ The reports were not major administrative documents, perhaps because they were so completely oriented, in the view of its chairman, toward "a reduction of $22,450,000 in the budget for 1932." In sum, it was proposed to abolish a handful of the thirty-two city departments and merge their activities with other units.

Cermak played an important role in the commission's deliberations, and his leadership is largely responsible for the results. He immediately had some of the recommendations embodied in the form of ordinances as well as administrative directives. "The recommendations as presented . . . have my approval and support. I shall insist upon action and sustained cooperation by every bureau and department head."

A year later (December, 1932) Cermak himself presented another set of proposals to his citizens' groups as well as to the city council. The objective was similar to the earlier attempt—this time a $2,500,000 annual saving—and the recommendations were equally innocuous. They called, for example, for the abolition of the license bureau (which Cermak had founded), the organization of a central trucking pool, and centralization of all inspection services. There was one rather more significant item, but this had not reached the state of presentation to the council. This was a proposal to establish a bureau of the budget which would exercise "centralized control of budget policies of all large local governments in Cook County." Professor Merriam was appointed to draft a resolution which was to be presented to all the governments involved. This plan did not come to fruition before Cermak's death —nor has it in three decades since.

Thus, Cermak did not cause vast reorganizations during his short term as mayor. A few units were eliminated, a few more merged with others; in one case, the sinecure board of zoning appeals positions were filled by other cabinet members instead of being distributed as patronage prizes. However, even these minor products were noteworthy results for a spoils politician. Since Cermak's death—even recently when both the mayor and governor were Democrats of reform caliber—no significantly greater reorganizations have been effected in Chicago government. There can be no doubt that Cermak was acutely interested in reorganization insofar as it did not seriously hamper party control.

Nor is there much doubt that he sincerely believed in consolidation of the many independent local governments. When he was president of the county board he often introduced legislation to this end. Further indication of this attitude is given in the plan for a county-wide bureau of the budget. He continued to lead in further consolidation plans as mayor. He was particularly in favor of merging the many local park boards into one—but did not rule out the idea of including other units of government as well.

When Henry Horner was elected governor, it seemed that Cermak would have an opportunity to demonstrate how honest had been his agitation for governmental consolidation. Because several of the park boards were appointed by the governor, most governors, especially if they were downstate Republicans, were not enamored of consolidation schemes. The patronage of the Lincoln Park and the West Park boards was too useful to them. However, with "Cermak's governor," this obstacle was largely eliminated. A month after Horner's election Professor Merriam told a legislative committee that Cermak and Horner would have "their own legislative program for drastic reorganization of government in Cook County."[42]

But these plans, like many others in Cermak's fertile mind, were cut short by his death. There is no way of knowing how extensive his planning would have been or how much much of it he could have succeeded in having adopted. To 1956, only one portion of his program had been enacted: the unification of park boards into a single park district, which, however, is independent of both city and county. But there is reason to suspect that the "Master Public Executive" might have done more. Only a few days after the new state Democratic officials took office, Cermak caused a unification of city and state license bureaus by a simple administrative agreement with his man Hughes, the new secretary of state.

Cermak might have caused greater government consolidation not only because his administrative mind was disturbed by the nonrational jungle of jurisdictions, but because in his position as undisputed party boss consolidation would have been advantageous for him. Had he continued as mayor, there is little doubt that the consolidations would have been directed toward aggrandizing the city. Such schemes would have strengthened the hand of the mayor-boss. Undoubtedly consideration of this kind explains his support of other reform measures in this period such as the short ballot, which would have had the effect of requiring the appointment of several officials hitherto popularly elected—court clerks, bailiff, coroner, and such. Most students of local government would agree that this measure is objectively desirable. For Cermak the mayor-boss, it was also a good thing. This was equally true of his scheme for the nonpartisan election of the mayor and the extension of the aldermanic term to four years. Considering Cermak's support in the 1931 elections, running for re-election as a nonpartisan candidate might have been advantageous.

The political element in his support for these various reform schemes is made clear by his continuing opposition to four-year terms for ward committeemen. As boss, his control was more secure if ward bosses had to fear defeat every two years in case they crossed Cermak. Naturally, all such schemes were rationalized on other grounds—often on grounds of economy. Economy was given as the reason for his suggestion to reduce the number of precinct election judges from five to three. It is easy to see that economy would be served by such a reduction; it is equally easy to see that election frauds might be facilitated—three persons are fewer to bribe than five.

But in spite of the political cast to Cermak's administrative and governmental reorganization plans, the current maze of Chicago governments would without doubt have been somewhat rationalized had he lived. That he went no further in reorganization schemes is less surprising than the fact that he went as far as he did. His position in these matters was well ahead of the majority of other local politicians and that of bankers, newspaper publishers, and industrialists. Gosnell, an astute observer of Chicago politics, has said that such business leaders used political bosses as the bulwarks for the status quo. It seems likely that Cermak would have proved a less stalwart bulwark than his successors have been. It also seems likely that had the equilibrium of political power continued to favor it, he would have led the powerful political forces toward reorganization rather than have allowed the fragmentization to persist. He certainly would not have had to be pushed in that direction.

MAYOR CERMAK AS CHIEF PERSONNEL OFFICER

Cermak's cabinet included more men of high caliber than those of most Chicago mayors, and was perhaps as good as the city ever had. This does not mean that considerations of political strategy were not included in the criteria for choice. On the contrary, in nearly every case it is easy to see who sponsored an appointee, or, alternatively, which group the appointment was calculated to recognize.

"I will be very careful in selecting my cabinet," A.J. said. And he was; the process of selecting cabinet members and other top personnel took him several cautious months. Furthermore, although he was willing to listen to the claims of groups and individuals who wished to make suggestions, he gave notice to ward committeemen and others of the party that "they should not expect me to put men in cabinet positions they cannot fill"—even if it meant going outside the party to find the properly qualified persons.

And, in spite of every pressure, A.J. was secure enough in his control of the party to follow through his plan for appointing good men. His first corporation counsel was Francis X. Busch, a professor of law, ex-president of the Chicago Bar Association, who had occupied the same position in Dever's cabinet. When Busch resigned (under amiable circumstances) he was replaced by William H. Sexton, also an ex-president of the Bar Association, who had been Harrison's corporation counsel. As generally expected, Colonel Sprague became commissioner of public works. Szymczak, to no one's surprise, was comptroller until appointed to the Federal Reserve Board. Bundesen, also as expected, was appointed president of the board of health.[43] After considerable delay, John P. Allman, "the iron man," was appointed commissioner of police. In this instance Cermak left the choice to his advisory commission. The building commissioner was J. E. Ericsson, who had held the same position in a Harrison cabinet. William Jackson, a manufacturer of electrical products, became commissioner of gas and electricity.

After the many promises of a "virile" civil service commission, A.J. made diligent efforts to fulfill at least a portion of his pledge. He offered the chairmanship to Professor Merriam, who declined.[44] He then offered it successively to several prominent businessmen, such as Edward F. Hurley. They did not accept it either. Finally he appointed Richard J. Collins, also a leading businessman, and formerly active in Cermak's campaign. For the two other members he named University of Chicago Professor Leonard D. White, a leading scholar in public administration, and J. V. Geary, a ward committeeman whose expertise in personnel matters was not well known.

Although these appointments (except for one member of the civil service commission) were good in the sense that these individuals were fitted for their positions by training, or were persons of integrity, or both, in nearly every case there was a valid political reason for appointment. For example, the appointment of Szymczak recognized the Poles; those of Sprague, Collins and certain others, the business community and "silk stockings"; White, the independents; Ericsson, the Scandinavians. Allman, the police commissioner, was "handed to" Cermak by his powerful advisory commission, and of course Bundesen's appointment was the payment of a political debt incurred in the mayoralty preprimary.

The rest of the cabinet was more clearly a case of patronage and recognition with qualifications and/or integrity definitely secondary. Elizabeth Conkey, Democratic national committeewoman, became commissioner of public welfare; Edward J. Kaindl, ward committeeman, was appointed city collector; B. F. Lindheimer was named to the board of local improvement; and Cervenka became commissioner of supplies. These are only a few indications of patronage at work. Of course, some of these persons may also have been qualified, but party and factional recognition was the basic criterion.

It was the heyday of Czech and generally of all Slav participation in city offices. All of the by-now familiar names were present: Cervenka, Kolar, Hruby, Tice, Denemark, and Sonnenschein.[45] Szymczak led the list of Poles and other Slavs which included Kielminski, Smietanka, Bobrytzke, and Dembrowski. Among the Jews were F. L. Lindheimer, Loebner, Lipsner, and Solitsky; and

Italians and Scandinavians were remembered in smaller quantities. In general the Irish (particularly the ex-Brennanites) fared much worse than in any other Democratic administration, as a comparison of Cermak's appointments with Dever's or Kelly's strikingly demonstrates.[46]

The Mayor's relation with his top-level advisers, including efficiency expert Jacobs and the citizens' committees, was generally excellent. Joshua D'Esposito, a member of the advisory commission, said that Cermak never interfered in the slightest with the commission's deliberations—even when the decision reached by it fell far short of agreeing with A.J.'s own predilections. This was the case, for example, when the commission recommended that an outsider "civilian" be appointed police commissioner.[47] Francis X. Busch offers an entirely different explanation. According to his view, Cermak pretended to be led by the commission when in reality he did the leading. By a judicious placement of his own men on the commission, by the control of the experts who performed the investigations on the basis of which the commission made its findings, and by virtue of his continuing interest and control of affairs in contrast to the sporadic interest and participation of commission members, Cermak in most cases was fairly able to engineer the kind of recommendations he desired. Mr. Busch said the eminent members of the commission were flattered by the Mayor's assumed deference but "never did a single constructive thing."[48] A hint of this state of affairs emerged when, after Cermak put into operation the large decreases in salaries, he told Avery and Jacobs that further dismissals were unnecessary.

Cermak evidently believed in keeping the experts on tap, not on top. In situations where political or practical expediency dictated, he did not hesitate to reject their recommendations. At the same time, he did not have the terror and distrust of reformers that the ordinary old-line politician manifested. He believed he could keep them within proper bounds. Therefore, he was largely responsible for the appointment of Jacobs as the powerful single assessor in the reformed tax administration, but again was not loath to take him to task for allegedly making excessively low assessments of the personal property of the wealthy.

Relations with other top-level administrators were similar. With those who were either important in their own right or who represented powerful groups, his behavior was correct, though distant. In most cases these men developed a grudging admiration for his capacities, although they were as one in their disapproval of his "grafting." A description by Mr. Busch of Cermak as mayor throws light both on Cermak and on his relations with his cabinet members, and is also a fair sample of the views of many "silk stocking," professional, and independent subordinates.

He had a quick brain and he was a resourceful, wonderful administrator. He loved administration. He had great pride in his administrative ability. As an administrator he was more astute than Dever, although both were keen for efficiency. But Cermak, knowing politics, was better in enforcing discipline. An appointee had to produce or his sponsors had to give him another man. He was independent and smart. He had a sense of people trying to use him. He was not polished or direct; he spoke plain English. He was more ruthless than Dever, not sentimental about getting rid of people. He was a great measurer of the political worth of an individual. You wouldn't fool him. He always knew how much influence each one had in his ward. I admired him, but I loved Dever. You couldn't love Cermak. He didn't have personal warmth. But had he lived he would have made a great mayor.[49]

A.J. was just as capable of calling "silk stockings" and millionaire subordinates on the carpet as he was of chastizing a delinquent janitor. In one instance, when he learned that his civil-service commissioners seemed on the point of issuing a directive to the effect that classified employees would not be forced to suffer political assessments, Cermak ordered both the wealthy chairman, Collins, and Professor White to his office. He did not bother with the formality of a greeting but began immediately to rant and bellow at his prestigious appointees. "What's this about political collections in the city hall? I'm against it!"[50]

Professor White was the author of the idea for issuing this instruction to the civil servants. He had written a sealed letter to Collins suggesting it. Cermak learned of the contents before Collins himself had read the letter—an excellent example of what Judge Jay Schiller described as Cermak's "Gestapo" organization. Although White had been appointed because of Cermak's gratitude to Merriam for his support, he now became *persona non grata*.

Cermak was in much closer contact with some of his cabinet

than with others, but he institutionalized some contact with all key cabinet members by initiating a practice new to Chicago mayors. He held regular weekly conferences with these persons, designed to "settle questions of jurisdiction and policy, apprise officials of Cermak's opinions and plans, and give Cermak an opportunity to keep departments working smoothly."[51]

From all accounts, A.J. was a strong administrator, exercising continuous and pervasive leadership vis-à-vis his top subordinates.

The Mayor and the Public Employees

In considering Cermak's relations with and attitudes toward the thousands of city workers, we must first note the general conditions of public employment and the state of civil service. The Chicago Civil Service Commission was a body of three members appointed by the mayor. Often these members were politicians who were "more anxious to evade the law than to enforce it," as Gosnell put it. As a result the practice had usually been to hold a few examinations and make thousands of sixty-day appointments which were renewed an indefinite number of times. There was also great favoritism in examinations and promotions, and disciplinary trials were often not seriously conducted. Besides, the commission's authority was shared with the council finance committee, the mayor, and department heads. Many of these were extralegal procedures, since the organic state legislation upon which the civil service system was based required great legal safeguards around classified employees. However, by Cermak's time many clever plans for circumventing the law had become standard procedure. The sixty-day appointment was the basic technique. Another tactic used to get around the provision requiring that the top eligible be appointed was the practice of obtaining waivers from persons at the top of the list. This allowed others who were well down the list to receive preferment. There were many kinds of pressure available to persuade the waiver of precedence.

During the mayoralty campaign Cermak had committed himself strongly to a "virile" civil service commission which he enthusiatically claimed would cure many ills of inefficient government—and stop the crime wave as well. We have seen that he made considerable attempts to appoint men of training and integrity to the commission but that he also named the ward boss Geary as a member. It seems obvious that Cermak believed he could control both the trained personnel expert (White) and the untrained but personally honest, wealthy member (Collins). He had no fears about the third member (Geary). When he learned that White was "no good," he did not hesitate to plan his removal, so that, although White was irritating in his efforts to correct abuses, he never had much opportunity to cause real harm to A.J.'s patronage schemes. Cermak completely controlled one commissioner, Geary, while the chairman, Collins, was a friend who was unfamiliar with his job. He also enjoyed the complete loyalty of the top permanent employee of the commission. This was its secretary and chief examiner, Osborne, who had also served under the worst spoils days of Thompson. The executive secretary of an organization of city civil servants described him as "Cermak's hatchet man."[52] This view of Osborne was corroborated by Professor White and others. Whereas White did not see Cermak for an entire year, Osborne reported to Cermak every morning. Cermak also saw Commissioner Geary daily and Chairman Collins frequently. But Osborne was the "chief patronage agent." He had full charge of the temporary appointments and also compiled the lists of eligibles which the Mayor requested. These lists were then manipulated via the waiver route.

All this was well known to the insiders, as was the resulting prostitution of the merit system. "Tony ran the civil service commission. Anybody could pass an examination."[53] Similarly for promotions. Whenever this was at issue the classic question was invariably put: "Who is his sponsor?" Again, however, bad as the situation was, it was at the very least a considerable improvement over the Thompson regime, when, as a Negro alderman put it, you "could go and talk a little." Although Osborne and Geary were completely under Cermak's control, with White and to a lesser degree with Collins, "There is absolutely no chance to get past. . . . They have it fixed so you have to take examinations on merit."[54]

During this whole time Cermak publicly professed great respect for and belief in the value of civil service. He often called for a "complete reclassification" to correct Thompson's utter disregard for the system. However, he showed some ambivalence when matters of economy obtruded. In such situations the merit system invariably had to give way. When the mass layoffs occurred in 1932, he admitted that 25 per cent of those laid off were civil servants, although thousands of temporary employees still remained. During the 1931 purge, when accused by an alderman of violating the civil service law, he denied it vehemently, although in the same breath he practically admitted it. "I take exception to the statement. It may be that we discharged civil service laborers who were paid seven dollars a day and who came to work with diamond studs and fur collars. We had no place for them, and there was no violation of the civil service law."[55]

It is fairly well authenticated that classified positions were for sale, as were promotions. The whole proceeding was highly systematized. Each job had its price. The executive officer of an association of civil servants described how employees would borrow money from the credit union so that they would have the purchase price. A carpenter foremanship cost $750, while $2,000 was needed to become a fire battalion chief.[56]

Cermak did not have a great respect for the merit system. Nor did he show much greater respect for individual employees, although he professed deep sympathy when they went payless. His complete lack of regard in reducing salaries and destroying other compensations such as sick leave and vacation has been noted. However, "He was not anxious to get crosswise with the employees as a group. He was pretty fair with them but only when he had to be. It was political to play ball with the Civil Service Association, but not with individual employees."[57] This concern with the Association did not prevent him from continually chastising and threatening public employees, or from pursuing ends he thought desirable at their expense.

It is therefore not strange that employees did not love him. It was not only that their jobs were in jeopardy; they actually feared any personal contact with him. One veteran employee of medium grade assessed employees' attitudes in this way:

There was a more definite dislike and distrust of him than for any mayor. Mayors like Dever and Dunne were considered theorists but naive. This was not felt about Cermak. They knew his political word was good—this was part of his complexity and animal cunning. They felt this cunning but feared it because the basis of his judgment was unpredictable. They didn't trust him, but despised him, except those making money through him.[58]

The civil service association official agrees with this description of the employees' attitudes.

They all hated his guts. They used to say that "the bastard is in for what he can get out of it personally." When his body lay in state in the city hall, a cop on guard asked one employee why he had made the circuit three times. He replied, "I want to make sure he's dead."[59]

In addition to fear of arbitrary dismissal there were pressures to join ward organizations. Many persons unknown to most employees came to collect dues—usually 1 or 2 per cent of the salary. One employee said he did not know of anyone who was discharged for failure to pay, but most of them paid because they were frightened.[60]

Manifestly, Cermak was better able to don the garments of the reformer in fiscal matters than in the personnel field. His was the prototype of the "bullwhip" school of administration. Authority undiluted with gentleness flowed unrelentingly downward, and only unquestioning obedience was expected in return. Not for Cermak was the human-relations type of personnel administration made famous by Elton Mayo and his Harvard group. Nor was he guilty of the sophisticated application of *Administrative Behavior* as propounded by Simon. For Cermak, administration was largely the use of authority and coercion as an extension of the will of the executive over his subordinates. It was manipulation in the crudest form—not the gentler variety of manipulation, which masquerades as respect for the human personality.

Consequently, Cermak's cabinet officials admired him while having no affection for him. And the rank and file of employees, who could not admire his abstract administrative capacities, simply feared and hated him. But no one among the dozens interviewed charged that his administration was less efficient than those of more popular mayors such as Harrison, Dever, Thompson, or even Kennelly.

THE MAYOR AND THE CITY COUNCIL

Just as on the county board, Cermak kept in constant and close touch with the city legislative branch, perhaps closer than any other Chicago mayor. In part this was a product of his long years as a council member and as leader of the council. No other mayor, at least in this century, had behind him comparable experience.

In his inaugural Cermak promised to fulfill his legal role as member of the council, and this pledge he kept faithfully. Whenever he was in the city he not only presided over plenary sessions but was a regular fixture at important committee sessions, where he invariably ran the show.

He was a good presiding officer. He knew parliamentary procedure and maintained a nice control over debate. He used no steam-roller tactics, but did not allow the council to run over him. His rulings were sharp and crisp. He was much superior to Dever. Kelly was as good, but he had nearly 100 per cent control over all the aldermen, while Cermak's was only two-thirds.[61]

However, his control was more than adequate. His hold on most of the local patronage made this inevitable, as did the generosity of Moe Rosenberg. The organization of the council reflected Cermak's control. Although the council was nominally nonpartisan, no Republican held any important committee chairmanship. In general there were few Republican committee chairmen. Even more important, the ex-Brennanites were well contained. Although Clark was allowed to retain the chairmanship of the finance committee, one of Cermak's floor leaders was vice chairman, while Arvey, the other floor leader, was also a member. Other members included Toman, Sonnenschein, and two other trusted Cermak men. Most other important committees were completely under the control of Cermak men. Bowler headed the rules and one other committee. Toman, Sonnenschein, and Landmesser headed others. When one compares the committee organization in 1932 with that in 1930 (Thompson's last year) or 1933 (Kelly's first year), it is easy to see Cermak's grasp on the council organization.

It is not surprising, then, that Cermak sometimes played the authoritarian role with the council. Such threats as this were commonplace: "I want your cooperation, and if I cannot have it I will go ahead anyway. I want to make it easier for you when the first of the year comes around."[62] Or he would scold the aldermen as if they were schoolboys.

You know that most of the time half of the members do not know what the other half is doing. Upon reflection you will agree it is a most ridiculous situation. Every member ought to know what is under consideration.

From now on I am going to insist you occupy your seats, and when you do not I shall call you by name.[63]

He was not at all averse to criticizing or punishing individual aldermen. The punishments might include loss of patronage and/or loss of office. Public chastisement, also, was frequently resorted to. The ferocious floor battles with Alderman Nelson, a Thompson man, were remarked by all observers. When another alderman criticized the wholesale abolition of jobs, Cermak revealed that there had been 350 men from the complainant's ward— all patronage employees—among the discharged. Perhaps his most celebrated public quarrel, on the Jacobs matter, was with his old nemesis, Clark. But friends, too, were the objects of public wrath. When several aldermen opposed the appropriation for Jacobs' work, Cermak described them collectively as "candidates for the psychopathic hospital." He singled out Toman for special censure at this time. The Mayor rode herd over all. No alderman who dared to oppose him was safe from attack.

THE MAYOR DEALS WITH CRITICAL PROBLEMS

Besides the terrible financial tangles, Cermak's short term as mayor saw him confronted with many other problem areas of importance. Primary among these were public assistance and crime.

Cermak and Public Assistance

Cermak's legal responsibility as mayor did not extend to this field; the city bureau of public welfare had only minor duties. Cook County administered almost the entire welfare program for Chicago. But Cermak could not stay out of the picture. The objective fact of incipient violence probably forced his hand somewhat, but even this need not have made him play such a prominent role in relief matters. Cermak valued his reputation as a humanitarian. It was a useful political attribute. What degree of actual sympathy he had for the impoverished can only be conjectured. Public welfare experts incline to give him the benefit of the doubt —Wilfred S. Reynolds, a top-ranking administrator in public and private welfare agencies in Chicago for over three decades, described Cermak as a "welfare statesman."[64] Although Cermak's public utterances in this connection have a certain coldness, it is certain he had no deep conviction against public assistance. And since it was so obviously politically expedient, if not necessary, there was little to lose and much to gain by wholeheartedly embracing the philosophy of governmental relief. Opposition could come from only one powerful political opinion: the wealthy. And Cermak shared many of the attitudes of this class. However, political expediency dictating, he felt certain he could convince the conservative rich that public assistance was to their advantage also in the long run.

Almost from the first Cermak was deep in the problems of relief, and until his death he was the central figure in the city and state in relief matters. Although the county was legally responsible, Cermak called the signals. His leadership was symbolized by his selection in 1931 as honorary chairman of the Joint Emergency Relief Fund of Cook County.

His real activities began after the eviction riots in August, 1931, in which several persons were killed and many wounded. In the beginning, and to a lesser degree in later months, he advocated using the existing nonpublic channels for assistance. He therefore led many drives and supported others. He soon found that this was insufficient, and he emerged as a full advocate of public assistance—by the municipality, the state, and the federal government.

Cermak's early commitment to great government programs of assistance is rather remarkable, given his businessman's social and economic philosophy. By July, 1931, he had arrived at supporting specific state taxes for relief purposes. From this date he suggested and supported a great variety of assistance by all levels of government. This included even the city government, which had virtually no legal power to deal with this problem and which in any event had no funds even for routine operations. But Cermak made ingenious use of existing city facilities. For example, he ordered that district police stations be used as informal employment agencies for odd jobs. (The state government, of course, had full power in this realm and the resources with which to operate.)

Cermak became a wholehearted supporter of action by the state government. He was among the leaders in recommending legislation and seeing it to successful enactment. The regular 1931 session of the legislature adjourned in June before Cermak became really active in this field and before his administration had an opportunity to present a legislative program. Nevertheless, such a program was presented during the 1931-32 special session. In a 1932 special session a much more complete program was presented, and Cermak made every effort to have it accepted. To a committee of unemployed he made the following pledge: "I agree there must be prompt action by the Legislature. . . . I can assure you I am urging every member of the Legislature to do his duty in this respect and I shall continue to do so."[65]

It was not so strange for Cermak to look to Springfield in this emergency. All his political career had served to indoctrinate him with the belief that all power was in Springfield and none in the Chicago area governments. As bailiff, as alderman, and as county president he had continuously filed bills in the legislature. But to look to Washington was another matter. After three decades it is difficult to recall the great fear of centralization that existed in the minds of many in 1931-33. But more recent controversies— federal aid to education, "socialized medicine," and integration in the public schools—serve to illustrate that state's rights is still not a dead issue.

Yet, within a few months of assuming office, Cermak was a firm advocate of federal intervention. [66] "It's up to the Federal Government now. . . . We can't do it. . . . The situation is desperate! The federal government must come to our relief!"[67] Beginning in June, 1932, he not only advocated federal assistance but made the first of the contacts with Washington that were to continue until his death. He made many trips to the national capital—to borrow money from the R.F.C., to lobby for direct federal loans to municipalities, and to urge federal relief programs.

He also instigated several schemes for direct federal-Chicago cooperative activities. One such scheme called for the federal government to supply the city with surplus grain which would be baked into bread by city and county institutions and then distributed to the needy. For Cermak, vigorous governmental action when a situation demanded it—even action by the federal government—was not *ipso facto* socialism or statism. To a large degree his economic conservatism was counterbalanced by a relative absence of distrust in government at any level and a recognition of the positive role government could play. However, he tried to draw a line; only in the existence of an emergency could such aid be invoked.

For A.J., the dole was "un-American." "The solution of the unemployment problem is in providing work. . . . If it [government] will make employment available through a big federal works program . . . private capital will receive the stimulation necessary to restore prosperity."[68] He made similar statements frequently. Upon his return from Europe he restated this point of view. "No, I certainly do not approve of the dole system. They all use the dole over there. Americans want work."[69]

He advocated public works even on the city level. He began negotiations with the R.F.C. for a loan in order to build the long-delayed Chicago subway. On his European trip he was much impressed by the Vienna slum-clearance public housing program. He tentatively visualized a similar program for Chicago. However, whereas he advocated federal assistance programs without reservations, his favorable reaction to the Vienna project was tempered by doubts stemming from his private-enterprise orientation. He was impressed enough to order an investigation to consider the feasibility of such a project in Chicago but made it clear that he considered it only because of the demands of relief.

I am not so sure that this socialistic idea could be worked out in Chicago because of economic problems involved. Such buildings would eventually cause a tremendous decrease in property value and the present owners of apartment buildings would find themselves holders of worthless piles of brick and stone.

But I'm not saying that the Vienna plan could not be adopted in Chicago as an unemployment measure.[70]

Cermak Fights Crime

There is generally little discussion of Cermak the crime fighter among his surviving colleagues, nor was much said even in journalistic eulogies. Perhaps the silence is due to the overwhelming acceptance of the stereotype of Cermak as a crude spoilsman. This is not a fair index of his activities in this area. Actually, he devoted much attention to crime and had considerable success as a police executive.

The supervision of police administration was highly specific and frequently public. The Mayor was always making surprise personal inspections (reminiscent of Theodore Roosevelt when he was New York police commissioner) and making his criticisms to newspaper reporters. The greatest part of his crusade was to clean out the dead weight of the department, to reduce administrative work by officers, and to have the maximum number of men out on the beat. There was no letup in this campaign.

> Here we are complaining that we have not sufficient policemen and I find many of them doing . . . clerk's jobs. This will stop. When I am through every policeman will be doing police duty.[71]
> We found there were certain captains had secretaries and assistant secretaries. If they are that busy, we can put extra captains on duty in the busiest stations. . . . They can work in eight-hour shifts and each captain will be responsible for the administrative work during his time on duty. I understand there are some captains on a "bench." I haven't been able to find [it] but those days are over. They will all be put to work.[72]

His supervisory activities were not confined to getting the "cops" out on the beat. The entire gamut of internal administration was fair game. To aid him in this work he instituted his own special squad and also made lavish use of undercover men. But these assistants in no way released Cermak from the duty of personal inspections. At the time that he began to become dissatisfied with Police Commissioner Alcock he announced that he was going to start a personal investigation of every police station. According to one reporter this was a "program unique in the history of metropolitan cities."

Even more persuasive than his detailed supervision of administration was his continuing participation in the direction of specific detail of operation and tactics. The day-to-day operation of the whole department was regarded as being in his direct purview. A.J. was in this context no more prone to the dogma of delegation of authority than in other areas of his concern.

His first direction of a drive was against crime conditions in Negro neighborhoods. He warned that if there were no results there would be a shake-up. Shortly thereafter a drive on the "policy racket" in the same territory was announced by the Mayor. But this was only one element in the greater drive on vice and gambling launched by Cermak. Next, he directed the organization of a vice and gambling unit. This was set up under the "personal direction of Cermak," who at this time took "personal charge of vice and gambling suppression."[73] Cermak had acted because he said he had had many complaints. "Up to this time I have had my own investigators look into them and ordered such places closed up."[74] But his own investigators were too few. Cermak used another approach to crime, borrowed from Thompson's political manual: the reiterated "There ain't no crime in Chicago" or words to that effect. Although he certainly was aware of the basic inadequacy of his statements, he utilized the identical statistics used by Thompson to show that the crime rate was higher in sixty-six American cities than it was in Chicago. He used this tactic frequently in speeches during his world's-fair-salesman tour of Europe. Also he tried to minimize the crime conditions by asserting that Chicago was no worse than any other place—only much more publicized. He was willing to go so far as to use censorship to prohibit the "maligning" of Chicago's reputation. Referring to a play which was alleged to expose Chicago crime, he said:

The crime situation must be dealt with. One of the things I'm going to do is suppress plays and pictures that depict crime in Chicago. Chicago is not the worst city in the world.... It must get rid of that reputation.

We are not going to get anywhere as long as these plays and pictures are put on....

That play I will prevent if it is what I believe it to be from the announcement. I am going to attend the first performance and will then decide what is to be done. There are going to be no plays in this city holding Chicago as a crime-ridden place.[75]

Cermak tried to portray himself as the true leader of the anticrime crusade in the Chicago area; and he was ready and willing to use whatever methods, tactics, and devices were available for fighting crime, as he defined it. Often he was irked, but not stopped, by niceties of due process.

What actual results did he obtain? Fortunately some relatively reliable data are available. The head of a private Chicago crime-fighting agency, the Secret Six, gave Cermak a relatively good score.

There has been a marked improvement in crime conditions in the city since Anton J. Cermak became mayor and James P. Allman commissioner of police. But the old alliance between politics and crime, so flagrant under the former city administration, still exists and is strong. The political-criminal alliance has been severely jarred on several occasions, but the same old "fix" is still working.[76]

The chief nonpublic crime-fighting organization, the Chicago Crime Commission, in the report of its operating director, was also commendatory toward Cermak. As of January 19, 1933, the report stated that "Chicago has advanced in its war with the criminal enemy."[77] It saw as "a most hopeful sign" the cooperation between the many local officials, Cermak among them, involved in criminal justice. The report said that the cooperation of these officials was more "inclusive than at any time in the commission's history." (There can be little doubt that Boss Cermak's control was instrumental in causing such inclusive cooperation.) It was emphasized that Cermak "is consistently pressing for results."

The 1934 edition of this same report was also laudatory. Of course, this report covers only two months of Cermak's regime, but most of the individuals singled out for praise were "made" by Cermak. Allman, Cermak's new police commissioner, was described in a quotation from Bruce Smith, director of research of the Citizens' Police Committee, as "a fine, enlightened and vigorous Commissioner who is giving us a remarkable administration." Mayor Kelly's name is not mentioned at all. It was estimated that 80 per cent of the one hundred recommendations of the Citizens' Police Committee were then in effect.

The *Report of the President* (Frank J. Loesch) for the same period was even more praiseful. The visitors to the World's Fair saw no gangsters, boasted Mr. Loesch.

To the visitors' astonishment, it was the gangsters who were hiding, and not the police.

The year has been notable for its vigorous law-enforcement against the organized criminal. . . .

For this favorable result we have to thank Mayor Cermak and the Committee of eminent citizens who in 1932 [*sic*] selected James P. Allman for head of the Police Department, with assurances that he could with his force, pursue and arrest without hindrance, any criminal under suspicion, no matter what might have been his former impunity.

The Mayor has strongly backed the Chief in that policy, doubtless, against much pressure from politicians seeking to remove Commissioner Allman for some more pliant head.[78]

[282]

In a very real sense most of the public acts of a politician are acts of public relations. The political man continually strives to construct in the public mind a picture of himself that is positive and attractive. His stand on issues, his relations with various political groups, and his day-to-day conduct are all greatly influenced by his estimate of the reaction of the great amorphous public and of its various relatively more homogenous parts. This factor is frequently a major consideration in supporting a policy, in appointing an official, and in many more private areas such as marriage, social and sex relations, recreational practice, religious attitudes and practices, and so forth. For Cermak, the 100-per-cent politician, these observations apply with particular force. He not only kept both ears to the ground—he all but lay prostrate in his efforts to absorb undefined changes of opinion. There are few of his private and public acts that cannot be understood in the light of unceasing role-playing.

But besides this generalized obeisance to the opinions of the masses and of groups, there is a more definite category of acts and observances in these days generally described as public relations. Business has a long history of recognizing the great importance of favorably influencing political persons. The fact that business groups pioneered in organizing lobbies is not accidental, and one of the well-known devices of early business gentlemen-lobbyists was lavish use of entertainment and the exertion of personal charm to convince legislators and administrators of the virtues of their corporations. From the recognition of the usefulness of lobbying to business stemmed the professions of lobbyist, press agent, publicity man, and, most recently, public-relations counselor. Politics recognized the utility of these new professions relatively early.

But the realization of the importance of public relations to public administration came much more slowly—and our concern here is with Cermak the metropolitan area administrator, though nonetheless a politician. Perhaps more precisely, the public-relations function was always dimly recognized, but its importance for public administration remained unrecognized until quite recent days. Needless to say, this nonrecognition of public relations as a function—in the same way as personnel or purchasing was recognized as a unique function—hampered the development of the arts and techniques of the field in its application in public administration. The recentness of the use of public relations function by public administrators and executives is best indicated by a vain search for its inclusion in the older writings on public administration.[79]

It is possible to make a case for the position that the art of public relations as applied to public administration is a contribution of the New Deal and the unique qualities of Franklin Roosevelt. At a minimum, the function grew to maturity during the long Roosevelt era. It is sometimes forgotten that the frequent radio addresses by public administrators, the weekly Thursday presidential press conference, and the steady avalanche of press releases from administrators have not always been with us. There is perhaps no better illustration that the several unsuccessful Congressional efforts to control such activities by federal departments. Also indicative is the prominence of the presidential press secretary (for example, Eisenhower's Mr. Hagerty) and of the public relations officers of various military men (for example, MacArthur's Whitney).

Only with the realization of the newness of public relations in administration can there be an appreciation of Cermak's activities in this field in 1931-33. We have by now seen Cermak's deference to public opinion in many political and administrative situations and his tireless efforts to win the support of certain groups. As mayor he operated as ambassabor-salesman-host-diplomat. All of these from a certain point of view can be included under the rubric of public relations, for in the final analysis Cermak was always trying to sell himself.

But in these roles Cermak was more ostensibly selling Chicago or a policy. It is fitting that the discussion of his administrative career be ended by a glance at techniques of public relations more directly aimed at selling himself. In several respects Cermak was a pioneer practitioner in this field—a true innovator. Although obviously lacking many of the personality attributes of some of the outstanding public-relations-oriented administrators such as the Roosevelts, he was persistent in the search for and trial of new techniques and devices. He was also unique in his recognition of the great value of public relations and the resulting fullness of his program in this realm. As county administrator he had given indications of his propensities in this field, but these developed to fuller flower in his brief career as mayor.

An early innovation was the Mayor's creation of the office of an official city greeter. In a great convention city like Chicago—a city, moreover, where hundreds of important personages, as well as ordinary travelers, of necessity had to change trains (and, more recently, airplanes)—the host duties of the mayor were enormous. To aid him in discharging the responsibility, Cermak invented this novelty in municipal affairs. His official greeter, with white accoutrements, white automobile, and siren-screaming white-motorcycle escort, did the honors for most second-rank dignitaries. This invention not only served to conserve Cermak's time and energy but was also a piece of useful public relations. The flamboyance of "Greeter" Gaw and his entourage was appreciated not only by the city, trained to Thompson's flamboyance, but by the entire national press. In his trips to New York, A.J. was invariably questioned about the Greeter by reporters; most obituaries include a mention of him.

Cermak was an indefatigable speaker before all sorts of local groups—the Chicago Bar Association, Czech and other ethnic groups, business groups—the whole urban miscellany. But group contacts are not novel, while Cermak used some extremely novel techniques for his time.

Not the least of these was the press conference. Cermak's realization of the importance of ample and favorable press coverage is indicated by his practice of giving daily group interviews—public reporting could hardly be more frequent than this! He also recognized the importance of more formal written reporting: *ergo,* his recommendation for regular and simplified reports by administrative departments, which he called for in his inaugural address.

Even more unusual was Cermak's extensive use of the radio. No public official of his day, and few since, made more extensive and varied use of this medium for reporting to his constituents. Early in his career he began weekly broadcasts to the citizens. These were true precursors of the famous Fireside Chats. They were even described as "intimate chats" in which the Mayor was to be heard "discussing his troubles, analyzing the problems to be met, asking advice, and in general talking over the job." There were not one, but two, fifteen-minute periods per week. At least one of these was reserved for Cermak, while the other was used by cabinet officers and other top administrators. There was perhaps good reason to describe this program as "a most unique experiment in broadcasting and city management."[80] Cermak described the purpose of the broadcasts in this way:

> There is no public official who does not need your help. We need your advice and your cooperation. We need your constructive criticism. We are interested in your opinions on governmental affairs.
> Further than that it is your right to know what we are doing so that you may form correct opinions and have the facts on which to base constructive suggestions.[81]

This program contained another innovation which was then, and is even now, unusual. The listener-citizens were specifically invited to participate in the broadcasts, and by extension a new channel of communication was opened between government and the governed. At the conclusion of the broadcasts "the listeners will be asked to write in and comment, not only on the broadcast, but to make suggestions as to how Chicago may be improved."[82] This sharply illustrates the great value Cermak placed on public relations. He wanted to know the views of citizens and the impact of his policies upon them. This is probably related to his personality attribute of extreme distrust of subordinates and associates. He wanted to know firsthand wherever possible: he wanted firsthand contacts with those whom he wished to manipulate. This trait was also responsible for another of his techniques: the open office door. Cermak at work in his shirt sleeves, perhaps with a sandwich and a glass of milk to serve for his hasty repasts, was always on view and personally accessible. So many people did he see and so much time was absorbed that finally, in desperation (within months of his death), he reduced calling hours so that he would have time to "transact the business of the mayor's office."[83]

Cermak's broadcasts were successful, despite his lack of a golden voice. The best indication of success is the doubling of the broadcast program in time and frequency. This was done by initiating a special series for women. Whereas the earlier programs were evening broadcasts, for the ladies they were scheduled during the morning hours twice weekly. Cermak spoke on each of these programs, followed by women city and county officials. He also accepted irregular and spasmodic invitations to appear on the air, taking part in programs with such nongovernmental persons as film star Pola Negri or describing his tour of Germany for the local German hour.

In public relations as in other areas of urban administration, Cermak displayed a high order of imagination and originality of technique impressive for a man whose general orientation was conservative. No complete assessment can be made of his administrative career in the short term as mayor. However, this term, taken together with his eight years as county president, reveals an administrator of uncommon talents, a great relish for administration, a willingness to try new methods and techniques, a recognition of the usefulness of new concepts of administration, considerable skill as a supervisor, and an almost superhuman store of energy and capacity for work.

· 13 ·

BOSS

OF

ILLINOIS

AFTER Cermak's election to the office of mayor and the winning of
the huge city hall patronage, nearly every local political prize was
in the hands of the Democrats—and almost completely in Cermak's
grasp.

The amount of political power in A.J.'s hands—flowing from his
elected offices and his party suzerainty—had never been equaled in
local political history. A.J. maintained tight personal control over
the city government but did not give up his hold on the county.
Although he resigned as county president,[1] his faithful ally of many
years, Whealan, became his successor. Moreover, Cermak did not
relinquish his seat as a member of the county board until February,
1932, when his successor was endorsed by the party machine.[2]

He held close reins over the local party machinery. Said one
ward committeeman: "The mayor controls the party in Cook
County. The mayor has forty-five of the fifty ward committeemen
and a majority in the country towns."[3] Although Cermak gave up
his position as chairman of the county central committee, the post
was assumed by Pat Nash, of whose loyalty Cermak was certain. To
make doubly sure, A.J. not only continued to sit as a member of
the committee (which necessitated running for the office of ward

committeeman biennially) but also had himself elected treasurer of the central committee. He was also in full command of the managing committee and of every other section of local party machinery.

As a consequence, he controlled the overwhelming majority of elected county officials and judges, the sanitary-district board, and the South Park board. The last two bodies were controlled by deals with Republicans, and he and State's Attorney Swanson were on the friendliest terms. In addition, A.J. had "made" J. Hamilton Lewis, the junior senator. The Democratic congressmen from Chicago districts needed his support for re-election, as did the Cook County Democratic members of the state legislature. The allegiance of the legislators was clearly indicated as they ratified Cermak's choice for Democratic floor leaders in both chambers—Igoe in the lower house, and Courtney in the senate.[4]

SELECTING A CANDIDATE FOR GOVERNOR

This was the situation when Cermak was inaugurated in May, 1931. But there was a major gap in Cermak's power position: the state government. All the state offices—with the exception of the state treasurer, who was a Chicago Democrat, albeit Irish—were held by Republicans; and the opposition party also controlled both houses of the legislature. The state offices were, then, the next obvious target. Not only were they desirable because of insatiable demands for power and patronage, but the historic Chicago-downstate controversies made Chicago Democratic control of Springfield a goal of tremendous significance.

Cermak as mayor was in an incredibly difficult administrative position. He had inherited a bankrupt city. The municipality had such slight administrative and legal discretion that at every turn permission from Springfield was necessary. Often this permission was not granted; when it was, it came after much delay. If ever a degree of home rule was to be had, it seemed that it demanded a Chicago Democrat in the governor's chair and a Democratic majority in the legislature. Therefore it is not strange that hardly had A.J. entered the mayor's office before discussion and speculation about the 1932 election began. This would be the first presidential election to come during Cermak's leadership. In addition to a new governor and every other state executive officer, all members of Congress, a senator, all the members of the state legislature, and several important county officers, including someone to fill the pivotal office of state's attorney, were to be elected. Many decisions had to be made.

From Cermak's point of view the most important office among these was that of governor—although this did not dim his vital interest in the presidential possibilities. There was little threat to his position as mayor-boss from any other Democratic officeholder except a governor. A vigorous Democratic governor, were he to stray from Cermak's control, would have sufficient patronage to make Cermak's crown sit uneasily.[5] The graveness of the problem and Cermak's indecision are indicated by the fact that, although discussion of candidates was lively from the spring of 1931, the Democratic organization was not ready to file its slate on February 6, 1932, the first day for filing. It was a week later that the organizational candidate was indorsed—Judge Henry Horner. From early 1931 to this date, there was much discussion, billingsgate, many compromises, many false alarms.

It is almost certain that Cermak wanted to take the gubernatorial nomination for himself. That his personal ambitions for office went only as far as the governorship had been demonstrated in 1927-28 by his grim desire for that office and his lack of enthusiasm for a seat in the United States Senate. Cermak's personality made him prefer an executive to a legislative role. For A.J., it was better to be the one governor of Illinois (from Springfield it was easy to guard the integrity of his Cook County organization) than the junior senator from Illinois, one of ninety-six senators. But if he were to climax his office-holding career with the governorship, what better time than now—when he had won such a smashing victory; when there seemed to be such promising Democratic weather; and when he not only controlled a powerful Democratic machine but had such a preponderance of the "decent" elements of Cook on his side? He was fifty-eight years old; by election time he would be fifty-nine. Over the last six or seven years he had been often and seriously ill. Could he afford to wait until 1936, when he would be sixty-two? The answer must have been obvious to him. If Illinois were to have a Czech governor, it would have to be now.

But there were real obstacles. Cermak had been elected to his third term as county president in November, 1930. He had electioneered for mayor from December, 1930, to April, 1931. What would be the public reaction were he to announce himself for governor in 1931 or in 1932—the third and progressively more prestigious office sought in two years? Surely Thompson would get a bigger hog from the stockyard, and the voters might begin to believe the cries about "Dictator Tony."

There was also the ethnic power problem within the party. It is probable that during the negotiations for the mayoralty indorsement Cermak had allowed the Brennanite Irish to believe that the nominee for governor would go to them, or, more specifically, to Igoe. At that time, when Igoe withdrew his claims to the mayoralty (but while Clark was still fighting), it was reported that an understanding had been reached, although "the nature of the deal has not been revealed."[6] Whether or not a promise had been made to Igoe, soon after A.J.'s election as mayor, Igoe made it clear he *was* a candidate for the organization's gubernatorial endorsement.

It was plain that Igoe would not do for Cermak. In spite of every appeasement, Igoe had given adequate indication that he chafed under A.J.'s leadership. Were Igoe to become governor, A.J. would have to wage continuous battle to retain command. Another objection to Igoe was that he was a loser. Democratic leader in the house since 1916, he had twice been defeated for state's attorney by large votes. Although Democratic prospects looked good, few visualized the Roosevelt landslide early in 1931. No, Igoe would not do.

But since Igoe was irascible and not to be controlled easily, something had to be done to contain him. What? How? Cermak did not know. He therefore played a waiting game. He did not openly oppose Igoe's candidacy, but he postponed decision. In the meantime, he let Igoe know that he would be extremely pleased to support him for attorney general—a post Igoe now did not want.[7] Conferences and clashes with Igoe were to continue until the slate was finally drawn.[8]

Cermak used the same delaying technique with the other pretenders who had gubernatorial bees in their bonnets. Most important among them, with A.J.'s tacit approval, was Judge Henry

Horner, a German Jew who had been probate judge since 1914, who had played an influential part in A.J.'s recent campaign, and who was supported by the Sprague businessmen's committee which had performed such yeoman service in the mayoralty contest. Francis X. Busch, prominent attorney, who was very close to Cermak, was an unannounced possibility.[9] Still another would-be candidate was Bruce Campbell, downstate politician and perennial seeker after office.

During these months of delay it seems evident that A.J. was trying to figure out some way of taking the candidacy himself without shattering the party. Reporter John Dienhart says that A.J. confessed to him, "I'm going to become the candidate. Why should I be mayor? I could run the city from Springfield." Another observer believes that Horner was merely a stalking horse used by Cermak because of a belief that the Irish leaders would prefer even Cermak to a Jew.[10] Jewish leaders Lindheimer and Adolph J. Sabath also thought that Cermak intended to jettison Horner,[11] and Horner himself feared this contingency.[12]

All these observers agreed that A.J.'s chief reason for being reluctant to claim the nomination openly was fear of Igoe. As in the case of the 1931 mayoralty election, he was not disposed to welcome a full-scale electoral battle with the dissident Irish. It was not that he doubted his ability to win in such a test of strength; rather to be feared was that the bitterness of the primary would so weaken party unity as to endanger chances of victory in the general election. Cermak seldom trifled with the main objectives—electoral victory for his forces and the ensuing power flowing from office and patronage.

This uncertain and psychologically wearing situation went on for nearly a year. Toward the end of November Cermak finally called party leaders to begin formal slatemaking. At the end of January, by which time the slates should have been completed, reports about Cermak's own candidacy were still in circulation. One headline ran: "Cermak Told He Should Run for Governor; State and Local Democrats Make Plea; Urge Mayor to Aid Chicago from Capital."[13] Significantly, A.J. said neither aye nor nay to these "pleas."

In February the state nominating committee "demanded" that

Cermak accept the candidacy. He refused. "Then they threatened to place his name on the . . . ballot but Cermak remained adamant. Then they indorsed Horner."[14]

The headline on the above news item stated that Cermak would still be drafted. But this was not to be the case. A.J.'s dream of the governorship undoubtedly died hard, but it was overwhelmed by too many real considerations. His fears about Igoe and the disruption of the party were only a part of the picture. There was, besides, the fact of having gone so far in the direction of encouraging Horner and his backers. Horner's powerful supporters, suspecting that A.J. might ultimately throw Horner over, importuned and threatened. According to the late Congressman Sabath, he and Moe Rosenberg told A.J. that they "wouldn't stand for it."[15] Cermak had some reason to fear that Rosenberg, Sabath *et al.* might swing to Igoe if Horner were jilted.[16] And Horner, from the point of view of A.J.'s power position alone, was certainly preferable to Igoe. There was little reason to expect that Horner, if elected, would challenge Cermak's leadership in the way Igoe was certain to do.

Finally, A.J. decided that it was the better part of political wisdom to settle on Horner. Chicago all but demanded a Chicagoan as candidate. Cermak, realizing the importance of an understanding governor for the grave fiscal problems of the city, could not have chosen downstater Campbell. But Horner was more than a Chicagoan. He was a "good" candidate of the kind Cermak so often declared he sought—indeed, it was often said that Horner was chosen because Cermak felt "there was a change on."[17] Horner's career of seventeen years on the probate bench has been described as "distinguished." Mayor Harrison said that "he was absolutely honest as a judge. There was never any criticism of his integrity,"[18] and other local political figures also placed him in that small band of good Chicago politicians, the Stevensons, Douglases, Dunnes, and Devers. There is a minority view that Horner was "not aggressively good or bad . . . [and was] ideally equipped to act as a rubber stamp."[19] Although there are grounds for believing that Horner never bucked the machine—that is, not until 1936—this does not gainsay the long years of unassailable public service which in the wilderness of American urban politics is no small virtue.

Horner had the enthusiastic backing of all the Chicago news-papers. Moreover, the same group of civic organizations, business-men, and "silk stockings" that had helped elect Cermak supported him—but with more enthusiasm for Horner. The money available for a Horner campaign, some believe, may have been a major factor in A.J.'s early encouragement of him.[20]

But there was one serious handicap to Horner's candidacy, or so it seemed. Horner was a Jew, and Jews had not held many import-ant elective offices. New York City, almost one-third Jewish, had never had a Jewish mayor, nor New York State up to that time a Jewish governor. No Jew had been governor of any state. Was Cermak sincerely convinced that he could elect a Jew? How would the ethnic groups organized by Cermak respond to such a candi-date? These questions were in the minds of many politicians and strengthened their belief that A.J. would eventually take the nom-ination himself. One intimate of A.J., when told by him that Horner would be the candidate, responded with disbelief, "Do you really intend to try to elect a Jew?" "Not only will I elect him," Cermak replied, "but he'll be the greatest governor Illinois has had."[21]

With the nomination of Horner, Cermak made his boldest at-tempt at recognition of ethnic groups. In a sense, he was also recognizing the Dunne-O'Connell-Harrison faction of the party, to which Horner had once been allied, as well as "the forces for good."

But he had to consider the requirements for recognition of the entire state. If the gubernatorial indorsement went to a Chicagoan, other portions of the state had to be remembered for other promi-nent positions—that is, if Cermak was interested in building a united state party and not just in maintaining his supremacy in Cook County. And Cermak was of course interested in building an integrated and victorious state machine.

The rest of the ticket was therefore admirably balanced. The state ticket did not neglect downstate but was carefully weighted to counter the expected Igoe diatribes. The candidate for lieutenant governor, Donovan, a Joliet resident, was chairman of the state committee (he had been national committeeman until Igoe had been given this position). The candidate for state treasurer was another downstater with a name to which the Irish were not likely to object, John C. Martin. The other three top state places went to Chicagoans Otto Kerner, Edward J. Hughes, and Edward J. Barrett. Here we note a Czech (Cermak's old friend Kerner) and two unexceptionable Hibernian gentlemen. The pattern of recognition continued among candidates for congressional offices. For United States senator, the Germans and the downstaters were remembered by the naming of W. H. Dietrich. For congressmen-at-large, Brennan and Nesbit were chosen.[22] The district congressmen from Chicago were also well balanced. Of course, Adolph J. Sabath was slated again, as was E. A. Kelly. James T. Igoe, who had been with Cermak in the struggle for leadership, was no longer *persona grata.* His replacement was, cleverly enough, T. J. O'Brien. Here Germans were again remembered by such names as Schuetz, Schlaegar, and Cermak's friend, Charles H. Weber, and the Poles, by Kocialkowski.

The long county slate was also carefully balanced, the top place going to Cermak's erstwhile protégé, Tom Courtney, another Irish representative; for coroner, there was Walsh; for circuit court clerk, Conroy; and for recorder, Clayton F. Smith. A Pole, Zintak, was the nominee for clerk of the superior court. On the slate for the sanitary district, Cermak allowed the nomination of two Irishmen, Touhy and Woodhull, who had joined the Igoe-Clark cabal to take the control of the district away from Cermak.

The slate for the state legislature showed a similar regard for Irish sensibilities. Nearly half of the nominees for the lower chamber had recognizably Irish names, and there was a sizable representation among the nominees for the state senate as well.[23] However, the city judicial slate showed greater attention to balance than to the fear of charges of anti-Irish bias. Of twelve nominees, there were only three with Irish names.[24]

Besides ethnic and geographic balance, the factor of party organization was not overlooked. There were at least eleven ward committeemen on the slate, and one from a country town. With the number on the city payroll, Cermak had about a third of the members of the county committee directly indebted to him for contemporary sponsorship. None of these could very well support Igoe in the ensuing battle.[25]

While the Democrats were girding themselves for a primary battle, it was clear that the Republicans were disorganized and demoralized. Governor Emmerson was not a candidate for re-election, but there were eight contestants for the gubernatorial nomination, including Brundage and Small. The fact that Small, after having had to repay $600,000 to the state because of his speculations, was nominated in this badly divided field offered conclusive evidence of Republican impotence.

In the Democratic primary the entire Cermak slate was nominated by large majorities. Igoe had little chance against the Cermak steamroller. Horner polled more votes than Igoe and Campbell combined.[26] Igoe led Horner downstate by 4,000, but this record was smashed by the nearly 150,000 Horner majority in Cook County. Campbell had only 5,000 votes in Cook County, but ran well ahead of both the others downstate. It is probable that had Campbell not run, most of his downstate votes would have gone to Igoe. But this would not have prevented Horner's nomination. The Cermak machine was simply too strong in Chicago for Igoe.[27] This strength was even more clearly seen in the overwhelming defeat of Scott Lucas by Cermak's candidate for the senate. Lucas received only 5,000 votes in Cook County, while Dietrich had 264,665. No downstater could hope to gain Chicago Democratic votes without Cermak's sanction. In the primaries Cermak had also conducted a little housecleaning among undependable ward committeemen. Igoe was among the casualties of this purge. He was also stripped of his national committeemanship, even though he now returned to the organization with a professed desire for harmony. After a show of coy reluctance, Cermak allowed himself to be persuaded to be Igoe's successor in this position.

Now that the party strife was settled, the real job was at hand—victory, and the end of Prohibition. Soon after the primary Cermak announced that the state platform would be dripping Wet and that the fight against Small as an Anti-Saloon League tool would begin immediately. The national convention also had to be Wet, Cermak declared. "I will give my vote to no man who is not an out-an-out Wet."[28] Thus the program aimed at victory in November through harmony—even including Igoe. But the boys had to be Wet.

THE DEMOCRATIC NATIONAL CONVENTION OF 1932

Cermak's interest in national politics had a relatively short history. Except for his part in the war hysteria of 1917-19 it is possible to note the beginning of his concern with national policy. The date was 1919-20, coincident with the start of Prohibition. But it was more than a coincidence. There was a direct causal relationship between the "noble experiment" and Cermak's involvement in national politics. Until individual thirst became a matter of federal fiat, Cermak's Wetness concerned itself with purely local and state regulation. Heretofore he had been concerned with the selection, influencing, and control only of state and local officials. His stand had been in the name of "personal liberty" and the United Societies—and in the interest of the breweries.

When the first shock of Prohibition passed, it was obvious that the field of action of the Wets had to move onto the national scene where the Anti-Saloon League had won its great victory. From 1920 on Cermak was intensely interested in the election of senators, congressmen, and, most of all, presidents. He was a delegate to every Democratic national convention from that date. In evaluating presidential candidates he seemed to have no other criterion than whether the man was Wet enough. This consideration had been solely responsible for his unsuccessful support of Governor Edwards in 1920 and was one of the major factors in his loyalty to Al Smith.

Cermak's interest in national policy apparently did not extend beyond this question. One of the founders of the National Association Against Prohibition, he considered repeal the outstanding issue for over a decade. His first election as county president was made on a Wet platform against the rabid opposition of the Anti-Saloon League; in two subsequent contests for the same office Cermak's position as acknowledged spokesman for organized and unorganized Wets was always brought to issue. And each of these campaigns was accompanied by a Cermak-sponsored Wet referendum calculated to demonstrate overwhelming Wet sentiment in Illinois. There had been two Cermak booms for mayor and one for governor in the past decade and a half, each based on his unquestioned and fearless Wetness. In two cases when he fought actively but unsuccessfully for nomination (in 1923 for mayor, and in 1928 for governor), he rationalized his desire for office in terms of opposition to "sumptuary legislation." And his campaign for senator was almost entirely based upon pledges to end Prohibition.

During this period Cermak had made contact with Wet leaders in other parts of the country. In the 1924 Democratic national convention he had been among those who fought for Smith in the famous 103-ballot deadlocked convention. The Wets lost; but in 1928 Cermak had again supported the "Happy Warrior," this time successfully. He had done all that was possible to induce each convention to take a frank stand against Prohibition. In these efforts he had also failed.

Now Cermak was mayor of Chicago and unquestioned boss. He had proved his power and his skill in bitter campaigns, and he had enginered a measure repealing the Illinois Prohibition acts. It looked like a good time for resolute action against the Eighteenth Amendment. And Cermak would be one of the most influential members of the convention, not only because he would head the third largest delegation, but also because, since his was the host city, he would control the galleries.

Immediately after the election as mayor, A.J. began activities leading to the selection of a presidential candidate of his choice. He spoke to Democratic leaders in Florida, and the deference of these men—hitherto among the Dryest of the bone Dry southern Democrats—seemed to be an omen of things to come. Cermak's attack on Prohibition in this speech was no different than such speeches of his had been for years—only now it seemed to carry conviction. He prophesied to his Florida associates that the Democratic party could construct "a mighty future on the national discontent with prohibition."[29]

By June, 1931, the various presidential aspirants were "beating the bushes." Cermak, unwilling to commit himself this early, convened a secret meeting of local party leaders in his office and compelled them to accept Senator J. Hamilton Lewis as favorite son. There was another reason for this extraordinary action. Not only did Cermak desire freedom of action with respect to the various aspirants for the nomination, he wanted to allay rumors connecting him with a Smith-Tammany stop-Roosevelt movement. Roosevelt's manager, Farley, came to Chicago to pay his respects to Cermak. The discussion ostensibly concerned the selection of Chicago as the convention site, but there can be no doubt that the astute Farley brought his candidate's merits into the discussion.

To test Farley's merchandise Cermak went to New York, where he was treated as a very important visitor. His views on possible candidates were eagerly sought. Cermak refused to commit himself but was not averse to issuing statements.

> Yes, there is a lot of sentiment for Governor Roosevelt, but I think there is more for Al Smith. Of course, the Illinois delegation ... will be pledged to Senator J. Hamilton Lewis. What will happen after the first ballot will depend on what happens at the convention.[30]

And,

> I cannot think of any issue that will transcend prohibition and hard times.
> I called on Smith and we talked politics among other things. He is ultra wet and I am wetter.[31]

A.J. did not think that Smith was in a "receptive mood" but believed that he was favorable to Roosevelt. But as for A.J., he was going into the convention as an "out and out Wet," and the candidates would be considered only after a Wet platform was assured. Was F.D.R. Wet enough? "I think he will be acceptable to the wets. I think he is wet enough."[32] He could not, however, completely conceal his personal preference for Smith. "The point is just this. Illinois Democrats, like a lot of other Democrats, are for Smith because they know that he is really and sincerely against prohibition."[33]

In the autumn he went to New York again. He had conferences with Mayor Walker, with New Jersey boss Hague, with national chairman J. J. Raskob, with Tammany boss John F. Curry. He had come, he said, to warn his New York colleagues "that the Democratic party cannot 'pussyfoot' on the prohibition question ... that it cannot win if it does and that any deviation from the standard of three years ago may result in a third party."[34] By this time the Smith-Roosevelt feud had become public, as Smith launched a bitter attack upon his former protégé. Cermak said he wished to find out the nature of the difficulty between Smith and Roosevelt. Was it something to do with Roosevelt's already suspect Wetness? "We always figured Governor Roosevelt was wet enough to satisfy anybody. That's what we want to find out about."[35] Cermak found out, but evidently was not convinced. During the conference with Roosevelt, Cermak talked little, listened much. When it was over, his mind was made up to be with Smith.[36] Then he visited Smith. Although he made no definite commitment, Mayor Kelly, who was present at the meeting, believed that Cermak allowed Smith to conclude that A.J. was in his camp.[37]

Whatever degree of actual loyalty he felt for Smith, in the succeeding months of 1931 and the spring of 1932 he reiterated his allegedly single-minded determination to nominate Senator Lewis. Not even Smith's eventual announcement of his candidacy caused him to shift ground. "I'm with Senator James Hamilton Lewis for President. It makes no difference here what Governor Smith said."[38] This continued to be his public attitude until the convention began.[39]

Cermak had much to do with the choice of the members of the Illinois delegation. However, he had not chosen to pack it solidly. In the first place, he had wanted to include as many factions of the party as possible, in the interest of harmony. There were such old stalwarts as Harrison and Dunne, who were outspokenly for Roosevelt. But they were useful to Cermak locally; and, like every other member of the delegation, they were as Wet as Cermak could desire. As proof, the state convention had adopted a dripping Wet platform.[40] However, the overwhelming proportion of the delegation were Smith men, and a great many were loyal Cermak followers.[41]

Illinois had fifty-eight votes. The delegation consisted of fifty-four district votes and four votes at large. The latter were divided among sixteen delegates-at-large, each with one fourth of a vote. This arrangement was intended to assure party "togetherness." Cermak was elected chairman of the delegation; and the indorsements of the county and state committees were ratified by the convention delegation, which elected Cermak national committeeman to replace Igoe.

But Cermak did not have full control of the delegation. His decision to allow wide factional participation resulted in Harrison and Dunne joining with downstate leader Dallman to control 15¼ votes for Roosevelt. (Illinois did not use the unit system.) That

A.J. would have difficulty with the elder statesmen became clear at the first meeting of the delegation, before the convention opened. Cermak angrily halted an attempt to cause the delegation to commit itself to Roosevelt as second choice. "We in Chicago have no second choice. We are with Senator Lewis so long as he stays in the field. . . . We are not attempting to coerce those of a different mind, but we do not want them to coerce us."[42] He was irritated by Harrison-Dunne tactics during the entire convention.[43] Nevertheless, as the convention began, Cermak controlled 40¼ votes.[44]

The Roosevelt forces arrived with a majority of the delegates pledged. However, they needed many more because party rules then required a two-thirds majority for nomination. The strategy of the Smith-Tammany stop-Roosevelt forces was to hold Roosevelt for three ballots. After that it was believed that the convention would move to Smith. As usual, the two main groups had had the preliminary skirmishes in the proceedings of the convention committee on permanent organization. The anti-Roosevelt forces supported Jouett Shouse for permanent chairman.[45] The Roosevelt managers wanted Senator Walsh, but in meetings of the convention arrangements committee they had agreed to Shouse in exchange for the approval of Senator Barkley as keynoter.

However, before the convention started it became known that Farley had changed his mind and was going to risk a test of strength by attempting to elect Walsh as well as Barkley. The Smith forces were indignant at this news, and so was Cermak, although he still claimed he did not belong to the anti-Roosevelt bloc. If Shouse were not retained, then why keep Barkley? There should be instead a good Wet keynoter like Senator Lewis.[46] On the morning the convention opened, he announced that fifty votes of the delegation would support the anti-Roosevelt forces on matters of convention organization.

By this time Cermak did not even have the alibi of loyalty to Lewis, for "Jim Ham" had neatly double-crossed Cermak by withdrawing his name. He had wired Cermak and Roosevelt-supporter Dallman. The latter told Farley,[47] who thought that now Illinois' fifty-eight votes would go to Roosevelt and all but insure the nomination. But Cermak had other plans. His prominent Chicago banker friend, Melvin Traylor, quickly emerged as the favorite son about a week before convention time.[48] Thus Cermak had a new stalking horse, although it was more and more difficult to pretend that he was not a charter member of the stop-Roosevelt boys. This was the situation as Mayor Cermak—chairman of the Illinois delegation, national committeeman, and undisputed leader of the Illinois Democracy—greeted the national convention.[49]

The Roosevelt forces struck first blood as they succeeded in electing Walsh permanent chairman. They demonstrated their strength by polling a large majority on the first ballot—450 ahead of the closest rival—but more than a hundred less than the number required for nomination.[50] The stop-Roosevelters were going well, and many states had to be polled—including New York.[51] There was no longer any doubt that Cermak and Tammany were together.

Farley was frantic. He tried to get McAdoo and California to switch, but he was unsuccessful. Then he buttonholed Cermak.[52] He had no better luck here, although he knew that if he could convince Cermak "the result would be inevitable."[53] Farley knew that if Cermak were moved, Indiana would go with him.

By this time the second ballot was in progress, and Cermak though "sympathetic" was also "regretful" because "his delegation could not switch without a caucus."[54] Farley did not believe this alibi: "I knew better, but could do nothing. He had everything in his hands at that moment—national prominence . . . possibly life itself—but he postponed the decision and political opportunity passed him by."[55]

Cermak sat tight during the first three roll calls, delivering $40\frac{1}{4}$ votes for Traylor each time. The Roosevelt forces gained a few votes on each roll call but could not reach the necessary total. The third ballot ended the famous all-night session, and the convention was adjourned until the evening. Farley was a busy man during the recess. He successfully negotiated the deal with Sam Rayburn and John Garner which netted both the Texas and California delegations. This broke the log jam. On the fourth ballot that evening, Roosevelt was nominated.[56] Of course, Illinois then joined the parade, but Cermak had missed the bandwagon.

But this is not the whole story, for by that time, one of his major aims had been accomplished. Although a candidate had been nominated whose Wetness was not quite dripping, the convention ratified the "Illinois plank"—the Wettest of Wet planks. Perhaps this was Cermak's chief aim. He had been mightily encouraged by the substantial vote in the Republican convention for a Wet plank, although—perhaps to Cermak's relief—only a Moist one was finally adopted.[57] Cermak stated that the Democrats had to outdo the opposition party in their "liberalism."[58] He was certain that the Wets were in the majority in his party.[59]

To insure a suitably Wet platform, Cermak had made his peace with Igoe and had him elected the Illinois member of the resolutions committee.[60] Igoe was a persuasive pleader, and he was able to have the resolutions committee adopt a truly Wet plank.[61] The plank read in part: "We advocate the repeal of the eighteenth amendment. . . . We demand that the congress immediately propose a constitutional amendment to truly representative conventions in the states called to act solely on that proposition."[62] Pending repeal, there was a demand for immediate modification of the Volstead Act to legalize beer.[63] The less outspoken Wets on the resolutions committee were outraged; Senator Glass called it a "barroom plank."[64] He and Cordell Hull sponsored a minority report, which was only Moist.

Two reports were submitted to the convention. The minority report had considerable support, but the dripping Wet plank was adopted by a large vote—934¾ to 213¾.[65] For the adoption of this plank Cermak must have most credit. Not only was his representative Igoe one of its authors, but Cermak's control of the gallery was instrumental in the defeat of the Moist resolution. Cermak had the galleries well packed with party workers who were enthusiastic Wets—and Smith followers.[66] A.J. controlled the police who determined who was to enter the convention hall. There were hundreds—or thousands—of courtesy admission cards signed by the mayor. "Delegates could not get tickets for their wives. Public men of high standing and influence were denied admission to the hall. Persons who had bought tickets found them useless.[67]

The galleries were disorderly beyond belief, especially when the Prohibition resolutions were being debated. They "shouted down the speakers who tried to head off the Democratic party in its mad rush to prohibition repeal."[68] Cermak's control of the galleries was recognized by Chairman Walsh. When McAdoo tried to speak for the Moist resolution and was drowned by boos and catcalls, Walsh turned to Cermak and said: "Mayor Cermak, I appeal to you . . . to control this convention."[69]

Thus Cermak accomplished one of his chief aims. But not even with the unruly, nearly unanimous Smith gallery was it possible to succeed in stopping Roosevelt.[70] When Farley finally succeeded in coaxing Garner, Hearst *et al.* to surrender Texas and California, Roosevelt was nominated without Cermak's help. Not only had he not delivered the president-making votes, but his refusal to accede to Farley's pleas was widely interpreted as "missing the boat"; and the best that was then available was an inconspicuous place upon the bandwagon. This was Farley's view. "There is an old saying in poker that a man frequently over-plays his hand by staying too long. It happens in politics also."[71] This same view of Cermak's stand has often been expressed by political reporters and by Cermak's political associates.

But had he actually "missed the boat"? Was it, as is often charged, his greatest political blunder? What was it that caused him to refuse Farley's blandishments? It is the position of the writer that Cermak's refusal to join the Roosevelt forces was a logical, understandably calculated risk, and that for him political expediency militated against deserting the stop-Roosevelt movement.

Of the greatest importance in his determination was his assessment of the attitude toward Smith of most local leaders, who had an almost mystical attachment to Smith and Smith's candidacy. Of course this was more true for the Irish leaders, but not much less so for others who were Catholics. Cermak himself had had much to do with the growth of the Smith mystique, although for other reasons than Smith's Irish ancestry and his Catholicism. In the struggle for leadership of the party the Irish who rallied to Cermak's side and opposed the Brennanites could rationalize their move in terms of Cermak's proven loyalty to Smith. During the mayoralty campaign Thompson's charges that Cermak was an enemy of the Irish were partially refuted by proofs of Cermak's great record as a Smith man. In the view of men who had reason to know, this factor loomed large in Cermak's thinking. He had just emerged victorious from the Igoe-Irish revolution in the 1932 primary. What would be the result of the next Irish *putsch* if he could be pointed to as a saboteur of the presidential aspirations of the Irish ideal, Smith?

To Henry Sonnenschien, Cermak's faithful adjutant, this fact alone explains his action in the convention. "He didn't think Smith would win, but he [Cermak] was scared of the Irish. Hague, Flynn, and most of the local Irish leaders were with Smith."[72] The identical view was held by the late Mayor Kelly, who was familiar with the attitude of the Irish leaders. His diagnosis of Cermak's "mistake" was in these words: "His mind was made up to be with Smith win or lose because it was helpful in Chicago and because he was Wet."[73]

In this evaluation we also find the second element for Cermak's determination. He simply did not have faith in Roosevelt's Wetness. We have seen how large a candidate's Wet views loomed in Cermak's thinking. Not only was Smith's candidacy popular with that portion of his local organization of whose control he was least certain, but Smith's sincere Wetness could not be doubted. Roosevelt was a different matter. We have seen Kelly's evaluation of the way Cermak reacted to Roosevelt's attempts to convince A.J. that he was Wet enough. Cermak was evidently not convinced. Although the convention had adopted a platform which was soaking Wet, A.J. knew well enough that the party candidate could either nullify the platform or honor the pledge. He believed that with Smith all of his Wet demands would be met; but with suave Roosevelt, this was not so certain.

There was also the factor of Cermak's personal reactions to Smith and Roosevelt. Smith, like Cermak, was a product of the lowest economic and social level. Both were self-made men, diamonds in the rough. There is no doubt that Cermak not only admired Smith but held him in genuine affection. What must his attitude have been to the urbane, aristocratic, cigarette-holder-wielding scion of old country gentry? Although the tragic circumstances of his death have linked his name irrevocably with Roosevelt's and have implied a great fondness for him, the facts seem to be otherwise. The night before the fatal shooting Cermak had given quaint expression of his attitude toward Roosevelt. He asked a colleague to accompany him to Cuba because he did not wish to be in Miami when the President-elect arrived. "Roosevelt is not only weak in the legs, he's also weak in the head," he told his political associate.[74]

There is also evidence to show that Cermak was not caught unaware by the switch of California and Texas. The assumption has been that, had he known of the negotiations, he would have delivered his own delegation (and Indiana's) rather than sink with the die-hard Smithites. As the delegates gathered on the evening of the fourth (and last) ballot, ex-Mayor Carter H. Harrison, the leader of the Roosevelt supporters in the Illinois delegation, was summoned by Cermak who sat a few seats away. Cermak bluffed to the end. He had tried his best to force Harrison and associates to join the majority of the delegation in opposing Roosevelt. Now he threatened Harrison again. "I'm going to vote the whole delegation against Roosevelt this time," he bullied Harrison. "You can't do that," replied Harrison, "I'll demand a roll call." "Don't do it," Cermak answered. "It's all fixed. It will be Roosevelt and Garner."[75]

Thus, Cermak knew that Smith's chances were finished. He might have rushed to Farley, offered his votes and got a preferred place among the president makers. The fact that he did not seems proof that he believed that for local reasons it was preferable to go down with Smith's ship. There would be later opportunity to demonstrate his loyalty to, and support of, Roosevelt. He could turn out a record Roosevelt vote in the fall if his local organization remained intact. But if he deserted Smith, he might have to carry the burden of Irish Democratic antagonism in the fall campaign. This could have endangered the chances of the Democratic presidential candidate, as well as of Horner and the rest of the ticket. No one expected the overwhelming Roosevelt landslide at this date.

So certain was Cermak of the results of the fourth ballot that he was not even in the hall when McAdoo made his famous offering to Roosevelt. There was consternation among the Illinois delegation. Kelly was able to get Traylor's assent to withdraw his name, but Horner was worried about this and insisted that nothing be done until Cermak returned.[76]

Thus, it seems that Cermak did not completely miss the boat. True, Farley was not overly friendly, but the subsequent support of Roosevelt by the Chicago Democratic organization was such that Cermak's successors did not lack influence in Washington. Cermak's Wet demands were satisfied, and Roosevelt honored the party's barroom plank. In his acceptance speech Roosevelt accepted the plank, and Cermak had nothing to complain of on this score. Finally, and most important, Cermak's convention behavior insured the continued unity of his local machine.[77]

THE 1932 GENERAL ELECTIONS

When the national convention ended, a very sick Cermak went abroad—not to recuperate from his most recent gastrointestinal attacks, but in order to sell the new and respectable Chicago to Europeans, so that the investments of his wealthy backers in the fair would not be jeopardized. As soon as A.J. returned, in mid-September, the full fireworks of the campaign began.

Thompson played a major part in Small's campaign and Cermak was made the chief issue. The viciousness of the personal attacks surpassed what had seemed the unsurpassable record of the 1931 canards. Not only was Cermak pictured as a dictator, not only did Thompson repeat every charge of graft from his 1931 tirades, but there were new charges of vote stealing in the primary, and even more ethnic slander. Thompson had evidently not learned from his errors of the year before. Cermak was "Tony Baloney the Dictator," "Anton the First, Emperor of Cook County," and worse. Nor were the candidates spared. Even a loyal Thompson publicist admits that Thompson, "desperate, overstepped bounds and got on thin ice more than once."[78] He told farmers that if Horner were elected the price of pork would fall—a not overly delicate anti-Semitic slur. He again dragged in Cermak's alleged exiling of the Irish. "Cermak to Szymczak to Zintak—and the Irish are out."

Cermak took up the cudgels; and, now that he was mayor, was much less careful of his dignity.

Big Bill is trying to get back to the public trough ... by sneaking into the governor's chair. ...

Now, I have no objection at all to an alliance between Small and Thompson. They are two of a kind. They belong together and I hope they enjoy each other's company.[79]

Cermak spoke extensively in Chicago, throughout the state and, since it was a national election, in adjacent industrial states where there were large foreign-born populations. He was a prominent participant in the presidential campaign. That he was now in full rapport with Farley was made clear in the announcement that Cermak, rather than one of the preconvention Roosevelt supporters, was to be in full charge of the national campaign in Illinois. Farley congratulated him publicly on the fine campaign organization which he was operating for Roosevelt. Cermak not only gave many speeches for Roosevelt—who was now for Cermak "the man of the hour"—he also organized the National Association of Roosevelt Czechoslovakian Clubs of America and became its president. But his most significant contribution was in fund raising. He was appointed the head of the Illinois division of the national campaign finance committee and was extremely active in finding dollars to match the tremendous amounts available to Hoover.

The 1932 contest was a very uneven one. The overwhelming combination of forces that had elected Cermak the year before had been significantly strengthened. The results of the election reflected the juggernaut character of the Democratic organization. The 1932 victory completely overshadowed the victories of 1930 and 1931. For the third time since the Civil War, Illinois went Democratic. Cermak succeeded in bettering considerably his boast of a 200,000 majority for Roosevelt. Actually, the majority was almost 550,000. In Cook County Roosevelt polled almost a million votes and accrued a 330,000 majority. The majority for Cermak's designee for senator was almost as great. The Democrats elected both congressmen-at-large and six of the ten congressmen from Cook County districts. They also elected seventeen of the total of twenty-five congressmen in the entire state.

The victories among state offices were even more overwhelming. Cermak had engineered a clean slate. Horner's majority in the state was scarcely believable—100,000 greater than Roosevelt's. Horner's majorities in Chicago and Cook County were also larger than Roosevelt's. He even carried traditionally anti-Chicago downstate by well over 100,000 votes. The results were similar for other state offices, although they ran somewhat behind the heads of the ticket. The Democratic victory also included the control of both houses of the state legislature.

The Cermak local ticket all but swept the field as well. It was led by the impressive victory of Thomas J. Courtney for state's attorney over Cermak's erstwhile friend, the incumbent Swanson. Courtney captured Chicago by nearly 300,000 votes and Cook County by considerably over 300,000. Although smaller majorities were gained by other local candidates, their victories were also impressive. Even the smallest majority (Zintak) was well over 100,000 in the city and 75,000 in the county. The only losses suffered by the Cermakites were two of twelve judges of the municipal court. It was a staggering victory for Cermak and for local and state Democracy—not to mention the unprecedented national success. The local and state Republicans were nearly annihilated, presaging their almost complete impotence for many years to come.

It is clear, however, that the victory was more than a symbol of Democratic strength and a sign of dissatisfaction with Republican "normalcy." Undoubtedly this generalized attitude played an important role. However, analyses of the election returns tend to show that it was Cermak's organization, not only of the party but of other local forces, which accounted for the hitherto matchless success of Illinois Democracy. In other words, the election did not demonstrate a wholesale weakening of Republican sentiment among Cook County and Illinois voters. There was some trend toward the Democrats but no sign of a complete change in the traditional Republican leanings of the county and the state. What can be more accurately inferred is that Cermak utilized the dissatisfaction with national and state Republican leadership and, on the local level especially, where national party labels are less important, cashed in by virtue of a highly efficient and articulate organization and by the presentation of some candidates who were objectively better qualified than those whom the bankrupt local and state Republicans were able to offer.

Therefore, although Cermak delivered handsomely enough for Roosevelt (it was the largest presidential vote in the history both of Illinois and Chicago), the traditional Republicanism can be seen as still operative. Roosevelt captured only 55.24 per cent of the total vote cast in the state and ran 70,000 votes behind Horner in the county and well over 100,000 behind in the state. Similarly, Horner's majority in the city was slightly larger than Roosevelt's, while in Cook County it was nearly double the Roosevelt majority.

The significant factor here is the much stronger Republican tradition—especially in presidential elections—among voters of the county as compared to Chicago voters. The reason for Roosevelt's smaller vote as compared to Horner and Courtney lies not in the greater zeal of the machine for the local candidates but rather in the willingness of a portion of the traditional Republicans to support local Democratic candidates in cases where they are of the opinion that the Democratic are superior to the Republican candidates.

However, even in the city, analysis has revealed that the traditional Republican vote had not weakened considerably.[80] Roosevelt lost nine wards in Chicago as against three lost by Horner (and five by Cermak in 1931), and in every case the wards lost by Roosevelt and won by Horner were traditionally Republican strongholds. Similarly, in the most Republican areas of Cook County—that portion outside of Chicago—Horner ran four to three as compared to Roosevelt. The explanation then of Roosevelt's great majority in the city, the county, and the state, lay in the ability of the Cermak machine to flex its muscles and deliver a very large percentage of the non-Republican vote—that percentage which usually did not vote.

The election results also offer some commentary on the relation between success in elections and ethnic candidates. The most noteworthy fact was the unprecedented victory of a Jew for governor—the first in the history of the country. Even more impressive was his record-breaking vote and near-record majorities in Chicago and the whole state. This would seem to indicate that ethnic bias—even against a member of a group which, next to the Negro, suffers most from prejudice—in a political contest can be minimized or overcome when the ethnic candidate is clearly the superior of the two contestants, when he is supported by a vigorous and active party, and when other powerful opinions are mobilized in his behalf.[81]

On the predominantly Irish county ticket, the Democrat with the smallest margin of victory was Zintak, a Pole. He had 25,000 fewer votes in the county than the next lowest victor.[82] The Democrats elected ten of the twelve judges of the municipal court. The two Democrats who were defeated were Bicek, a Czech, and Urbanski, a Pole.[83] In none of these cases were the candidates who were more successful than Kerner, Zintak, Bicek, and Urbanski, conspicuously more qualified or even more prominent. One can draw a tentative conclusion from these facts (or at least conclude that more investigation into this area might be fruitful). It is possible that candidates from the less assimilated ethnic groups in order to succeed in urban elections have to demonstrate more than ordinary qualifications for office (like Horner), or must be fortunate enough to face a totally discredited candidate (as did Cermak in 1931).

CERMAK AND HORNER

Cermak had done what many had deemed impossible: he had elected a Jew as governor. Before and during the election and ever since there has been considerable interest in the relationship of these two very dissimilar men. Although Horner was supported by all the newspapers and even a greater array of "decent" elements than Cermak had enjoyed in 1931, many wondered about the extent of Cermak's control over the "Lincolnian" judge. We have noted the Thompson charges to the effect that Cermak would become dictator of Illinois were Horner elected—in effect, that Cermak had a halter on Horner. Was this the case? On balance, it seems that Horner was not such a spineless creature that he could be owned by Cermak. Only persons with great animus and with inadequate information have made this charge. It is true that Horner had immense admiration for Cermak and was grateful to him for his election.[84] It is also true that Horner had not hitherto shown himself to be an assertive person. It is for this reason that when Cermak publicly indorsed Horner's candidacy, "people ribbed him . . . said at least Tony could control him."[85]

However, a great many competent observers who know both Cermak and Horner believe otherwise. Carter H. Harrison said that "no man could control Horner, he was very determined."[86] Another informant said:

Horner turned Tony down when he was even the least bit out of line. Cermak asked him only for regular patronage, but Horner would not allow key positions to be used for patronage. If Cermak gave him qualified men they were appointed; if not, he would have to give Horner some other names.[87]

A veteran political reporter believed that Horner gave Cermak several important appointments initially, but from then on "he was on his own."[88] James C. Denvir, a stout Igoe man, said that had Cermak lived, he and Horner would have fallen out. Professor Gosnell, who is not a great Horner admirer, admits that "Horner did not follow Cermak's suggestions on all occasions."[89] But the answer can never be known because of Cermak's early death. However, in the light of Horner's subsequent and successful revolution against Cermak's successors in 1936, it seems unlikely that Cermak could have controlled Horner completely.[90]

But it is clear that Cermak intended to wield great influence in the executive mansion. When Horner went to Florida to draft his inaugural address, Cermak accompanied him, obviously not as a ghostwriter. Despite Cermak's insistence that patronage had not been determined, upon their return Cermak repeatedly announced Cook County's preferences for legislative leaders. There was an announcement of a patronage conclave, and Cermak also gave instructions to the Cook County members of the legislature. It seems clear that whether or not Cermak could have controlled Horner, he was determined to do his best to run the state from the city hall—since he could not run city hall from Springfield.

The first appointments by Horner were unexceptionable from Cermak's point of view. Cermak's son-in-law, Dr. Frank J. Jirka, was appointed director of the department of health; son-in-law Graham was selected as president *pro tem* of the state senate; and good Czech friend Joseph Triner was named chairman of the Illinois Athletic Commission. Besides these nepotistic appointments (and Kerner was attorney general), Horner appointed others to whom Cermak was indebted. Martin P. Durkin[91] became head of the department of labor, and labor leaders Victor Olander, Agnes Nestor, and Anton Johannsen received positions.

But Horner also appointed many persons who were closer to him than to Cermak. B. F. Lindheimer (whom Cermak had also placed in his cabinet) became chairman of the Illinois Commerce Commission; Barnet Hodes received a place on the Illinois Tax Commission; and Joseph L. Lisack and Alfred K. Stern were also appointed.[92] Cermak was understanding about these appointments. After all, these men had also supported him in 1931. However, it is not unlikely that it irked him considerably not to have complete control over the plums. This feeling was abetted by constant prodding from Nash and Kelly to hurry Horner, who was not making appointments as rapidly—and in some cases not as "wisely" —as he might. One who was present at a conference when Kelly and Nash were baiting Cermak about this matter reports that Cermak turned upon them and exploded: "Neither you or I will push him. He's going to take his God damn sweet time."[93]

But there were exceptions to Cermak's admirable restraint. One such, which is still talked about among Chicago politicians, was Cermak's anger when he learned that Ernest Lieberman had been appointed state highway engineer. A.J. telephoned "his" governor and proceeded to show Horner his displeasure. "Where did you get that fellow—they tried to hand him to me when I was elected Mayor. Where did you get . . . ?"[94] Cermak was in bed with an ear ailment when this conversation took place.[95] Nevertheless, two days later he went to Springfield to talk to Horner.[96] It was no surprise that the conference concerned patronage.[97]

Whatever the future might have held, no break between Cermak and Horner took place. Cermak received a goodly share of the new patronage, adding to his already huge quantities.

Now he was truly boss of Chicago and Illinois. Even before the state officers became Democrats, his great political power was frequently noted: ". . . one of the most powerful leaders in Democratic politics and the most successful 'boss' in the history of Jeffersonian ranks. . . . Since the history of modern Democracy in Chicago, no leader has enjoyed such victories."[98] Or, "At the close of the [1932] convention, it was apparent that Cermak was one of the most powerful and resourceful leaders of the Democratic Party in the United States. . . . Cermak is . . . not only one of the most powerful, but one of most sinister and portentous figures in the political life of America!"[99] In January, 1933, with the new avalanche of offices under his control he was "absolute boss of that city and the state of Illinois."[100]

Not only were the Republicans completely demoralized but there was no threat of insurgency within Cermak's party. The ignominious defeat of Igoe—even by a Jew—had insured this result. Although some of the Irish leadership was still secretly unreconciled, and although a few were actively champing at the bit of

Czech overlordship, there was little they could do. No longer did Cermak have to deal so gently with would-be Irish usurpers as he had from 1928 to 1931. His power was so well consolidated that any who planned an uprising had to reckon with the good possibility of being ruined. They had seen the Igoes mercilessly disciplined—both M. L. and James T. were henceforth finished as local leaders, even after Cermak had passed from the scene. Even those most envious of "the — Bohunk" had to admit grudgingly that none among them had ever matched A.J. as an organizer,[101] and as a creator of Democratic victories and Democratic power.

But even if they did not admire him, they were frightened. He was the complete boss. He held every center of power in his own hands. There was no longer, as in the time of Brennan or Sullivan, one or several autonomous local governments whose spoils were controlled by chieftains opposed to the machine, from which these recalcitrants could attempt a sabotage of those in control of the party machinery. Nor could they find any such patronage havens which could be used as sanctuary to escape the wrath of the machine. Finally, it was no longer possible to attempt to snipe at the machine directors or to organize their overthrow through bipartisan arrangements. Cermak had largely destroyed the Republicans, had stripped them of control over all local pelf, and where a few held out—as in the case of judges—they were completely subservient to his demands.

Cermak's control of the formal machinery of the party was equally complete. Never had such an iron grip been held on local party organs by any boss, Democratic or Republican. Nor was this only a shadowy, back-room grasp of the Brennan variety. For example, Brennan was national committeeman only briefly and was not an officer of the state, county, or managing committees. Here, as with public office, Cermak openly held many responsible positions, and those he did not himself hold were in the grip of lieutenants whose loyalty was unquestioned. After Cermak resigned as chairman of the county central committee, Nash became chairman—but Cermak became treasurer. Moreover, Cermak had direct control over the destinies of the overwhelming number of the ward committeemen who constituted the central committee. Either they were Cermak appointees, or they owed their election to public office, their places of prominence on legislative committees, and elsewhere, to Cermak sponsorship. And Cermak could break them as he had made them. This had been demonstrated in the case of the Igoes and lesser ward chieftains. Cermak completely "owned" the central committee.

This was also true of the managing committee. In Brennan's time this had been the most authoritative party mechanism, since Brennan had seen fit to have Cermak as county chairman. Now that Cermak was boss, the managing committee was not superior to the central committee, but it too was entirely in Cermak's grasp. Clayton F. Smith, whose reliability had been proved in 1929 and in the Igoe schism of 1932, was chairman, and A.J.'s old friend McDonough was secretary. Cermak also dominated the state committee, as the bitter complaint of downstate legislators over Horner's nomination indicates. Not only did he control its Chicago members in the degree that he "owned" ward committeemen, but the state chairman, Donovan, was now a Cermak man and had become lieutenant governor as a consequence. Also, Cermak had the friendship of downstate leader Campbell, whose candidacy in the gubernatorial primary had so usefully drawn downstate anti-Jewish votes away from Igoe. But to make things even more snug, Cermak had created the office of treasurer of the state committee and filled it with old reliable Pat Nash. In this manner A.J. had both local and state party machinery securely in his pocket. Finally, Igoe's national committee post had been forfeited as a result of his quixotic rebellion. To no one's surprise, the party chieftains coaxed Cermak to move into the vacancy. Most indicative of his desire to have his thumb on every valve of party power was his continued holding of the office of ward committeeman of his own ward. A.J. was nothing if not thorough in anticipating and insuring against risk of rebellion. Few individuals in the history of American urban politics had united in one person this degree of power.

A.J. had the whip hand. The Irish were in line. They dared not oppose him. In the words of an Irish police captain, bitter in his hate for the "no-good Bohunk" because "he won't let anyone else make a dollar," revolt was out of the question because "the son-of-a-bitch would crucify you!"[102]

· 14 ·

MARTYR

MAYOR

AFTER the matchless victories in November, 1932, and after coming to some *modus vivendi* with Governor Horner regarding the degree of influence Cermak was to wield over state matters, A.J. had only federal matters to worry him. Throughout December and January discussion was rife concerning the first Democratic distribution of federal patronage since 1916. Cermak was vitally interested. In December there were reports of Cermak's patronage requests to Democratic National Chairman Farley in New York, where Cermak attended a meeting of the national committee.[1]

But it became evident that A.J., in spite of the great Roosevelt vote in Illinois, was not as close to the Roosevelt entourage as some others. It must have been unbearably galling to Cermak to read in the newspapers J. Hamilton Lewis' announcement of the list of persons who were to be first recommended. It was probably even more annoying that Lewis included Cermak's name among the favored.

This was only one of several indications that many people would have liked to see Cermak receive a cabinet appointment. Many would have been pleased to see him promoted to the highest honorific position—away from Chicago. Thus, there were persistent reports that Cermak would be offered the office of Secretary of Commerce. "Several members of Roosevelt's board of strategy desire the mayor in the cabinet, it was said, because of his demonstrated ability, and to give recognition to the great army of foreign-born voters."[2] It was not remarkable that it was also reported that Cermak would refuse the position were it offered.

But he was extremely interested in positions for others. Although it is doubtful that his hegemony could really have been endangered by federal patronage inhering through Lewis to the nearly extinct Harrison-Dunne forces, Cermak could not let the federal spoils go without battle. Cermak and Lewis had had differences concerning the distribution of patronage. Lewis was considered to be the most favored Illinoisian for federal patronage, and his Senate term had four more years to run. He might risk a show of independence against Cermak's dictates. Cermak was definitely uneasy about federal patronage; there were many vacancies he was interested in —district attorney, federal judge, postmaster, collector of internal revenue—and many people he wanted to reward. And it was clear that others were getting ahead of him. Nonmachine men Harold Ickes and Donald Richberg were to have big jobs; so was Carter Harrison, as well as several downstate persons—and obviously not through Cermak.[3]

Cermak's uneasiness about the federal patronage and about his begging expedition to Farley was clearly indicated just before he left for Florida. He told his plans to a number of people and also confided his doubts about the success of his mission. He asked Edward Kelly whether or not he should even make the trip, inasmuch as he was not a member of Roosevelt's inner circle.[4] And after he had conferred with Farley in Miami, he was still so reluctant to see Roosevelt that he invited a colleague to accompany him to Cuba, in order that he might avoid seeing the president-elect. "Walsh is going to be attorney general and he's a friend of Igoe. I don't want to have to take a lot of guff."[5]

But being what he was, Cermak had to go to Florida, and he had to see Roosevelt. Not only was it necessary for him to try to get the patronage, he also wanted federal aid for the financially desperate city.[6] Apparently the talks with Farley were satisfactory—so he informed lieutenants Arvey and Szymczak via long distance.

All he now had to do was to see Roosevelt and to make certain that Farley's pledges would be honored.

THE ASSASSINATION

Roosevelt landed from his yachting trip on February 15, 1933. That night a reception was arranged in Bayfront Park in Miami. A great crowd awaited the President-elect on makeshift grandstands. Cermak was in the front seat of the reviewing stand. The President-elect rode by in the usual open car. Seeing Cermak, he beckoned to him, but Cermak did not approach him at that moment. Roosevelt gave a short speech from the automobile. When he had finished, amidst the roar of applause Cermak along with other dignitaries approached him. Cermak and Roosevelt exchanged a few remarks. Roosevelt's auto was about to start when shots rang out. Cermak was hit, as well as four others.

Pandemonium was let loose. The crowd took after the assassin, but police rescued him. The wounded lay screaming or wandered about streaming blood. Roosevelt's car shot ahead, as Cermak cried: "The President: get him away!" Still standing erect, Cermak was walked by two companions to Roosevelt's car, which had been halted.

The question of whether the assassin was aiming at Roosevelt or whether he indeed intended his bullet for Cermak has been asked too often, and too many replies have been hazarded, to allow the matter to be overlooked. The contention that the assassination was planned for Cermak is mainly based upon charges of a connection between Cermak's administration and gangsters. The argument is recorded in many places and, together with contributions made by many persons interviewed, may be generalized as follows.[8] Chicago had highly integrated criminal organizations which habitually worked with politicians of both parties. Because of the needs of the various gangster syndicates for protection, new agreements and new alliances became necessary whenever there was a change in administration—whenever a new mayor or state's attorney took office. The Cermak administration permitted the status quo to continue until the 1932 elections were over. Then there was a redistribution of territory and protection.

Cermak had his own friends on the West Side . . . in the heart of Cermak territory.... Radical changes were to be made in the North Side syndicate situation. Ted Newberry, North Side gang chief, had found favor with the new administration and was to be further strengthened according to accepted reports.[9]

Cermak was virtually his own police commissioner; "he kept himself informed in phases touching gambling, liquor and other underworld branches."[10]

Mayor Cermak was a master of detail. He dealt closer with the mysterious, menacing line of the underworld than any mayor in Chicago's history. This phase was something the bankers, big business, were not concerned in. Cermak was in full control in this sector; in other lines . . . he would take orders from, work with, the bankers. But Traylor and the rest were not interested in booze, gambling, and other activities of the underworld. The high hats did not want to know about it, beyond seeing that they got their share of deposits from that business as well as from legitimate business. . . . It was apparent that Cermak had no conscientious aversion to the business of gambling and beer running. . . . He was mayor now, but that made no difference to Cermak.[11]

But Cermak's connections with gangland were more particularly adduced from the notorious Nitti case. In December, 1932, Frank Nitti, "The Enforcer," cousin of Capone and regent for the by-then incarcerated gang lord, was shot by a member of Cermak's personal police detail during a raid upon the Capone headquarters. But Nitti, although shot three times, did not die; and he was arraigned for assaulting detective Lang, who had shot him. Lang had sustained a wound in one finger. Nitti denied that he had assaulted Lang and refused to testify on the ground that he might incriminate himself. Thereupon Lang was indicted for perjury and for an assault on the gangster.

Gangland rumor and police reporter gossip murmured that Lang had acted for the alleged gang leader favorite of Cermak, Ted Newberry. It was rumored that Newberry had offered $15,000 for Nitti's death and reported that Newberry had threatened to run the "greaseballs" (Capone gang) out of town. These rumors were substantiated, in the view of some, when Newberry met his end in true gangland tradition a few weeks later.

Lang's trial was held after Cermak's death. One of the raiding policemen upheld Nitti's contention that he was unarmed and charged Lang with shooting himself for camouflage purposes. The third policeman testified that after the shooting he had visited

Cermak's office. Lang claimed that he had shot Nitti in self-defense and that the raid had been ordered by Cermak. Cermak's orders had been that Lang arrest Louis (Little New York) Campagna, who had been brought from New York by the Capone syndicate to kill Cermak. "Lang testified to Mayor Cermak's deadly fear of assassination."[12] Lang's lawyer attempted to substantiate this on the testimony of a manufacturer of bulletproof vests to the effect that Cermak had bought such a garment. This testimony did not enter the record. At other sessions Lang testified that Cermak was afraid of Capone violence because Cermak "planned to stop all gangster operations during the fair."[13]

Lang was found guilty of assault, but then given a new trial, which was never held. After many continuances, the charges were "striken from the call with leave to reinstate."[14] Although Lang was discharged from the police department he has never been tried again. Many hold the opinion that this mercy has been shown because of his threat to "blow the lid off Chicago politics" and to tell "enough to wreck the Democratic party."[15]

The theory is, then, that Cermak was shot in retaliation for the Nitti shooting, as well as because of other gangland connections inimical to the Capone syndicate. It is believed by some that the Capone gang hired the assassin, Guiseppe Zangara, who was not a gangster, and planned the shooting to occur when it did in order to divert suspicion from the gangsters themselves.[16]

An alternate theory also holds that the assassin was a Capone hireling. However, this theory emphasizes Cermak's antigangster activities as the cause of the shooting. Thus, the assault on Nitti is seen as only one act among Cermak's activities to end the gangster reign. Two of the policemen who were chosen by Cermak for his hoodlum squad said that Cermak spoke to the following effect: "I am having trouble with the gangsters and I need your help in shoving them out of town before the fair begins. I am going to have you sworn in as deputy coroners so you can go all over Cook County picking up those hoodlums."[17] Nitti, it is said, "gambled that the crime crusade would blow up if they got rid of Mayor Cermak."[18]

There is some evidence that Cermak believed that he was in danger before the shooting occurred and that he was of the opinion that Zangara had aimed at him. Alderman James B. Bowler, who was one of the first to reach Cermak after he was hit, said that shortly after arrival at the hospital Cermak told him that he had had a premonition of some such occurrence.[19] Cermak expressed similar sentiments to John Dienhart, a reporter friend of long standing. According to Dienhart, the day after the shooting Cermak was convinced he had been threatened before leaving Chicago because of his intention to break up the syndicate's control. Cermak told Dienhart that he had purchased a bulletproof vest, but had not worn it on the fatal day.[20]

Much is made of the story of the bulletproof vest. As sophisticated an observer as the late Harold Ickes based his contention that Cermak was Zangara's intended victim almost solely upon the story of the vest.[21] Also often pointed out are the special precautions which had been taken to secure Cermak's safety following Nitti's shooting. A.J. had moved from the Congress Hotel to the bungalow at the top of the Morrison Hotel, to which there was access only by a private elevator. Even before the Nitti incident the Mayor had had two detectives as personal bodyguards, while a third guarded his home. This force had been increased to five, and for a while the homes of his daughters had also been guarded. Two city detectives had accompanied Cermak to Miami. These are in the main the arguments in support of the theory that Zangara was hired by Capone mobsters to assassinate Cermak. They have been given wide credence and great circulation, particularly by persons who disliked or hated Cermak.

What actually seems to be the case, however, is that, regardless of what connections might have existed between Cermak and Chicago gangdom, the shooting was neither planned by gangsters nor executed by a gangster hireling. It is the personality and statements of Guiseppe Zangara as they were revealed after the shooting that do the most violence to the hired-assassin theory. Zangara was a 105-pound, five-foot-five-inch, thirty-three-year-old Calabrian immigrant. He had been in this country for nine years and had become a citizen only two years previously. A few days prior to the attack he had purchased a thirty-two-caliber pistol for eight dollars with the intention, he said, of killing President Hoover. When he read that Roosevelt was expected in Miami, he changed his plans.[22]

Zangara consistently voiced definitely recognizable, if incoherent, Nihilist attitudes.

> I'm sorry I didn't kill him. I want to kill all presidents—all officers.
>
> I don't know whether I shot Mr. Roosevelt or not but I want to make it clear I do not hate him personally. I hate all Presidents, no matter where they come from, just like I hate all officers and everybody who's rich.
>
> I am sore at government—because as a kid I had to work instead of going to school, and I'm sick now because I had to work.
>
> I am a member of no party. I believe bolshevism is all right.
>
> I have done my own thinking and I reached this decision by myself.[23]
>
> I have always hated the rich and powerful. When I read ... the President-elect was coming to Miami I determined to kill him. I hoped I would have better luck than I had ten years ago, when in Italy I bought a pistol to kill King Emmanuel.[24]
>
> By a queer trick of fate the same thing that foiled me at that time was the same thing that prevented me tonight from killing Mr. Roosevelt—there was too dense a crowd around and I couldn't shoot properly.[25]

Zangara described how he got to the park early so as to get a seat as close to the reviewing stand as possible.

> I sat there waiting and my stomach kept aching me. I kept thinking that if the crowd didn't get too thick around I wouldn't fail like I did ten years ago. I meant to shoot Mr. Roosevelt while he was talking, but the people in front of me were standing up. I was too short. Finally, some of the people got tired of standing and my big chance came, when I stood up on a bench and pointed the gun at Mr. Roosevelt.
>
> Somebody was pushing against the bench and made it wobble. The gun was shaking in my hand but I pulled the trigger anyhow.[26]

On Zangara's person were found clippings describing Roosevelt's movements; in his quarters there were many more of the same, as well as clippings describing the assassination of McKinley. Also reported in his possession, by the chief of the Secret Service, were reprints describing Lincoln's slaying. He called attention to similarities between Zangara and Czolgosz, McKinley's assassin.

Zangara remained defiant to the end and never changed his story or his attitude one iota—not when he was arraigned, not when he was sentenced to eighty years in prison (before Cermak died), and not as he was strapped into the electric chair. Over the days before the execution took place, he scribbled feverishly in notebooks, penning what he called his autobiography. He laughed when he was sentenced to die. At the hour of execution, he yelled at the guards, "Take your hands off me. I sit in chair. I not afraid to die."[27]

No one has ever attempted to refute the general picture of the pitiful, crazed creature Zangara was—an almost classic paranoid who should have been committed to an institution instead of being made to suffer the supreme penalty at the hands of a revengeful citizenry.[28] He was the sort of man who neither would have found it in conformity with his ideas and purposes to hire himself out to gangsters nor, on the other hand, would have been considered by gangsters as a reliable or likely person to entrust with their commissions. Gangsters do not operate in this haphazard way.[29] The "one-way ride," the machine-gun tattoo, the shotgun blast—these are their customary and foolproof methods. No plot similar to this shooting is recorded in the annals of gang murders.

That Cermak was not Zangara's target, however, does not do away with the theory that the Capone mob had reason to desire Cermak's death. There remain the questions of his alleged part in the Nitti assault, his alleged relationship with Newberry, such evidence of fear on his part as the precautions taken in Chicago, and certain statements he made following the shooting. What of these? The only evidence of Cermak's involvement in the Nitti assault was the testimony of the two policemen—discharged from the police force for their part in the incident—that Cermak had ordered the raid. It must be taken into account that this testimony offered a convenient alibi for the man who had shot an unresisting gangster; his whole defense was based upon the plea that he was obeying orders from a superior officer, that superior by that time being dead. But even in this testimony Lang said that Cermak had ordered the arrest of another gangster, not Nitti.

There was no evidence beyond unsubstantiated rumor that Cermak sponsored Newberry or any other evidence of Newberry's alleged offer of a reward for Nitti's life. Assuming, however, that Newberry had made such an offer, there is no particular reason for supposing that Cermak was involved. It was very much within the realm of possibility for a direct connection to be made between Newberry and Detective Lang.[30] (Detective Lang was a "tough cop," according to Mayor Kelly.) As for Lang's threats to "blow the lid off Chicago politics" and to wreck the Democratic party—Cermak, although immensely powerful, was not the entire party; there were others who might easily have been connected with deals along the lines of the Nitti incident.

Although there is no reason to suppose that Cermak's moral scruples were especially pronounced, there is every reason to suppose that his caution was. A.J. was ambitious and eager to profit, but his avoidance of rash conduct and his shrewd calculation of risks was very noticeable. The Nitti affair was not the type of thing in which Cermak would characteristically have been willing to entangle himself. Carter Harrison was positive that Cermak could not have been involved in the Nitti case on just these grounds. "He was too conservative to get mixed up in murder." The study of Cermak as a personality tends to bear this out.

Although there is little doubt that Cermak feared gangsters, there is no evidence that he feared them because of involvement in the Nitti shooting. The special precautions taken to guard him after Nitti was assaulted were undoubtedly a product of fear. But there is reason to believe that he had a general fear of retaliation for his threats to wipe out gangster operations before the fair, and he may easily have supposed that the gangsters would take the Nitti assault as his doing.

Actually, the only statement of fear Cermak is alleged to have made *before* the shooting was that quoted by Detective Lang (who was, under the circumstances, a not entirely disinterested party) that Cermak was in deadly fear of assassination. To none of the people with whom Cermak spoke before leaving for Miami and upon his arrival there did he speak of a fear of being attacked by gangsters. All of his quoted statements to the effect that he feared gangster violence were made after Cermak had already been wounded, most of them while he was in intense pain, some of them when he was incoherent.

THE FINAL ILLNESS

Cermak's martyrdom was born with his intuitive cry as the bullet pierced his side: "The President: get him out!" It was either during the ride to the hospital or shortly after his arrival there that he uttered to Roosevelt the typically ungrammatical phrase which has since often been quoted—"I am glad it was me instead of you."[31]

Cermak was driven to the hospital supported in Roosevelt's arms. Roosevelt said that during the first few blocks of the ride A.J. slumped. Then he shocked Roosevelt by sitting bolt upright. Thus began Cermak's greatest fight. It was during the nineteen-day ordeal beginning on February 15 that A.J. displayed qualities of stubborn strength which earned him the admiration and respect of people the world over.

After early examination by physicians, Cermak was given a fifty-fifty chance of recovery. In the beginning, the only cause for worry was the bullet, which had pierced the right lung and become lodged in a vertebra. Soon other complications developed. First some of the heart fibers became paralyzed. Shortly, Cermak's condition was announced to be "precarious"; then in quick succession came warnings or announcements of pneumonia, gangrene of the heart, and septic pneumonia. On February 21 he suffered a setback and his condition was described as critical. The next day he had a serious sinking spell caused by an intestinal ailment. On February 26 it was announced that he definitely had pneumonia. Two days later his "amazing recuperative powers" halted the pneumonia, and he was given solid food. Prior to this time he had been given blood transfusions and oxygen, had collapsed, and was reported to be in great distress, groaning with pain. He continued to improve after February 28. But on March 1 he was placed in an oxygen room; and there more transfusions, another heart attack, more injections. Cermak scarcely emerged from the oxygen treatment until the early morning hours of March 6, when it was apparent that death was imminent. Toward the end, more and more attention was given to his gastrointestinal disorders. One of the doctors was quoted as saying, "If we could only stop the accompanying enteritis we could get him on the road to recovery."[32]

The entire country interested itself in Cermak's struggle for survival—seven telegraph machines were set up in the hospital to feed the hungry presses. During this period of most acute pain, while suffering from several major ailments, Cermak displayed a high order of physical courage and vitality. His effort had begun with the moment he was struck, when he "did not wince, he did not yield, he did not collapse. He kept to his feet until he got in the Roosevelt car." This was the description of Miami's city manager, whose arm was linked with A.J.'s as the bullet struck.

After Cermak's momentary collapse in the automobile and his quick recovery, he remained conscious, and spoke to Bowler, Roosevelt, and others. Bowler described his attitude on this first day: "The Mayor is a Trojan. While everybody else was excited and alarmed, he was absolutely calm. He ordered me to call his children in Chicago and tell them not to worry."[33] Roosevelt talked to Cermak the night of the shooting and stayed to visit him the next day, trying to cheer him up. Cermak joked with him a bit; then he urged Roosevelt to guard his welfare: "Better be careful Mr. President; you know the condition of the country today . . . please be careful." He expressed great concern to Roosevelt about the unpaid Chicago teachers. On this point Roosevelt was quoted as saying: "It seemed to be the one thing that was troubling him. Weak as he was, he went on to describe the school teacher situation." It was reported that in the delirium of his first night in the hospital Cermak constantly babbled about the teachers.

The next few days A.J. was able to put on a more cheerful and optimistic attitude. When his daughters, arriving from Chicago with their husbands, wept at his bedside, he chided his sons-in-law, "Why don't you keep the girls in good spirits? Take them out dancing. Or do I have to get up and take them places myself?" With Governor Horner, who said that Cermak looked like a man on the way to recovery, Cermak was also jovial, joking about the hospital regimen. "I thought I was Mayor of Chicago," he said, "but with all the nurses around, this is the one place in the world I can't do anything I want to." The next day the good spirits and apparent optimism continued, as Cermak greeted his stenographer, Mrs. Beasley, who had just come in from Chicago. The exchange went this way:

Cermak: So you arrived all right. I thought maybe they'd shot up the office in Chicago too.
    You've brought your typewriter, I hope, and plenty of stationery. We've got a lot to do. And say, I could eat a good steak.
Mrs. Beasley: Or some nice liver and dumplings?
Cermak: Yes, that's an idea. That ought to plug up this bullet hole.[34]

The live spirit and the eagerness to work were not warranted by the physicians' bulletins, and by the next day were overwhelmed by the torments of illness. Clutching his stomach and groaning, Cermak confessed, "I am in terrible pain. This is an old trouble of mine. It's causing me terrible pain." On the same day he gave his last full interview. His newer pessimism was evident in it. The accent of the suffering martyr—the last public portrait he was to create for himself—weighted every syllable.

> I do not know whether I'm going to get well. I hope whoever succeeds me will make his first duty the payment of money owed [the teachers].
>
> If this will have helped me get loans . . . I'm glad I was shot.
>
> This bit of lead is not too burdensome for me to carry. For a long time I have had lead in my heart over their distress.
>
> Don't worry about me or whether I get well.
>
> I am sure I can suffer . . . for the sake of Chicago, particularly when it spared the life of our great President-to-be.
>
> . . . The lesson the nation should learn from this incident . . . is that we should all work together for the common good. Every citizen should try to believe in his public officials and should give them a chance. Public officials don't want to fail. They want to succeed.
>
> It may be that I will carry this bullet with me for the rest of my days. If this in any way makes just a few people understand the need for greater co-operation at this time, I should almost thank the poor unfortunate who shot me for giving me this opportunity to make my contribution to the great American nation which has given me my opportunities.
>
> And if there is a change in my condition and they tell me I cannot recover, I will pass along happy in the feeling that the great President-elect of the United States has been spared to the American people, whom I love with all the love that must be in the heart of a man who came to this country a poor immigrant baby and was allowed to go so far under the stars and stripes.[35]

Two days following this interview, Cermak, still in great pain, signed an authorization for a proxy to sign tax warrants which were to be used to pay the teachers; and on the day following, he dictated a telegram thanking the officials who had distributed the tax warrants. His attitude at this time, when he was as ill as he was to be at the end, was indicated in the report of an interview with his son-in-law Graham. "Do you think I'm going to live?" he asked. Upon receiving a reassuring reply, he went on, "Well, I've got things in Chicago well on their way. I'm fighting. I'm doing the best I can." He did fight; the doctors were "amazed" by his "will to live." The last days of his life were purely a gargantuan struggle to survive, duly reported by the press.

The Mayor fought on for days after the doctors had been seized by despair. His great heart ... kept beating against overwhelming odds while a corps of physicians looked on with awe.... He spent the last four days in an oxygen room.... But these measures would have been futile without the cooperation of a mighty will to live.

Death could have triumphed days ago if the mayor had not defied fate.... His spirit kept death from his bedside indefinitely.... Days before, they [the physicians] admitted they realized that only a miracle could save him, but they were buoyed up by the patient's astonishing vitality and mental strength.... He was very near death immediately after the transfusion, but pulled himself back from the portals of death to keep himself alive by sheer will power for a few more precious hours.[36]

Cermak died in the early morning of March 6. He had been in a coma for hours and had scarcely recognized his family. Near the end he asked to see his favorite grandchild, Vivian Graham, but he did not know her when she was brought in.

THE MARTYR MAYOR

In death Cermak was honored more than in life. A special train brought his body to Chicago. The casket was escorted to the train by local political dignitaries. It was met near Chicago by Horner, the city council, and Cermak's cabinet. Cermak was first brought to his home in Lawndale, where great crowds passed his bier. Then the body lay in state in the city hall for twenty-four hours.

Cermak's was "the most spectacular funeral demonstration in Chicago history." There were 500,000 spectators along the line of march; 30,000 participated in the procession proper; 23,000 attended the ceremonies at the Chicago Stadium; and 50,000 witnessed the interment in the Bohemian National Cemetery. In the city hall 76,000 viewed Cermak's body, and many more thousands in his home. The floor of Chicago Stadium, which had so recently been the scene of Roosevelt's nomination, was transformed with a sea of lawn and flowers in the form of great cross. The procession itself, from the city hall to the stadium and then to the cemetery, was as grand as A.J. would have wanted; it put to shame his 1915 Wet parade.

The huge pageant escorted him to the grave in near-zero temperature. Military units of all kinds, detachments of police and firemen, representatives of the veterans' organizations which had so often aided and abetted him—all these and thousands of others marched in the most impressive funeral procession the city had ever witnessed. There were representatives of large numbers of Czech organizations, a guard of honor of Czechs, and the band of the predominantly Czech Harrison High School from Lawndale. Nor did his other ethnic supporters forget their loyalty. There were representatives of ninety-two "hyphenated" organizations, and a delegation of fifty-two silk-hatted gentlemen, each representing a different "nationality." The identity of the pallbearers also reflected Cermak's leadership of the foreign born, and the primacy of his ties to his own Czech people: there were Courtney, Kerner, Toman, Rosenberg, and Szymczak, and one nonpolitician—Serhant, Cermak's Czech, Republican real-estate partner. Other groups were recognized in the long list of honorary pallbearers.

Cermak's Czechness was given chief recognition; the names of his pallbearers and the choice of cemetery bear this out. In every phase of the ritual Czechs were pre-eminent. The Bohemian Odd Fellows Lodge was there, as well as the Lawndale Masonic Lodge, and young representatives of the Bohemian Orphanage.

The political motif was clearly present in the persons of other participants. Not forgotten were Cermak's gifts to Democracy. James A. Farley, by then chairman of the Democratic National Committee, represented the national organization, and symbolic was the presence of Tammany Chief Corry and Brooklyn Boss McCooey. The local machine was represented not only by the chief eulogist, Horner, and the pallbearers but by the official presence of the holders of nearly every public office—the incumbents of which had become Democrats in recent years in large part by dint of Cermak's efforts. Also in evidence were members of the state and local Democratic committees.

The funeral services proper were posthumous evidence of A.J.'s genius for combination. The service in the stadium was nonpartisan and nonreligious. Even in death Cermak had a balanced ticket and recognized the major organized religions. In addition to Horner's, eulogies were presented by a priest, a minister, and a rabbi. Horner praised Cermak's "tireless industry," his "sound

[329]

judgment of men," and his ability to do his own thinking—"men could not frighten nor cajole him." He, as well as the clergymen, made much of Cermak's rescue of Chicago. "Cermak took command of his own political party and vitalized it into an instrument for unselfish public service. With this instrument [he] met the public foes in battle array and attacked with such force and rapidity that the well organized army of the underworld was soon confused and scattered."

Cermak was also seen as a "symbol of democracy," because of his humble origin and limited opportunities in a foreign land in contrast to the opportunities in this mobile society, which he readily embraced. No speaker failed to underline the obligations of the city and its citizens to Cermak's martyrdom. There were tributes by the hundreds—from Czechoslovakia, from businessmen, from "silk stockings," from political colleagues. "There was no sham or hypocrisy about Mayor Cermak," said financier James Simpson. Banker George M. Reynolds described the death as a "calamity." "It is hard to estimate the loss suffered by the city." D. F. Kelly, he of the Kelly Bill, stated that: "Chicago has never had a man whose passing will be felt in so many directions." Political friends were also kind. William L. O'Connell called the dead mayor a "splendid executive," and T. J. Bowler described him as "the greatest leader the Democratic Party ever had." Emmett Whealen praised his "will of steel." "Underneath his brusqueness and determination there was a sentimental streak that few people were allowed to witness." Clarence Darrow's farewell was probably the most honest. "I knew Mayor Cermak pretty well for a good many years. I always liked him . . . . On the whole, he was a pretty good man."

But after the laudatory eulogies and the hundreds of high tributes, in death as in life Cermak was engaged in controversy. The unfinished colloquy about the actual shooting has already been mentioned. In addition, after Cermak's burial there was considerable argument as to the cause of his death. Although at first an attempt was made to ascribe as the direct cause of death the assassin's bullet, it later emerged that Cermak had died not of a gunshot wound but of ulcerative colitis. The first efforts to suppress this fact may be laid to the objective of obtaining the death penalty for the assassin.[37] Nine physicians, consequently, had signed an autopsy report stating that the direct cause of death was a gunshot wound, with contributing causes being colitis, gangrene, peritonitis, collapse of lungs, and partial failure of heart. Later, however, when Dr. Karl Meyer (an old friend of Cermak) gave a report stating that the direct cause of death was ulcerative colitis, of the nine who had signed the autopsy report those physicians questioned admitted that the bullet wound was "not directly responsible but indirectly responsible."[38] They went on to confirm completely the statement given by Dr. Meyer. Dr. Meyer's report stated that peritonitis from an ulcerative colitis was the direct cause of the mayor's death; that the assassin's bullet partly induced, but did not directly cause, a series of complications which all the efforts of the physicians could not overcome; that the gunshot wound itself had been completely and cleanly healed; that the mayor did not die from gangrenous pneumonia as announced following the autopsy; that the autopsy showed that the mayor's heart was in good condition and would have carried him along for at least another ten years. "The mayor's life," Dr. Meyer stated, "could have been saved if even a few days before he died the colitis could have been stopped."[39]

In Memoriam

After the great funeral and the paeans of praise, friends of Cermak attempted to establish more lasting tributes to the Czech mayor. This time the responses were not conspicuously favorable. The aldermen renamed Twenty-second Street Cermak Road; the forest preserves had a Cermak Wood and later a Cermak Pool, but this was all the government in Chicago and Illinois were willing to do in perpetuation of the memory of the greatest boss Chicago has produced.

An attempt was made to have a Cermak monument erected in Chicago's Grant Park, but Republican legislators were less than cooperative. They suggested that Cermak be buried in Lincoln's tomb. This ended the agitation for a publicly erected monument. A tag day was held to collect funds for a memorial. This was also a failure. The city of Miami Beach planned to erect a memorial in Bayshore Park, but this was never done by the city. It remained for

Cermak's fellow Czechs to build this Bayfront Park memorial. And indeed, ironically—perhaps justly—whatever permanent symbols of Cermak's life exist have been created by the Czechs.

But Cermak left two very imposing legacies which could be considered a kind of memorial to his name. These he created by his own efforts; they were not dependent upon the posthumous efforts of his successors. They were the conquering local and state Democratic machine, and the undying and ultimately successful enmity to national Prohibition.

The machine to which Kelly and Nash fell heir was virtually invincible. It proved this convincingly in local elections in 1933 and in county and congressional elections in 1934. In the 1933 "nonpartisan" aldermanic election, the organization captured a great majority in the council; only a handful of captive Republicans remained. Twenty-one of the fifty seats were not even contested, eighteen of these "free rides" going to Democrats and the remaining three to Republicans in name only.[40] In the judicial elections of the same year the entire Democratic ticket was swept in by better than two to one.

The 1934 county and congressional elections served even more to illustrate the control of the organization which Cermak had left. At this election the remnant of the Republican party attempted to make a stand, but it was fearfully routed. The Democratic congressional delegation was increased (including M. L. Igoe, who finally won an election, as he was promoted to congressman-at-large). The entire local Democratic ticket won by great majorities. "Every Democrat on state, city, Sanitary District and Municipal Court tickets was elected—and the four-year Alderman's term, which the people repeatedly had beaten by an overwhelming majority . . . won."[41] In no other election of municipal court judges in the history of that court (since 1906) had the Democrats swept the slate of twelve at biennial elections. (Hitherto the largest number elected was ten, in Cermak's last campaign.) But this time no Republican judicial candidate escaped defeat. The might of the local Democrats was further demonstrated by the fact that in the election of state representatives in fifteen of nineteen Chicago districts the results were decided at the primary, in most cases redounding to the exclusive advantage of the Democrats. The delivery in most wards was tremendous, the first place going to Arvey's ward, which turned in 92.21 per cent Democratic votes.

The Democrats were indeed reaping what A.J. had sown. The harvest was even more fruitful in the 1935 mayoralty election. Edward J. Kelly, rather obviously not a Czech, had been named mayor to finish Cermak's unexpired term by Cermak's chief first lieutenant, Nash, who in traditional boss fashion decided to stay in the background.[42] The machine's power was shown as the state legislature passed an extraordinary measure allowing the city council to elect Cermak's successor. Of course the council validated Nash's choice. Thus began the Kelly-Nash continuation of the organization Cermak had built and perfected. When in 1935 Kelly had to present himself to the electorate (for the first time in a political career going back at least to 1902), the organization was powerful enough to select its Republican opponent.[43] Kelly won by a majority so huge that it surpassed Cermak's by over 100,000 votes—his majority was 543,853.

However, the work of eliminating the Republicans, finished off by Kelly-Nash, had almost been accomplished by Cermak from 1929 to 1932. "Not since the formation of the Republican party in the city had the Democrats so dominated the political scene."[44] Kelly was re-elected in 1939 and in 1943 to the position which Cermak could have in all likelihood retained, had his health allowed it. When in 1947 Kelly was persuaded to retire, his successor, Martin Kennelly, was the true businessman type so dear to Cermak for advisory purposes. (Indeed, Martin Kennelly had been a member of the Cermak businessmen's committee in the 1931 campaign.) Kennelly was reelected in 1951, and was succeeded by Richard Daley, another Irish Democrat, who is still mayor in 1961. Although Kelly-Nash made some serious mistakes, by and large the grip of Democrats over Chicago has continued. Cermak's legacy to local Democracy proved a valuable one and stands as a monument to an archpolitician. Mayor Daley, so important in the successful nomination and election of Kennedy, is in a very real sense a beneficiary of Cermak.

His second legacy and self-created memorial was the defeat of Prohibition. It is doubtful that any other person in the nation did as much as this ex-coal miner to discredit the perhaps greatest single victory of any pressure group and to cause repeal of the Eighteenth Amendment. Certainly no one in Illinois could challenge his supremacy as an extradripping and unfailingly consistent Wet. We have described his constant struggle against strict liquor-law enforcement prior to 1919 and his tireless campaign of public education and agitation against the Eighteenth Amendment in later years. He fathered three state-wide initiatives from 1922 to 1930 (coinciding in each case with his own campaign for office) to demonstrate that Prohibition was against the wishes of the majority. No weapon of propaganda, no technique of persuasion was left unused by him to cause the defeat of this piece of "sumptuary" legislation and cause the return of "personal liberty."

Ironically, Cermak did not live long enough to see the actual fruits of his long crusade. Although he had engineered the repeal of the Illinois Prohibition acts of 1931, the Republican governor vetoed the bill. Although he had been a principal agent in the adoption of the "barroom plank" in the 1932 Democratic national convention, his untimely death prevented him from seeing the Democratic administration validate the pledge. Indeed, in December, 1932, the House of Representatives failed to pass a repeal resolution by a great vote (272-144), as earlier that year the Senate had refused to modify the Volstead Act to permit 2.75 per cent beer. However, the Collier Bill, authorizing the manufacture of beer, had been passed by the House at the end of 1932, and the end of the "noble experiment" was obviously nigh. On February 16, 1933, the day after the shooting in Miami, the House passed the resolution calling for repeal (Illinois congressmen voted seventeen "aye" to six "nay") and on February 20, the day Cermak gave his last public interview, the Senate ratified the lower chamber's action. A week after Cermak's death, the Cullen Bill, allowing 3.2 per cent beer, was passed by a huge vote (316-97); and a month after his death Illinois and twenty-two other states had beer legally for sale. How Cermak would have rejoiced; for in his view, this would have signified the end of the depression and the attendant automatic disappearance of all other ills of society.

The repeal amendment went into effect in November; and now Cermak would have felt completely vindicated, as he would have by the Cook County and Chicago vote on the amendment. The voice of democracy was at last being heard. It also was ironic that Cermak did not live long enough to become a member of the Illinois convention which considered the repeal amendment. It would have been fitting for him to have led the repeal delegation —along with Nash, Toman, Arvey, and Mrs. Conkey—and to introduce the repeal resolution. Instead, the honor went to Nash.[45] Cermak might have considered the convention's fifty to zero vote for repeal as the ultimate reward for thirty-one years of arduous political work. But A.J. was gone; this achievement he did not see and enjoy as he had seen and enjoyed the coming of age of the Cook County Democratic juggernaut.

THE

MAN

WHO

STAYED

IN

LAWNDALE

ANTON Joseph Cermak's success as a political leader was a function of the interaction of his personality, his membership in a particular ethnic group, general social and cultural factors operative in the larger society, certain social and political institutions, a given choice of political roles, and certain situational and chance factors.

The most important basic facet of Cermak's personality for our purposes is that he was, as the biographical material illustrates clearly, a power seeker. His entire life effort was dedicated to his career. He appears to have had no other powerful needs or desires outside of gaining, maintaining, and expanding his political power and prestige. When persons interviewed compared him to contemporary or past political figures, they invariably assessed Cermak as being, in their experience, the figure with the fewest soft spots, the fewest extraneous demands on his time and energies, the fewest interests outside the realm of political power. From the first Cermak had to seek power; it was never thrust upon him. He continually fought for position and control in the party and for public offices of increasing prestige and responsibility. On at least two separate occasions in Cermak's career, events seemed to pose objectively desirable alternatives to continued active party work and office holding. In neither instance did Cermak give evidence of seriously or sincerely considering the alternatives, although on both these occasions he was extremely ill, and on one of them his wife was dying.

Cermak fits perfectly into the pattern of Harold Lasswell's construct of the political power seeker.

> The notion of a political type is that of a developmental type who passes through a distinctive career line in which the power opportunities of each situation are selected in preference to other opportunities. As such a person moves from infancy through maturity, he becomes progressively predisposed to respond to the power-shaping and power-sharing possibilities in each situation in which he finds himself.[1]

Lasswell, in company with numbers of psychologists seeking to discover the reasons for the formation of the power-seeking personality, suggests that the power urge is a "compensatory reaction against low estimates of the self."[2] Certain infantile experiences are of importance in the generation of this feeling of inferiority. Although we cannot reconstruct Cermak's infancy, we do know that he later suffered from colitis, a psychosomatic dysfunction in which the basic conflict is that of the ego seeking to overcome extreme inner demands for inactivity, dependence, love, help, and care, to which the ego reacts with feelings of guilt and inferiority.[3] As a result of this conflict, the individual often strives to overcompensate by being overly aggressive, independent, dominant, and active.[4]

Whatever Cermak's infantile experiences, it is certain that the social conditions of his childhood and youth were not of the sort to allay existing fears, doubts, and insecurities. The poverty of the family; the eventual recognition of low social status; the presence of the more assimilated Irish groups in the Braidwood community —all of these were sufficient to force comparisons in which Cermak's youthful self-estimate may well have suffered. The behavior of his adolescence was marked to an extreme degree by the sort of compensatory mechanisms likely to appear as the result of this conflict; he was a bully, a fighter, a "tough," apparently unable to win feminine affection or to form relationships in any but the dominance-subservience pattern.

Cermak's situation in Chicago as towboy and kindlingwood

peddler, was not much improved in the early days, from the point of view of status, over what it had been in Braidwood. Eager to assert himself, what fields lay open to him? His poverty excluded him from any endeavor requiring training or education. But both politics and business might be entered without formal training; and both were, moreover, among the acceptable prestige vocations, both in the American ethos and in the estimate of the American-Czech community. Cermak entered the two fields simultaneously.

Although nominally Cermak remained a businessman to the end of his life and even rationalized his political activity in terms of his business welfare, ultimately he sacrificed the latter to the former. His choice seems to have been determined in the main (1) by his own personality and (2) by the social and cultural environment.

For an aggressive egocentric like Cermak politics was the preferred choice because it offered more direct satisfactions of the power demand. Within the structure of government there were opportunities for the exercise of as nearly naked power as is sanctioned in modern society. It has often been pointed out that government in modern urban society enjoys the monopoly of legally sanctioned coercion.

As a poor, young, semi-illiterate Czech-American in the urban setting, Cermak had the best chance—perhaps the only chance—for gaining power and prestige through politics. The evidence was there before his eyes. Pilsen had few successful businessmen beyond the level of saloonkeeper or shop owner—no merchant princes, no utilities moguls, no meat-packer magnates. But there were some Czechs in politics who enjoyed both power and prestige.

Cermak's own ethnic group, moreover, set an unusually high premium upon political power, in part no doubt because of their history of forcible detention from political participation in the old country.

Politics and political leadership and aspiration have suppressed all other aims and achievements and . . . during the past thirty years the Czechs of Chicago have made of their political highlights a matter of hero-worship.

. . . the glamour of politics . . . in the community of Chicago's Czechs . . . has dimmed all other accomplishments.[5]

So Cermak made his choice, in part an unconsciously conditioned one, in part consciously determined by foreseeable rewards.

Just as Cermak's ethnic group was influential in determining his final choice of politics as an outlet, so was it instrumental in his achievement of success as a political leader. His first contact with the preordained Democratic organization was through the Czechs; his first party superiors were Czechs; his superiors in early appointive patronage jobs were Czechs. His Czech contacts, especially business contacts, as well as his connection with the ward Democratic organization were responsible for his first nomination to elective office.

By this time the population of Lawndale and the senatorial district of which it was part were changing. The Czechs were overtaking the Germans in the ward, and the Germans, Poles, and Irish in the senatorial district. Thus, by the time of Cermak's first nomination, although the ward boss was a German, Cermak had already attained the position of chairman of the ward organization. It was the pressure of the populace which caused Cermak and the Zoldaks to demand a place on the ticket in 1902, and which was responsible for the Irish leadership's acquiescence to the demand.

Cermak continued to use the Czechs as a vehicle in his rise to power and prestige. By 1908 he was ward boss of the predominantly Czech Twelfth Ward. This position was to remain the anchor of his power to the end of his life. The control of this Czech ward not only was responsible for giving him a preferred place in the Democratic party hierarchy but was also an important factor in his repeated successes in quest of elective office. His ward retained him as ward committeeman for well over twenty years. It elected him alderman five times. Its votes were largely responsible for his four terms as state representative. The Czechs in adjacent wards and their ward leaders soon acknowledged Cermak's position as the spokesman for all the Czechs, increasing his influence in party councils. His role as Czech boss also gave him control of a sizable and relatively dependable body of votes in his search for city and county-wide offices.

From the first, the Czechs admired Cermak; "The Czechs would go to him."[6] The male proletariat as well as Czechs of the lower middle class particularly admired the figure of the aggressive gang leader, successful businessman, and hearty drinker.

When Cermak began to climb among the Czechs, there were few Czechs of ward-leadership status; rather, the political leaders of the Czechs were Czech Jews. In the train of these were the Novaks and the Cerveneys, who were creatures of these leaders. Cermak, along with several contemporaries, began to vie for the political leadership of the Czechs. Most of Cermak's rivals were, like John Cervenka, lacking the common touch. Most of them were not power seekers of the Cermak caliber; they were as much interested in business as in politics. Such men as Vopicka, Sokol, and Triner did not manifest the persevering interest in political power and office holding manifested by Cermak; they did not fight either to gain or to maintain power and offices as Cermak did. Others, like Kerner, seemed absolutely reluctant to accept political office or party responsibility; and although this type achieved a certain degree of political success, upon Cermak's death these men voluntarily left the political fray. But regardless of the intentions or potentialities of these men, Cermak, once in power, developed techniques for containing any major ambitions they may have had. Each of the aforementioned individuals, and many others of the same classification, received appointive office through Cermak sponsorship.[7] Not only did this tactic tend to neutralize would-be rivals, but Cermak could also use these appointments as evidence of his success in gaining recognition for the Czechs and of his faithfulness in rewarding the political service of these persons.

But many of Cermak's rivals of the sort mentioned above forfeited all real chances of succeeding Cermak. Most of them, upon achieving a degree of business or professional success, left Lawndale, either physically or socially. It has been pointed out that this is often the case with the sort of leaders who rise in minority groups: "In a minority group, individual members who are economically successful, or who have distinguished themselves in their professions, usually gain a higher degree of acceptance by the majority group."[8] This places them culturally on the periphery of the underprivileged group and makes them more likely to be marginal persons. They are fearful of having their good connections endangered by too close contact with the relatively underprivileged components of their ethnic group, who are not acceptable to the cultural majority. Nevertheless, because of their status and power, such persons may often gain and maintain leadership, in the absence of leaders more closely identified with the people.

Cermak offered the Chicago Czechs a real alternative to the lukewarm assimilationist type of leader, and they were eager to accept the alternative. For the Chicago Czechs, at the same time that they accepted American middle-class standards and values, insisted upon retaining their cultural individuality, preserving it in the numerous institutions previously discussed. Thus, a cardinal reason for Cermak's three decades of leadership of the Czechs was his willingness to remain one of them and among them. He stayed in Lawndale, in body and in spirit.

He succeeded in convincing his Czech constituency that their power and status were inextricably bound up with his. Luckily, shortly after he became leader of the Czechs, his position in the party hierarchy was influential enough to enable him to distribute sufficient patronage and secure enough places on the ballot to demonstrate his probable future success.

But just as Cermak used the Czechs in his rise to power, so the Czechs had their influence upon his political development. Although it was true that they accorded their political leaders a great deal of honor and deference, they nevertheless kept a jealous and critical watch on them. Although the Chicago Czechs as a group were ambitious and eager to win political recognition, they accepted certain American ideals of "clean" government. Beginning with the earliest days, the Czech wards were among the "most decent."[9] Studies of dishonest elections have consistently omitted the predominantly Czech wards. Moreover, Cermak's ward voted intelligently on public issues.[10] Thus, it was incumbent upon Cermak to maintain a reputation of at least minimum political cleanliness. This restraint eventually served as one of the factors making him acceptable to "the forces for good" as an alternative to Thompson.

Cermak was fortunate in rising among an ethnic group that was ready, willing, and able to accede to political power, and that had certain advantages over other urban minority groups. First of all, the Czechs set great value upon participation in the processes of government. And in spite of the exclusion from political processes that they had suffered in their history on both sides of the Atlantic, their tradition also included ancient memories of independent ethnic government, as well as more recent successful demands for recognition from a dominating foreign group—Bohemia having been by the end of the nineteenth century the most autonomous non-German, non-Hungarian entity in the Austro-Hungarian Empire. Thus, exclusion from participation in government was not sufficient to cause a feeling of group hopelessness. Moreover, the tradition of participation, plus the experience in self-government in voluntary associations, fitted the Czechs as a group for political activity. The group was also highly literate, had a high rate of naturalization, and showed great aptitude in adjusting itself to American life. At the same time, the Lawndale Czechs remained cohesive, stable, self-contained, and self-sufficient. They demanded recognition as a distinct group, and were enraged at being lumped with other Slavs and Eastern and Southern Europeans.

Since the 1890's, the Chicago Czechs had been overwhelmingly Democratic. Thus, the vehicle for group political recognition was the Democratic party, in the same way that Cermak's own party vehicle was predetermined. The Democratic party in Chicago by that time was the party of the immigrant. The chief ethnic components were the entrenched Irish, the Germans, the Jews, and the Poles. During this period the number of Italians in the party was negligible, and the total Italian population in Chicago was not significant. Among the other numerous ethnic groups in the city, the Scandinavians and the Negroes at that time were even more overwhelmingly Republican than the Czechs were Democratic.

Although the Irish, Poles, Jews, and Germans all were larger population groups than the Czechs, within the Democratic party itself the Czechs were not so greatly outnumbered. A very large part of the Germans, and perhaps 50 per cent of the Poles, were considered Republican voters at the beginning of Cermak's rise and in general up to his death. The Jews as Jews, because of internal cleavages (recently somewhat obscured by the advent of the state of Israel and the resultant efforts at solidarity), cannot be considered a homogeneous ethnic group. None of the Jewish subgroups equalled the Czechs in numbers. Further, a significant group of Jews who were members of higher economic classes tended to be Republican.

These other ethnic groups within the Democratic party labored under certain handicaps when compared to the Czechs in the race for group political preferment. In the case of the Jews, without reference to internal division, all labored under the disadvantage of anti-Semitism. Up to the time of Cermak's death few Jews rose to positions of greater power and prestige than the leadership of overwhelmingly Jewish wards. The case of Horner is really no exception, inasmuch as Horner was more a creature of Cermak's making than a reflection of the political power of the Jews as a group.

The Poles had a less favorable tradition of political prestige and participation than did the Czechs; moreover, the proportion of peasants pure and simple was much higher among the Poles than among the Czech group, which contained so many skilled workmen, artisans, and small businessmen. As a result, the group feelings of deprivation in the political sphere was much less pronounced among the Poles, and their demands as a group for recognition much less intense and heartfelt during most of Cermak's career.[11] The internal community structure of Chicago Poles was less favorable for gaining political power as a group than that of the Czechs. In contrast to the Czech community, the Polish community was hierarchically organized, with a high degree of control exercised by the church. Apparently the most important end served by church, family, and voluntary associations was the resistance to contamination of the Polish-American community by the larger culture. This end appears to have been considered far more important than group participation in the political process and the winning of political prestige. The Czechs, in contrast, although wishing to retain their cultural identification, were nevertheless able to accept American standards and ideals, perhaps because these closely approximated their own cultural standards and ideals. Among the measurable results of the Polish-American cultural rigidity was the less accelerated rate of naturalization as compared to the Czechs, and a greater reluctance to allow symbolic assimilation, such as, for example, the use of the English language. This cultural rigidity put certain inflexible boundaries in the paths of

Polish political leaders in their attempts to form alliances with other groups. Because of the combination of these factors, until recent years the Polish vote has been considered, next to that of Negroes, the most "deliverable" in Chicago. All of these conditions taken together made the Poles as a group less likely than the Czechs to gain political power in the first two decades of this century.

The Germans, besides dissipating their ethnic strength by the adherence of a great many to the Republican party, were among the highest in point of assimilation of all immigrant groups not from the British Isles. This reduced their strength as a distinctive group, as did an ethnic organization relatively less cohesive than that of the Czechs. Moreover, the degree of influence exercised by the Germans in the Democratic party was sharply reduced as a result of the anti-Hun feelings engendered by the First World War.

Cermak was thus the beneficiary of the advantages and aptitudes of his group, of its mass feeling of discontent, and its self-conscious determination to win political recognition. He was fortunate in that no entrenched indigenous non-Jewish leadership existed among the Czechs prior to his rise. From the beginning he acted as leader—to capture his ward from German leadership; to gain recognition for the Czechs (and for himself) from the Irish in his nomination to the state legislature; and following this, to go on in similar fashion to offices of increasing importance.

Concurrently with his rise among the Czechs, Cermak began to play the role of the leader of the entire foreign-born population. His earliest vehicle for this role was his office in the United Societies (1906). It is important to note that he acceded to this office in part because of his already acquired status among the Czechs, although at that date his undisputed leadership was several years away.

The United Societies, as we have noted, was a huge conglomeration of constituent ethnic societies and individual members. At different times the number of member societies was well over a thousand, and the number of individual members for whom the United Societies was spokesman was well over 200,000. Obviously, at a time when Chicago's population was closer to two million than to three million, this was a sizable number of votes. Of course, it was not a bloc. Among the ethnic members there were mutual antagonisms and hostilities. Nevertheless, on two policy issues they stood as one against nativists and Americanists; these were their unanimous support of the unrestricted sale and use of liquor and their resistance to antiforeign legislation.

Cermak's position in the United Societies was important in several ways. It brought him in contact with other ethnic leaders as well as the rank and file of self-conscious ethnic groups. As the recognized spokesman for the organized liquor industries, he had at his disposal large sums of money to use as he saw politically fit. The United Societies provided him a platform from which to publicize himself and gave him an opportunity to make a name for himself with regard to the issue that was to be conspicuous throughout his career—that of "personal liberty." This was an issue which could be relied upon for rallying the support not only of ethnic groups but also of Chicago voters in general, who were as a whole overwhelmingly Wet in sentiment. Ultimately, Cermak was able to weld already Democratic elements among the United Societies membership into a bloc within the Democratic party which was able to challenge the entrenched Irish for party leadership. Also in part owing to his United Societies connections—as well as to judicious use of patronage—he was able to convert large groups (some Germans, many Poles, some Scandinavians, some Italians) and their leaders from Republicanism to Democracy. Several of these ethnic groups had their own history of feelings of aggression against the Irish because of their virtual monopoly of the Democratic party. Cermak's roles as leader of the foreign born and leader of the Wets were given the largest share of credit not only for his accession as Democratic leader but for his entire political career by Mayor Kelly, Mayor Harrison, and many others.[12]

Although Cermak's roles as leaders of the Wets, the Czechs, and the foreign born generally were of great importance in his political rise, the institution of the political party was also indispensable. Shortly after his arrival in Chicago, we have seen that Cermak made his initial contact with the Democratic party. From that time to his death he held successively nearly every party position in the local and state party organizations. As he rose from court attaché to mayor of Chicago, he also rose from assistant precinct worker to boss of the local and state party and national committeeman from

Illinois. What factors were instrumental in his success within the party?

The tremendous amount of experience in the intricacies of party organization at every level and the accumulated knowledge of the most successful kinds of manipulation at every level must be reckoned as a major factor. Closely connected with this were Cermak's long and varied experiences as an office holder. The combination of these two elements gave him an intimate and rich fund of information concerning the complicated local government structure, which was second to none among local politicians. The continuous office holding also gave Cermak a steady stream of personal patronage which was used to satisfy not only the demands of the Czechs but the expediencies of party and factional advancement. Cermak was always careful to distribute patronage methodically, fairly, and with nice attention to payment of political obligations.

His early rise in his ward was a product of his aggressive personality, his limitless willingness to work, and a higher level of intelligence than that of competing precinct captains. Once he was ward committeeman, his ward became and continued to remain one of the best Democratic wards. Later, when he became spokesman for all of Chicago and Cook County Czechs, his influence in the party and in the various factions thereof was immeasurably increased.

In his rise within the party his use of the existing factionalism could scarcely have been improved. When he joined the party, the Harrison faction enjoyed the allegiance of Chicago and Cook County Czechs. Thus Cermak became a Harrison man. He maintained this connection as long as it was profitable; however, even before the Harrison faction was destroyed, Cermak had made important contacts with other Democratic factions. In these contacts his role as Wet spokesman was invaluable. From the demise of the Harrison faction, Cermak became an important member of the Regular Democrats (the Regulars from 1916 on *were* the party); and he was to remain such until the end of his life. But this did not imply blind party loyalty. During this entire period Cermak mastered and practiced the fine art of bipartisan trading. In the practice of this art he played no favorites. From time to time he made alliances with every faction of the fragmentized Republican party.

For years Cermak was recognized as the chief among the Democratic ethnic bosses, as well as the custodian of the Democratic party's "liberal attitudes" and later their Wet planks. This dual source of influence—Wet and foreign born—greatly enhanced his intrafactional influence vis-à-vis the Irish leadership.

His prestige within the party was further reinforced by his widely recognized vote-getting ability. Few Democratic party functionaries could match him in this regard. Similarly, he was looked upon as one of the most able Democratic officeholders. Given the level of performance of most party hacks who were nominated for office by Chicago Democracy, the general approval won by Cermak from civic groups and newspapers, especially in the last fifteen years of his life, was a welcome boom to the local machine.

All of the preceding elements were brought together and reinforced by certain of Cermak's forceful personal qualities. His fellow politicians were in general much impressed by his political know-how; his wide knowledge of governmental affairs; his manifest physical strength; and his reputation for a willingness to indulge in personal violence—"You dasn't monkey with Tony." They were also impressed by his seemingly endless fund of energy and by his practically limitless willingness to devote himself to party affairs.

Finally, Brennan and the Irish leadership were confident of their ability to control the "Bohunk." Although by the mid-twenties Cermak's power was acknowledged to be great, Mayor Kelly stated that he was considered by the Brennan leadership as only an "errand boy."[13] This attitude was held in spite of Cermak's leadership of the foreign born, his pre-eminence as a Wet, his control after the defeat of Dever of the most powerful patronage office in the hands of a local Democrat. The attitude of the Irish showed misjudgment not only of Cermak's capacities but of the temper of the non-Irish elements of the Democratic party. Historically, Chicago Irish Democrats, although usually not completely united, were so much more united than the other ethnic elements of the party that they had succeeded in dividing and conquering.

Of Cermak's skills, aptitudes, capacities, techniques, and attitudes that were important in his political life, perhaps most vital was his mastery of the art of manipulation, what has been called group diplomacy. He was able to create favorable power balances by creating or reinforcing support and by successfully wooing or neutralizing the apathetic or the hostile.

He had considerable sensitivity to the strength and direction of social and economic tendencies and their probable impact upon the well-being of political parties. Frequently he displayed acute perception of possible courses of action to meet a pending crisis and then took quick and positive measures.

He rarely made errors in his selection of personnel, either as public official or party functionary. As public official it was his habit to make some very good appointments. There is no case on record of any important Cermak-appointed subordinate who had to be removed for dereliction of duty. It is true that Cermak never allowed good appointments to occur in such numbers as to hamper his freedom of action in matters of patronage and spoils; nevertheless, such appointees made possible a minimum of effective government by the various Cermak administrations, lending the color of respectability to Cermak as public official. As party functionary Cermak selected workers largely on the basis of effectiveness, but it is noteworthy that most of the men closest to him could be described as being of mediocre talent. Cermak took no chances on building up a rival or possible successor. In a very few cases when some lieutenant showed either unusual qualifications or ambition, he was eliminated, either by a promotion to a nonlocal office or by less subtle means. As a result of his policy of personnel selection Cermak at no time in his career had to face rebellion in his own ranks; and upon his death no Cermak lieutenant was qualified to step into his shoes.

Every qualified observer interviewed by the writer emphasized Cermak's qualities as a peerless party organizer and as an administrator. Usually attention was called to the organization of the ethnic groups and the country towns, and to the great dent Cermak's efforts made in local Republican ranks. By the time of his death he had even begun to make some inroads on the solid Republican Negro vote.

Cermak could by no stretch of the imagination be described as an orator. In the latter years of his career, however, he developed into an effective impromptu haranguer. Even in the earliest years, when speaking to his own or other immigrant constituencies, or when discussing his favorite issue, he was unusually effective. Other audiences, such as women's organizations or "silk stockings," were often impressed by his forthrightness and apparent seriousness of purpose.

One of Cermak's chief techniques as officeholder was his continual use of citizens' advisory committees, invariably packed with distinguished names. Through these committees Cermak went through the motions of public consultation and power sharing. However, the committees were usually so well organized, through the appointment of a few key Cermak men plus the control of the agenda and of full-time committee experts, that recommendations to which Cermak himself was opposed seldom eventuated. The use of these committees may be reckoned as a chief weapon in Cermak's successful drive to enlist the support of "the forces for good."

Another technique of first importance was Cermak's habit of giving a minimum of effective administration in every elective office. This was especially noteworthy in the field of public welfare during his terms as president of the county board. As a result, when Cermak ran against Thompson, he was able to campaign as a master public executive. Whenever Cermak was accused of graft or inefficiency, the ubiquitous citizens' committees were summoned. They investigated and often cleared Cermak; and they made recommendations for corrective action, which Cermak immediately accepted. He was never caught twice in an embarrassing situation in the same administrative area.

Cermak was a tireless worker in every public and party position. It was partly owing to this willingness to exert himself and partly owing to his refusal to delegate to others any responsibility that he could carry himself that he gained his deserved reputation as a master of detail.

Cermak also had a reputation for scrupulous payments of political debts. It was widely admitted, even by his enemies, that his political word was good. He rarely gave off-the-cuff assent to requests for favors or jobs; but once he had made a promise, he rarely failed to abide by his pledge.

In Cermak's long career he was careful not to become wedded to many issues or policies. The few that he embraced, such as Wetness or home rule, were overwhelmingly popular. There is no case on record where Cermak was a proponent of a measure not favored by the majority. Cermak was a true conservative. His entire social, political, and economic orientation reflected the views of the dominant groups in America with the possible exception of his attitudes concerning liquor. Although he rose from a proletarian background, his thinking was entirely that of the rugged individualistic, laissez-faire entrepreneur. He was not guilty of proposing any major social innovations. This steady conservatism, however, was not inflexible. Thus, in the emergency of the depression he was one of the first local politicians to recognize not only the permissibility but the desirability of federal assistance.

In Cermak's political life, as in the lives of all men, chance and certain situational factors over which he had no control played an important part. "We must not forget that fortune, chance, or luck . . . is always playing in the process of sifting men for leadership."[14] In the preceding chapters an attempt has been made in every given situation to identify the situational and chance factors. These included: the change of population in Lawndale, coinciding with Cermak's arrival on the scene; the lack of many able Czech leaders; the split among the Germans during the organization of the United Societies, which allowed Cermak's accession as a compromise candidate; the fact of the national split in the Republican party, which was partially responsible for Cermak's first election to a city-wide office; the advent of Prohibition, which gave him an issue that was foolproof and for which he was completely qualified to speak; his possession of the biggest patronage office held by a local Democrat during the lean twenties, when Democrats locally as nationally were the chronic out-party; the death of Brennan in 1928, at which time Cermak held this office, and the fact that Brennan had no strong and able heir-designé; the circumstance of Brennan's death coinciding with the time in Cermak's political development when he was more than ready to take over and when his continued frustration by the Irish leadership could no longer be borne by him; the coincidence in time of an ever greater revulsion against Prohibition and the complete discrediting of the local Republican organization; the further coincidence of the world-wide economic depression at the peak of Cermak's career, a depression which political fortune had made a Republican one.

Cermak had personal qualities and skills which were suited to his time and place. In many ways he was similar to his colleagues of both parties. His main difference lay in his more single-minded dedication to the quest for power, political position, and prestige; in his role as representative of a cohesive, fairly large, relatively capable, and highly ambitious ethnic group; in his role as official leader of the organized Wets and as spokesman for the unorganized proponents of free-flowing alcohol; and in his high level of administrative ability in party affairs and in public office.

APPENDIX I:

CHICAGO

AND

COOK COUNTY

LEADERS can scarcely be understood outside the context of their total environment. Physical habitat has long been recognized as an indispensable factor in the development of ethnic character and nationality.[1] In the development of an individual the environment provided by the city or the town of lifelong residence holds an unquestionably important place. Cermak was a Chicagoan from his young manhood to his death; every step of his career was taken within the framework of this environment. Developing as a politician and as a personality, he both affected and was affected by that framework. It is important to specify some of the principal facets of the city in which he rose to political power.

POPULATION; ECONOMIC GROWTH

When Cermak reached Chicago in 1889 its population was about 1,000,000. By 1900 it was 1,698,575; in 1910, 2,185,283; in 1920, 2,701,-705; and by the time of Cermak's death, well over 3,000,000. The figures for Cook County and for the entire metropolitan area are, of course, greater still.[2]

This rapid growth paralleling Cermak's life was a counterpart of the economic growth of mid-America and the Mississippi Valley, in the process of which Chicago became the economic capital of one of the foremost agricultural producing territories in the world. With the industrial revolution it came to be a rail center as well as a water-traffic terminal; it was a great agricultural clearinghouse; and from the period of 1890, industries—primarily iron and steel, but also printing, the needle trades, and electric supply manufacture—came to the city and its environs.

A producer and a market on this scale required financing. The city built up its own financial structure, featuring such famous names as Armour, McCormick, Field, Yerkes, and Insull. It is not surprising that these leaders and others of the industrial group made an impact on local politics. From this time the Commercial Club, the Association of Commerce, the Illinois Manufacturers Association, the Commonwealth Club, and similar bodies were centers of power which had to be considered.

To counter the organization of industry, workers also organized. Eventually the Chicago Federation of Labor was set up; and, compared to other large cities, Chicago was a union town. This was not done without struggle and sometimes bloodshed. The Haymarket Massacre of 1886, the Pullman Strike of 1894, the violence connected with the organization of the garment workers and the building trades —all are landmarks of the period, not to mention later battles during the CIO organization campaign in the early thirties.

Landmarks in the physical growth of the city were the fire of 1871 and the Columbian Exposition of 1893. From the havoc of the fire the city arose with increases in population, area, and wealth; and this ideal of building a bigger and better Chicago was continued in the form of the exposition around the Midway and the organization of an ambitious city plan, many of the provisions of which were in time partially realized, such as the improvement of the lakefront and the reclamation of large areas of the lake itself.

MUSHROOM GROWTH OF GOVERNMENT

While improvements of this kind were being sought, another force was active in effecting a disruption of effective local government. Owing largely to the state legislature's unwillingness to give the city adequate powers to deal with the growing complexity and scope of municipal affairs, one could see many governments emerge where only one had existed. There were, in addition to the city and county, the virtually autonomous sanitary district, three major park boards and several minor ones.

THE MOVEMENT TO THE SUBURBS

Another disruptive force occurring at the same time was the dispersal of the population to the suburbs. At first this was controlled by annexation; but after 1889 the tide could not be controlled; and, with

better transportation and increased wealth, many dormitory settle-
ments drained off some of the better educated and more politically
conscious elements of the population. By 1910 Chicago's population
was 2,185,284, and that of the metropolitan region 3,047,324; in 1920
Chicago included 2,701,705 persons, and the region had 3,858,818. The
suburbs increased 30 per cent between 1920 and 1930, while Chicago
grew by only 25 per cent.[3] Thus about one third of Chicago's potentially political citizens lived outside the municipal boundary; and the
impact of this situation on governmental affairs was not in the direction of honest, vigorous government.

THE IMMIGRANT TIDE

The constant outward mobility of Chicago's citizens cannot be considered without noting its connection with the immigration into Chicago. As the exodus to the outlying districts took place, the dwellings
and neighborhoods in the city were successively taken over by other
groups, usually later arrivals on the American scene. And as successive
waves moved on and were replaced by newer groups, new problems of
ethnic organization and integration arose. From its founding by the
French up to the mid-nineteenth century, Chicago was settled largely
by native Americans, who were then augmented by Germans, Irish,
and Scandinavians, while the bulk of the immigrants after 1890 consisted of Italians, Poles, Russians, and Bohemians.[4] World War I
stopped the great mass of immigration from abroad, but a new and
large native group culminated the population pyramid during and
after the war. This was, of course, the Negroes.

By the time Cermak arrived in Chicago the earlier groups were
firmly entrenched in the life of the city—socially, economically, and
politically. Although the South and Central European groups were
soon to outnumber the earlier immigrants, still in 1929, near the end
of Cermak's career, the Northwestern Europeans were more numerous,
if one considers the second generation.[5] The problem of multiple
ethnic groups having to act in concert in the framework of a single
government is not simple. This question has been more complex in
Chicago than anywhere in the world except New York; and it would
be impossible to overestimate the impact of this situation on the political, social, and economic history of the city. These matters have
been dealt with in detail.

CITY VERSUS DOWNSTATE

Chicago's history has been characterized by two major struggles:
one for home rule and the other for honest and efficient government.

Beginning as a village in 1833, it received its first city charter in 1837; but very soon the sharp population increases outmoded this grant. Not until the adoption of the constitution of 1870 was the city able to get a new and somewhat appropriate grant of power. This, however, soon proved inadequate; and from that time to the present repeated efforts have been made to cajole, threaten, and coerce the state government into granting Chicago adequate powers to meet her needs. From time to time some minor concessions were made, but nothing really significant was done to alleviate the situation.

With two million population, the city was still unable to grant a concession for checking hats or selling popcorn on the new municipal pier without a special act of the Legislature, to say nothing of powers adequate to deal with the complicated question of transportation and communication in a growing city, dependent for its life on free and rapid circulation of persons and goods.[6]

All this may have been due to indifference; however, when the great population and wealth of the city began to be noticed, fear replaced the original neglect on the part of the downstate as represented in the legislature. There began a campaign to curtail representation of Chicago in the state's legislative body. Although the constitution requires representation based on population, from 1900 to the end of Cermak's career no reapportionment was authorized by the legislature.[7] Consequently, Chicago's population increase of 1,500,000 from 1900 to 1930 remained unrepresented in Springfield. A compromise by the Constitutional Convention of 1920, permanently limiting the representation of the city in exchange for home rule, was convincingly turned down by the voters of Chicago.

As time went on many concrete issues added fuel to the city-downstate rivalry. Among these were the gasoline tax and the control of the city milk supply, but most important, the questions concerning liquor and liquor regulation. That Cermak understood these matters and used them in order to gain power have been documented.

STRUGGLE AGAINST CORRUPTION

The other great political problem of Chicago has been its effort to gain efficient and responsible government. By the time of its birth the spoils system had begun to gain foothold in the United States at large; it is not surprising that Chicago did not escape the blight. Like other great American metropolitan centers, it has suffered the levies of the usual political connivers, grafters, dishonest contractors, hoodlums, and other "lice on the body politic," but it can be distinguished from other American cities in one important respect. Never until the advent of Cermak was Chicago in the control of one highly organized and integrated political machine. It may be that its local chieftains were as unscrupulous and avaricious as members of any graft ring; but it was never possible to organize one permanent, Tammanylike superstructure.[8]

THE PEOPLE AND THEIR LEADERS

Even to the twenties and thirties Chicago had many of the characteristics of a frontier city.[9] "Liberty" was a word having diverse interpretations, including that of lawlessness.

The majority of the people were from the earliest days proponents of the wide-open town, meaning little regulation of drinking, gambling, and prostitution. Blue laws were uniformly opposed, except by a small minority. This situation was in part due to the fact that from 1860 to 1920 roughly one third of the population was born in those parts of Europe where matters of this kind were not viewed from the standpoint of traditional Puritan moral dicta.[10]

The industrial and political leaders who emerged during this period did much to encourage and maintain such "liberal" attitudes. These leaders were characteristically the type of self-made men, the "rugged individualists," a type which has seemed to flourish and persist longer in Chicago than in comparable large cities. "Chicago, in contrast to New York, has been a center abounding in self-made men—industrialists, grain merchants, large department-store owners, and real estate speculators."[11]

The self-made politicians shared the outlook of the self-made businessmen and identified themselves with them; and the reverse is also true, though perhaps to a more limited extent. Cermak is from this point of view typical enough. It is certainly no overstatement to say that "he had the social philosophy of a businessman."[12] At any rate there existed between the businessmen and the politicians a point of contact and a basis for understanding. Each side was quite willing to act as though a *de facto* mutual nonaggression pact were in effect: "You don't interfere in our affairs, and we won't interfere in yours."

Both kinds of self-made men were ruthless and less than completely committed to the public interest. Which group, the businessmen or the politicians, was less faithful is a nice question. All seemed to have inherited the dog-eat-dog philosophy of the earlier generation of robber barons. They were boosters—violent, flashy, offensive. "A want of deference for ceremony and tradition corresponded to a sometimes brutal disregard for the values inherent in human life, a defiance of established moral codes."[13]

Probably no one better illustrates the actual spirit behind the city's slogan of "I will" than Samuel Insull, the financial buccaneer whose artificially constructed empire of watered stock was instrumental in bringing on the worst effects of the depression in Chicago. Whatever may have been his contribution to the technology of public utilities, it cannot be doubted that in his eyes bigness was goodness, whether in fiscal deals or opera houses, and that in order to achieve size nothing like orthodox morality was allowed to stand in his way. Everyone and everything had a price in Insull's eyes, including public officials, politicians, newspapers, lawyers, and civic leaders.[14]

Although no complete case can be made, it is not unlikely that politicians were partially responsible for the Insull fiasco and its chaotic effect on the Middle West. It is certain that both parties assisted his rise, that neither party interfered with his manipulations, and that both parties were beneficiaries of substantial campaign contributions from him.[15]

Cynical of politicians, political reform, or parties and factions and political promises, he nevertheless became a center of political influence and power cutting across the lines of party and faction and focusing in the central point of control, control sometimes for advantage and sometimes for immunity, sometimes positive and sometimes negative, yet in any case, control.[16]

Insull has been singled out not as an isolated example; rather is he a symbol of the larger group of bold, crude, self-seeking leaders of the respectable business world. On the one hand these men were civic fathers, important church leaders, prominent in the exclusive set, righteously indignant in public, in pulpit, and in press against political corruption; and on the other hand, they were the handmaidens and partners and financial angels of the political bosses whose corruption they denounced. Some have rationalized their practices on the ground that these were eminently practical men faced with the distasteful status quo of dishonest and incompetent government, who replied to power with power in an attempt to allow their legitimate business concerns to grow and prosper, so that the whole community might profit therefrom. It has been said that they had to save themselves and their enterprises from possible sabotage and certain levy from political pirates; and that therefore it was legitimate for them to buy off such parasites as a measure of self-defense. One might readily question the moral coherence of such an argument; and certainly little defense can be made of the hypocritical pose on the part of these men as pure knights of civic uprightness, save on the grounds that they were paranoiac enough to believe the myth themselves. This, of course, may very well have been the case. In any case, in the Chicago of the first three decades of this century, Lincoln Steffens' theories concerning the alliance of corrupt politicians and decent big businessmen did find persuasive evidence. That Insull's attitudes were, however, merely symptomatic of a prevailing atmosphere in Chicago may perhaps be illustrated by the fact that after his trial, at which he had stated quite openly, "I'd do it again," he was acquitted without delay, and with no protests of any size or intensity.[17]

SCRAMBLED GOVERNMENT

The Chicago metropolitan area, in common with other such areas in this country, has unbelievable lack of integration in government. Of course we shall not begin to consider the 1,600 governments, the 7,700 elective officials, and the 85,000 employees who worked in this political wonderland.[18] Our attention will be directed only to the governments in Cook County and the City of Chicago; for it is with knowledge of their intricacies that Cermak climbed to his position of power.

There were in 1909 eight major governments in this area and twenty-five minor ones.[19] The major ones were the City of Chicago, Cook County, the board of education, the public library board, the sanitary district, Lincoln Park board, West Park board, and South Park board. In addition, there were about seventy-five elective judges. Chicago voters had to elect 161 officials during a six-year period.

Each of the eight major governments had independent taxing and financial powers, its own officers, and its own rules for governing itself. The governing bodies of all were appointive, except for those of the city, the county, and the sanitary district, which were elective. The board of education and the public library board were appointed by the mayor but after appointment were virtually independent. The boards of Lincoln Park and West Park were appointed by the governor, while the South Park board was appointed by the judges of the circuit court of Cook County.[20] These were all major governmental units from the point of view of budgets, numbers of employees, and amount of patronage, favors, and perquisites. The board of education had budgets of nearly $100,000,000; the city, $209,000,000; the county, $34,000,000; the South Park board, $5,000,000; while the sanitary district's budget in 1931 was $73,946,000. The payroll of the sanitary district sometimes reached 3,000; that of the city, 20,000[21] One should also bear in mind that these are largely independent jurisdictions; therefore, in complex municipal affairs, each of them may have to be consulted. Thus, these and many lesser and competing "city halls" blur boundaries of party, social, and ethnic groups, and make the understanding of Chicago politics a tour de force. For there may be little integration between these governments, inasmuch as frequently different parties and party factions hold power in these different centers of influence. Control over these entities was then to a great degree the immensely rich stakes in the game, and involved possession of

... payrolls "taking care" of thousands of party workers; appropriations running into the hundreds of millions; power to give or withhold in many of the daily incidents of life which make or destroy individual happiness or fortune; influence leading into state and national politics, affecting the political fortunes of governors and senators and strengthening or weakening the power of national parties.[22]

To describe properly the workings of the crazy-quilt pattern would take volumes; but perhaps a brief sketch of the structure of two of these important jurisdictions, the city and the county, would be useful for our purposes; for not only are the governments of these of the first importance, but it was with them that Cermak had the longest and most intimate connection.

THE GOVERNMENT OF THE CITY OF CHICAGO

The government of the corporate City of Chicago is basically the mayor-council type. The two most important elements are the nearly coordinate branches, the council and the mayor. The other elective officers are the thirty-seven justices of the municipal court, the clerk and bailiff of this tribunal, the city clerk, and the city treasurer.

The council has always been a body of great power, both legally and traditionally.[23] It was empowered to make the budget, set up new departments, and legislate on a wide scope. As a result of a legislative act originally passed in 1919, aldermen were elected in a technically nonpartisan election for two-year terms; the term was lengthened to four years in 1958. The same law changed the number of wards from thirty-five to fifty and reduced the representation of each ward from two to one alderman.[24]

Many lines of division were present in the council. There were the blocs representing the different sections of the city, the divisions between the parties, and the ones who could be bought and those who could not. An eminent alumnus has estimated that one third was generally purchasable, one third could not be bought, and one third vacillated with one eye on public opinion and the other on the tempting bait.[25]

The mayor presides at council sessions, and in cases of personally strong mayors considerable control over the council has been exhibited. Most of the work is performed by committees, composed largely on a nonpartisan basis. Thus it has happened that powerful committees have had chairmen of the opposition party. Committe recommendations were not at all certain of adoption and even if passed were liable to veto by the mayor. Moreover, some measures such as bond issues and amendments to the charter must be submitted to the electorate in the form of a referendum.[26]. The council ratifies all mayoral appointments; it grants franchises and regulates public utility rates; it appropriates funds. Since 1957 it has surrendered its power over formulation of the city budget to the mayor.

The office of the mayor is a demanding position. "The Mayor of Chicago is the City's most impressive show-piece; he is its chief personnel agent; he is its city manager; he is its chief lawmaker, its chief financier, its diplomat, its leader, all in one; or he should be, if he did all that is expected of him."[27]

He has the normal duty of executing the laws; he presides at council meetings; and he has broad powers of appointment, including the board of education, the civil service commission, the public library board, the heads of all city departments, and all nonelective, noncivil-service officials.[28] He has broad powers of removal over most of these positions, although he must inform the council concerning each dismissal. The mayor has important administrative responsibilities in supervision of the extensive municipal services.

His legislative duties, besides that of presiding over the council, include the duty of delivering an annual message and the privilege of other such communications. As presiding officer, he casts the deciding vote if there is a tie. He has broad veto powers, which extend to the item veto in fiscal matters, and may only be overturned by a two-thirds vote of the council. In case of a veto, he may substitute his own bill, which must be considered immediately if the veto is upheld. The substitute bill needs only a simple majority. At other times, too, he may initiate legislation.

THE GOVERNMENT OF COOK COUNTY

Cook, one of the most populous counties in the United States, having an area of nearly one hundred square miles, has the disintegrated type of government typical of American counties. The county includes most of Chicago as well as the most important suburbs. Within the city limits were 90 per cent of its population and over 90 per cent of its tax potential.[29] In its diffused government it is difficult to locate responsibility and centers of integration, for though most of the legislative function is vested in the board of commissioners, the executive function is divided between the latter and a galaxy of independently elected officials.[30]

The principal agency is the board, consisting of fifteen members elected for four-year terms. Ten are elected from the portion of the county within the city; the remaining five are elected from the part outside the city. The president of the board is elected both as a member and as president. It is in the person of this official that any possible coordination of the county government is possible. The chief device available for this purpose is an effective veto power, perhaps the most effective such power in the state.[31] The president may veto any money resolutions, contracts, or anything incurring fiscal liabilities; and this can be reversed only by four fifths of all the elected members. This provision includes the item veto. Some influence is also possible in the president's capacity as presiding officer and in his membership on important committees where the veto threat can be voiced.

"With the advice and consent" of the county board he appoints many administrative officials. The appointment power is greatly increased by the fact that no board concurrence is required to appoint the three members of the county civil service commission. They are removable at his discretion.[32] Since the merit system in Cermak's time was little more than façade, it is clear that of the several thousand positions in agencies responsible to the county board and the president, there was no little patronage available.[33] Cermak made extremely successful use of this situation.[34] Many of his political contemporaries believe that control of this strategic job-dispensing position was most instrumental in his rise to power.[35]

In sum, the president of the county board is much stronger than similar officers in the rest of the state, his office resembling in many important respects that of the mayor in a mayor-council government.[36] Notwithstanding the powers vested in the president and the county board and their important responsibilities in the area of public welfare, public health, and highway construction, some most vital responsibilities are discharged by independent officers who have no responsibility to the president or to the county board. These include the influential positions of state's attorney, sheriff, county clerk, treasurer, coroner; the tax-assessment officials, the judicial officers; and the clerks of the various courts.

The president and the county board also function in a like capacity for the Cook County Forest Preserve District, which administers great park areas. The president is also chief executive officer of the forest-preserve district, and in this position his veto can be overridden only by unanimous vote of the entire board.[37]

POLITICAL PARTIES

As already indicated, the Chicago pattern in both parties consisted of feudal baronies rather than the Tammany system, although there was more disintegration among the Republicans than among the Democrats.

The Republicans had since the turn of the century been clustered around three powerful factions, each led by a dominating figure and each roughly representing one of the city's great sections. Charles Deneen, senator and ex-governor, was perhaps the strongest in the south side and outlying areas, mostly supported by the middle class, the press, business, and reform elements. Deneen, though considered the most respectable and responsible, nevertheless was a professional who knew all the rules of the game, recognized the lubricant nature of patronage, and at times was not averse to less than snow-white alliances.

The west-side coterie, originally founded by the "blond boss" Senator Lorimer, gained footholds in other parts of the city and made use of all the weapons in the rough-house arsenal of urban politics without much attention to the niceties. This organization and its techniques were captured by "Big Bill" Thompson and his political mentor Fred Lundin, the "poor Swede."

The third contingent's power was firmly rooted in the north side. Originally headed by Mayor Busse, it was later taken over by Edward J. Brundage, ex-corporation counsel and attorney general. Medill McCormick was also important in this group. This clan was seldom as strong as the first two and most frequently allied itself with one or the other depending upon the booty dangled before it.

The Thompson-Lundin crowd was closely connected with the downstate machine of Governor Len Small (one of Lorimer's protégés), but in 1923 this relationship was severed and Lundin left Thompson for the Small camp. After 1920 the situation became more complicated, as two new names rose to prominence in the ranks of the west-side crowd. These were Robert E. Crowe, state's attorney, and George V. Barrett, county reviewer.

In the late twenties and early thirties these factions constantly grouped and regrouped, broke old treaties, and made new alliances for nearly every primary. In the political news of this period one reads of the Crowe-Barrett faction, the Small-Thompson, the Brundage, the Deneen-Small-Thompson, and every other possible combination of these elements.

During the same period Chicago Democracy was usually in two main camps. One of these was led by Roger Sullivan and later by George Brennan, while the other was led by the two Carter Harrisons (father and son, each five times mayor) and Edward F. Dunne, former mayor and governor, and his assistant, William L. O'Connell. Sullivan, a utility operator, was more nearly the classic boss, being a candidate for office only once, losing the race for United States Senator in 1916. After his death and Brennan's assumption the same nongenteel tactics were used as under Sullivan; but in 1923 a temporary truce between the Brennan and Harrison forces resulted in the election of a Democratic mayor, William Dever. The alliance was soon broken over patronage difficulties and harmony of a permanent nature was not effected until Cermak took the reins.

These various factions divided federal, state, county, and other patronage, and rose and fell with the currents of political fortune. Their connections and combinations constitute an intricate tangled skein—at times they rallied to the support of their respective parties, and at times they crossed party lines and fought together, especially in local contests, where the national party lines were shot to pieces. Almost any combination of these elements was possible and actual. There was no boss strong enough to control all of these factions even in one party, and as a rule each man fought at the head of his own faction. . . . In general the Deneen faction was the strongest in Republican times, and the Brennan in Democratic times, and these two factions were most generally supported by the press.[38]

The stakes of the game, given the factor of scrambled government, although incalculable, were astronomic. Appropriations in the hundreds of millions, patronage in the many thousands,[39] access to so many forms of privilege made local government not only a big business but a vehicle to power and fortune.

APPENDIX II:

LEADERSHIP

AND

PSYCHOSOMATIC

ANALYSIS[1]

THE dynamic concept of personality as propounded by Freud and enlarged or elucidated by other psychologists and analysts, although it has scarcely begun to be exploited by political scientists, has to some degree affected the work of students of political leadership. It is true that most writers, faced with the problem of dealing with the relation between political power and personality, continue to fall back in the main upon describing the manifest traits of the successful politician; but there are few among the more serious students of leadership who do not give at least a passing glance at childhood circumstances, family relationships, and striking evidences of personality disorders in a subject, where these are available.[2]

An additional avenue of insight into the relationship between power and personality has been opened up by clinical research in the field of psychosomatic medicine. The theory underlying the psychosomatic approach to illness is that emotional factors play a causative role in disease. No valid correlation between personality types and diseases has been made; that is to say, there has been found no typical "asthmatic personality," "rheumatoid arthritic personality," etc. On the other hand, correlation does appear to exist between specific emotional conflicts and specific diseases; e.g., in the unconscious of asthmatics a typical conflict-situation will be found.

The writer, in a study of the career of the Chicago politician Anton J. Cermak, found the literature on psychological factors in disease of great assistance in an effort to determine the emotional background of the subject's behavior. Among the most conspicuous of Cermak's characteristics were closemouthedness and the absence of personal friendships. He kept no diary, wrote few personal letters, and was the author, with assistance, of only one manuscript. Thus, while many descriptions of the overt features of personality were available from surviving associates and from contemporary newspaper articles, only the crudest sorts of inferences as to the interior organization of personality could be made.

Newspapers some three weeks following Cermak's death carried the story that the immediate cause of his death had not been, as had at first been given out, the bullet wound inflicted by Roosevelt's would-be assassin, but rather a case of ulcerative colitis fatally aggravated by the bullet injury. Reports of illnesses, recuperative trips, confinements to bed or hospital, begin to punctuate the record of Cermak's career consistently beginning with the year 1925, when he was fifty-two years old. These illnesses, even in the more garbled newspaper reports, are described as "gastro-intestinal." Dr. Frank Jirka, Cermak's son-in-law and one of his physicians, stated that the politician's chronic ailment was colitis. These various bits of medical information, which at first appeared to be of no more than ordinary biographical interest, eventually provided a key to the specific emotional needs which had led the subject to seek and fight to maintain political power, which influenced his conduct of political office, and which to some degree were responsible for his winning of a following, for his choice of political role, and for the extent and limitations of the power he achieved.

I

Cermak was born in Kladno, Czechoslovakia, the eldest son of Anton Cermak, a coal miner, and his wife, Katherine. The couple emigrated to America in 1874, when Anton, Jr., was a year old, settling near Chicago in Braidwood, Illinois, a mining community heavily populated by Czechs. Moves from Braidwood to Chicago and back again, brought on by the instability of employment in the mines and in the city, recurred throughout Cermak's poverty-ridden childhood. His formal education amounted to a total of approximately three years of elementary school, attended sporadically in Braidwood and Chicago.

Both Cermak parents were physically vigorous, hard-working, and long-lived. The father was the more outstanding personality; he was remembered for his powerful physique even in his old age. The mother was most frequently described as "like everybody else," or "like any other mother." In his own marriage, Cermak repeated the pattern of his parents, choosing a shy, undistinguished partner who, by choice, played absolutely no role in his public life. Cermak's six siblings—four boys and two girls—like the parents, were hard-working and reliable, but demonstrated none of the unusual aggressiveness or ambition of the eldest brother. Although his brothers were young men at the time when Cermak began to gain significant political power, none of them attempted to use his influence to any end beyond the retention of the minor public positions Cermak obtained for them. Both sisters married within the ethnic group; their husbands were men of no special prominence.

The Bohemian-American family, like the Bohemian-American community, is a close-knit unit; and in details of behavior relating to the family Cermak was not atypical of his group. He maintained amicable relations with the members of his immediate family throughout his life. He saw to it that his brothers were put into positions as fortunate as their capabilities allowed; prior to his entrance into politics, he welcomed them into the wood-and-hauling business he established as a youth. As soon as he was able, he became the support of his father and mother; moreover, both lived under his roof in Chicago until their deaths. It is said that Katherine Cermak was often approached by friends to intercede with her son for favors, and that he never refused a request made through her. With his own children, Cermak's indulgence—even overindulgence—was marked.

Very early—as early as elementary school age—the young Cermak began to exhibit an interest in leading his fellows. Although there was intense enmity between the Czechs and the second largest (and socially dominant) ethnic group in Braidwood, the Irish, Anton, Jr., not only established friendship relations with Irish boys, but became a ringleader among them. He appears to have accomplished this through a combination of brash derring-do, a quick wit, and a superior physical strength, which he did not hesitate to use in physical encounters. In the acts of vandalism and the gang fights which occupied boys of his age and economic circumstances in Braidwood, his personal pugnaciousness as well as his strong, stocky physique stood him in good stead.

Cermak entered the Braidwood mines at the age of thirteen—not an unusual age, among Braidwood boys of that time, to leave school and become so employed. His social life, like that of his friends, now centered largely about the Braidwood saloons, although minors were presumably not allowed. In this period, Cermak continued to have a following of youths who regarded him as spirited, popular, and affable. Not all observers, however, were so impressed.

He didn't get along with people. He was always getting into fights. He thought he was a tough guy and could fight. He couldn't leave people alone, and most were afraid of him. Girls were very scared. He would always ask to take them home from dances, and they were afraid because he was mean and drunk, and would say "No." He would then "lay" for the girl and the boy who was walking her home, beat him up, and land in jail. The cop used to say that he never had to go into a tavern and haul him out. All he had to do was wait by the door, and soon he would be thrown out because he was making trouble.[3]

At sixteen, he went to live with a relative in Pilsen, a predominantly Czech neighorhood on Chicago's near southwest side. It was not long before he gained the leadership of one of Pilsen's "gangs" of young men—an ascendancy which was influential in securing for him his first petty job with the local Democratic organization. By the time he was nineteen, he had purchased a horse and wagon and had launched an independent business. He had also become a busy "ward heeler." Within two years, his business had prospered sufficiently to allow him to marry; and in two years more he had built a home that was the equal of any in his new neighborhood of Lawndale—the Czech community where he was to maintain residence to the end of his life.

In the years that followed, as his young family and his young business grew and flourished, Cermak was carefully working his way up the party ladder—always rationalizing his political activity on the ground that it was "good for my business"—going from the position of precinct election official to assistant precinct captain, to precinct captain, to bailiff in a justice-of-the-peace court.[4] All the while, he was assiduously building a personal following among his own ethnic group, a following which eventually widened to include Chicago foreign-born in general. In 1902, at the age of twenty-nine, he reaped the rewards of his efforts in the form of nomination and election to his first elective office, that of state representative.

Thereafter, for the thirty-one remaining years of his life, Cermak held virtually uninterrupted elective office—legislative, executive, and administrative, in city, county, and state governments. He rose to the mayoralty in a city which for nearly a hundred years had not recruited

a single one of its forty mayors from among the foreign born, and
which has not done so again in the twenty-one years since his death.
He died, according to Edward J. Kelly, his successor as mayor and
ultimately as party chief, the most powerful figure in the State of
Illinois and in the history of Chicago.[5]

Needless to say, Cermak did not win his successive political laurels
in the guise of the brawling, undisciplined "plug-ugly" he had been
as a youth. At the same time, the traits which had characterized his
adolescence did not utterly vanish.

His pugnaciousness survived as a dormant threat in his bearing and
his manner, which intimidated many people. Even though, as an
adult, he did not engage in fisticuffs, "People were afraid he would
crack them one."[6] He was, moreover, capable of violent states of rage,
in which he hurled at those who had offended him not only verbal
abuse, but whatever heavy objects happened to be handy.

In his maturity, he by no means took on charm, refinement, or
suavity, nor did he learn to cultivate the gentler arts of diplomacy. In
interviews with former associates and critics, the descriptive terms,
"crude," "blunt," "outspoken," "bullying," "tough," "aggressive," regularly occurred. He appeared to take pride in his own absence of
polish. "[The Mayor] . . . is sure of one thing and that is that it is not
through any charm of personality that he has arrived" is only one of
many statements made in the same vein throughout his career.[7]

For his success in impressing associates and followers, Cermak depended upon other qualities. A man without formal education, he
showed an amazingly wide knowledge of governmental affairs. He
was always thoroughly conversant with the remotest aspects of any
public problem; he earned, and capitalized upon, the title of "a master
of detail." He was also a talented and effective party organizer and
administrator. In the mayoralty campaign against Thompson, he ran
as a "master public executive." In this campaign, as in others, he made
little or no attempt to create for himself a "colorful" personality. Far
from being jovial, hearty, or outgoing, he gave an impression of withdrawn, absorbed seriousness, even of lumpishness and melancholia—
"You couldn't love him."[8]

He was described, even by enemies, as a "man of his word." He
never made promises lightly or hastily, but once he had committed
himself to a program he could be depended upon to act decisively
about it. He was frequently described as "courageous" or "fearless."
Again, the facts seem to be that he was slow to espouse any public
policy, and in his political life cannily wed himself only to issues whose

popularity was assured. But he would fight all opposition to defend those measures in which he had come to "believe."

"He trusted no one"; he "permitted nothing to happen without his personal knowledge." Cermak's intimate acquaintance with the details of so many public matters was in part the result of his mistrust of co-workers and subordinates, a mistrust which appears to have been compounded of the convictions (1) that no one could be trusted to do any given job so well as he; and (2) that no one could be trusted not to attempt to do him personal injury—he was "suspicious," "hostile." He did not like to "rely" upon people. Since delegation was inevitable in the complicated hierarchy of governmental and party affairs, he did a prodigious amount of checking and overseeing. He is known to have employed espionage agents. In addition, he saturated himself with information on any subject with which he was concerned. Thus he was much less at the mercy of the words and judgments of others.

Cermak is said to have "worked constantly." Journalists, coworkers, other politicians, all commented on the phenomenon of his indefatigable attachment to work. Frequent illness was not allowed to interfere; even on his deathbed, five days after the shooting, in extreme pain and weakness, he said to Clara D. Beasley:[9] "So you arrived all right . . . you've brought your typewriter, I hope, and plenty of stationery. We've got a lot to do. . . ."[10]

Cermak's ability to work almost literally around the clock was made possible not only by his tremendous reserve of physical energy but by his absolutely undivided concentration upon gaining, maintaining, and expanding his political power and prestige. When persons interviewed compared him to contemporary or past political figures, they invariably assessed him as being, in their experience, the figure with the fewest "soft spots," the fewest extraneous demands upon his time and energies. With the exception of his doting affection for his three daughters, he appears to have had no life and no serious interests outside the political arena. His wife had little in common with him, and he was not in the habit of spending a great deal of leisure time with her—in fact, from the time he became president of the county board, he maintained a downtown hotel room in which it was his habit to work through the night, often not returning home. It was remarked again and again that "he had no personal friends." Such cronies as he did have were always men with whom there was a definite political or business tie; and even with these he "always talked business," he "confided in no one." His apparent indifference to sex was also commented upon: he did not attempt to be gallant, or even sociable, with women. During his long career, no breath of scandal relating to his sexual behavior ever touched him; and in the course of many interviews with enemies who would have been delighted to add to their criticisms of him the charge of sexual looseness, not one made this accusation. In short, Cermak indulged few human claims that could be considered a "waste" from the point of view of power. In line with this sort of orientation, it is notable that characteristically his strongest emotional reactions, in anger or in enthusiasm, were called forth by *groups* and *stereotypes* (as, the Czechs, the poor, the Irish), or by *causes* and *ideas* (as "personal liberty," World War I, America, the City of Chicago), rather than by particular *individuals*.

Cermak's attitudes toward wealth deserve some special attention because of the psychologic significance of money in the illness from which he suffered. There is no doubt that he revered wealth and respected those who possessed it. He did not "take to" people who were "cultured," but he stood in awe of "culture" and "learning" generally, and it may be conjectured that his respect for these was as symbols of wealth. This conjecture is strengthened by the fact that culture without wealth impressed him much less: his respect and deference went to such figures as wealthy banker Melvin A. Traylor, rather than to scholars Charles E. Merriam and Leonard D. White.[11]

Cermak was an excellent businessman and a successful one. His business enterprises, quite apart from any money he made in politics, were sufficient to make him a well-to-do man: he was director of two banks and co-owner of a flourishing real-estate business; his property-holdings and other investments were large. It seems clear that he regarded it as of the greatest importance to accumulate wealth. And yet, although he was described by one of his associates as "the most acquisitive man I know,"[12] it is significant that he never seriously considered deserting politics for business, even when his political fortunes were at their lowest.

Cermak seems to have had some genuine feeling of obligation to the "less fortunate." He was greatly preoccupied with the "deserving poor" in both his public and his private acts. His charitable activities began in the earliest stages of his career, with the founding and presidency of two organizations devoted to charity—the Bohemian Charitable Organization (1910) and the Bailiffs' Benevolent Association (1912). He also dispensed private charity. According to his eldest daughter, there were often foundlings in the Cermak home, whom Cermak supported until he found homes for them. Gifts were given to poor families every Christmas; and Mrs. Cermak did a great deal of sewing "for the poor."[13] Cermak was very active in initiating, organizing, and supporting public welfare projects during his tenure as county board president—thus gaining, incidentally, a good deal of his support from Chicago "reform elements." Many unofficial charitable activities—such as the presidency of the All-Chicago Christmas Fund and the presidency of the United Charities of Chicago—also figured in this period. Efforts of the official sort in public welfare continued during the mayoralty, growing more prominent as the depression rolled on and the need for them increased. The unofficial charities also kept pace, with Cermak's realty firm donating money to twenty-eight charities, and "Mayor Revealed as Food Provider for Hundreds of Youngsters."[14]

Cermak was often described as "ruthless." He himself made no secret of his policy of overlooking both personal liking and personal enmity in the conduct of his political affairs. He cooperated with enemies and attacked friends, as political necessity indicated—"You don't keep books in politics," being his favorite and often iterated maxim. He showed no sentimentality about firing incompetent employees and eliminating party rivals. Although neither his stated ethics nor any of his practices was at all uncommon among his fellow-politicians and fellow-businessmen, the completeness of his dedication to protecting his position, and his seeming impassivity in so doing, impressed all observers.

Cermak's emotional stolidity, his apparent seriousness of purpose, his intimidating manner, his absolute refusal to allow his authority to be questioned in any of the various posts he held—all these doubtless contributed to a central impression of him, held by the greatest number of observers—that of a "dominating," "autocratic," "czar-like" personality.

II

Having described, in brief, the traits of this political personality as they appeared to others, the questions arise: what shaped this character; what necessities lay behind the aggressiveness, painstakingness, ruthlessness, personal coldness, hostility, and so on? It is insufficient to answer, as it is often answered, that this man, "like most politicians," was formed by the "love of power," or the "desire for financial gain." To have said this is actually to have said very little, inasmuch as "power" and "money" are not ends in themselves, but serve more deeply rooted complexes of psychological needs which may vary greatly from individual to individual.

No answer could be anything but partial. Regardless of what psychiatry has to say about the importance of infantile experiences in shaping personality, it cannot be doubted that certain later life experiences, certain social and economic factors, play a determining part. The data offered here are not intended to "explain" the life-behavior of the subject, but only to suggest the category of psychological dynamisms into which this behavior fits.[15]

III

The literature on the influence of psychic factors in intestinal disturbances includes cases ranging from chronic diarrhea to cases of mucous and spastic colitis. Ulcerative colitis, in which ulceration of the large bowel develops, is the most extreme and dangerous form of the disease. The symptoms of colitis are painful cramps and frequent evacuations. It is not known to what extent the different forms of colitis are related.

The general theory underlying the investigations of the influence of psychic factors on the gastrointestinal system is that those emotions which cannot, for various reasons, be expressed in overt behavior or through the sexual apparatus will express themselves through the only outlet left to them, the internal organs. Diseases of these organs are referred to as "organ neuroses." "Neurosis" as a general term has been conveniently defined as "the fixed repetition of inappropriate behavior in response to conflict."[16] In the case of an organ neurosis, this "inappropriate behavior" is not a matter of overt action, as it is in, for example, the case of a compulsion neurosis, but takes place within the body. It is the affected organ that behaves "inappropriately"; i.e., functions improperly, its dysfunction being the response of the individual to a conflict situation. Although inherent constitutional factors may play a part in vulnerability to the disease, certain individual experiences are nevertheless causative.

Three "elemental tendencies" in emotional life are of importance in dysfunctions of the gastrointestinal system. These are: (1) the wish to take or receive; (2) the wish to give or eliminate; (3) the wish to retain. Alexander associates these three emotional tendencies with three types of patients. They are, corresponding to the emotional tendencies just listed: (1) the gastric type; (2) the colitis type; and (3) the constipation type.[17] We will here consider only the gastric and colitis types, in which the same conflict situation is typically found.

In the unconscious of both these types are found intense "oral-receptive" and "oral-aggressive" wishes; that is, exaggerated desires to

[373]

be loved, to be taken care of, to be dependent and passive, as well as to take, to grab, even to rob. To these desires the patient reacts with a sense of guilt and inferiority, because of the incompatibility of such longings with the aspirations of the adult ego for independence and activity. The unconscious dependent wishes are strongly repressed in the case of the gastric patient, whose conscious attitude is usually one of extreme independence, self-sufficiency, activity. Unable to gratify his unconscious longing for help, love, passivity in his conscious behavior, the patient reverts to the infantile mode of gratifying these desires: "the wish to be loved becomes converted into the wish to be fed"; the stomach, under these conditions, "behaves all the time as if it were taking or about to take in food."[18] It is this chronic stimulation of the stomach which leads to such disturbances as epigastric distress, "heartburn," "nervous stomach," and in many cases, ulcer formation.

The colitis patient, like the gastric patient, wishes to overcompensate for his passive, dependent, in-taking wishes with great activity, with giving, and with independence. Where the two types usually differ is in their solutions to this conflict. While the gastric type overcompensates for his dependent receiving and taking desires by real activity and accomplishment, the typical colitis patient has a "violent reluctance to exert himself, to engage in systematic strenuous work, and to fulfill those obligations to which he feels compelled emotionally."[19] Unable to compensate for his dependent desires by real activity and accomplishment, he expresses these in the "tacit language of the body." Whereas the upper end of the gastrointestinal tract is peculiarly suited for expressing thwarted desires for receiving, for taking, for dependence and passivity, the lower end of the intestinal tract is especially adapted for expressing thwarted desires, on the one hand, to give and accomplish, on the other hand, to attack.[20] The colitis patient, then, overcompensates for his passive, dependent wishes not through actual efforts to accomplish, but by reverting to the infantile expression of achievement: that is, with attacks of diarrhea. The chronic eliminative pressure on the colon may result in colitis, in the same way that the chronic stimulation of the stomach may lead to ulcer.

Colitis, however, appears not only in patients who manifest this surface flight from activity and responsibility, but also in individuals who for most of their lives manifest the independent, "go-getting" attitudes of the typical ulcer patient. It appears that the desire to give and accomplish may be thwarted, not by the patient's neurotic inhibitions against exerting himself, but by external circumstances. The loss of material wealth figures very prominently among such external circumstances.[21] Patients to whom the power to meet financial obligations is very necessary as a means of overcoming guilt over repressed receptive desires, once deprived of this means, often substitute the infantile "valuable possession." Thus, colitis appears not only in individuals whose dynamic formula is: "I have the right to take and demand, for I always give sufficiently. I do not need to feel inferior or guilty on account of my receptive and grasping wishes because I am giving something in exchange"; but also in those with the typical gastric type attitude; i.e., "I do not want to receive or to take. I have no such wishes. I am independent, active, and efficient."[22]

Colitis frequently indicates the patient's fixation on the anal phase of his libidinal development;[23] and thus, many of the prevailing traits of the "anal character"—as they have been delineated by Freud, Abraham, Jones, Brill, and other writers—may be found in patients suffering from the disease.

IV

Cermak's surface attitudes throughout his life were those most typical of the ulcer patient rather than of the colitis patient. He showed anything rather than a "violent reluctance to exert himself," dependence, or direct demands for affection in most relationships. Occasionally, in illness, he articulated a desire to throw off responsibility ("I'm through, exhausted, and tired of it all"); in particular, Mayor Kelly recalls his having stated to him, not long before the shooting in Miami, when he was in the most deplorable physical condition, that he had no desire "to be mayor or anything else."[24] For the most part, however, even in illness, his active, aggressive, independent manner did not desert him. It is particularly noteworthy that, in spite of the inevitable publicity given his many periods of illness, he was never taunted by political enemies with the accusation of physical infirmity. Of all the people interviewed, only two seemed so much as aware that he was a sick man. One was his son-in-law and private physician, Dr. Frank Jirka; the other was the reporter, John Dienhart, a more than commonly acute observer, who accompanied Cermak on the trip he took to advertise the World's Fair to Europe, during one of his severest periods of illness.

A careful survey of Cermak's power situations at the time of his attacks reveals that the attacks occurred during crises of the kinds described by Alexander as being typical of situations precipitating the disease.[25] The attacks of colitis began at the stage of his career when he had gained most and had most to lose; interestingly, up until this time, he had usually manifested gastric symptoms as well. His attacks occurred in situations where his leadership was being actively challenged; but they continued after he had firmly established his dominance over the party and had gained the mayoralty. It is notable that this period coincided with the worst phase of the depression, when he was continually preoccupied with financial worries, both public and personal. The period of the mayoralty, assumed as it was in 1931, was a time of unceasing anxiety, of public responsibilities that could not be met satisfactorily, no matter what dogged efforts were made, of public problems that had no solution. In Cermak's final illness, he appears to have been haunted principally, both in delirium and in his clear moments, by the fear that Chicago's schoolteachers would not be paid.

The dynamic background of Cermak's illness as formulated by Alexander and other writers allows us to place this politician rather squarely in the category of power-seeking personalities suggested by Lasswell and a number of psychologists; viz.: those persons in whom the power-urge is a "compensatory reaction against low estimates of the self."[26] Further, the formation of certain specific personality traits, although doubtless influenced by other factors, can be traced to the conflict-situation characteristic of gastrointestinal disturbances. Among these may be counted the propensity to "give to the poor," related to the hidden desires to take, to grab, or to rob, which can only be compensated for in "giving"—in this case, in acts of personal charity as well as through above-average performance in the sphere of public welfare. Again, Cermak's refusal to exert himself to be outgoing, charming, or "colorful," his creation of the relatively uninteresting and austere role of the "master public executive," his insistence upon relying on his record of dependability, hard-workingness, and thorough acquaintance with any job undertaken, is of a piece with the preoccupation of some colitis patients with giving "real values."[27]

Cermak demonstrated the characteristics of the "anal" person in a whole congeries of related traits: his hostility, suspiciousness, lack of warmth, reluctance to delegate responsibility, unswerving adherence to courses of action agreed upon; and finally, in the central characteristic of his personality, the demand for power.

Cermak's anal characteristics were of the "sublimation" type rather than of the "reaction-formation" type. In the former type of orientation, the infantile pleasure in the bowel function and resistance to interference with its control, instead of being repressed to the degree that entirely opposite surface attitudes are formed (i.e., cleanliness, orderliness, parsimony, gentleness, overcompliance, as in the case of a reaction-formation) simply pass over into other areas of life which are structurally analogous. Thus, the "sense of power that accompanies control of the sphincters . . . may be obtained through self-control or the control of other persons."[28] The more intense this infantile experience, the greater may be the subsequent need to satisfy the essentially sadistic urge to wield power.

The explanation of why Cermak should have sought to gratify his power-demands in the area of government must be sought elsewhere than in his individual infantile experiences. It may be said in passing that government in the modern urban environment, as has often been observed, offers opportunities for the exercise of as nearly naked control and power as is sanctioned in our society. Moreover, Cermak's own ethnic group, the Czechs, set an unusually high premium upon political power, their adulation and respect going first not to the businessman, the intellectual, or the artist, but to the politician.

The anal personality has been described as "withdrawn from others"; he "seeks security by making himself an autarchic, self-sufficient system, and feels love or any other outgoing attitude as a threat to his security."[29] Abraham explains the inability to love thus: the child will have the earlier-mentioned sense of pleasure and accomplishment in its bowel function if the period of training is not forced upon him before he is "psychically ready for it." This psychical preparedness only appears when the child begins to transfer to others—its mother, for example—the feelings that were originally bound narcissistically. If the child has acquired this capacity to identify with others, it will perform its function "for the sake of" others; but if the training is forced upon it too soon, it will acquire the habit through fear, its inner resistance remains; "its libido will continue in a tenacious narcissistic fixation, and a permanent disturbance of the capacity to love will result."[30]

It seems fair to assume, then, on the basis of the foregoing summary, that a number of related traits manifested by Cermak—his suspiciousness, his hostility, the apparent impoverishment of his personal relations, his seeming indifference to sex—had deeper roots than the conscious desire to protect his political position. It is significant, however, that all these traits, so negative from the point of view of human intercourse, should have proved useful in the career of a political power-seeker.

Cermak's desire to rely upon no one but himself, his insistence upon "checking" all personnel and all details of every operation, and his adherence to his "political word" are characteristics commonly found in certain types of anal personalities. Jones says that such persons are "equally hard to move to a given course of action as to bring them from it once they have started on it," and relates this stubborn persistence to the infantile pleasure in control of the sphincters.[31] In all these traits there is manifest the "self-willed independence" of some anally fixated personalities, a confidence in personal powers which makes it difficult for the individual to believe that anyone delegated to do a task can do it properly. Jones cites the case of Napoleon as an example of the type who

... organizes an elaborate system which functions marvellously well while its author, with tireless energy, attends in person to every detail, but which runs the risk of collapse as soon as the master hand is inactive; for, having assumed it all himself, he has given no one else the chance of being trained in responsibility.[32]

Cermak's career offers a microcosmic parallel here. He was responsible for the organization of the first cohesive, city-wide party machine, comparable to Tammany Hall, that Chicago had ever known. So complete was his grasp of the organization, so tirelessly had he eliminated possible pretenders, that upon his death there was no one to "step into his shoes."

As will be apparent from the material presented here, it should be possible, given an acquaintance with the literature of psychoanalysis, to form a working theory as to the psychological background of the behavior of a given political figure out of descriptions of his overt behavior or direct observation of it. The presence of disease offers a slightly more reliable guide, in that the fact of disease—provided it is firmly established—is irrefutable, while the impressions of observers with regard to the behavior of any political subject are subject to certain biases. The literature on psychic factors in disease is as yet incomplete, but the material thus far published should prove valuable in many individual and comparative leadership studies.

NOTES

Chapter 1

1. Harold Zink, *City Bosses in the United States* (Durham, N. C.: Duke University Press, 1930), p. 10. While some other municipal politicians may have had less or more formal education than Cermak, those studied by Zink all had much more. On the Chicago scene, the Harrisons, Crowe, and Deneen all were college men; Brennan and Sullivan had at least completed high school. Even in Cermak's own Czech-American group, the next most eminent politician, Otto Kerner, was judge of the United States Circuit Court of Appeals for many years.

2. This was the situation of George E. Brennan, who preceded Cermak as leader of Chicago and Cook County Democracy. Despite popular Chicago legend, the records fail to reveal that the maimed Brennan was at any time Cermak's teacher. The alleged sponsorship of Cermak by Brennan, also a part of Chicago political mythology, seems to be apocryphal as well.

3. H. K. Barnard, *Anton the Martyr* (Chicago: Marion Publishing Co., 1933), p. 17.

4. J. R. Commons, "Slavs in the Bituminous Coal Mines of Illinois," *Charities,* XIII (December 3, 1919), 227.

5. Local #1 was founded in the Lower Braidwood Bohemian Hall.

Many national and state mine leaders emerged from Braidwood because labor conditions there caused much agitation. A.J. was personally acquainted with John Mitchell, founder and first president of the UMW, who lived in Braidwood across from Cermak's friends, the MacElroys.

6. Statement of a Braidwood contemporary, personal interview.

Chapter 2

1. Anton J. Cermak, "Why Businessmen Fail in Politics," *Nation's Business,* XXI (1933), 25.

2. H. K. Barnard, *Anton the Martyr* (Chicago: Marion Publishing Co., 1933) p. 24.

3. For an explanation of factions in the Democratic party, see Appendix I.

4. C. E. Merriam and H. F. Gosnell, *The American Party System* (New York: Macmillan Co., 1949), p. 175.

5. Sonja Forthal, "Relief and Friendly Service by Political Precinct Leaders," *Social Service Review,* VII (1931), 608-18. The multiplicity and frequency of this kind of benevolent service have been demonstrated by Harold F. Gosnell, *Machine Politics: Chicago Model* (Chicago: University of Chicago Press, 1937), p. 71. Also see Jane Addams, *Democracy and Social Ethics* (New York: Macmillan Co., 1902).

6. Sonja Forthal, "The Small Fry and the Party Purse," *American Political Science Review,* XXXIV (1940), 66-76.

7. Gosnell, *Machine Politics,* p. 68; cf. H. D. Cherry, "Effective Precinct Organization" (Master's thesis, University of Chicago, 1952), pp. 105 ff.

Chapter 3

1. Emily Greene Balch, *Our Slavic Fellow-Citizens* (New York: Charities Publications Committee, 1910), p. 6.

2. *Ibid.,* pp. 8 ff.

3. Thomas Capek (ed.), *The Czechoslovaks: The Czech (Bohemian) Community of New York* (New York: Czechoslovak Section of America's Making, Inc., 1921), pp. 9 f.

4. Thomas Capek, Jr., "Have the Bohemians a Place in the Sun?" in *Bohemia Under Hapsburg Misrule,* ed. Thomas Capek (New York: Fleming H. Revel Co., 1915), p. 22.

5. Herbert A. Miller, "The Bohemian Character," *ibid.,* p. 135.

6. B. Simek, "Why Bohemia Deserves Freedom," *ibid.,* p. 126.

7. *Ibid.*

8. Ferdnand Perontka, "A Portrait of Czechoslovakia," in Karel Capek *et al., At the Crossroads of Europe: A Historical Outline of the Democratic Idea in Czechoslovakia* (Prague: PEN Club, 1938), p. 253.

9. *Ibid.*, p. 256.

10. Emily Greene Balch, "The Bohemians as Immigrants," *Bohemia Under Hapsburg Misrule*, pp. 185 ff.

11. Czechs generally were not opposed to women's suffrage until it became connected with the Prohibition issue.

12. Balch, *Our Slavic Fellow-Citizens*, p. 395.

13. Robert E. Park and Herbert A. Miller, *Old World Traits Transplanted* (New York: Harper and Bros., 1921), p. 219; Kenneth D. Miller, *The Czecho-Slovaks in America* (New York: George H. Doran Co., 1922), p. 107.

14. Kenneth D. Miller, *The Czecho-Slovaks in America*, p. 219.

15. Balch, *Our Slavic Fellow-Citizens*, pp. 365-70.

16. *Ibid.*

17. Harold R. Mayer, "South Lawndale," Chicago Plan Commission, *Forty-Four Cities in the City of Chicago* (Chicago, 1942), pp. 25-27. In this treatment South Lawndale is the name given to the community.

18. *Ibid.*

19. *Ibid.*

20. "Cermak Tells His Countrymen's Spirit of Cooperation Is Helping City to Take Rank as World's Metropolis," *Chicago Herald and Examiner,* October 27, 1927.

21. Mayer, "South Lawndale," pp. 25-27.

22. *Ibid.*

23. Jakub Horak, "Assimilation of Czechs in Chicago" (Ph.D. dissertation, University of Chicago, 1920), p. 41.

24. *Ibid.*, p. 44.

25. *Ibid.*, p. 45.

26. *Ibid.*, p. 46.

27. Kenneth D. Miller, *The Czecho-Slovaks in America*, p. 75.

28. Quoted in Miller, *The Czecho-Slovaks in America*, p. 93.

29. Cf. Nelson Algren, "A Lot You Got to Holler," *Penguin New Writing*, No. 36, ed. John Lehman (Harmondsworth, England: Penguin Books, 1949). Mr. Algren is the best observer of this phenomenon as it has been experienced by Chicago Poles.

30. Horak, "Assimilation of Czechs in Chicago," p. 48. For treatment of this problem among the Irish, see the fictional works of James T. Farrell, notably *Young Lonigan* (New York: Vanguard Press, 1932).

31. In 1922 fully 60 per cent of urban Czechs had a working knowledge of English, in contrast to 30 per cent for other Slavs. See Kenneth D. Miller, *Czecho-Slovaks in America*, p. 107.

32. Horak, "Assimilation of Czechs in Chicago," p. 54.

33. *Ibid.,* p. 52.

34. *Ibid.,* p. 55.

35. An especially vehement one is held by R. A. Ginsburg, "Czechs in Politics," in *Czech and Slovak Leaders in Metropolitan Chicago,* ed. Daniel D. Droba (Chicago: Slavonic Club of the University of Chicago, 1934), pp. 262-64.

36. Josepha H. Zeman, "The Bohemian People in Chicago," *Hull House Maps and Papers* (New York: T. Y. Crowell and Co., 1895), pp. 115-28.

37. Horak, "Assimilation of Czechs in Chicago," p. 55.

38. *Ibid.,* p. 68.

39. A. J. Cermak in *Chicago Herald and Examiner,* October 26 and 27, 1927.

40. Cf. the case of the funeral services for Sinclair Lewis, a vehement agnostic. "News and Notes," *The Humanist,* Vol. XI (August, 1951).

Chapter 4

1. For an analysis of factions of the Democratic party, see Appendix I.

2. *Chicago Daily Times,* February 16, 1933.

3. Fletcher Dobyns, *The Underworld of American Politics* (Kingsport, Tenn.: privately printed, 1932), p. 37.

4. "Political opinion" is used here and will be used subsequently in place of that ambiguous term "public opinion." The attempt is to distinguish between the inarticulate and unarticulated opinions and attitudes of unorganized individuals, and the well-formulated, highly organized views of individuals as members of groups and the attitudes of certain powerful and articulate individuals. The latter is what I mean by political opinion. On the other hand, public opinion frequently does not recognize this distinction, tends to blur it, to identify public opinion with an undefined, inchoate, almost mystical force.

5. Personal interview.

Chapter 5

1. Harold F. Gosnell, *Negro Politicians* (Chicago: University of Chicago Press, 1930), p. 74. Among the city council's important pre-

rogatives may be included power to pass the budget, create new departments, grant franchises, reject mayoralty appointments, and enact city ordinances.

2. Each district had three representatives.

3. Letter from A. J. Cermak to the Municipal Voters' League, 1909.

4. Harold F. Gosnell, *Machine Politics: Chicago Model* (Chicago: University of Chicago Press, 1937), pp. 49 f.

5. The primary law of 1910 neglected to specify the length of his term or the time of his election. The primary law of 1919 decreed four-year terms but was found unconstitutional. When the 35-ward system gave way to 50 wards, the confusion was compounded. The primary law of 1927 specified two-year terms. *Ibid.,* p. 28.

6. When Cermak was mayor, redistricting caused Negroes to lose control of one ward. Gosnell, *Negro Politicians,* pp. 76 f.

7. Charles E. Merriam and Harold F. Gosnell, *The American Party System* (New York: Macmillan Co., 1948), p. 179.

8. For an analysis of factions of the Democratic party, see Appendix I.

9. For an analysis of factions of the Republican party, see Appendix I.

10. Charles E. Merriam, *Chicago, A More Intimate View of Urban Politics* (New York: Macmillan Co., 1929), p. 282. Cf. the account of another candidate in this election, Carter H. Harrison, *The Stormy Years* (Indianapolis: Bobbs-Merrill Co., 1935), pp. 266-95.

11. Merriam, *Chicago, A More Intimate View,* p. 284.

12. *Chicago Examiner,* March 30, 1912.

13. *Ibid.*

14. H. K. Barnard, *Anton the Martyr* (Chicago: Marion Publishing Co., 1933), p. 33.

15. Coughlin believed that Cermak was a good friend, and Kenna was later one of A.J.'s political advisers. Lloyd Wendt and Herman Kogan, *Lords of the Levee* (Indianapolis: Bobbs-Merrill Co., 1943), p. 350.

16. *Chicago Tribune,* October 11, 1911.

Chapter 6

1. Personal interview.

2. See *infra,* this chapter.

3. *Chicago Tribune,* June 19, 1917.

4. Quoted in *Chicago Tribune,* December 29, 1917.

5. *Chicago Evening American,* June 28, 1917.

6. Lloyd Wendt and Herman Kogan, *Lords of the Levee* (Indianapolis: Bobbs-Merrill Co., 1943), p. 324.

7. *Chicago Evening American,* October 21, 1915.

8. *Chicago Tribune,* November 3, 1915.

9. *Chicago Evening American,* February 9, 1916.

10. *Ibid.*

11. *Chicago Evening Post,* January 4, 1917.

12. *Chicago Examiner,* November 10, 1917.

13. *Chicago Evening American,* November 1, 1918.

Chapter 7

1. Much of the foregoing is based on interviews with Judge Kerner. Kerner said that Cermak offered him at this time a place on the Cook County circuit bench. This he refused but later accepted. In 1932 Kerner was elected Attorney General of Illinois, along with Horner and the rest of the Cermak ticket. Subsequently, he was appointed to the United States Circuit Court, where he served with distinction for many years. His son was elected governor in 1960. This man, Otto Kerner, Jr., thus became the first Czech-American governor of Illinois, and perhaps the first such governor of any state. Governor Kerner's wife is one of Cermak's daughters.

2. Joseph Houdek, long-time acquaintance of Cermak, summed up the attitude of numbers of Lawndalites in this remark, which was often repeated at this time. Personal interview.

3. Charles E. Merriam, *Chicago, A More Intimate View of Urban Politics* (New York: Macmillan Co., 1929), p. 22.

4. Judge Landis later became the "czar" of organized baseball.

5. William H. Stuart, *The Twenty Incredible Years* (Chicago: M. A. Donahue and Co., 1935), p. 135.

6. *Ibid.*

7. *Ibid.,* p. 138.

8. Judge Harry Fisher, personal interview.

9. Stuart, *Twenty Incredible Years,* p. 143.

10. Statement by John Dienhart, personal interview.

11. Charles S. Eaton, personal interview.

12. *Ibid.*

13. Statement by Judge Thomas J. Courtney, personal interview. Judge Courtney was elected state's attorney in 1932 on Cermak's ticket. During the period under consideration, he was a page in the council.

14. Charles S. Eaton, personal interview. This account of Cermak

as junketing alderman is based upon descriptions by Alderman Eaton and several other then members of the council.

15. *Ibid.*

16. *Ibid.*

17. *Ibid.*

18. *Ibid.*

19. *Ibid.*

20. *Ibid.*

21. Quoted in Merriam, *Chicago, A More Intimate View,* p. 74.

22. As, for example, A. J. Liebling. For an amusing if distorted treatment of the physical and the spiritual Chicago, see his "Second City," *New Yorker,* January 12, 19, and 26, 1952.

23. Ferdinand W. Peck, quoted in *Chicago Evening American,* October 27, 1922.

24. For specific proposals, see Stuart, *Twenty Incredible Years,* pp. 88, 123.

25. John Dienhart, John Delaney, Henry Sonnenschein, Clayton F. Smith, personal interviews.

26. *Chicago Herald and Examiner,* April 18, 1920.

27. *Ibid.,* June 9, 1919.

28. *Chicago Tribune,* June 9, 1919.

29. *Ibid.,* July 4, 1919.

30. *Chicago Herald and Examiner,* February 28, 1920.

31. *Ibid.,* February 9, 1922.

32. *Chicago Tribune,* May 21, 1922.

33. *Ibid.,* May 25, 1922.

34. *Chicago Herald and Examiner,* January 12, 1922.

35. *Ibid.,* April 9, 1922.

36. *Ibid.,* March 12, 1922.

37. *Chicago Daily News,* February 18, 1920.

Chapter 8

1. John Dienhart, personal interview.

2. Joseph Gill, personal interview. Mr. Gill was Brennan's brother-in-law, a ward committeeman and party leader. It was he who conveyed Brennan's political "testament" to the party after Brennan's death.

3. Statement by Henry Sonnenschein, personal interview.

4. Charles E. Merriam, *Chicago, A More Intimate View of Urban Politics* (New York: Macmillan Co., 1929), pp. 182 f.; cf. Fletcher Dobyns, *The Underworld of American Politics* (Kingsport, Tenn.:

privately printed, 1932), pp. 50 f., and *passim*.

5. James C. Denvir claims that A.J. was an unwilling candidate—so unwilling that Brennan paid his assessment. Cermak had money, but Denvir says Cermak did not believe he could defeat the Irish Ryan.

6. *Chicago Herald and Examiner*, April 16, 1922. Cermak was very grateful. "It is always a pleasure to deal with a generous opponent. . . . I may be pardoned for entertaining a suspicion that, perhaps, the best man didn't win the race."

7. October 16, 1922.

8. *Chicago Evening American*, November 6, 1922.

9. *Ibid.*

10. Parke Brown, *Chicago Tribune*, October 16, 1922.

11. *Ibid.*

12. Quoted, *Chicago Tribune*, September 19, 1922.

13. *Chicago Evening Post*, November 3, 1922.

14. *Ibid.*

15. Charles Wheeler, *Chicago Herald and Examiner*, October 21, 1922.

16. *Ibid.*, November 3, 1922.

17. November 3, 1922.

18. November 4, 1922.

19. *Chicago Evening American*, October 20, 1922. During his term as president, Cermak worked very closely with M. S. Szymczak, a young Polish political leader. Cermak helped him gain a county office during these years, and later, when he was mayor, appointed him city comptroller. Cermak also sponsored Szymczak's original appointment as Governor of the Federal Reserve System in 1933, a position that Szymczak held as of 1952. M. S. Szymczak, personal interview.

20. *Chicago Daily News*, December 4, 1922. For a description of the government of Cook County, see Appendix I.

21. Proceedings of the Board of Commissioners of Cook County, 1922-23, p. 2.

22. *Chicago Evening American*, December 21, 1922; *Chicago Herald and Examiner*, December 22, 1922.

23. William Busse, personal interview.

24. Carroll H. Wooddy, *The Chicago Primary of 1926* (Chicago: University of Chicago Press, 1926), p. 91.

25. A large number of persons agree on the rough outlines of this version of the Murray deal. Among these are Mr. Denvir, Commissioner Busse, and Mr. Busch. Denvir, however, gives Brennan all or most of the credit for engineering the scheme. Personal interviews.

26. One of the two appointees was a good friend, Henry A. Berger; the other William F. Struckman. Significantly, neither was Irish.

27. *Chicago Tribune,* December 4, 1923.

28. Wooddy, *The Chicago Primary of 1926,* p. 91; *Chicago Herald and Examiner,* January 19, 1926. This report stated: "Pelke is acceptable to the Democrats."

29. Wooddy, *The Chicago Primary of 1926,* p. 91.

Chapter 9

1. Carter H. Harrison, personal interview. Mr. Harrison was outspoken about the "double-cross."

2. Charles N. Wheeler, *Chicago Herald and Examiner,* January 30, 1924.

3. Parke Brown, *Chicago Tribune,* March 26, 1924. The headline of the story stated: "Cermak . . . Ends Harmony Debate Among Democrats."

4. *Chicago Tribune,* May 20, 1924.

5. William H. Stuart, *The Twenty Incredible Years* (Chicago: M. A. Donahue, 1935), p. 190.

6. *Ibid.,* p. 192.

7. *Ibid.*

8. Fred D. Pasley, *Al Capone, The Biography of a Self-Made Man* (Garden City: Garden City Publishing Co., 1930), p. 41.

9. See chapter 14, pp. 330, 331.

10. Charles N. Wheeler, *Chicago Herald and Examiner,* November 6, 1925.

11. *Chicago Herald and Examiner,* January 22, 1926.

12. The 1926 Chicago elections offer perhaps one of the most interesting examples of an urban political campaign, with all its noise, personal vilification, irrelevant ballyhoo, real and fake issues, ruthless tactics, and various personalities. An excellent treatment of this campaign is in Carroll Wooddy, *The Chicago Primary of 1926* (Chicago: University of Chicago, 1926). Wooddy's study deals only with the primary and almost exclusively with Republican matters.

13. James C. Denvir, Judge Harry Fisher, William Busse, Henry Sonnenschein, Joseph L. Gill, John S. Clark: personal interviews.

14. The foregoing technique was described by James C. Denvir, Cermak's appointee to the presidency of the county Civil Service Commission during personal interviews.

One of Cermak's nephews, John Kalal, corroborates Denvir's account, and amplifies Cermak's conscious planning to build a real

Democratic organization in the country towns. This nephew was involved in some of the negotiations with individual Republicans; personal interviews.

15. Stuart, *Twenty Incredible Years,* p. 281.

16. Warren Phinney, *Chicago Daily News,* December 6, 1926.

17. Statement in personal interview.

18. Personal interview.

19. See Stuart, *Twenty Incredible Years,* pp. 280-320.

20. Charles E. Merriam, *Chicago, A More Intimate View of Urban Politics* (New York: Macmillan Co., 1929), p. 289.

21. Both the Drucci alliance and the cooperation of Capone are admitted by Thompson-admirer Stuart, who says: "The time for statements was over; only sterner stuff counted now. Capone men, an army of them, spread through the bad lands of the West Side that night and in the early hours of election morning. . . . Steal the election from Thompson? Not where the Capone mob was marshaled!" *Twenty Incredible Years,* p. 317.

22. The *Chicago Evening American,* April 5, 1927, described the start of election day as witnessing one alderman hiding, political workers intimidated, two bomb explosions.

23. Professor Merriam, personal interview. Others, such as Fletcher Dobyns, explicitly make this charge. *Underworld of American Politics* (Kingsport, Tenn.: privately printed, 1932), pp. 71 ff.

24. *Chicago Herald and Examiner,* May 13, 1927.

25. *Ibid.*

26. Parke Brown, *Chicago Tribune,* July 17, 1927.

27. August 29, 1927.

28. *Chicago Herald and Examiner,* December 5, 1927.

29. *Chicago Evening American,* January 30, 1928.

30. Edward L. Gorey, *ibid.,* February 11, 1928.

31. *Ibid.*

32. John Dienhart, *Chicago Herald and Examiner,* February 14, 1928.

33. Quoted by a close associate, personal interview. Similar remarks were reported by many other colleagues.

34. John F. Delaney, personal interview.

35. Quoted by John Dienhart, *Chicago Herald and Examiner,* June 25, 1928.

36. *Ibid.,* June 26, 1928.

37. *Ibid.,* June 29, 1928.

38. *Chicago Tribune,* September 15, 1928.

39. *Ibid.,* September 22, 1928.

40. *Chicago Herald and Examiner,* September 28, 1928.

41. For detailed accounts, see Merriam, *Chicago, A More Intimate View of Urban Politics,* pp. 292-98; Stuart, *Twenty Incredible Years,* pp. 355-89.

42. Merriam, *Chicago, A More Intimate View,* p. 293.

43. Lloyd Lewis and Henry J. Smith, *Chicago, the History of Its Reputation* (New York: Harcourt, Brace and Co., 1929), pp. 465 f.

44. Merriam, *Chicago, A More Intimate View,* p. 297.

45. Quoted in Dobyns, *Underworld of American Politics,* p. 1.

46. *Ibid.*

47. *Twenty Incredible Years,* p. 368.

48. *Ibid.,* p. 369. Italics added.

49. Lewis and Smith, *Chicago, the History of Its Reputation,* p. 481.

50. *Chicago, A More Intimate View,* pp. 293, 297.

51. However, it is true that relatively heavy votes were cast for Small, Smith, and Crowe in the Republican primary in many "good" Democratic wards, such as the First, Fifteenth, Eighteenth, Twenty-first, Twenty-fourth, Twenty-fifth, Twenty-sixth, Twenty-seventh, Thirty-first. This was not true of Cermak's ward or Toman's heavily Czech ward. Both had larger votes for Swanson than for Crowe and larger votes for Emmerson than for Small, but Cermak's ward showed a slight preference for Smith over Glenn, while the reverse was true for Toman's ward. *Chicago Daily News Almanac and Year Book,* 1929, p. 733.

52. This was necessitated by the aforementioned death of the incumbent Haas, Deneen candidate for renomination, the appointee being Mrs. John W. Jaranowski.

53. Judge Crowe and other Crowe-Barrett-Thompson-Brundage cohorts, personal interviews.

Chapter 10

1. Igoe had been leader of the Citizens' Democratic party faction which had so ineffectually opposed Brennan in the 1922 primaries, the first important election following Brennan's succession to the bossdom.

It will be recalled that Cermak, then running for his first term as county board president, had clashed violently with Igoe, then city clerk. This is another classic example of a favorite Cermak dictum: "You don't keep books in politics." As for Igoe, now a congressman, his district was a west-side one, and friendship with Cermak was almost obligatory. In the following discussion it will be observed that many

other west-side leaders formerly considered Cermak's foes also joined
Cermak in his struggle to capture the Democratic party. The best
example is old rival Congressman A. J. Sabath. Cermak soon repaid
them for their support and foresight. He saved both Igoe and Sabath
from opposition in the 1930 primaries. *Chicago Herald and Examiner,* March 9, 1930.

2. *Ibid.,* September 21, 1928.

3. *Chicago American,* October 26, 1928.

4. William H. Stuart, *The Twenty Incredible Years* (Chicago: M.
A. Donahue, 1935), pp. 391 ff.

5. Clark was only an alderman, albeit chairman of the powerful
finance committee. T. J. Crowe had just been defeated for re-election
as president of the sanitary district, the only one of four Democratic
candidates for trustee failing to be elected. O'Brien held no public
office; he had lost his 1926 campaign for sheriff.

6. For some time now, since the demise of the Harrison forces,
Sabath and Cermak had had a rapprochement. Although the coolness
between them continued—on Sabath's part at least reaching the point
of complete antipathy—a working cooperation was useful to both.
Sabath's Twenty-first Ward was in Pilsen and still contained a considerable number of Czechs amenable to Cermak influence. A.J.
might conceivably have unseated him, as Roger Sullivan had attempted to do without success. But Sullivan was not a Czech, nor did
he use a Czech cat's-paw. Furthermore, Sabath's congressional district
included parts of Cermak's ward and still other Czech areas.

7. John F. Delaney said that Cermak's confidence in Whealan was
such that he even trusted him with his money. When Cermak became
mayor, Whealan's services were rewarded by promotion to A.J.'s vacated presidency. Personal interview.

8. McDonough had been "friendly" with Cermak since the 1919-22
days in the city council, where he had been one of Cermak's chief lieutenants. In the 1924 Democratic national convention he had been
alone with Cermak to fight the "pussyfooting" Wet plank. Cermak is
alleged to have promised McDonough the nomination for county
treasurer. Judge Jay Schiller, personal interview. McDonough was
nominated for treasurer in 1930 without opposition. *Chicago Daily
News Almanac and Year Book,* 1931, p. 713. In 1930 he also became
committeeman of the Thirteenth Ward. *Ibid.,* p. 715. Mulcahy and
Collins held lucrative appointive positions by the grace of Cermak.
In 1930 Collins became committeeman of the Twentieth Ward. *Ibid.*
Both McDonough and Collins replaced Irishmen.

Boetius Sullivan was the son of Roger Sullivan and had never been satisfied with his relative power position in the Brennan group.

Courtney had been a candidate for attorney general in 1928 upon Cermak's insistence. In 1932 he was to become state's attorney owing to Cermak's manipulations.

9. For a complete list see *Chicago Daily News Almanac and Year Book*, 1927, p. 765. This is a minimum figure. It includes only those whom the writer knows to be Irish or with such typical Irish names as Walsh, Brady, and Ryan. Cf. Harold Gosnell, *Machine Politics: Chicago Model* (Chicago: University of Chicago Press, 1937), p. 45. Gosnell found that over one half of Democratic ward committeemen (more than 25) between 1928 and 1936 were Irish.

10. See *Chicago Daily News Almanac and Year Book*, 1927, pp. 776 ff., for appointments during the Dever administration.

11. Carroll H. Wooddy, *The Chicago Primary of 1926* (Chicago: University of Chicago Press, 1926), p. 185, n. 21. The Germans had five representatives; Jews, four; Poles, three; and Czechs, two.

12. Edward M. Martin, *The Role of the Bar in Electing the Bench in Chicago* (Chicago: University of Chicago Press, 1936), p. 237. Martin's estimated statistics are for 1932, except for those on the Jews, which are for 1926. It is probable that the 1928-30 situation was not significantly different. The estimated voting strengths were as follows: Poles, 262,621; Germans, 247,347; Jews, 212,680; Irish, 126,662; and Czechs, 79,895. These figures include the first and second generations.

13. Charles J. Vopicka was appointed to the school board; Cermak's son-in-law, Richey V. Graham, became superintendent of the house of correction; Ptacek, the police captain Cermak had allegedly protected when he was bailiff, became deputy superintendent of police; John A. Sokol was appointed city Civil Service Commissioner; close friends Hajicek and Denemark received other appointments. *Chicago Daily News Almanac and Year Book*, 1927, pp. 776-81.

14. Every politician interviewed agreed as to his chagrin at the time. Joseph Gill said "there was a hell of a set-to in the committee" when Cermak learned he had again been finessed.

15. *Chicago American*, January 25, 1929; *Chicago Tribune*, May 6, 1929.

16. Igoe was to be the thorniest rival in A.J.'s struggle for dominance.

One of the two men Cermak then placed on the judicial ticket was his friend and Czech protégé Otto Kerner, who had stepped down from his alderman's post in 1919 to make a place for Cermak after A.J. lost the election for sheriff. Prior to this time, Kerner had been attorney for the county board.

Igoe was also allowed to nominate his candidate by the simple expedient of axing one of the incumbent Democratic judges. *Chicago Daily News,* May 10, 1927. Cf. Martin, *The Role of the Bar,* pp. 75 f.

17. See Cermak's own article describing Czech contributions to the life of Chicago, *Chicago Herald and Examiner,* October 27, 1927.

18. *Chicago Herald and Examiner,* March 13, 1934.

The Rosenberg investigation disclosed that in 1929-30 he had distributed nearly $500,000 to Democratic politicians, the largest part to Cermak. The money was obtained from profits of the Rosenberg Iron and Metal Company which were improperly reported for tax purposes. Rosenberg could afford much largesse because by virtue of Cermak's efforts he was able to buy scrap metal so cheaply from local utility firms that his profits were enormous. Rosenberg admitted that his company received 90 per cent of all utility scrap in Cook County and all the scrap of the Illinois Bell Telephone Company in the entire state. For accounts of the Rosenberg confessions see all Chicago newspapers, March 12, 13, 14, and 15, 1934, especially the *Chicago Daily News, Chicago Herald and Examiner,* and *Chicago Evening American.*

19. *Chicago Herald and Examiner,* March 17, 1934.

20. Statement by Judge Jay Schiller, personal interview. Judge Schiller may be presumed an authoritative source in this connection. In Rosenberg's confession he was listed as recipient of a $5,000 Rosenberg donation. *Chicago Herald and Examiner,* March 13, 1934.

21. Quoted in the *Chicago Herald and Examiner,* March 17, 1934. The party's financial deficit was corroborated by ex-alderman Bailiff A. J. Horan, a member of the Irish brotherhood. He had been a protégé of T. J. Crowe. Mr. Horan was listed by Rosenberg as having received $5,000 from him in 1929-30. Horan said Cermak liquidated the party's debts at thirty cents on the dollar. Personal interview.

Cermak's son-in-law, Richey Graham, richer by $2,500 of Rosenberg's money, agreed with Rosenberg that the party deficit had been $200,000. Contrary to Horan, he claims that Cermak accomplished the liquidation at fifty cents on the dollar. Personal interview.

22. *Ibid.*

23. James C. Denvir, professing to be a loyal O'Brien-Crowe man, although at the time a Cermak appointee, was one of those making this point. Personal interview.

Another was John Dienhart, closest to Cermak of all reporters.

Dienhart explains it simply. "Cermak raised the money and bought the organization." Statement in personal interview.

Dienhart's statement has a high degree of persuasiveness when one considers a partial list of Rosenberg's recipients as published in the *Chicago Herald and Examiner,* March 13, 1934.

Cermak	$95,000	Arvey	(Jewish)	$12,000
Co. Treas. J. B. McDon-		Ald. B. A. Cronson		
ough (Irish)	6,000	(Jewish)		5,000
Former Ald. Al Prignano		Bailiff A. J. Horan (Irish)		5,000
(Italian)	5,000	Tom Byrne, Sanitary		
Ald. John Toman		District trustee (Irish)		5,000
(Czech)	5,000	Former Ald. L. B. Ander-		
Ald. Oscar F. Nelson		son (Negro)		5,000
(Scand.)	5,000	Joe Przybylo, 1929 ald.		
Former Ald. Max Adam-		candidate (Polish)		5,000
owski (Polish)	5,000	Former Ald. Joseph Cepak		
Former Ald. Harry Van-		(Czech)		5,000
Norman	5,000	Geo. Seif, crim. ct. clk.		5,000
Former Ald. Frank Sloan	5,000	Mun. Judge J. Schiller		
Ald. Dorsey Crowe (Irish)	5,500	(Jewish)		5,000
St. Rep. Frank Ryan		St. Rep. John Bolton		2,500
(Irish)	2,500	St. Rep. John R. Mc-		
Former St. Rep. An-		Sweeney (Irish)		2,500
thony Pintozzi (Italian)	2,000	St. Rep. Ray O'Keefe		
St. Rep. John R. Hruby		(Irish)		2,500
(Czech)	2,500	St. Rep. John J. O'Brien		
St. Rep. Don Griffith		(Irish)		2,500
(Irish)	1,000			
St. Sen. Richey V. Graham				
(Cermak's son-in-law)	2,500			

24. John Dienhart, *Chicago Herald and Examiner,* December 12, 1928.

25. "The Kelly-Nash Machine," *Fortune,* August, 1936, pp. 14-47.

26. *Chicago Tribune,* September 1, 1925.

27. Statement in personal interview.

28. Statement in personal interview.

29. For example, see *Chicago American,* November 8, 1928, and Arthur Evans, *Chicago Tribune,* December 12, 1928.

30. Personal interview.

31. John S. Clark and Henry Sonnenschein, personal interviews.

32. Statement by James C. Denvir, personal interview.

33. Statement in personal interview. This informant claims that two T. J. Crowe-O'Brien-Clark men, Harry Kohl and William R. O'Toole, swore to him that their names were forged. The charges of forgery are doubtful. In the 1930 election of ward committeemen when several anti-Cermak men were beaten by Cermak friends, both Kohl and O'Toole were elected. *Chicago Daily News Almanac and Year Book,* 1931, pp. 715 f.

34. Arthur Evans, *Chicago Tribune,* December 12, 1928. The headline read, "Scramble to Get New Jobs Widens Democratic Rift." The rift was clear to those in the know.

35. *Chicago Herald and Examiner,* August 1, 1929. Later Cermak was to symbolize his *de facto* control by having the party headquarters removed from the famous "Parlor A."

36. Edward L. Gorey, *Chicago Evening American,* November 8, 1928.

37. *Chicago Herald and Examiner,* December 12, 1928.

38. This would have been convenient for O'Brien and Crowe, both of whom were now out of office but in control of the managing committee. Interestingly enough, Cermak had proposed such a patronage committee two years before. But Brennan was alive then, and he had controlled most of the patronage. A. J. no longer agitated for his earlier plan.

39. Arthur Evans, *Chicago Tribune,* December 12, 1928.

40. For instance, at this time he was accused of helping Cermak deal with the Deneen Republicans by offering the Deneenites favored places on future primary ballots. *Ibid.*

41. *Ibid.*

42. John Dienhart, *Chicago Herald and Examiner,* December 12, 1928.

43. Joseph Gill, personal interview.

44. *Chicago Daily News Almanac and Year Book,* 1927, p. 794. At the same time Kelly also was chief engineer of the sanitary district, at a salary of $15,000 a year. This too was by virtue of a Brennen-Crowe-Barrett-Thompson bipartisan agreement.

45. *Chicago Evening American,* December 14, 1928.

46. John S. Clark, personal interview.

47. Kelly's attitude toward Cermak, as revealed in personal interviews, was heavily tinged by condescension and not very well-veiled contempt. There seems little doubt that personal friendship and sen-

timent would have placed him with the O'Brien-Clark crowd had he been a free agent.

48. *Chicago Evening American,* February 28, 1929. In both the sanitary district and the case of the circuit judges it would have been possible to deal with the other Republican faction.

49. Statement by John S. Clark, personal interview.

50. *Ibid.* Clark alleged that through this promise Cermak had been able to coax Berger to his side in the struggle for leadership.

51. *Chicago Herald and Examiner,* April 27, 1929.

52. For some of the charges see *Citizens Association of Chicago Bulletin No. 77,* January 18, 1929. Martin, *Role of the Bar,* pp. 300-10, gives a useful summary of the whole case.

53. Another defendent was Martin Edelstein, former real-estate agent of the district and a relative of Moe Rosenberg. Eventually Edelstein was found guilty, sentenced to six months' imprisonment, and fined $2,000. This sentence was passed by Judge Harry Fisher and two other judges sitting *en banc.* Later Fisher granted a new trial. Still later the case was nol-prossed. Such action can only be taken on the initiative of the state's attorney. Martin, *Role of the Bar,* p. 309. Evidently in this instance Rosenberg's support of Cermak had paid off, as had Cermak's deal with Swanson.

54. During the legislative investigation State Senator McCauley's questions revealed great sensitivity to the deals, including an alleged Cermak demand to halt projected grand jury investigations not only of the sanitary district but also of the county board and the forest preserve. *Chicago Herald and Examiner,* April 27, 1929. The investigation of Cermak's jurisdiction was never made.

55. The prosecutor, Assistant State's Attorney John E. Northrup, made frequent charges of "political attempts to ruin the prosecution," and once temporarily quit the case for this reason.

56. Senator McCauley intimated in the investigation of the sanitary district that Cermak had demanded that Whalen and Touhy agree to help bring about the removal of Martin J. O'Brien as chairman of the managing committee. *Chicago Herald and Examiner,* April 27, 1929. Whalen and Touhy probably acquiesced—at least their names do not figure prominently in the struggle in 1929. However, in December, 1930, they joined Igoe—who had also temporarily not opposed Cermak—in an attempt to recapture the sanitary district from Cermak. The attempt failed. *Chicago Herald and Examiner,* December 3, 1930.

57. After his conviction Crowe was re-elected ward committeeman.

58. In addition to the political influences mentioned, others in-

cluded: seven months' delay from the time indictments were voted until trial began; before Judge Fisher assigned the case to himself, attempts to have the case tried by two judges who were also in political debt to the defendants (one of these quashed the Kelly indictment) ; agreement by the defense to dispense with a jury trial; attempts to buy off the prosecutor by offering him a judgeship.

59. *Chicago Evening American,* December 14, 1925. Cermak characterized such reports as "lies circulated for a purpose."

60. *Ibid.* A.J. denied that Igoe's name even entered the discussion during conferences with the Deneenites and claimed that he had not talked to a single judge concerning Igoe's re-election or disposal. This seems less than perfect candor on his part.

61. *Chicago Evening American,* December 14, 1928.

62. John Dienhart, *Chicago Herald and Examiner,* December 20, 1928. County Clerk Sweitzer denied he would deliver the places Barrett was offering. However, Sweitzer frequently shifted his loyalty during this period. Barrett's plot stemmed from a desire to become the Republican mayoralty candidate in 1931. It would be to his advantage to weaken Cermak, who seemed likely to be one of the Democrats who would get the Democratic nomination. But there is another plausible explanation. There seems good reason to believe that Barrett was not acting alone but in conjunction with the Brennan heirs, who would also have gained by damaging Cermak. Barrett had good friends among the Irish Democrats—being himself Irish, as was his ally Robert E. Crowe. Barrett and Robert E. Crowe constituted the west-side element of the Crowe-Barrett-Thompson-Brundage combine and thus had many intimate contacts with the Sherman Hotel boys. The Fleming Coal Company, of which the president was a former secretary of Maclay Hoyne and two of whose directors were brothers of Mr. Barrett, had held the exclusive contract for coal with the sanitary district. In the 1926 primaries it was charged that the year following the start of the Fleming contract the district's coal bill was more than doubled. See *Chicago Daily News,* March 30, 1926; *Lightnin',* publication of the Better Government Association, Vol. I, no. 5, 1926.

That Chicago politics made even stranger bedfellows than other places is in part illustrated by the fact that in 1930 Mrs. E. J. Fleming, wife of the president of the company, was one of Cermak's nominees for the county board.

63. In Rosenberg's confession he alluded to one sum of $20,000 he gave Cermak in 1930 in order to "take care of" certain aldermen. He

was reported as stating "some of the money he gave Cermak found its way into the pockets of certain county commissioners." *Chicago Herald and Examiner,* March 13, 1934. There are grounds for believing that Cermak would have used money had it been necessary to thwart Barrett's scheme. And Rosenberg had a seemingly inexhaustible supply all in $500 and $1,000 bills in the vaults of the Foreman Trust and Savings Bank, at another bank, and still another vault at the Sherman Hotel headquarters.

64. *Chicago Herald and Examiner,* January 30, 1929.

65. *Chicago Daily News,* February 13, 1929; *Chicago Evening American,* February 13, 1929.

66. *Chicago Tribune,* May 6, 1929. During this time he had also gone to Johns Hopkins University for treatments.

67. *Chicago Evening American,* March 8, 1929. *Chicago Herald and Examiner,* March 9, 1929.

68. *Ibid.* O'Brien declared that: "the party will be better served if each group puts a complete slate of candidates for ward committeemen before the voters next April. The side which wins a majority will control the party. That should satisfy everybody, and not injure the chances of the candidates who will be on the county ticket."

O'Brien was evidently stalling for time, and also reckoning with the well-known difficulty of defeating incumbent committeemen—thirty-three of whom were Irish.

69. John Dienhart, *Chicago Herald and Examiner,* April 20, 1929. Dienhart reported that this action was in retaliation for an attempt by Toman to seek a place on the committee on committees. The O'Brien-Crowe-Clark forces interpreted this as a device to prevent Clark from being re-elected chairman of the key finance committee.

70. *Ibid.* This squabble between Clark and Toman was also related to the 1931 mayoralty, as had been Barrett's plot against Cermak. Clark's name was often being mentioned as a possible candidate. Clark said: "Two years is a long time ahead and many things might happen in the meantime.... Toman was taken off the chairmanship of his committee because we felt the place was more deserved by Alderman Albert J. Horan."

Clark did not explain in what way Horan, protégé of M. J. O'Brien, was more deserving. He did comment on Cermak's alleged attempt to have him removed from the finance committee. "I, of course, heard that Cermak was trying to take me off the finance committee, but that is all I know about it."

Horan was not one of the Sherman Hotel bitter-enders. He was named by Rosenberg as having received $5,000. *Chicago Herald and Examiner*, March 13, 1934.

71. Rosenberg said he gave $30,000 to Cermak directly to be used in this election and that he himself had spent $8,000 in his own ward. *Chicago Herald and Examiner*, March 17, 1934.

72. *Ibid.* Perhaps Rosenberg thought he was "building up Cermak," intimating that Cermak was his man. In truth, Mr. Rosenberg was mistaken!

It has been said that P. A. Nash had similar designs. "He thought he could control Tony." Statement by James C. Denvir, personal interview.

73. One was made up of lawyer members of the central committee, and headed by M. L. Igoe, who was at that time not actively opposed to Cermak. Also on this committee were Cermak men Sabath, Busch, Mulcahy, and Lewe.

To head what was designated as a committee of "high-class lawyers," Cermak chose his old friend of many Wet battles, Alfred S. Austrian. The committee included a few lawyers who were not primarily politicians; but the politicians, almost exclusively Cermak men, predominated. These were: Judges Fisher, Sullivan, Schwaba, and Floyd E. Thompson; Alderman Arvey; and country-town committeemen Hall and Mason.

74. Igoe was chairman of this unit. What troubled A.J. was the inadequate share of the judicial positions Igoe's committee was allegedly settling for in the agreement with the Crowe-Barrett-Thompson-Brundage Republicans. Either Cermak had overestimated his control over Igoe, or Igoe had misjudged the relative strength of Democrats and the Crowe-Barrett-Thompson-Brundage factions.

75. *Chicago Herald and Examiner*, September 5, 1929.

76. With whom he had been negotiating. See *Chicago Tribune*, September 9, 1929; *Chicago Evening American*, September 9, 1929; William H. Stuart, *Chicago Evening American*, September 13, 1929.

77. *Chicago Evening American*, October 15, 1929. The committee was headed by Harry Eugene Kelly, prominent member of the bar association, executive vice-chairman of the Civic Safety Committee, which had functioned so well in electing Swanson in the "Pineapple Primary," and an influential member of the Union League Club. The secretary of this committee was William Rothmann, a lawyer whom Cermak had appointed to the advisory committee of lawyers during the preparation of the slate.

78. One small local indication of this political-economic myopia is

the fact that the Illinois Democrats were having a difficult time finding someone who was willing to run for the United States Senate.

Said Cermak: "I never saw anything like it. In days gone by a detail of guards would be stationed in front of headquarters to keep the candidates from knocking each other down in trying to win the organization's indorsement." John Dienhart, *Chicago Herald and Examiner,* July 14, 1929.

79. For an uncomplimentary sketch of Lewis, see Fletcher Dobyns, *The Underworld of American Politics* (Kingsport, Tenn.: privately printed, 1932), pp. 91-101. Dobyns describes Lewis during a case he was pleading before the United States Supreme Court when he was a corporation counsel for Chicago. He was interrupted by Justice Holmes during his argument, Mr. Holmes remarking, "Mr. Lewis, I can't get the slightest idea of what you are talking about." To this Lewis replied, "Your Honor, I can only furnish the argument—not the capacity to understand it."

In reply to the author's question as to whether or not Cermak could control Lewis, Mayor Carter Harrison replied, "No one could control him. He was the biggest blankety-blank liar." Statement in personal interview.

One informant alleged that Cermak nominated Lewis because he thought he might win, but also because of Lewis' age (he had been a congressman from Washington in the late 1890's and was no longer young). This informant states that after Cermak's death, Lewis telephoned all the newspapers to announce that he had caught cold at Cermak's funeral. Mrs. Lloyd Lewis, interview.

80. Edward L. Gorey, *Chicago Evening American,* January 30, 1930.

81. *Chicago Evening American,* March 3, 1930.

82. It was at this time that he spared Congressman Sabath and Igoe, son-in-law Graham, and several ward committeemen from being opposed.

83. *Chicago Evening American,* March 12, 1934.

84. John Dienhart, *Chicago Herald and Examiner,* March 19, 1930. A.J. was referring to the Better Government Association, of which Davis was the chief official.

85. *Ibid.*

86. Parke Brown, *Chicago Tribune,* March 19, 1930.

87. Quoted in *Chicago Herald and Examiner,* April 11, 1930.

88. However, Barrett, although supported by important Irish sentiment, lost both Chicago and Cook County to the unknown Zacharias. When a Pole with a Greek name can accomplish this in a Chicago

Democratic primary against a contender with a name like Barrett, it is convincing proof of a functioning political organization. It was Zacharias' prominence among the Poles that led A.J. to select him. Like Syzmczak and Zintak, he was another bid for the large Polish vote.

89. *Chicago Daily News Almanac and Year Book*, 1927, p. 737.

90. *Ibid.*, 1931, p. 714. Of the rest there were four Jews, one Italian, and one Pole. Now names like Schiller, Edelman, Scheppler, Graber, Lisack, Bonelli, Kadow, and Green dominated the McCarthys and O'Connells. Green was a Negro.

91. *Ibid.*, 1929, p. 736; 1931, p. 715.

92. Mrs. McCormick spent about $300,000 for the primary, it was discovered by the Nye Committee. For the investigation of these expenditures, see *Hearings Before a Select Committee on Senatorial Campaign Expenditures, 71st Congress, 2nd Session*, Part II, Illinois.

93. For a detailed account of Thompson's antics in the campaign, see Stuart, *Twenty Incredible Years*, pp. 437 ff.

Part of his attack was a broadside called, "To the Negroes of Illinois," which described the *Tribune's*—and, by inference, Mrs. McCormick's—anti-Negro bias. These handbills were distributed outside Negro churches by city policemen.

The *Tribune* attacked Thompson in turn. Thompson decided on the most telling reply of his career. According to apologist Stuart, friends of Thompson warned the mayor that if he delivered the speech he was planning, Colonel McCormick would have him killed. But these good friends assured him that if that eventuated they would kill McCormick. Nevertheless, Thompson decided to give the speech, and, although he became very sick, he wrote the speech and had one of his cabinet members deliver it.

The speech was demagoguery itself. The theme was, "The *Tribune* Always Gets Its Man." By innuendo, the *Tribune* was credited with responsibility for every violent death that had occurred in Chicago within the last fifty years. It was even intimated that Mayor Harrison's assassin in 1893 had been driven to his act by the *Tribune*.

The speech was later included in a campaign pamphlet entitled, "William Hale Thompson's Deathbed Speech on the *Chicago Tribune*." The opening paragraph was as follows:

"The arrogant, conceited, overly rich snobs who own and control the Lingle-Evangelistic institution brazenly and boastfully and heartlessly assert like the Canadian Mounted Police, 'We always get our man,' but the *Tribune's* slogan is, 'We always get our man, be we right or wrong. . . .' "

94. The *Tribune* offered a reward of $25,000 for the killer; the *Herald and Examiner* a similar amount; and the *Post*, $5,000. The publishers of all the Chicago newspapers met and acceded to Col. McCormick's request to allow the *Tribune* "to get" the murderer of its reporter. McCormick had State's Attorney Swanson appoint a *Tribune* attorney as special prosecutor.

After Lingle was buried, it developed that he had been a racketeer, with close connections to Capone. It also developed that he had speculated in grains and stocks as a partner of Police Commissioner Russell.

These events led to a mutual exchange of recriminations among all the local newspapers.

For the Lingle case see all Chicago newspapers from June 10 to July 11, 1930—especially the *Tribune*, June 18 and July 1, and the *Daily News*, July 11, 1930.

95. *Chicago Daily News*, July 14, 1930.

96. *Chicago Herald and Examiner*, July 18, 1930.

97. *Ibid.*, Oct. 27, 1930.

98. *Chicago Tribune*, May 17, 1930. Nor did A.J. relinquish the ridicule he was wont to use in referring to the Drys: "About all that remains for the drys to do is to classify the possession of a bottle-opener a felony and to make the carrying of a corkscrew equivalent to carrying a deadly weapon and the vote against the fanatics will be unanimous among thinking voters."

99. *Ibid.*, May 19, 1930.

100. *Ibid.*, Aug. 13, 1930.

101. *Chicago Herald and Examiner*, Nov. 3, 1930.

102. He received the support of the United Charities of Chicago, the Juvenile Protective Association, and Dr. Graham Taylor, of the Chicago Commons.

103. *Chicago Evening American*, Oct. 31, 1930. Cermak was highly lauded: "Of all civilians in public life, Mr. Cermak has been the most helpful to veterans.... He may well be called the 'man who never forgets.'"

Cermak was indorsed by the normally Republican leaders of the American Legion.

104. *Chicago Daily News Almanac and Yearbook*, 1931, pp. 727 f.

105. The Republicans salvaged one congressman-at-large, but he narrowly defeated the Democrat who ran third. *Ibid.*, pp. 622 f.

106. Brennan's brother-in-law, Joseph L. Gill, was elected clerk. He won by one of the smallest majorities. *Ibid.*, p. 729.

107. The votes were: Cermak, 620,245; Reich, 389,175. *Ibid.,* p. 728.

108. This was in tremendous contrast to 1926, when Cermak had had only three Democratic colleagues. Included among the new members was Cermak's good "German friend Charles H. Weber; F. J. Kaspar, a Czech; at least one Pole; and three women. One of the women was Amelia Sears, director of the United Charities; another was Mrs. Edward J. Fleming, wife of a good Crowe-Barrett-Thompson-Brundage supporter. *Ibid.*

109. *Ibid.* One of the judges elected was Rudolph F. Desort, a Czech; others were Ross C. Hall, a loyal Cermak country-town committeeman, and Judge Prystalski, Polish leader.

110. *Ibid.,* p. 674. Among the members were many reliable Cermak men, not the least of whom Cermak's major-domo Henry Sonnenschein, and Cermak's son-in-law, R. V. Graham. A.J.'s legislative interests were not to be unguarded while Igoe was Democratic leader in the lower chamber.

111. For the Illinois vote see *ibid.,* p. 623; for the local vote, *ibid.,* p. 729.

For repeal of the Eighteenth Amendment:

	Chicago	Cook County	Illinois
Yes	535,071	624,712	1,054,432
No	145,401	186,861	506,741

For modification of the Volstead Act:

	Chicago	Cook County	Illinois
Yes	528,962	614,341	968,652
No	132,218	169,218	506,973

For repeal of the Illinois Prohibition Act:

	Chicago	Cook County	Illinois
Yes	546,428	634,013	1,060,004
No	134,250	173,527	523,130

112. *Ibid.,* p. 729.

Chapter 11

1. Some, however, believed that Cermak and Thompson had had such a cordial relationship in recent years that Cermak would not look askance upon a fourth term for "Big Bill." "[Cermak] had been far from unfriendly with the City Hall organization, had received much in City Hall favors—in fact some had expected Cermak would make it as easy as possible for Thompson to win again." William H.

Stuart, *The Twenty Incredible Years* (Chicago: M. A. Donahue and Co., 1935), p. 453.

This kind of thinking represented great unfamiliarity with Cermak the power seeker, and also a general kind of political naïveté. That Cermak had had Thompson favors was indisputable. Such good Czech friends as Hajicek, Denemark, and Kolar held positions of prominence in the Thompson administration.

2. Carroll H. Wooddy, "Jubilee in Chicago," *National Municipal Review*, XX (June, 1931), 321.

3. In order to give Igoe the national committeemanship it was necessary to remove incumbent Thomas F. Donovan, who was originally "made" by Brennan. Donovan was, and continued to be, chairman of the state committee. According to John S. Clark, he was an O'Brien-Clark-Crowe man. Personal interview.

In 1932, Cermak was to nominate and elect Donovan lieutenant governor. By that time he was at war with Igoe.

4. *Chicago Evening American,* November 5, 1930.

Smith and Bundesen had scored impressive victories in the 1930 elections, for recorder and coroner, respectively. *Chicago Daily News Almanac and Year Book,* 1931, p. 728. Bundesen had given several indications of being on Cermak's side in the struggle for party leadership. Smith, originally a member of the Sherman Hotel group, had nevertheless impressed A.J. enough to have him replace O'Brien as chairman of the managing committee.

5. Edward L. Gorey, *Chicago American,* November 19, 1931.

6. *Ibid.,* December 8, 1930.

7. *Ibid.* The reference is to the efforts of Igoe and Clark to capture the control of the district from Cermak-Deneen.

8. *Ibid.,* December 12, 1930.

9. Mayor Kelly, personal interview.

10. William H. Sexton, Cermak's second corporation counsel. Personal interview.

11. Edward L. Gorey, *Chicago Evening American,* December 12, 1930.

12. *Ibid.,* December 15, 1930.

13. *Ibid.,* December 17, 1930.

14. *Ibid.,* December 12, 1930.

15. *Ibid.,* December 17, 1930.

16. Personal interview. The names of these persons were not divulged.

17. *Ibid.*

18. Edward L. Gorey, *Chicago Evening American,* December 17, 1930. Whatever happened to the alleged $250,000 bribe to Clark, another part of the deal was revealed in this article—the nomination of Municipal Judge Allegretti, Clark's close friend, for the superior court. The nomination was unopposed, and Allegretti was subsequently elected.

19. *Ibid.,* December 24, 1930. It is worth noting that this article describes the indorsement as a result of a conference between Cermak and the Clark-A. J. Horan-Judge John J. Sullivan combination. Horan and Sullivan had during the last days of the lethal struggle for leadership occupied relatively neutral positions, but Sullivan's name had also been prominently mentioned as a mayoral possibility.

20. Parke Brown, *Chicago Tribune,* December 25, 1930.

The reason for the slating of each candidate is easily determined. Kaindl was a ward committeeman from a largely Polish constituency but had a German name. Brady was Irish and also a ward committeeman. Smietanka was a Slav, while Allegretti, besides being Italian, was Clark's friend. There were also geographical considerations. Cermak of course came from the near southwest side; Brady was from the farthest southwest corner; and Kaindl was from the northwest side.

21. *Chicago Daily News Almanac and Year Book,* 1932, pp. 699 ff. The votes were as follows: Thompson, 296,294; Lyle, 227,986; Albert, 99,137.

22. *Ibid.,* p. 699.

23. Charles H. Weber, personal interview.

24. *Ibid.* Besides Mr. Weber, Bert A. Massee, head of Palmolive-Peet, Eugene McDonald, head of Zenith Radio, and Harry Hollingshead, wealthy Nash distributor, were present at this discussion. These men were representative of the businessmen who were important among Cermak's supporters in this campaign.

Another version of Bundesen's withdrawal was given by a close Cermak associate. According to this story, Dr. Bundesen, in addition to receiving assurances of the health commissionership, was also paid handsomely in cash. Although Bundesen rationalized his withdrawal in terms of ensuring a Democratic victory and the prime necessity of getting rid of Thompson, and although he gave frequent campaign speeches for Cermak, in private he was not completely reconciled to the smothering of his mayoralty ambitions. Asked by Cermak to sign a "health book" recounting Cermak's great accomplishments in the field of public health, Dr. Bundesen refused, according to a Cermak associate. Personal interview.

See Elmer L. Williams, *That Man Bundesen* (Chicago: Better Government Association, 1931). Bundesen was appointed by Cermak the city's chief public health official. As of 1960, he was, as he had been for more than two decades, president of the Chicago Board of Health.

25. Wooddy, "Jubilee in Chicago." After Cermak's election a suit was filed by a "taxpayer" charging conspiracy between Cermak and the election commissioners in order to eliminate the independent candidates. *Chicago Evening American*, May 9, 1931; *Chicago Herald and Examiner*, May 10, 1931.

26. Quoted by Edward L. Gorey, *Chicago Evening American*, February 24, 1931.

27. Caspar Nathan, personal interview.

28. Warren H. Pierce, "Chicago, Unfinished Anomaly," *Our Fair City*, ed. Robert S. Allen (New York: Vanguard Press, 1947), p. 175.

29. In this connection, Robert E. Crowe's charge that the B.G.A. promised Brennan, among other *quid pro quo's*, Ku Klux Klan support in 1924 in exchange for money, becomes somewhat persuasive. Judge Crowe, personal interview.

30. Edward W. Martin, "Chicago's New Deal in Municipal Affairs," *National Municipal Review*, XX (May, 1931), 310.

31. From stenographic notes of campaign speeches, quoted in Wooddy, "Jubilee in Chicago." Unfortunately, no complete political study of Thompson has ever been made. Some quite useful Thompsoniana are available nonetheless. One of the most complete is Stuart, *Twenty Incredible Years*. A complete journalistic work, but written before the end of Thompson's career, is John Bright's *Hizzoner Big Bill Thompson* (New York: Jonathan Cape and Harrison Smith, 1930). The best short analysis of Thompson the politician is "Mayor Thompson, the Second Lincoln," chapter 3 of Harold Gosnell's *Negro Politicians* (Chicago: University of Chicago Press, 1930). Other useful material is found in Victor S. Yarros, "Presenting Big Bill Thompson of Chicago," *Independent*, November 5, 1927; and in the many campaign pamphlets.

32. Quoted by Charles E. Merriam in manuscript of campaign speech, in author's possession. "Silas the grafter" was Silas Strawn, a prominent "silk-stocking" civic and business leader.

33. *The People's Choice* (New York: Duell, Sloan and Pearce, 1944). Other more recent attempts in the same vein are no more definitive.

34. Congressman A. J. Sabath, personal interview.

35. Charles E. Merriam, personal interview.

36. Paul V. Colianni headed the Italian-American Regular Democratic Organization of Cook County, very active in A.J.'s behalf. Other Italian-American party supporters were A. J. Prignano, Judges Bonelli and Borelli, John Vacca, and Anthony Pintozza. Prignano and Pintozza had both been identified as recipients of Rosenberg money.

37. A. S. Smietanka; Edward J. Kaindl; the powerful banker and professor M. S. Szymczak; Judge E. K. Jarecki; Frank V. Zintak; Judge Prystalski; former judicial candidate Derdzinski; and Benjamin Adamowski. Cermak subsequently appointed Szymczak to his cabinet and later was to arrange his appointment to the Federal Reserve Board. Adamowski was to become a swashbuckling Cook County State's Attorney in the 1950's.

38. Charles H. Weber was A.J.'s closest contact. Sweitzer's support was also important. Others were Frank H. Landmesser, Committeeman Voss of the Fiftieth Ward, and "Paddy" Bauler. John Traeger was a member of the campaign advisory committee. In 1959 Bauler was elected to another four-year term as alderman.

39. The most influential Scandinavian Democratic leaders were Chief Justice Sonsteby of the municipal court, County Architect Eric Hall, and Ward Committeeman Christ A. Jensen who owed his ward committeemanship to Cermak. Sonsteby and Jensen were elected in the Cermak era, and Hall was a Cermak appointee. During the campaign Thompson frequently accused Cermak of having allowed Hall exorbitant fees for plans for the county jail.

The most prominent of the Negro Democratic leaders was Michael Sneed, his importance being recognized by his election as ward committeeman in 1932—the first Negro Democratic ward committeeman in the country. Mr. Sneed, personal interview.

40. Crowe's support may be gauged by the fact that when Cermak was mayor, he retained Crowe's brother in his city job, making him one of the very few Republicans who escaped discharge. Crowe's protégé, Joseph P. Savage, was now an attorney for the forest-preserve district. *Chicago Herald and Examiner,* March 22, 1931.

41. Stuart, *Twenty Incredible Years,* p. 544.

42. Si Mayer, personal interview. Mr. Mayer was present during a discussion on election night when Barrett demanded ten jobs in payment for his double-cross of Thompson.

43. James C. Denvir, personal interview. Ettleson's nephew, Alderman Cronson, retained an important council chairmanship after Cermak was mayor. He was also a Rosenberg beneficiary to the tune of $5,000.

44. Parke Brown, *Chicago Tribune,* February 28, 1931. Said Lundin, in part, "I'm willing to indorse the rest of the nominees but not Thompson. That's ... because he's the father of the crime wave.... I'm for Cermak."

45. Edward L. Gorey, *Chicago Evening American,* March 31, 1931.

46. Parke Brown, *Chicago Tribune,* March 12, 1931.

47. *Ibid.,* March 3, 1931. In this report the election of a Deneenite as South Park commissioner by Cermak-controlled judges was noted.

48. Edward L. Gorey, *Chicago Evening American,* March 27, 1931.

49. In 1931 he was a South Park commissioner; after Cermak's election he, too, was to find a place in the cabinet; and after Horner became governor, he was promoted to be head of a department of the state government.

50. A full-page advertisement in a metropolitan journal even then cost perhaps $1,000 per day. Maybe the friendly *Tribune* and *Daily News* contributed their bit by lower advertising rates.

51. Also actively campaigning for Cermak were Michael J. Galvin, head of the Teamsters and Chauffeurs Union; Leslie G. Grandee of the same organization; Joseph A. Ryan of the Sheet Metal Workers; William F. Quinlan, president of the Chicago Street Car Men's Union; Mary McEnerney of the Bindery Workers; and Richard J. Wren, head of the Operating Engineers.

52. However, Cermak at least attempted to woo Nelson, who was on Rosenberg's gift list at the rate of $5,000.

53. See Stuart, *Twenty Incredible Years,* pp. 235 ff. and 319.

54. *Chicago Herald and Examiner,* January 28, 1931.

55. Stuart, *Twenty Incredible Years,* p. 406.
Brunker and Kelly had been leaders of the Civic Safety Committee, under whose leadership the "Pineapple Primary" was won by the "forces for good."

56. *Ibid.,* p. 502.

57. Manuscript of campaign address.

58. As, for example, the Irish-American Good Fellowship Club and the Illinois Irish-American Club.

59. *Chicago Evening American,* March 25, 1931.

60. Mrs. Conkey was president of the Illinois and the Cook County Women's Democratic Clubs as well. She was to become A.J.'s commissioner of public welfare.

61. Mr. Ickes, personal interview. He and Professor Merriam were accompanied by Mrs. Fairbank.

62. "Finishing the fifth year as alderman, being one of the council

leaders, probably superior to any alderman in push and driving power." See its *Report,* 1921.

63. Gosnell concluded that "the press eliminated the strong Thompson machine." Harold Gosnell, *Machine Politics: Chicago Model* (Chicago: University of Chicago Press, 1937), p. 157.

64. *Ibid.,* chapter 8.

65. Circulation figures are for 1931.

66. Lorimer was Thompson's first political mentor and in later days became a Thompson supporter. The *Tribune* was responsible for the crusade which eventually led to ousting Lorimer from the United States Senate.

67. Gosnell, *Machine Politics,* p. 163, table 17.

68. *Ibid.*

69. February 18, 1931.

70. Gosnell, *Machine Politics,* p. 163, table 17.

71. Quoted in Edward L. Gorey, *Chicago Evening American,* March 28, 1931.

72. *Ibid.,* April 4, 1931.

73. Merriam, *Chicago, A More Intimate View of Urban Politics* (New York: Macmillan Co., 1929), p. 146.

74. *Chicago Daily News,* April 2, 1931.

75. Paul V. Colianni, a Cermak official, quoted by Edward L. Gorey, *Chicago Evening American,* March 28, 1931.

76. Quoted in the *Chicago Evening American,* March 12, 1931.

77. *Ibid.,* March 21, 1931.

78. Edward L. Gorey, *ibid.,* March 26, 1931.

79. *Ibid.,* March 23, 1931.

80. *Ibid.,* March 31, 1931.

81. Quoted by Rev. John Evans, *Chicago Tribune,* March 30, 1931.

82. *Ibid.*

83. Gosnell, *Negro Politicians,* pp. 94-100.

84. *Ibid.*

85. Parke Brown, *Chicago Tribune,* April 5, 1931.

86. Stuart, *Twenty Incredible Years,* p. 454.

87. Charles E. Merriam, personal interview. Although Merriam refused all offers, at his suggestion Professor Leonard D. White was appointed to the city Civil Service Commission by Mayor Cermak.

88. See reports of his speeches to the Interfraternity Club, the City Club Forum, and the University of Chicago Forum. Edward L. Gorey, *Chicago Evening American,* March 19, 1931; *ibid.,* March 20, 1931; *Chicago Herald and Examiner,* April 3, 1931.

89. *Chicago Herald and Examiner,* March 20, 1931.

90. *Ibid.*

91. This was in marked contrast to Thompson, who was constrained to search far afield for his issues. His favorite whipping boy, King George, was again much employed. In the *Chicago Herald and Examiner,* March 15, 1931, he was reported as stating that the campaign "resolves itself down to a fight between Uncle Sam and Great Britain." He continued, in the same vein, that if Cermak were elected, "it will make him a most powerful ally of the King of England. . . . If the people of Chicago want a dictator and a tool of international bankers, let them vote for 'Dictator Tony'; if they want a real American who fights for the people and against international bankers, let them vote for Bill Thompson."

92. John Dienhart, *Chicago Herald and Examiner,* April 5, 1931. Cermak must have paid a fearful psychic price for this fidelity to his role. "When the mayor compared their lineage he wanted to make other comparisons. But he stuck his tongue in his cheek and discussed what he contended were the issues."

93. Quoted by Edward L. Gorey, *Chicago Evening American,* April 6, 1931.

94. John F. Delaney, one of the authors of the document, personal interview.

95. Among these were James C. Denvir and Judge Jay Schiller. Personal interviews. Mr. Denvir, who was very active in the campaign, said that things were going "sour," that Thompson's vilifying attacks were starting to be felt, and that the frequent "granddad" speeches of eleven-year-old Vivian Graham were starting to backfire. He also said that the *Tribune's* attacks on Thompson were recoiling in an unfavorable way. Before the campaign began, according to Mr. Denvir, Cermak had asked him, "How will I run?" Denvir had replied, "You'll win if the *Tribune* doesn't attack Thompson too much." Denvir says that Parke Brown, *Tribune* political editor who was present at this discussion, asked permission to carry this insight to Colonel McCormick.

Judge Schiller said that Cermak's own public appearances had started to work against him. According to him, Cermak was such a poor speaker that he alienated audiences in certain neighborhoods by gaucheries and mispronunciations. To A.J. the Ti'voli theater continued to be the Tivo'li.

A number of other observers did not agree with the analysis of these two gentlemen as to the effectiveness of Cermak's speeches, or the negative effects of Vivian's addresses and the *Tribune* attacks. Included in this group were such veteran observers as Mayor Kelly and Harold Ickes.

96. Gosnell, *Negro Politicians,* pp. 80, 115.

97. *Chicago Tribune,* April 3, 1931.

98. However, two of his fellow candidates, Kaindl and Smietanka, were defeated. Both lost by relatively small votes—Kaindl by 65,000 and Smietanka by 20,000 out of over a million votes cast. Since Kaindl lost to Kearns, a Deneen candidate, some charged Cermak with a deal. However, this is unlikely. In Deneen's own ward Cermak won by only a handful of votes. What is more likely is that Kearns' Irish name, as well as that of Casey, the other Republican winner, carried him to victory. The only Irish candidate on Cermak's ticket, Brady, also won. *Chicago Herald and Examiner,* April 8, 1931.

99. *Chicago Daily News Almanac and Year Book,* 1932, p. 704.

100. The Second, Third, and Fourth Wards gave Thompson a total of 57,469 votes and Cermak only 17,145, a majority of over 40,000. *Ibid.* However, in 1927 the same wards had cast more than 60,000 Thompson votes. Arthur Evans, *Chicago Tribune,* April 8, 1931. Subsequent references to the votes in the 1927 mayoralty election are based upon this article.

101. Toman's ward cast the largest majority for Cermak among these wards, and Cermak's, the second largest. However, the largest Cermak majority came from a northwest-side ward.

102. Wooddy, "Jubilee in Chicago," p. 321.

103. The fact that the Democratic leaders in Thompson's winning wards were Irish in four out of five cases is not necessarily significant. It is likely that these men—Walsh, Collins, Burke, and Geary—did as well as could be expected.

104. The other banner wards were as follows: Cermak's, better than 6 to 1; Sabath's 13 to 3; Toman's, about $3\frac{1}{2}$ to 1; Rosenberg's, better than 4 to 1; and Kocialkowski's, better than 3 to 1.

105. However, the other three wards in this group had been carried by Thompson in 1927.

106. But the wards of each of these three leaders had given Thompson great pluralities in 1927. Jensen's ward had been won by Lyle in the 1931 primary.

107. For example, Noonan's ward was carried by more than 4 to 1 over Lyle.

108. Even "Hinky-Dink's" First Ward, which was carried by Cermak by 5 to 2, had given Dever a much larger majority in 1927.

109. Thompson's forces were bitter in defeat, as their behavior in the 1932 elections was to illustrate. Even in 1950 there were grumbles about a stolen election. One Thompson supporter, James Breen, told the author that the stealing of the election for Cermak had been engineered at a meeting held at the Union League Club. Every Democratic leader was there, according to Mr. Breen, and most Republican leaders, including Brundage and representatives of Governor Emmerson. The same story was told to the writer by other Thompsonites; and Stuart states that frauds worked against Thompson. However, even he does not say that Thompson would have won were he to have received every vote cast for him. *Twenty Incredible Years*, p. 471. According to Charles S. Eaton, Thompson's commissioner of police told him that Cermak had lost by 100,000 votes and that he could "put the finger on it." According to Eaton he did not "put the finger on it" because Thompson did not want the mayor's office any more. Mr. Eaton, personal interview. In the light of Thompson's 1932 performance such an attitude on his part appears most unlikely.

It is not improbable that there were frauds in Cermak's favor in some wards, but it is equally possible that there were frauds in Thompson's favor, especially in the Negro wards.

On balance, it is not likely that 200,000 votes were stolen without considerable repercussions either then or subsequently. Of the dozens of Cermak enemies interviewed by the writer only the most rabid Thompson men repeated the story of the stolen election.

Chapter 12

1. Statement in personal interview.
2. *Inaugural Message of Honorable A. J. Cermak, Mayor* (Chicago, 1931) ; also reprinted in *Chicago Herald and Examiner*, April 28, 1931.
3. The members included such good Cermak friends as Kerner, Kaspar, Burt A. Massee, and Oscar Mayer. Others who had served on other Cermak committees included Professor Merriam, Sewell Avery, Mrs. Fairbank, Mr. Olander, D. F. Kelly, Joshua D'Esposito, Elmer T. Stevens, and William R. Dawes. Francis X. Busch was appointed permanent counsel of the commission.
4. Harold F. Gosnell, *Machine Politics: Chicago Model* (Chicago: University of Chicago Press, 1937), p. 3.
5. Charles E. Merriam, *Chicago, A More Intimate View of Urban Politics* (New York: Macmillan Co., 1929), p. 254.
6. *Ibid.*
7. Statement by the late Mayor Kelly, personal interview.

8. Statement by Francis X. Busch, personal interview.

9. *Ibid.*

10. Edward L. Gorey, *Chicago Evening American,* May 2, 1931. Cervenka admitted that he was going to help Cermak "reorganize"— and that he would report directly to Cermak. Cermak at least once publically admitted that he used "undercover men." See *Chicago Evening American,* December 10, 1932.

11. "Right" is used here in the sense in which it is regularly utilized by politicians and other political activists when evaluating someone's attitudes on issues. Cf. Theodore Roosevelt's use of "right" in Henry Cabot Lodge, *Selections from the Correspondence of Theodore Roosevelt and Henry Cabot Lodge, 1884-1918* (New York: Charles Scribner's Sons, 1925), Vol. II, p. 228.

12. Carroll H. Wooddy, "Jubilee in Chicago," *National Municipal Review,* XX (June, 1931), 321.

13. Statements by Joseph Triner, Francis X. Busch, several others. Personal interviews.

14. See Albert Lepawsky, *Home Rule for Metropolitan Chicago* (Chicago: University of Chicago Press, 1935), chapter 7. Cf. Appendix I, *infra.*

15. See Herbert D. Simpson, *Tax Racket and Tax Reform in Chicago* (Chicago: Institute for Economic Research, Northwestern University, 1930); J. L. Jacobs, *Assessment of Real Estate and Personal Property in Cook County, Illinois* (Chicago: Office of the Assessor, 1934); and O. L. Altman, "Chicago's Experiment in Personal Property Taxation, 1931-1936" (Ph.D. dissertation, University of Chicago, 1936); Dennis J. Fleming, "The Relation of Mayor to Budgetary Controls in Chicago" (M.A. thesis, University of Chicago, 1949).

16. Lepawsky, *Home Rule for Metropolitan Chicago,* p. 103.

17. *Chicago Evening American,* June 3, 1931.

18. Cf. the 1959 unpleasantness suffered by Michigan and its governor, G. Mennen Williams, because that state was presumably "broke."

19. Edward L. Gorey, *Chicago Evening American,* April 28, 1931.

20. See William H. Stuart, *The Twenty Incredible Years* (Chicago: M. A. Donahue, 1935), pp. 472 ff.

21. Personal interviews.

22. Charles Wheeler, personal interview. Mr. Wheeler, of the non-Cermak-loving *Daily News,* could in no sense be described as a Cermak admirer.

23. Personal interview.

24. Quoted in Edward L. Gorey, *Chicago Evening American,* December 30, 1931.

25. Quoted in *Chicago Evening American,* February 17, 1932.

26. See *ibid.,* February 18, 1932; *Chicago Tribune,* February 19, 1932.

27. Quoted in Edward L. Gorey, *Chicago Evening American,* July 16, 1932.

28. Quoted in *Chicago Tribune,* March 22, 1932.

29. *Chicago Herald and Examiner,* July 23, 1932.

30. *Ibid.,* December 7, 1932.

31. Cermak was not unique among responsible state and local executives who simultaneously opposed and supported sales-tax legislation. Many 2 per cent depression-caused sales taxes not only were maintained through the 1950's but are approaching 5 per cent. The governor of Washington State was only one avowed foe of the sales tax who urged increases in the sales-tax rate in 1959.

32. Quoted in Edward L. Gorey, *Chicago Evening American,* May 25, 1932.

33. *Ibid.*

34. *Chicago Evening American,* June 23, 1932.

35. *Chicago Herald and Examiner,* July 27, 1931. Cermak had no legal control of any kind over judges, although the City Council appropriated for the court's expenses. At this time Cermak also slapped at the board of education, also exempt from his direction. "There can be no continuance of the School Board's spending orgy of the past four years." (However, the mayor appoints school board members.)

36. Cermak chided Thompson's practices in a more jovial way than he had during the campaign. He said that Thompson must have had a "very loose political organization," because he had found 350 unnecessary employees at one city institution, and all from one ward. The ward committeeman of that ward had been superintendent of the institution. "Well, that surely seemed like a lot of people from one ward to have on the city payroll. We fired all of them except one. He was a laborer who wore a diamond in his tie and was sitting around the office of the institution. We didn't fire him, but gave him a shovel, and he quit." *Chicago Daily News,* August 18, 1931.

37. Quoted in Edward L. Gorey, *Chicago Evening American,* December 1, 1931.

38. *Chicago Herald and Examiner,* February 18, 1932.

39. This attitude vis-à-vis a recalcitrant city legislature is remark-

ably similar to the attitude subsequently to be shown by Franklin Roosevelt vis-à-vis Congress—"Do it, or else. . . ."

40. *Chicago Herald and Examiner,* October 6, 1932.

41. Mayor's Advisory Commission on Administrative Reorganization, *Summary Report* (transmitted by Mayor A. J. Cermak to the City Council, December 1, 1931), and *Preliminary Report* (concurred in by the City Council, December 22, 1931).

42. *Chicago Herald and Examiner,* December 10, 1932.

43. The Chicago Medical Society vigorously protested this appointment, but in 1960 Bundesen was still on the job. The Society did not want Bundesen because he was not a member. It had asked Cermak during the campaign to pledge himself against appointing Bundesen. *Chicago Herald and Examiner,* May 2, 1931. Nor was Cermak quite pleased at having to make this appointment. As a result, the department of health under a health commissioner was changed to a board of health having four members. Bundesen was head, while two other members, Dombrowski and Probrytzke, were good Slavs.

44. Professor Merriam, personal interview. Merriam was also offered a position on the board of education, and ultimately the presidency of this body, when Cermak gained control of it.

45. Sonnenschein was still Cermak's secretary, although he was now also alderman of Cermak's ward. As alderman his salary was $5,000; as mayor's secretary, $6,000. Son-in-law Graham was also included, as was Hajicek. Of course, several retained their county jobs, such as Venecek, Stasny, and Joseph Cermak.

46. Although the share of the ex-Brennanites equaled that of any other group, the highest position granted to them was the relatively minor one of commissioner of public service. The Irish of the Dunne-O'Connell wing were not neglected. O'Connell was offered the fire commissionership but did not accept.

47. Mr. D'Esposito, personal interview.

48. Statement in personal interview.

49. *Ibid.*

50. Quoted by Professor L. D. White, personal interview.

51. *Chicago Herald and Examiner,* May 3, 1931.

52. James Errant, personal interview.

53. Statement by John Dienhart, personal interview.

54. Quoted in Harold Gosnell, *Negro Politicians* (Chicago: University of Chicago Press, 1930), p. 222.

55. *Chicago Evening American,* August 17, 1931.

56. James Errant, personal interview.

57. *Ibid.*

58. Statement by Howard C. Brodman, personal interview.

59. Statement by James Errant, personal interview.

60. Howard C. Brodman, personal interview. Mr. Brodman did not "kick in," but never suffered as a consequence.

61. Statement by Francis X. Busch, personal interview.

62. *Chicago Evening American,* August 17, 1931.

63. *Chicago Herald and Examiner,* May 14, 1931. It was reported that the scolded councilmen cheered.

64. Mr. Reynolds, personal interview.

65. *Chicago Evening American,* October 11, 1932.

66. *Ibid.,* August 19, 1931.

67. A. J. Sloan, *ibid.,* June 1, 1932.

68. *Chicago Herald and Examiner,* May 11, 1932.

69. *Ibid.,* September 12, 1932.

70. *Ibid.* The conflict between Cermak's laissez-faire economic philosophy (and his real-estate interests) and his belief in positive government is demonstrated here. The "economic problems involved" seemed sufficient to bar low-cost public housing although he had been so favorably impressed by the Vienna plan which had completely eliminated slums and, in A.J.'s words, reduced the death rate 70 per cent.

71. *Chicago Evening American,* July 6, 1931.

72. Quoted in Edward L. Gorey, *ibid.,* July 27, 1931.

73. *Chicago Evening American,* September 3, 1931.

74. Parke Brown, *Chicago Tribune,* September 3, 1931.

75. Edward L. Gorey, *Chicago Evening American,* April 28, 1931.

76. *Chicago Herald and Examiner,* October 31, 1932.

77. Chicago Crime Commission, *Report of Operating Director* (Henry Barrett Chamberlain), Annual Meeting, January 19, 1933.

78. Chicago Crime Commission, *Report of the Director.*

79. Thus Leonard D. White omitted public relations as a function from his pioneering textbook *Introduction to the Study of Public Administration* (New York: Macmillan Co., 1926), and did not really discuss it until the 1948 edition. The ubiquity of "public relations" during the Eisenhower years (and the rise of television) has been the subject of much discussion and scholarship. Its role in Richard Nixon's career, culminating in the famous "Checkers" speech, has become part of political folklore. So with the public-relations-engineered defeat of Senator Tydings in the Maryland election of 1950 by the forces of the late Senator McCarthy. Many observers give "public relations" major

credit for President Kennedy's election following his television victories over Mr. Nixon. Pertinent, too, is the great position of power of many press secretaries and public-relations men of presidents and other officeholders. Names like James C. Hagerty and Pierre Salinger are widely familiar. It was commonly assumed that Mr. Hagerty's position of power in the Eisenhower administration was challenged only by Sherman Adams, the President's chief-of-staff. However, Robert Montgomery, film personality, also had access to the President in his role as television consultant. When discussing the forensic style of Mr. Eisenhower, or others of his administration, it was not uncommon to make references to the "Robert Montgomery school of acting."

Television as political "public relations" is also being used widely by the Kennedy administration. Mr. Kennedy, for example, has pioneered in the use of the "live" television press conference. Cf. Stanley Kelley, Jr., *Professional Public Relations and Political Power* (Baltimore: Johns Hopkins Press, 1956).

80. *Chicago Evening American,* June 13, 1931.

81. *Chicago Herald and Examiner,* June 16, 1931.

82. *Chicago Evening American,* June 13, 1931.

83. *Ibid.,* December 15, 1932.

Chapter 13

1. Edward L. Gorey, *Chicago Evening American,* April 7, 1931.

2. *Chicago Evening American,* February 3, 1932; *Chicago Herald and Examiner,* February 4, 1932.

3. Quoted in Paul R. Leach, *Chicago Daily News,* October 13, 1931.

4. This was only one of a series of appeasement measures toward Igoe which Cermak was constrained to make.

5. This is precisely the situation that developed after Cermak's death. Governor Horner broke with Kelly-Nash, Cermak's successors as party bosses, and decisively defeated the organization's candidate in a pitched battle primary. See "The Kelly-Nash Machine," *Fortune,* August, 1936, p. 47.

6. Edward L. Gorey, *Chicago Evening American,* December 15, 1930.

7. Joseph L. Gill, personal interview.

8. See John Dienhart, *Chicago Herald and Examiner,* August 27 and September 12, 1931.

9. Mr. Busch, personal interview. According to Busch, as far as he knew, Cermak intended to choose between him and Judge Horner. Igoe was not seriously considered—nor, according to Mr. Busch, was Cermak.

10. James C. Denvir, personal interview.

11. Personal interviews.

12. William H. Sexton, Charles H. Weber, John Dienhart, personal interviews.

13. John Dienhart, *Chicago Herald and Examiner,* January 29, 1932.

14. *Ibid.,* February 13, 1931. There is little doubt that Cermak wished to be governor, if only as a legacy to his daughters, to whom he was a more than ordinarily doting father. It is also very likely that the Czech in him strongly desired that a man of his antecedents reach that high office. What he himself could not achieve was achieved by another of Czech descent in 1960. Otto Kerner won the Illinois governorship by a huge vote, not only vastly larger than Kennedy's but also much greater than Senator Paul Douglas'. Kerner not only is the son of A.J.'s old ally, but he is the husband of one of Cermak's daughters.

15. Statement by the late Congressman Sabath, personal interview.

16. Horace Lindheimer, personal interview. Mr. Lindheimer is a brother of Benjamin F. Lindheimer, who had been secretary of the Sprague committee and became a member of Cermak's cabinet, as well as a member of the South Park Board. Benjamin Lindheimer was one of Horner's most important backers at this time. In the subsequent election, he succeeded to Igoe's position as ward committeeman of the Fifth Ward. After Cermak's death, when Horner had broken with Kelly-Nash, Lindheimer stood with the Irish leaders, as did his west-side colleague, Arvey.

17. Albert J. Horan, personal interview.

18. Statement in personal interview.

19. Fletcher Dobyns, *The Underworld of American Politics* (Kingsport, Tenn.: privately printed, 1932), pp. 117 ff. Dobyns was a rabid Cermak foe. See also Harold F. Gosnell, *Machine Politics: Chicago Model* (Chicago: University of Chicago Press, 1937), p. 21.

20. A. J. Horan and Joseph L. Gill, personal interviews. Gill quotes Cermak to this effect: "Every rich Jew from New York to San Francisco will contribute to his campaign."

21. Quoted by Joseph Triner, personal interview.

22. The pattern continued in the nominees for trustees of the state university. In addition to Cermak's good German friend and physician, Dr. Karl A. Meyer, there was O. M. Karraker; and the sole woman on the entire ticket was Mrs. Nellie V. Freeman.

23. Polish names were next most numerous, then German, then Italian, and finally Czech.

24. These were Rooney, Dunne, and McGarry. There were two Czechs, Bicek and Kaspar; one Pole, Urbanowski; one Italian, Bonelli; one Jew; and a German, Gutknecht, whose wife was Jewish.

25. But the slate did not meet universal approbation—especially downstate. The downstate Democratic members of the state House of Representatives in caucus censured the slate, amidst frantic cries of "dictator" against Cermak. A strong condemnatory resolution was adopted. It charged that the slatemaking was not the result of "free and voluntary expression of individuals," but was "the operation of a political machine speaking through proxies . . . said action is un-American, un-Democratic, and an insult to the intelligence of every voter. There is not sufficient room in the Democratic Party for any dictator or any set of men to dictate to the people of Illinois." *Chicago Evening American*, February 16, 1932.

26. Horner, 397,499; Igoe, 255,527; Campbell, 134,972. The votes in Cook County were as follows: Horner, 317,286; Igoe, 170,563; Campbell, 5,660. *Chicago Daily News Almanac and Yearbook*, 1933, p. 888.

27. The vote in the Twenty-fourth Ward is revealing: Horner, 15,614; Igoe, 241; Campbell, 17. This was Rosenberg's ward, but it is clear that *organization*, not ethnic sympathy, was chiefly responsible for this fantastic vote. The vote for congressman in the same ward illustrates this sharply: T. J. O'Brien, 9,392; J. T. Igoe, 661; Cohen, 637. Stuart, *The Twenty Incredible Years* (Chicago: M. A. Donahue, 1935), p. 489.

28. Quoted by Parke Brown, *Chicago Tribune*, April 19, 1932.

29. *Chicago Herald and Examiner*, April 28, 1931; cf. Edward L. Gorey, *Chicago Evening American*, April 17, 1931.

30. William E. Lawry, *Chicago Herald and Examiner*, July 23, 1931.

31. *Chicago Herald and Examiner*, July 24, 1931.

32. *Ibid*.

33. *Chicago Tribune*, July 24, 1931.

34. Quoted in the *Chicago Tribune*, July 24, 1931.

35. Quoted in *Chicago Herald and Examiner*, November 2, 1931.

36. Mayor Kelly, personal interview. Kelly was a participant in the discussion. Upon emerging from the interview, the two were swamped by reporters. So dissatisfied with Roosevelt's Wetness was Cermak that he nearly divulged his opinions to the press. Said Kelly: "I had to keep kicking his heels to keep him quiet."

37. *Ibid.* Mayor Kelly told of another Cermak-Smith conversation when Kelly was present. This took place after the convention. Kelly and Cermak, accompanied by Hague, called upon Smith. Cermak requested that Smith make a radio speech supporting Horner and Courtney. Smith became overcome by anger. He shouted and swore and ranted about Cermak's disloyalty. And Cermak kept explaining that he had been powerless to hold the Illinois delegation from Roosevelt after the favorite son withdrew.

38. Quoted in *Chicago Tribune,* February 8, 1932. A.J. would make no comment on whether Smith's candidacy would harm Roosevelt's. However, Igoe did comment, and his reply is indicative of the strong pro-Smith sentiment among local Irish leaders. Igoe said Smith's candidacy did not hurt Roosevelt's because Roosevelt's candidacy had "fallen by the wayside." "Smith, more than any other candidate, speaks the language of the people."

39. John Dienhart, *Chicago Herald and Examiner,* May 9, 1932. Lewis was the only candidate. There was no second choice. However, two days later, although he was still for Lewis "to the last ditch," a second choice did emerge—his banker friend, M. A. Traylor. *Ibid.,* May 11, 1932.

40. Stuart, *Twenty Incredible Years,* p. 490.

41. Cermak's clique included Nash, Toman, Rosenberg, Whealan, McDonough, Clayton Smith, Walter LaBuy, and others. These had full votes. Judge Horner was a delegate-at-large. For the full list see *Chicago Daily News Almanac and Yearbook,* 1933, p. 889.

42. Quoted in *Chicago Herald and Examiner,* June 3, 1932. Cermak added that Cook County was not trying to control the delegation, and that if the unit rule were in force he would be the first to vote against it. Nor, he said, was Chicago (Cermak) trying to dominate Democratic politics in Illinois.

43. One writer described his discomfiture with their cheers for Roosevelt in the convention with this interesting bit of dialogue— even if probably apocryphal:

"Tell 'em to shut up and use some sense," Tony whispered to Chief Bailiff Al Horan. "Didn't I put 'em on the delegation?"

"You ought to have known better," Horan whispered back. "You can't shut 'em up. That's one time you slipped, Tony."

"Yes," muttered the mayor, "that's one time I slipped." W. A. S. Douglas, "Kindling Wood Peddler," *American Mercury,* XXIX (July, 1933), 341-47.

44. There were $2\frac{1}{2}$ votes for minor candidates.

45. Charles Michelson, *The Ghost Talks* (New York: G. P. Putnam's Sons, 1944), pp. 4-8.

46. *Chicago Evening American,* June 9, 1932.

47. James A. Farley, *Behind the Ballots* (New York: Harcourt, Brace and Co., 1938), pp. 120 ff.

48. *Ibid.,* p. 120. Farley was not pleased by this development. "Although there was a large body of sentiment in the Illinois delegation for Roosevelt—the opposition used every stratagem to keep fifty-eight votes out of our column. . . . It is very seldom that a state is fortunate enough to have two favorite sons qualified for the Presidency, but the Illinois leaders were equal to the occasion."

49. *Chicago Herald and Examiner,* June 28, 1932. Cermak delivered a notable welcome speech—written by Judge Harry Fischer. He reminded the delegates that "millions of hungry men, women and children crave a return to the simplicity and freedom of American life that have all but disappeared. They believe we will have more respect for our constitution with the eighteenth amendment eliminated."

50. Farley, *Behind the Ballots,* p. 141.

51. This was made upon the demand of Tammany leader Curry. *Ibid.*

52. One account of this hectic conference is of some interest. Farley, "flushed and plainly emphatic," was "very very earnest about something. . . . He talked—whispered rather—with visible effort to obtain some agreement. Cermak nodded once or twice, and once shook his head slightly, but gave no real indication of what his response was to Farley's appeal to him." *Chicago Evening American,* June 30, 1932.

53. Farley, *Behind the Ballots,* p. 120.

54. Farley, *Jim Farley's Story: The Roosevelt Years* (New York: McGraw-Hill Book Co., 1948), pp. 21 ff.

55. *Ibid.*

56. Farley, *Behind the Ballots,* p. 151.

57. *Chicago Daily News Almanac and Year Book,* 1933, p. 662.

58. John Dienhart, *Chicago Herald and Examiner,* June 19, 1932. The Republicans had voted to submit a repeal amendment to the states. But Cermak felt this would take too long. There also had to be immediate action to allow beer.

59. Tom Pattey, *Chicago Tribune,* June 21, 1932.

60. *Chicago Herald and Examiner,* June 3, 1932. Igoe also enjoyed the privilege of nominating Traylor.

61. This was considerably Wetter than the original draft which had been prepared by A. Mitchell Palmer, formerly Attorney General of the United States, notorious for the Palmer raids. See Roy V. Peel and T. C. Donnelly, *The 1932 Campaign, An Analysis* (New York: Farrar and Rinehart, 1935), p. 100.

62. *Chicago Daily News Almanac and Year Book,* 1933, p. 663.

63. *Ibid.*

64. Dobyns, *The Underworld of American Politics,* pp. 128 ff.

65. *Ibid.*

66. Mayor Kelly, personal interview. Kelly said packing the galleries was normal procedure. He himself was experienced in convention trickery. It was under his auspices that the famous "voice from the sewers" disrupted a later Democratic convention in Chicago.

67. Willis J. Abbot, *Christian Science Monitor,* quoted in Dobyns, *The Underworld of American Politics,* p. 135.

68. *Ibid.*

69. Dobyns, *The Underworld of American Politics,* p. 135.

70. A somewhat similar scenario was enacted in the 1960 Democratic National Convention. Here the gallery once again overwhelmingly favored a candidate (Stevenson) who could not win the nomination. However, in contrast to 1928, Stevenson had virtually no "organization" support and the clamor from the bleachers availed him less than it had Smith in 1928.

71. Farley, *Behind the Ballots,* p. 142.

72. Mr. Sonnenschein, personal interview.

73. Mayor Kelly, personal interview.

74. Personal interview.

75. Statements by Mayor Harrison, personal interview.

76. Mayor Kelly, personal interview.

77. The risk entailed in an earlier attempt to switch to Roosevelt was demonstrated by the lusty booing from the galleries which accompanied the final switch by the Illinois delegation, although by this time Roosevelt's nomination was assured.

78. Stuart, *Twenty Incredible Years,* p. 496.

79. *Chicago Herald and Examiner,* October 29, 1932.

80. H. F. Gosnell and N. H. Gill, "An Analysis of the 1932 Presidential Vote in Chicago," *American Political Science Review,* XXIX (1935), 984.

81. However, Horner proved in 1936 that he was capable of being renominated even in the face of the most determined opposition of

the city machine, and of winning re-election although enjoying less than the wholehearted support of that organization. Of course by this time Cermak was dead.

82. *Chicago Daily News Almanac and Yearbook,* 1933.

83. *Ibid.* However, Kaspar, another Czech, was elected, as was an Italian, Bonelli.

84. Joseph Triner and Milburn Akers, the latter a publicity man for Horner, personal interviews.

85. Statement by Mayor Kelly, personal interview.

86. Personal interview. A. J. Horan also doubted that Cermak could dominate Horner. Personal interview.

87. Statement by Joseph Triner, intimate of Cermak and one of Horner's department heads. Personal interview.

88. Statement by Charles Wheeler, personal interview.

89. *Machine Politics,* p. 21.

90. For Horner's revolt, see "The Kelly-Nash Machine."

91. Durkin was later Eisenhower's first secretary of labor.

92. *Chicago Daily News Almanac and Year Book,* 1934, pp. 767-70. All these men were Jewish.

93. Quoted by Joseph Triner, personal interview.

94. Quoted by Stuart, *Twenty Incredible Years,* p. 515. This was one of the times that Cermak "bawled Horner out like a baby" in the words of one observer. Statement by John Dienhart, personal interview.

95. *Chicago Evening American,* January 26, 1933.

96. Edward L. Gorey, *ibid.,* January 28, 1933.

97. *Chicago Herald and Examiner,* January 29, 1933.

98. *Chicago Evening American,* April 7, 1931.

99. Dobyns, *Underworld of American Politics,* pp. ix f.

100. Douglas, "Kindling Wood Peddler," p. 341.

101. Statements by Mayor Kelly, A. J. Horan, Clayton F. Smith, and many other Irish leaders. Personal interviews.

102. Statement reported by Howard C. Brodman, personal interview.

Chapter 14

1. *Chicago Tribune,* December 9, 1932. At this time he was presenting, among others, the claims of—as he said—"one of the greatest sons of democracy," Bruce Campbell, for attorney general.

Cf. Edward L. Gorey, *Chicago Evening American,* December 7, 1932. Vopicka was among Cermak's nominees.

Cermak was also greatly interested in the position of Speaker of the House of Representatives. His man for this powerful position was Representative Rainey. Cermak was reported in conference with Tammany leaders attempting to line up congressional support for this man. *Chicago Herald and Examiner,* December 10, 1932.

2. John Dienhart, *Chicago Herald and Examiner,* December 8, 1932.

3. Mayor Harrison revealed one position and one individual of vital interest to Cermak. A.J. wanted his son-in-law, Graham, just selected as president *pro tem* of the state senate, to be collector of internal revenue for Chicago. Harrison was approached by Farley, who insisted against Harrison's wishes that Harrison take the job. Harrison wanted another position. Farley indicated that the Harrison appointment was to be only temporary, but that it was a "must." Cermak had demanded the job for Graham, and Farley was reluctant to refuse a job for A.J.'s own son-in-law. If a deserving Roosevelt man like Harrison were to get it, Farley could save face. Harrison accepted reluctantly but kept the job for many years. Personal interview.

The great urgency about refusing this job to A.J. reinforces the report that Cermak at this time was being investigated for income-tax evasion. In the 1930 campaign he himself admitted this. The investigation of his tax returns was corroborated by an individual whose official job gave him access to this kind of information. Personal interview.

4. Mayor Kelly, personal interview.

5. Quoted by Charles H. Weber, personal interview. Before leaving Chicago, Cermak had called Triner, Kerner, and Mrs. Jirke and told each of them he was going to see Roosevelt. To one he said he was going to get help to pay the teachers, to another, that he wanted to see about a job for Szymczak. The Szymczak quest succeeded.

6. *Chicago Herald and Examiner,* February 8, 1933. For a photograph of one of the Cermak-Farley conferences at the Hialeah race track, see *ibid.,* February 14, 1933. At this time Cermak was reported negotiating for an R.F.C. loan for paying city employees and for a civil-service commissionership for Szymczak. *Ibid.,* February 16, 1933. For Farley's own account of the conferences, see his *Jim Farley's Story* (New York: McGraw-Hill, 1948), p. 35.

7. L. L. Lee, *Chicago Evening American,* February 16, 1933. Mr. Lee was city manager of Miami. At the moment of the shooting his arm was linked with Cermak's. The account of the shooting has been based on this participant's report.

8. For one statement of the argument, see William H. Stuart, *The Twenty Incredible Years* (Chicago: M. A. Donahue, 1935), pp. 501 ff.

9. *Ibid.*, p. 502.

10. *Ibid.*

11. *Ibid.*

12. *Chicago Herald and Examiner,* September 28, 1933.

13. Milton S. Mayer, "Corrupt and Discontented?" *Survey Graphic,* XXIII (October, 1934), 480-81.

14. Stuart, *Twenty Incredible Years,* p. 518.

15. Milton S. Mayer, "Corrupt and Discontented?"

16. This was the belief of crime fighter Frank J. Loesch. In an interview that was not published until after Loesch's death, because of his wife's fear of reprisals, he was quoted as follows: "Because of gambling and other mob war in Chicago, there was one hoodlum element which wished to eliminate Mayor Cermak. They were not brazen enough to do it themselves." Robert Kleckner, *Chicago Daily Times,* August 7, 1944.

17. Statement by Captain Tom Connell and Lt. Bill Drury, *Chicago Herald-American,* November 4, 1948.

18. *Ibid.*

19. *Chicago Herald and Examiner,* February 16, 1933.

20. Mr. Dienhart, personal interview.

21. Personal interview.

22. *Chicago Herald and Examiner,* February 16, 1933. Zangara's statements were made through interpreters to police officers.

23. *Ibid.*

24. *Ibid.*

25. *Chicago Evening American,* February 16, 1933.

26. *Ibid.*

27. Bob Crossland, "I Saw Zangara Die," *True Detectives Magazine,* November, 1949. Cf. Robert J. Donovan, "The Long Stomach Ache," Annals of Crime, *New Yorker,* November 27, 1954, p. 115.

28. Zangara insisted that he was sane. At least two physicians agreed with him. *Chicago Evening American,* February 18, 1933. More recently one of the members of the sanity commission that examined Zangara said, "Medically he was *not* sane. Legally he was considered sane. ... I am sure if he were alive today and we had the modern facilities for examining him psychiatrically, he would be adjudicated as a very insane person and probably hopelessly insane."

29. This point was made by Mayor Kelly—who did not hold with the gangster theory.

30. The possibility of direct connection between Chicago policemen and gangsters is given greater credibility by the 1952 investigations of such connections, led by Alderman Robert Merriam. See any Chicago newspaper of July 15, 1952, through July 25, 1952.

31. There are several versions of the exact wording as well as the time of the statement. Alderman Bowler first quoted the statement in his signed article in the *Chicago Herald and Examiner*, February 16, 1933, saying that it had been made on the ride to the hospital. *Chicago Evening American*, February 16, 1933; *Chicago Tribune*, March 6, 1933.

32. John Dienhart, *Chicago Herald and Examiner*, March 2, 1933.

33. James B. Bowler, *Chicago Herald and Examiner*, February 16, 1933. Roosevelt was also requested by Cermak to notify his daughters and assure them that he was all right. Mrs. Frank Jirka, personal interview.

34. *Chicago Herald and Examiner*, February 20, 1933.

35. John Dienhart, *ibid.*, February 21, 1933; reprinted March 7, 1933.

36. *Chicago Tribune*, March 6, 1933.

37. Zangara received quick "justice." Even while Cermak was still thought to have a good chance for recovery he was tried for attempted manslaughter and sentenced to eighty years in prison. Within a day of Cermak's death a Miami coroner's jury found that he had died of the bullet wound, and on March 20 Zangara was executed.

38. These physicians were Cermak's old friend, appointee, and family physician, Dr. Tice, and his son-in-law, Frank J. Jirka.

39. Quoted in *Chicago Evening American*, March 31, 1933.

40. Stuart, *Twenty Incredible Years*, p. 547.

41. *Ibid.*, p. 533. For the congressman-at-large election, see Harold Gosnell, *Machine Politics: Chicago Model* (Chicago: University of Chicago Press, 1937), p. 94.

42. Nash had difficulties in his selection. With the "Bohunk" gone there were plenty of pretenders to the throne. James B. Bowler came roaring back from Miami insisting that Cermak had designated him. John S. Clark was again a "candidate." When Nash chose Kelly these others were furious. Bowler called Nash an "insipid old man" and Kelly a "thief." Statement by Charles H. Weber, personal interview. Mayor Kelly said Bowler and Clark were "very abusive." Personal interview.

43. This was charged by the independent candidate (*Chicago Daily*

News, Chicago Tribune, March 27, 1933), and "substantiated" by Professor H. F. Gosnell. See his *Machine Politics,* p. 19, n. 26.

44. Gosnell, *Machine Politics,* p. 8.

45. For a list of the delegates see *Chicago Daily News Almanac and Year Book,* 1934, p. 800. Again ironically, in this convention he would have had opposing him such formerly useful "silk-stocking" bankers as Harry Eugene Kelly.

Chapter 15

1. Harold P. Lasswell, *Power and Personality* (New York: W. W. Norton, 1948), pp. 21-22.

2. *Ibid.,* p. 53.

3. Franz Alexander and T. M. French, *Studies in Psychosomatic Medicine* (New York: Ronald Press, 1948), pp. 121-22.

4. *Ibid.;* cf. Alexander, *Psychosomatic Medicine* (New York: W. W. Norton, 1950), p. 119; Karl Abraham, *Selected Papers* (London: Hogarth Press and Institute of Psychoanalysis, 1927), p. 376.

5. R. A. Ginsburg, "Czechs in Politics," *Czech and Slovak Leaders in Metropolitan Chicago* (Chicago: Slavonik Club of University of Chicago, 1934), pp. 262-64.

6. Statement by Joseph Houdek, personal interview.

7. John A. Cervenka, whose career ran parallel with Cermak's for many years, was very specific in describing the many devices Cermak used for achieving these ends. Cermak kept Cervenka continuously in office from 1910 on; Mr. Cervenka charges that this was among Cermak's devices for neutralizing him as a serious rival. The most extreme instance occurred during Cermak's tenure as county board president. One appointment he offered Cervenka was as superintendent of one of the county institutions, which would have required Cervenka's residence on the institutional premises, some distance from Lawndale. Personal interview.

8. Kurt Lewin, "The Problem of Minority Leadership," *Studies in Leadership,* ed. Alvin W. Gouldner (New York: Harper and Bros., 1950), p. 193.

9. Mayor Harrison, personal interview.

10. Harold Gosnell, *Machine Politics: Chicago Model* (Chicago: University of Chicago Press, 1937), pp. 138-42, especially figure 9.

11. The attitude of the Polish community in this respect has sharply altered over the past thirty years.

12. Personal interviews.

13. Statement in personal interview.

14. William B. Munro, *Personality in Politics* (New York: Macmillan Co., 1924), p. 117. Cf. James Bryce, *Modern Democracies* (New York: Macmillan Co., 1924), p. 559: "That which we call chance... has more to do with the course of events than the builders of scientific history have generally recognized."

Appendix I

1. Ernest Barker, *National Character and the Factors in its Foundation* (New York: Harper and Bros., 1927), pp. 48 ff.

2. U.S. Bureau of the Census, *Fifteenth Census of the United States: 1930.* Vol. I. *Population* (Washington: Government Printing Office, 1931), p. 280. Cf. Helen R. Jeter, *Trends of Population in Chicago* (Chicago: University of Chicago Press, 1927), pp. 17 ff.

3. Albert Lepawsky, "Chicago, Metropolis in the Making," *National Municipal Review*, XXX (April, 1941), 211.

4. Paul F. Cressy, "The Succession of Cultural Groups in Chicago" (Ph.D. dissertation, University of Chicago, 1930), p. 10.

5. *Ibid.,* p. 11.

6. Charles E. Merriam, *Chicago, A More Intimate View of Urban Politics* (New York: Macmillan Co., 1929), p. 14.

7. This entire struggle is well described by W. B. Phillips, "Chicago and the Downstate: A Study of Their Conflicts" (Ph.D. dissertation, University of Chicago, 1940).

8. Merriam, *Chicago, A More Intimate View,* p. 18: "It is a curious fact that Chicago has never had an effective boss of the New York or Philadelphia type, with a well-organized machine capable of holding out against public opinion for any length of time." Also see chapter 2. Cf. Edward M. Martin, *The Role of the Bar in Electing the Bench in Chicago* (Chicago: University of Chicago Press, 1936), pp. 288-310.

9. This atmosphere is noted, somewhat romantically, by Claudius O. Johnson, *Carter Henry Harrison I* (Chicago: University of Chicago Press, 1928), p. 30: "To it the venturesome were drawn; by it adventurers were attracted. Many choice spirits were numbered among its population, but it had the frontier town's proportion of riffraff. The timid feared it; the pious prayed for it; the robust, vigorous, loud, coarse and irreverent, albeit good-hearted, enjoyed it."

10. The proportion of foreign-born persons in the Chicago area was significantly larger than that of the United States as a whole. See Jeter, *Trends of Population,* p. 33; also see Table XXV, p. 34, and Table

XXVII, p. 44, for additional statistics on the ratio of native born to foreign born in the Chicago region, in Cook County, and in the City of Chicago.

11. Harold F. Gosnell, *Machine Politics: Chicago Model* (Chicago: University of Chicago Press, 1937), p. 25.

12. *Ibid.*, p. 14. See Anton J. Cermak, "Why Businessmen Fail in Politics," *Nation's Business*, XXI (January 1, 1933), 25. Besides the views expressed in this article by Cermak himself, this inference is drawn from comments made by his friends and associates in numerous personal interviews.

13. Louis Wirth, "Chicago: The Land and the People," *Survey Graphic*, XXIII (October, 1934), 22.

14. Donald Richberg, "Gold-Plated Anarchy: An Interpretation of the Fall of the Giants," *Nation*, CXXXVI (April 5, 1933), 368-69. Mr. Richberg tells of an alleged offer of $500,000 by Insull to George E. Brennan for the Democratic party of Chicago.

15. Carroll H. Wooddy, *The Case of Frank L. Smith* (Chicago: University of Chicago Press, 1931), is a fascinating account of Insull's role in the 1926 primary. Insull's political expenditures on that election amounted to $238,735, all but $15,000 having been given to the Republicans. See pp. 56-57: "I gave $15,000 to my friend George Brennan, and I feel ashamed it wasn't more."

At least $125,000 was given to Frank L. Smith, the candidate for the Republican nomination for United States senator. At the time Colonel Smith was chairman of the Illinois Commerce Commission, the administrative body that regulated utility rates.

Democratic forces were also nurtured through deals for the junk of Insull's empire, which was handled by Moe Rosenberg. Profits from this arrangement, amounting to $500,000 annually, came to light during the investigation of Rosenberg's income by internal revenue agents. From this source Rosenberg made disbursement to all deserving Democrats. On this point see *Chicago Daily News*, March 12, 13, 14, and 15, 1934. Also see chapter 10, this volume.

Also see Merriam, *Chicago, A More Intimate View*, pp. 196 ff.

16. Merriam, *Chicago, A More Intimate View*, p. 201.

17. Mitchell Dawson, "Insull on Trial," *Nation*, CXXXIX (November 28, 1934), 611.

18. C. E. Merriam, S. D. Parratt, and A. Lepawsky, *The Government of the Metropolitan Region of Chicago* (Chicago: University of Chicago Press, 1933), p. 8. This section relies heavily on this excellent study.

19. Merriam, *Chicago, A More Intimate View*, p. 90.

20. *Ibid.*

21. These figures are taken from Carroll H. Wooddy, *The Chicago Primary of 1926* (Chicago: University of Chicago Press, 1926), pp. 2, 6, 10-11; and from Merriam, Parratt, and Lepawsky, *Government of the Metropolitan Region of Chicago*, pp. 19-20.

22. Leonard D. White, introduction to Wooddy, *The Chicago Primary of 1926*, p. 1.

23. Merriam, *Chicago, A More Intimate View*, p. 222.

24. Walter F. Dodd and Sue H. Dodd, *Government in Illinois* (Chicago: University of Chicago Press, 1923), pp. 256 ff.; cf. E. Dennis Conroy, "The Electoral System of Chicago and Cook County" (Master's thesis, University of Chicago, 1951), p. 48. See also Neil F. Garvey, *The Government and Administration of Illinois* (New York: Thomas Y. Crowell Co., 1958).

25. Charles E. Merriam, personal interview.

26. Merriam, *Chicago, A More Intimate View*, p. 228.

27. *Ibid.*, p. 225.

28. City of Chicago, Municipal Reference Library, "Mayor, City of Chicago" (unpublished manuscript). See also Garvey, *The Government and Administration of Illinois*, pp. 543-45.

29. Paul Studenski, *The Government of Metropolitan Areas in the United States* (New York: National Municipal League, 1930), p. 224.

30. Merriam, Parratt, and Lepawsky, *Government of the Metropolitan Region of Chicago*, p. 33.

31. Dodd and Dodd, *Government in Illinois*, p. 249.

32. Clyde F. Snider, *County Government in Illinois*, a report prepared for Illinois Tax Commission, reprinted from 23rd and 24th Annual Reports, p. 60; cf. Garvey, pp. 552-57.

33. Wooddy, *Chicago Primary of 1926*, p. 11.

34. Statement by former county civil service commissioner, personal interview.

35. Of the employees in departments under the president's control, less than 50 per cent were in the classified service in 1929. See Studenski, *The Government of Metropolitan Areas*, p. 224.

36. Snider, *County Government in Illinois*, p. 60.

37. Dodd and Dodd, *Government in Illinois*, p. 225.

38. Merriam, *Chicago, A More Intimate View*, pp. 97 ff.

39. Cf. Harold F. Gosnell, *Negro Politicians* (Chicago: University of Chicago Press, 1935), pp. 202 ff.

Appendix II

1. This Appendix appeared as "The Use of Psychosomatic Categories in a Study of Political Personality," *Western Political Quarterly,* VIII (June, 1955), 234-47, and was published in *Political Behavior,* ed. Heinz Eulau, Samuel J. Eldersveld, and Morris Janowitz (Glencoe, Ill.: Free Press, 1956), pp. 125-33.

2. Harold D. Lasswell, *Power and Personality* (New York: W. W. Norton, 1948), includes brief biographical sketches and analyses of a number of politicians. Alexander L. George, "Woodrow Wilson: A Study of Political Personality" (unpublished manuscript) is an exhaustive psychoanalytic study of a single figure. Harold Zink, "A Case Study of a Political Boss," *Psychiatry,* I (1938), 527-33, is a psychological analysis of Klan leader David C. Stephenson.

3. Statements of a Braidwood contemporary, personal interview.

4. Anton J. Cermak, "Why Businessmen Fail in Politics," *Nation's Business,* XXI (1933), 25.

5. Mayor Kelly, personal interview.

6. Statement by Charles Eaton, personal interview. Mr. Eaton served on the city council contemporaneously with Cermak. He was alderman from the Fifth (University of Chicago) Ward, which at another period was represented by Charles E. Merriam.

7. Philip Kinsley, *Chicago Tribune,* March 22, 1931.

8. Statement by Francis X. Busch, personal interview. Mr. Busch was corporation counsel for the City of Chicago during Cermak's mayoralty.

9. Cermak's secretary.

10. *Chicago Herald and Examiner,* February 20, 1933.

11. According to descriptions of Cermak's behavior by both of the latter gentlemen in personal interviews. Mr. Merriam knew Cermak in numerous governmental connections, as did Mr. White.

12. Statement by Caspar Nathan in a personal interview. Mr. Nathan was for many years assistant corporation counsel for the City of Chicago, a position he held during Cermak's tenure of the mayoralty. He served in a public-relations capacity for Cermak during the mayoralty campaign.

13. Mrs. Frank Jirka, Cermak's eldest daughter, personal interview.

14. *Chicago Evening Post,* April 4, 1932.

15. The discussion that follows is based, except where otherwise noted, upon Franz Alexander, *Psychosomatic Medicine* (New York: W. W. Norton, 1950), and Franz Alexander and T. M. French, *Studies*

in Psychosomatic Medicine (New York: Ronald Press, 1948), with special reference to sections dealing with disturbances of the gastrointestinal tract.

16. Alex Comfort, *Authority and Delinquency in the Modern State* (London: Routledge and Kegan Paul, 1950), p. 83.

17. Alexander and French, *Studies in Psychosomatic Medicine*, p. 108.

18. *Ibid.*, pp. 116-17.

19. Alexander, *Psychosomatic Medicine*, p. 119.

20. These two meanings correspond to two important stages in infantile development. The first is the period of stool-training. Up to this time, the child has had sovereignty over the bowel function, which he finds pleasurable; he develops a "sense of independence which soon becomes associated with the excremental act." *Ibid.*, p. 116. In complying with the wishes of adults to regulate himself, the child comes to look upon the intestinal content as a kind of donation to them, for which he often receives rewards in praise or in gifts. The intestinal content itself in this way comes to be regarded as a "valuable possession ... and something which can be exchanged for other goods." "This explains its close relation to money, which is one of the best-established facts uncovered by psychoanalysis." *Ibid.*, p. 117. Later, however, the pleasurable attitude toward the bowel function becomes inhibited through educational procedures and is "changed into its opposite, disgust and depreciation, which becomes the basis of the sadistic aggressive-and-soiling connotation of the excremental act." *Ibid.* In this way, two psychologic meanings come to be attached to the bowel content: on the one hand, it is a symbol of giving, accomplishment, and independence; on the other hand, it is a symbol of hostility and attack.

21. See note 20.

22. Alexander and French, *Studies in Psychosomatic Medicine*, p. 128.

23. Otto Fenichel, *The Psychoanalytic Theory of Neurosis* (New York: W. W. Norton, 1945), p. 246. Cf. Alexander and French, *Studies in Psychosomatic Medicine*, pp. 103-72, *passim*.

24. Quoted by Mayor Kelly in a personal interview.

25. "Two emotional factors are conspicuous in the precipitation of the disease and in the provocation of relapses. One is the frustrated tendency to carry out an obligation, be it biological, moral, or material, and the second is a frustrated ambition to accomplish something

which requires the concentrated expenditure of energy." Alexander and French, *Studies in Psychosomatic Medicine*, p. 125.

26. Lasswell, *Power and Personality*, p. 53.

27. Alexander and French, *Studies in Psychosomatic Medicine*, p. 150.

28. Otto Fenichel, *Outline of Clinical Psychoanalysis*, trans. Bertram D. Lewin and Gregory Zilboorg (New York: W. W. Norton, 1934), p. 430.

29. Erich Fromm, *Escape from Freedom* (New York: Rinehart, 1941), p. 293.

30. Karl Abraham, *Selected Papers* (London: Hogarth Press, 1942), p. 374.

31. Ernest Jones, *Papers on Psychoanalysis* (Baltimore: Williams and Wilkins, 1938), pp. 415-16.

32. *Ibid.*, p. 417.

BIBLIOGRAPHY

BOOKS AND PAMPHLETS

Abbott, Edith. *Historical Aspects of the Immigration Problem.* Chicago: University of Chicago Press, 1926.

———. *Immigration.* Chicago: University of Chicago Press, 1942.

Abraham, Karl. *Selected Papers.* London: Hogarth Press and Institute of Psychoanalysis, 1927.

Addams, Jane. *Democracy and Social Ethics.* New York: Macmillan Co., 1902.

———. *Forty Years at Hull House.* New York: Macmillan Co., 1935.

Adler, Alfred. *Understanding Human Nature.* Garden City, New York: Garden City Publishing Co., 1927.

Alexander, Franz. *Psychosomatic Medicine.* New York: W. W. Norton and Co., 1950.

Alexander, F. and T. M. French (eds.). *Studies in Psychosomatic Medicine.* New York: Ronald Press Co., 1948.

Allen, Robert S. (ed.). *Our Fair City.* New York: Vanguard Press, 1941.

Andrews, Wayne. *Battle for Chicago.* New York: Harcourt, Brace and Co., 1946.

Asbury, Herbert. *Gem of the Prairie, an Informal History of the Chicago Underworld.* New York: Alfred A. Knopf, 1940.

Balch, Emily Greene. *Our Slavic Fellow Citizens*. New York: Charities Publications Committee, 1910.

Barker, Ernest. *National Character and the Factors in its Formation*. New York: Harper and Bros., 1927.

Barnard, Chester I. *The Functions of the Executive*. Cambridge, Mass.: Harvard University Press, 1938.

Barnard, H. K. *Anton the Martyr*. Chicago: Marion Publishing Co., 1933.

Baruch, Hugo (Jack Bilbo). *Carrying a Gun for Al Capone; The Intimate Experiences of a Gangster in the Bodyguard of Al Capone*. New York: G. P. Putnam's Sons, 1932.

Bean, Louis H. *How to Predict Elections*. New York: Alfred A. Knopf, 1948.

Beasley, Norman. *Frank Knox, American*. Garden City, New York: Doubleday, Doran and Co., 1936.

Berman, L. *The Glands Regulating Personality*. New York: Macmillan Co., 1928.

Bird, Charles. *Social Psychology*. New York: Appleton-Century Co., 1940.

Bishop, Glen A. and Paul T. Gilbert. *Chicago's Accomplishments and Leaders*. Chicago: Bishop Publishing Co., 1932.

Bogardus, Emory S. *Essentials of Americanization*. Los Angeles: University of Southern California Press, 1919.

———. *Immigration and Race Attitudes*. Boston: D. C. Heath and Co., 1928.

Bowen, Louise De Koven. *Fighting to Make Chicago Safe for Children*. Chicago: Juvenile Protective Association of Chicago, 1920.

———. *Growing Up With a City*. New York: Macmillan Co., 1926.

———. *The Public Dance Halls of Chicago*. Chicago: Juvenile Protective Association of Chicago, 1917.

———. *Safeguards for City Youth at Work and Play*. New York: Macmillan Co., 1914.

———. *Some Legislative Needs in Illinois*. Chicago: Juvenile Protective Association of Chicago, 1912.

Bowers, Claude G. *Beveridge and the Progressive Era*. Boston: Houghton Mifflin Co., 1932.

Bowers, David F. *Foreign Influences in American Life*. Princeton: Princeton University Press, 1944.

Bregstone, Philip P. *Chicago and Its Jews*. Chicago: Privately published, 1933.

Bright, John. *Hizzoner, Big Bill Thompson.* New York: Jonathan Cape and Harrison Smith, 1930.

Brill, A. A. *Lectures on Psychoanalytic Psychiatry.* New York: Alfred A. Knopf, 1948.

———. *Psychoanalysis.* Philadelphia: W. B. Saunders Co., 1913.

Britt, S. H. *Social Psychology of Modern Life.* New York: Farrar and Rinehart, 1941.

Brown, F. J. and J. S. Roucek. *Our Racial and National Minorities.* New York: Prentice-Hall, 1937.

Bryce, James. *The American Commonwealth.* New York: Macmillan Co., 1910.

———. *Modern Democracies.* New York: MacMillan Co., 1924.

Burgess, E. W. (ed.). *The Urban Community.* Chicago: University of Chicago Press, 1926.

Burgess, E. W. and C. Newcomb (eds.). *Census Data of the City of Chicago, 1920.* Chicago: University of Chicago Press, 1931.

———. *Census Data of the City of Chicago, 1930.* Chicago: University of Chicago Press, 1933.

Burns, Walter N. *The One-way Ride; The Red Trail of Chicago Gangland from Prohibition to Jake Lingle.* Garden City, New York: Doubleday, Doran and Co., 1931.

Capek, Karel *et al. At the Crossroads of Europe: A Historical Outline of the Democratic Idea in Czechoslovakia.* Prague: PEN Club, 1938.

Capek, Thomas (ed.). *Bohemia Under Hapsburg Misrule.* New York: Fleming H. Revel Co., 1915.

Capek, Thomas. *The Czechs (Bohemians) in America.* Boston: Houghton Mifflin Co., 1920.

———. *The Czechoslovaks: The Czech (Bohemian) Community of New York.* New York: Czechoslovak Section of America's Making, 1921.

Capek, Thomas, Jr. *Origins of the Czecho-Slovak State.* New York: Revel Press, 1926.

Champernowne, Henry. *The Boss.* New York: George H. Richmond Co., 1894.

Comfort, Alex. *Authority and Delinquency in the Modern State.* London: Routledge and Kegan Paul, 1950.

Cooley, Charles H. *Social Organization.* New York: Charles Scribner's Sons, 1929.

Counts, George S. *School and Society in Chicago.* New York: Harcourt, Brace and Co., 1928.

Crane, R. T. *The Autobiography of Richard Teller Crane.* Chicago: Privately printed, 1927.

Dennis, C. H. *Victor Lawson: His Life and His Work.* Chicago: University of Chicago Press, 1935.

Dobyns, Fletcher. *The Underworld of American Politics.* Kingsport, Tennessee: Privately printed, 1932.

Dodd, Walter F. and Sue H. Dodd. *Government in Illinois.* Chicago: University of Chicago Press, 1923.

Drake, St. Clare and Horace R. Cayton. *Black Metropolis: A Study of Negro Life in a Northern City.* New York: Harcourt, Brace and Co., 1945.

Drnec, Gustav and J. V. Welcl. *Nás Cermák.* Chicago: Privately printed, 1933.

Droba, Daniel (ed.). *Czech and Slovak Leaders in Metropolitan Area.* Chicago: Slavonic Club of the University of Chicago, 1931.

Dunbar, Flanders. *Mind and Body.* New York: Random House, 1947.

Dunne, Edward F. *Illinois, The Heart of the Nation.* Chicago: Lewis Publishing Co., 1933.

Farley, James A. *Behind the Ballots.* New York: Harcourt, Brace and Co., 1938.

———. *Jim Farley's Story: The Roosevelt Years.* New York: McGraw-Hill Book Co., 1948.

Fenichel, Otto. *The Psychoanalytical Theory of Neurosis.* New York: W. W. Norton and Co., 1945.

———. *Outline of Clinical Psychoanalysis.* Translated by Bertram D. Lewin and Gregory Zilboorg. New York W. W. Norton and Co., 1934.

Flynn, Edward J. *You're the Boss.* New York: Viking Press, 1947.

Forthal, Sonja. *Cogwheels of Democracy: A Study of the Precinct Captain.* New York: William-Frederick Press, 1946.

Frazier, E. F. *The Negro Family in Chicago.* Chicago: University of Chicago Press, 1932.

Freud, Sigmund. *Leonardo Da Vinci: A Study in Psychosexuality.* New York: Random House, 1947.

———. *New Introductory Lectures in Psychoanalysis.* New York: Carleton House, 1933.

———. *Three Contributions to the Theory of Sex.* Washington, D.C.: Nervous and Mental Disease Publishing Co., 1930.

Friedhrich, C. J. *Constitutional Government and Democracy.* Boston: Ginn and Co., 1946.

Fromm, Erich. *Man for Himself, An Inquiry into the Psychology of Ethics.* New York: Rinehart and Co., 1947.

Garvey, Neil F. *The Government and Administration of Illinois.* New York: Thomas Y. Crowell Co., 1958.

Gavit, John P. *Americans by Choice.* New York: Harper and Bros., 1922.

Gilbert, Hiram T. *The Municipal Court of Chicago.* Chicago: Privately printed, 1928.

Gosnell, Harold F. *Boss Platt and His New York Machine.* Chicago: University of Chicago Press, 1924.

————. *Machine Politics: Chicago Model.* Chicago: University of Chicago Press, 1937.

————. *Negro Politicians.* Chicago: University of Chicago Press, 1930.

Gouldner, Alvin W. (ed.). *Studies in Leadership.* New York: Harper and Bros., 1950.

Hamilton, Henry Raymond. *The Epic of Chicago.* Chicago: Willett, Clark and Co., 1932.

Handlin, Oscar. *The Uprooted.* Boston: Little, Brown and Co., 1952.

Harrison, Carter H. *Growing Up With Chicago.* Chicago: R. F. Seymour, Publisher, 1944.

————. *The Stormy Years.* Indianapolis: Bobbs-Merrill Co., 1935.

Horney, Karen. *The Neurotic Personality of Our Time.* New York: W. W. Norton and Co., 1937.

Hostetter, Gorden L. and Thomas Beesley. *It's a Racket!* Chicago: Les Quinn Books, 1929.

Hull House Residents. *Hull House Maps and Papers.* New York: Thomas Y. Crowell and Co., 1895.

Ickes, Harold. *The Autobiography of a Curmudgeon.* New York: Reynal and Hitchcock, 1943.

Jacobs, J. L. *Assessment of Real Estate and Personal Property in Cook County, Illinois.* Chicago: Office of the Assessor, 1934.

Jeter, Helen. *Trends of Population in the Region of Chicago.* Chicago: University of Chicago Press, 1927.

Johnson, C. O. *Carter Henry Harrison I.* Chicago: University of Chicago Press, 1928.

Johnson, Philander C. *Senator Sorghum's Primer of Politics: Helpful Hints on the Science of Not Getting the Worst of it.* Philadelphia: Henry Altemus Co., 1908.

Jones, E. *Papers on Psychoanalysis.* New York: William Wood and Co., 1933.

Jung, C. *Psychological Types*. New York: Harcourt, Brace and Co., 1922.

Kelley, Stanley, Jr. *Professional Public Relations and Political Power*. Baltimore: Johns Hopkins Press, 1956.

Kent, Frank. *The Great Game of Politics*. New York: Doubleday, Page and Co., 1923.

Key, V. O. *Politics, Parties and Pressure Groups*. New York: Thomas Y. Crowell and Co., 1948.

Kraus, Adolf. *Reminiscences and Comments*. Chicago: Toby Rubovits, 1925.

Kluckhohn, Clyde and Henry A. Murray. *Personality in Nature, Society and Culture*. New York: Alfred A. Knopf, 1948.

Lasswell, Harold D. *Power and Personality*. New York: W. W. Norton and Co., 1948.

Lasswell, Harold D. and Abraham Kaplan. *Power and Society*. New Haven: Yale University Press, 1950.

Lawrence, David. *Who Were the Eleven Million*. New York: Appleton-Century, 1936.

Lazarsfeld, Paul F. *et al. The People's Choice*. New York: Duell, Sloan and Pearce, 1944.

Lepawsky, Albert. *Home Rule for Metropolitan Chicago*. Chicago: University of Chicago Press, 1932.

———. *The Judicial System of Metropolitan Chicago*. Chicago: University of Chicago Press, 1932.

Levinson, Paul. *Race, Class and Party*. London: Oxford University Press, 1932.

Lewis, Lloyd and Henry J. Smith. *Chicago: The History of Its Reputation*. New York: Harcourt, Brace and Co., 1929.

Lippman, Walter. *American Inquisitors*. New York: Macmillan Co., 1928.

Litchfield, Edward H. *Voting Behavior in a Metropolitan Area*. Ann Arbor: University of Michigan Press, 1941.

Loth, David G. *Public Plunder: A History of Graft in America*. New York: Carrick and Evans, 1938.

Lynch, D. T. *Criminals and Politicians*. New York: Macmillan Co., 1932.

MacIver, R. N. *The Web of Government*. New York: Macmillan Co., 1947.

McKeon, Dayton D. *The Boss: The Hague Machine in Action*. Boston: Houghton Mifflin Co., 1940.

McKinely, Michael L. *Crime and the Civic Cancer*. Chicago: Chicago Daily News, 1932.

Martin, Edward M. *The Role of the Bar in Electing the Bench in Chicago*. Chicago: University of Chicago Press, 1936.

Masters, Edgar Lee. *The Tale of Chicago*. New York: G. P. Putnam's Sons, 1933.

Mayo, Elton. *The Human Problems of an Industrial Civilization*. New York: Macmillan Co., 1933.

——. *The Social Problems of an Industrial Civilization*. Cambridge, Mass.: Harvard University Press, 1945.

Mead, George Herbert. *Mind, Self, and Society*. Chicago: University of Chicago Press, 1934.

Mead, Margaret. *Coming of Age in Samoa*. New York: New American Library, 1949.

Merriam, Charles E. *Chicago, A More Intimate View of Urban Politics*. New York: Macmillan Co., 1929.

——. *Four American Party Leaders*. New York: Macmillan Co., 1926.

——. *The Making of Citizens*. Chicago: University of Chicago Press, 1931.

——. *Non-Voting, Causes and Methods of Control*. Chicago: University of Chicago Press, 1924.

——. *Scrambled Government: Who Rules What in Chicagoland?* Chicago: League for Industrial Democracy, 1934.

——. *Systematic Politics*. Chicago: University of Chicago Press, 1945.

Merriam, Charles E. and Harold F. Gosnell. *The American Party System*. New York: Macmillan Co., 1948.

Merriam, Charles E. and Louise Overacker. *Primary Elections*. Chicago: University of Chicago Press, 1928.

Merriam, C. E., S. D. Parratt, and A. Lepawsky. *Government of the Metropolitan Region of Chicago*. Chicago: University of Chicago Press, 1933.

Merton, Robert K. *Social Theory and Social Structure*. Glencoe, Illinois: Free Press, 1949.

Michels, Robert. *Political Parties*. New York: Hearst's International Library, 1915.

Miller, Herbert A. *Races, Nations and Classes*. Philadelphia: J. B. Lippincott Co., 1924.

Miller, Kenneth D. *The Czecho-Slovaks in America*. New York: George H. Doran Co., 1922.

Mills, C. Wright. *The New Men of Power*. New York: Harcourt, Brace and Co., 1948.

Moberg, Vilhelm. *The Emigrants*. Translated by Gustav Lannestock. New York: Simon and Schuster, 1951.

Moore, B. F. *A History of Cumulative Voting and Minority Representation in Illinois*. Urbana: University of Illinois Press, 1909.

Morganthau, Hans J. *Politics Among Nations*. New York: Alfred A. Knopf, 1948.

Mosca, Gaetano. *The Ruling Class*. New York: McGraw-Hill Book Co., 1939.

Munro, William B. *Personality in Politics*. New York: Macmillan Co., 1924.

Murphy, Gardner. *Personality; A Bio-Social Approach to Origins and Structure*. New York: Harper and Bros., 1947.

Orth, Samuel. *Our Foreigners*. New Haven: Yale University Press, 1921.

Ostragorski, M. Y. *Democracy and the Party System in the United States*. New York: Macmillan Co., 1910.

Overacker, Louise. *Money in Elections*. New York: Macmillan Co., 1932.

————. *Presidential Campaign Funds*. Boston: University of Boston Press, 1946.

Park, Robert E. *The Immigrant Press and Its Controls*. New York: Harper and Bros., 1922.

Park, Robert E. and Herbert A. Miller. *Old World Traits Transplanted*. New York: Harper and Bros., 1921.

Pasley, Fred D. *Al Capone: The Biography of a Self-Made Man*. Garden City, New York: Garden City Publishing Co., 1930.

————. *Muscling In*. New York: Ives-Washburne, Publishers, 1931.

Patterson, Haywood and Earl Conrad. *Scottsboro Boy*. New York: Doubleday and Co., 1950.

Peel, Roy V. *The Political Clubs of New York City*. New York: G. P. Putnam's Sons, 1935.

Peel, Roy V. and T. C. Donnelly. *The 1928 Campaign*. New York: R. R. Smith, 1931.

————. *The 1932 Campaign, An Analysis*. New York: Farrar and Rinehart, 1935.

Pierce, B. L. *A History of Chicago*. New York: Alfred A. Knopf, 1937.

Pierce, B. L. and J. L. Norris. *As Others See Chicago*. Chicago: University of Chicago Press, 1933.

Pigors, Paul. *Leadership or Domination*. Boston: Houghton Mifflin Co., 1935.

Pollock, James K. *Party Campaign Funds*. New York: Alfred A. Knopf, 1926.

——. *Voting Behavior: A Case Study*. Ann Arbor: University of Michigan Press, 1939.

Reckless, Walter C. *Vice in Chicago*. Chicago: University of Chicago Press, 1933.

Reichman, John J. (ed.). *Czechoslovaks in Chicago*. Chicago: Czechoslovak Historical Society of Illinois, 1937.

Reynolds, G. M. *Machine Politics in New Orleans, 1897-1926*. New York: Columbia University Press, 1936.

Salter, J. T. (ed.). *The American Politician*. Chapel Hill: University of North Carolina Press, 1938.

Salter, J. T. *Boss Rule, Portraits in City Politics*. New York: McGraw-Hill Book Co., 1935.

Salter, J. T. (ed.). *Public Men In and Out of Office*. Chapel Hill: University of North Carolina Press, 1946.

Schriftgiesser, Karl. *The Lobbyists*. Boston: Little, Brown and Co., 1952.

Sheldon, W. H., S. S. Stevens, and W. P. Tucker. *The Varieties of Human Physiques*. New York: Harper and Bros., 1940.

Simon, Herbert A. *Administrative Behavior*. New York: Macmillan Co., 1947.

Simpson, Herbert D. *Tax Racket and Tax Reform in Chicago*. Chicago: Institute for Economic Research, Northwestern University, 1930.

Smith, H. J. *Chicago, A Portrait*. New York: Century Co., 1931.

——. *Chicago's Great Century*. Chicago: Consolidated Publishers, 1933.

Smith, H. L. and L. M. Kreuger. *A Brief Summary of Literature on Leadership*. Bloomington: Bureau of Cooperative Research, Indiana University, 1933.

Spranger, Edward. *Types of Men; The Psychology and Ethics of Personality*. Translated by Paul Pigors from the fifth German edition. Halle: M. Niemeyer, 1928.

Stead, W. T. *Satan's Invisible World Displayed*. New York: R. R. Fenno and Co., 1897.

Steadman, Robert Foster. *Public Health Organization of the Chicago Region*. Chicago: University of Chicago Press, 1930.

Steffens, Lincoln. *The Autobiography of Lincoln Steffens*. New York: Literary Guild, 1931.

Stonequist, Everett V. *The Marginal Man*. New York: Charles Scribner's Sons, 1937.

Stuart, William H. *The Twenty Incredible Years*. Chicago: M. A. Donahue and Co., 1935.

Sullivan, Edward Dean. *Chicago Surrenders*. New York: Vanguard Press, 1930.

———. *Rattling the Cup in Chicago Crime*. New York: Vanguard Press, 1929.

Tead, Ordway. *The Art of Leadership*. New York: McGraw-Hill Book Co., 1935.

Thomas, W. I. and F. Znaniecki. *The Polish Peasant in Europe and America*. New York: Alfred A. Knopf, 1927.

Thrasher, Frederick M. *Chicago's Gangland*. Chicago: University of Chicago Press, 1923.

———. *The Gang*. Chicago: University of Chicago Press, 1927.

Van Devander, Charles W. *The Big Bosses*. New York: Howell Sosken, 1944.

Wallas, Graham. *Human Nature in Politics*. New York: Alfred A. Knopf, 1921.

Weber, Max. *Essays in Sociology*. Translated by H. H. Gerth and C. Wright Mills. New York: Oxford University Press, 1946.

———. *The Theory of Social and Economic Organization*. Translated by A. M. Henderson and Talcott Parsons. New York: Oxford University Press, 1947.

Wendt, Lloyd and Herman Kogan. *Lords of the Levee*. Indianapolis: Bobbs-Merrill Co., 1943.

White, Leonard D. *Conditions of Municipal Employment: A Study in Morale*. Chicago: University of Chicago Press, 1925.

———. *The Prestige Value of Public Employment in Chicago*. Chicago: University of Chicago Press, 1929.

Whitehead, T. N. *Leadership in a Free Society*. Cambridge, Mass.: Harvard University Press, 1936.

Whyte, William F. *Street Corner Society*. Chicago: University of Chicago Press, 1937.

William, Elmer Lynn. *The Curious Career of Tom Courtney Unveiled: A Documented Report of the Little Known Political History of a Payroll Patriot*. Chicago: Better Government Association, 1944.

———. *That Man Bundesen*. Chicago: Better Government Association, 1931.

Wirth, Louis. *The Ghetto*. Chicago: University of Chicago Press, 1928.

Wooddy, Carroll H. *The Case of Frank L. Smith*. Chicago: University of Chicago Press, 1931.

————. *The Chicago Primary of 1926*. Chicago: University of Chicago Press, 1926.

Young, Donald R. *American Minority Peoples*. New York: Harper and Bros., 1932.

Young, Kimball. *Social Psychology*. New York: F. S. Crofts and Co., 1947.

Zink, Harold. *City Bosses in the United States*. New York: Macmillan Co., 1939.

Zorbaugh, H. W. *The Gold Coast and the Slum*. Chicago: University of Chicago Press, 1929.

ARTICLES

Allport, G. W. and H. S. Odbert. "Traitnames: A Psychological Study," *Psychological Monographs*, No. 211, 1936.

Bernard, Jessie. "Political Leadership Among North American Indians," *American Journal of Sociology*, XXIV (September, 1928), 296.

Bunch, R. J. "The Thompson-Negro Alliance," *Opportunity*, VII (March, 1929), 79.

Cermak, Anton J. "Why Businessmen Fail in Politics," *Nation's Business*, XXI (January, 1933), 25.

"The Chicago Tribune," *Fortune* (May, 1934), pp. 14-25, 101-13.

Commons, John R. "Slavs in the Bituminous Coal Mines of Illinois," *Charities*, XIII (December 3, 1919), 227.

Conroy, Jack. "Boyhood in a Coal Town," *American Mercury*, XXIII (July, 1931), 83-92.

Douglas, W. A. S. "Kindling Wood Peddler," *American Mercury*, XXIX (July, 1933), 341-47.

Forthal, Sonja. "Relief and Friendly Service by Political Precinct Leaders," *Social Service Review*, VIII (1931), 608-18.

————. "The Small Fry and the Party Purse," *American Political Science Review*, XXXIV (1940), 66-76.

Frank, L. K. "The Dilemma of Leadership Psychiatry," *Journal of the Biology and Pathology of Interpersonal Relations*, II (August, 1939), 343.

Gates, Alfred. "Chicago Unravelling Fiscal Snarl," *National Municipal Review*, XXI (April, 1932), 261.

Ginsburg, R. A. "Czechs in Politics," *Czech and Slovak Leaders in Metropolitan Chicago,* ed. Daniel D. Droba. Chicago: Slavonik Club of the University of Chicago, 1934. Pp. 262-64.

Hallgren, Mauritz A. "Chicago Goes Tammany," *The Nation,* CXXXII (April 22, 1931), 446-47.

Gosnell, H. F. and N. N. Gill. "An Analysis of the 1932 Presidential Vote in Chicago," *American Political Science Review,* XXIX (1935), 984.

"The Kelly-Nash Machine," *Fortune* (August, 1936), 47.

Kingsbury, J. B. "The Merit System in Chicago From 1915 to 1923," *Public Personnel Studies,* IV (November, 1926), 306-19.

Lasswell, Harold D. "The Theory of Propaganda," *American Political Science Review,* XXI (1927), 627.

Lepawsky, Albert. "Chicago, Metropolis in the Making," *National Municipal Review,* XXX (April, 1941), 211-16.

Ligget, W. "The Plunder of Chicago," *American Mercury,* XXV (March, 1933), 269-79.

Martin, Edward W. "Chicago's New Deal in Municipal Affairs," *National Municipal Review,* XX (May, 1931), 310.

Masaryk, Alice G. "The Bohemians in Chicago," *Charities,* XIII (December 3, 1904), 206-10.

Mayer, Harold R. "South Lawndale," *Forty-four Cities in the City of Chicago.* Chicago: Chicago Plan Commission, 1942. P. 25.

Mayer, Milton S. "Corrupt and Discontented?" *Survey Graphic,* XXIII (October, 1934), 480-81.

Munro, William B. "The Boss in Politics—Asset or Liability?" *Annals of American Academy of Political and Social Sciences,* CLXIX (September, 1933), 12.

Overacker, Louise. "Campaign Funds in a Depression Year," *American Political Science Review,* XXVII (1933), 776.

———. "Campaign Funds in the Presidential Election of 1940," *American Political Science Review,* XXXV (1941), 273.

———. "Presidential Campaign Funds, 1944," *American Political Science Review,* XXXIX (1945), 534-35.

Park, Robert E. "Mentality of Racial Hybrids," *American Journal of Sociology,* XXXVI (January, 1931), 534-35.

Richberg, Donald S. "Gold-Plated Anarchy: An Interpretation of the Fall of Giants," *The Nation,* CXXXVI (April ᵣ 1933), 368-69.

Robinson, George F. "The Negro in Politics in Chicago," *Journal of Negro History,* XVII (April, 1932), 180-229.

Roucek, J. S. "A Study of Czecho-Slovaks in the United States," *Sociology and Social Research*, XVII (September-October, 1932), 62-71.

Seligman, Lester G. "The Study of Political Leadership," *American Political Science Review*, XLIV (December, 1950), 904-15.

Smith, Bruce. "Politics and Law Enforcement," *Annals of the American Academy of Political and Social Science*, CLXIX (September, 1933), 67-74.

Szymczak, M. S. "Poles and Their Aptitude in American Politics," *Poles in America*. Chicago: Polish Day Association, 1933. Pp. 93-95.

Wirth, Louis. "A Bibliography of the Urban Community," *The City*, ed. Robert E. Park, E. W. Burgess, and R. D. McKenzie. Chicago: University of Chicago Press, 1926. Pp. 161-228.

Wooddy, Carroll H. "Jubilee in Chicago," *National Municipal Review*, XX (June, 1931), 321.

Yarros, Victor S. "Presenting Big Bill Thompson of Chicago," *Independent* (November 5, 1927).

Zink, Harold. "A Case Study of a Political Boss," *Psychiatry*, I (November, 1938), 527-33.

NEWSPAPERS

Chicago Defender.
Chicago Daily News.
Chicago Daily Times.
Chicago Evening American.
Chicago Evening Post.
Chicago Examiner.
Chicago Federation News.
Chicago Herald.
Chicago Herald-American.
Chicago Herald and Examiner.
Chicago Inter-Ocean.
Chicago Journal.
Chicago Morning Mail.
Chicago Record-Herald.
Chicago Tribune.
Chicago Whip.
Denni Hlastel (Czech).
Narod (Czech).
Spravdlnost (Czech)

BIBLIOGRAPHY

PUBLIC DOCUMENTS

Bureau of the Census. *Fifteenth Census of the United States,* 1930.

Chicago Commission on Race Relations. *The Negro in Chicago.* Chicago: University of Chicago Press, 1922.

Chicago Plan Commission. *Forty-four Cities in the City of Chicago.* Chicago: Chicago Plan Commission, 1942.

Chicago Plan Commission. *Land Use in Chicago,* Vol. II. *Chicago Land Use Survey.* Chicago: Chicago Plan Commission, 1943.

Chicago Plan Commission. *Population Facts for Planning Chicago.* Chicago: Chicago Plan Commission, 1942.

Chicago Plan Commission. *Residential Chicago,* Vol. I. *Chicago Land Use Survey.* Chicago: Chicago Plan Commission, 1942.

City of Chicago. *Chicago's Report to the People.* 1947.

City of Chicago, City Council Committee on Crime. *Report,* 1915.

City of Chicago, City Council. *Proceedings,* 1908-1933.

City of Chicago. *Inaugural Message of Honorable A. J. Cermak, Mayor, 1931.*

City of Chicago. *Municipal Code of Chicago,* 1931.

Cook County Commissioners. *Annual Message of the President,* 1922-32.

Cook County Commissioners. *Official Records of the Proceedings,* 1921-32.

Democratic National Convention. *Official Records of the Proceedings,* 1932.

Forest Preserve Commissioners of Cook County. *Annual Report of the President,* 1921-32.

Illinois Blue Book, 1902-33.

State of Illinois Constitution, 1870 (revised).

State of Illinois House of Representatives. *Journal,* 1902-10; 1922-33.

United States Senate. *Hearings Before a Special Committee Investigating Campaign Expenditures in Senatorial Primary and General Elections, 1926, 69th Congress, 1st Session,* Part II. (Reed Committee.)

PUBLICATIONS OF CIVIC AND OTHER AGENCIES

Anti-Saloon League. *American Issue.*

Better Government Association. *Bulletins,* 1926-33.

———. *Lightnin',* 1926-33.

———. *Statement of the Better Government Association Concerning the Mayoralty Campaign,* 1931.

————. "The Strange Case of Judge E. K. Jarecki," Campaign pamphlet, June 21, 1933.

Chicago Crime Commission. *Annual Report of the Operating Director,* 1922-33.

————. *Annual Report of the President,* 1922-33.

————. *Criminal Justice,* 1919-33.

Chicago Recreation Commission. *Local Community Fact Book,* ed. Louis Wirth and Margaret Furez. Chicago: Chicago Recreation Commission, 1938.

Chicago Teachers Federation. *Bulletin,* 1919-33.

Citizens Association of Chicago. *Annual Report,* 1922-33.

————. *Bulletin,* 1901-33.

Cook County Democratic Organization. *Chicago Standard Opinion.*

————. *Public Service Leader.*

Council of Social Agencies. *Census Data of the City of Chicago, Community Areas.* Chicago: Council of Social Agencies, 1930.

Illinois Association for Criminal Justice. *The Illinois Crime Survey.* Chicago: Illinois Association for Criminal Justice, 1929. See especially Part III, "Organized Crime in Chicago," by John Landesco.

Illinois Municipal Review, Vols. I-XII, 1922-33.

Municipal Voters League. *Report,* 1909-33.

DIRECTORIES AND ENCYCLOPEDIAS

Appleton's Cyclopedia of American Biography.

Chicago Daily News Almanac and Year Book, 1900-33.

National Cyclopedia of American Biography.

The University of Chicago Library: *Chicago and Cook County, A Union List of Their Official Publications,* 1934.

Who Was Who in America.

Who's Who in Chicago.

Who's Who in Government.

UNPUBLISHED MATERIALS

Altman, O. L. "Chicago's Experiment in Personal Property Taxation." Ph.D. dissertation, Department of Economics, University of Chicago, 1936.

Cherry, H. Dicken. "Effective Precinct Organization." Master's thesis, Department of Political Science, University of Chicago, 1952.

Conroy, E. Dennis. "The Electoral System of Chicago and Cook County." Master's thesis, Department of Political Science, University of Chicago, 1951.

Cressy, Paul F. "The Succession of Cultural Groups in Chicago." Ph.D. dissertation, Department of Sociology, University of Chicago, 1930.

Edwards, Mrs. L. "My Twenty Years Experience in Streeterville District of Lake Michigan." Manuscript in the Library of the University of Chicago.

Fleming, Dennis J. "The Relation of the Mayor to Budgetary Controls in Chicago." Master's thesis, Department of Political Science, University of Chicago, 1949.

Horak, Jakub. "Assimilation of Czechs in Chicago." Ph.D. dissertation, Department of Sociology, University of Chicago, 1920.

Leiserson, Avery. "The Study of Leadership." Manuscript, Department of Political Science, University of Chicago, 1950.

McCarthy, E. R. "The Bohemians in Chicago and Their Benevolent Societies: 1875-1946." Master's thesis, Department of Sociology, University of Chicago, 1946.

McLemore, Francis Williams. "The Role of the Negroes of Chicago in the Senatorial Election of 1930." Master's thesis, Department of Political Science, University of Chicago, 1930.

Peel, Roy V. "James Gillespie Blaine: A Study of Political Leadership." Ph.D. dissertation, Department of Political Science, University of Chicago, 1926.

Philip, William B. "Chicago and the Downstate: A Study of Their Conflicts, 1870-1934." Ph.D. dissertation, Department of History, University of Chicago, 1940.

Robertson, Pearl. "Grover Cleveland as a Political Leader." Ph.D. dissertation, Department of Political Science, University of Chicago, 1937.

Slayton, William L. "Chicago's House of Lords." Master's thesis, Department of Political Science, University of Chicago, 1943.

Stevenson, Marietta. "William Jennings Bryan." Ph.D. dissertation, Department of Political Science, University of Chicago, 1926.

INDEX

[449]

passim; campaign for sheriff, 82, 90, 92-96; bailiff, 77-80, 83-84, 87-89; Gemmill investigation, 87-91; president, Cook County Board of Commissioners, 122, 123, 124-32, 143, 144, 145-46, 197, 402; charged with complicity in graft, 144-45; desire for governorship, 153-56, 290-91, 292-93, 417; drafted for 1928 senatorial campaign, 155, 157-61; use of citizens' committees, 349, 411; mentioned, 346
issues and attitudes: utilities, 75, 178; home rule, 84, 289; war work, 92, 96; support of Al Smith, 137, 152-53, 155, 158, 159, 297, 298-99, 300, 304-5, 306; organized crime, 140-43, 219 *(see also* Crime); taxation, 194, 196, 413; welfare work, 371-72; prohibition, see Cermak: *Prohibition (and liquor issue);* mentioned, 219, 350
legislative accomplishments: redistricting plan, 73-74; reorganization of police department, 110, 112; Chicago City Plan, 112-13; Bureau of Licenses, 113-14; park district plan, 265
as mayor of Chicago: desire for mayoralty position, 133; gaining the nomination, 199-204; primary election for, 203; campaign for, 204-37, 408; and public relations, 230-32, 283-87, 327; first day as, 239; descriptions of, 239, 240, 243-44, 245, 270, 319, 328, 330, 430; fiscal problems, 240, 241, 246-57, 258-63, 289, 327; and public assistance, 242, 257, 258, 276-78, 279, 415; bureaucratic management, 244-45, 258-66; appointments made, 245, 267-69; and advisory commission, 250, 263-64, 269; and state legislature, 252-54, 256, 278, 423; and civil service commission, 268, 270, 271-74, 362; relations with city council, 274-76; and crime, 279-82, 318-21, 323-24; role in 1932 presidential elections, 298-306, 307-10, 419, 420; election returns, 410; depression problems other than fiscal, *see* Depression; mentioned, 288, 289, 298

personal life: marriage, 17-19, 368; as family man, 37, 41, 58, 326, 328, 367, 370; religion, 46, 329; health, 86-87, 92, 143, 154, 157, 176, 187-89, 192, 194, 249, 325-28, 366, 375-78; psychology, 337, 338, 366, 375-78; brothers and sisters, 367
Prohibition (and liquor issue): "personal liberty," 55, 84, 138, 297; "Mr. Wet," 60, 85; United Societies, 82-83, 84, 85, 119, 125, 297; anti-Prohibition policy, 115, 137, 142, 143, 223; Anti-Saloon League, 119, 125-26, 160, 161, 197, 296-97; as issue in 1928 elections, 158-61; National Association against Prohibition, 297; A.J.'s interest moves to national level, 297-98, 299; as issue in 1932 elections, 303, 390, 418; defeat of Prohibition, 333-34, 420; mentioned, 53, 54, 56, 124-27, 150, 196, 197, 222, 296, 305, 345, 347, 351, 356
supporters and critics: Municipal Voters' League, 63, 100, 110, 216; press, 78, 79, 93, 216-17, 233; United Societies, 94-95; labor, 100, 212; Anti-Saloon League, 110, 125-26; *Chicago Tribune,* 124, 127, 217; *Herald and Examiner,* 127, 153, 218; *Chicago Evening American,* 127, 218; ethnic groups, 127, 200, 201, 202, 207, 208, 214, 225-26, 234, 236, 406; Citizens Association, 145; Better Government Association, 191-92, 194, 205, 216; "Silk Stockings," 200, 201, 215-16, 228-30; anti-Thompson Republicans, 209-10; business, 210-11, 228-30, 404; underworld, 212-13; women's groups, 214-15; civic organizations, 216, 228-30; *Daily News,* 217; religious groups, 226-28; bankers, 250-51; public-welfare leaders (1930), 401; American Legion, 401
Cermak, Antoinette, 9
Cermak, Anton (A.J.'s father), 3-4, 6-7, 8-9, 366
Cermak, Catherine, 3, 8-9, 366, 367
Cermak, Ella, 41
Cermak, Emilie, 9